Basics of

WEB WITHDRAWN

DESIGN

HTML5 & CSS3

Basics of
WEB
DESIGN
HTML5 & CSS3

Terry Ann Felke-Morris, Ed.D.

Harper College

Addison-Wesley

Boston   Columbus   Indianapolis   New York   San Francisco   Upper Saddle River
Amsterdam   Cape Town   Dubai   London   Madrid   Milan   Munich   Paris   Montreal   Toronto
Delhi   Mexico City   São Paulo   Sydney   Hong Kong   Seoul   Singapore   Taipei   Tokyo

Editorial Director: Marcia Horton
Editor-in-Chief: Michael Hirsch
Acquisitions Editor: Matt Goldstein
Editorial Assistant: Chelsea Bell
Vice President, Marketing: Patrice Jones
Marketing Manager: Yezan Alayan
Marketing Coordinator: Kathryn Ferranti
Vice President, Production: Vince O'Brien
Managing Editor: Jeffrey Holcomb
Production Project Manager: Heather McNally
Senior Operations Supervisor: Alan Fischer
Operations Specialist: Lisa McDowell

Art Director: Kristine Carney
Text Designer: Susan Raymond
Cover Designer: Rachael Cronin
Manager, Rights and Permissions: Michael Joyce
Text Permission Coordinator: Joanna Green
Cover Photograph: David Sutherland/Alamy
Media Editor: Daniel Sandin
Media Project Manager: Wanda Rockwell
Full-Service Project Management: Dennis Free, Aptara®, Inc.
Composition: Aptara®, Inc.
Interior Printer/Bindery: R.R. Donnelly/Willard
Cover Printer: Lehigh-Phoenix Color/Hagerstown

Credits and acknowledgments borrowed from other sources and reproduced, with permission, in this textbook are listed below, or appear on appropriate page within text.

Microsoft® and Windows® are registered trademarks of the Microsoft Corporation in the U.S.A. and other countries. Screen shots and icons reprinted with permission from the Microsoft Corporation. This book is not sponsored or endorsed by or affiliated with the Microsoft Corporation.

W3C is a registered trademark of the Massachusetts Institute of Technology, European Research Consortium for Informatics and Mathematics, or Keio University on behalf of the World Wide Web Consortium.

The author has created a variety of fictitious names, company names, e-mail addresses, URLs, phone numbers, and other similar items for purposes of illustrating the concepts and techniques described within this textbook. Any resemblance of these fictitious items to any person, company/organization, or location is unintentional and purely coincidental.

The Web Design Best Practices Checklist (Table 4.1) on pages 92–93 is copyrighted by Terry Ann Morris (http://www.terrymorris.net).

All photographs except those noted below are copyrighted by Terry Ann Morris.

Photo Credits: Figure 1.4, Page 5 © Maridav/Shutterstock Images LLC; Figure 1.6, Page 8 http://www.gliffy.com; Figures 1.7 & 10.7, Pages 9 & 260 Viktor Gmyria\Shutterstock, jossnat\Shutterstock; Figure 4.9, Page 77 © Shutterstock Images LLC; Figure 12.2, Page 314 Viktor Gmyria\Shutterstock, Lightvision, LLC\Shutterstock, jossnat\Shutterstock, portfolio\Shutterstock, valkos\Shutterstock; Figure 12.6, Page 324 © Monkey Business Images/Shutterstock Images LLC.

Library of Congress Cataloging-in-Publication Data

Morris, Terry (Terry A.)
  Basics of web design : HTML5 & CSS3 / Terry Felke-Morris.
    p. cm.
  ISBN-13: 978-0-13-700338-9
  ISBN-10: 0-13-700338-2
  1. XHTML (Document markup language) 2. HTML (Document markup language) 3. Cascading style sheets.
4. Web site development--Computer programs. 5. Web sites--Design. I. Title.
  QA76.76.H94M6548 2011
  006.7'4--dc22

                                                                        2010046199

10 9 8 7 6 5 4 3 2—RRDW—15 14 13 12 11

Addison-Wesley
is an imprint of

www.pearsonhighered.com

ISBN 10:   0-13-700338-2
ISBN 13: 978-0-13-700338-9

Preface

Basics of Web Design: HTML5 & CSS3 is intended for use in a beginning web design or web development course. Topics are introduced in two-page sections that focus on key points and often include a hands-on practice exercise. The text covers the basics that web designers need to develop their skills:

- Introductory Internet and World Wide Web concepts
- Creating web pages with (X)HTML and HTML5
- Configuring text, color, and page layout with Cascading Style Sheets
- Configuring images and multimedia on web pages
- Exploring new CSS3 properties
- Web design best practices
- Accessibility, usability, and search engine optimization considerations
- Obtaining a domain name and a web host
- Publishing to the web

Student files are available for download from the companion website for this book at http://www.pearsonhighered.com/felke-morris. These files include solutions to the Hands-On Practice exercises, starter files for the Hands-On Practice exercises, and the starter files for the Case Study. See the access card in the front of this book for further instructions.

Features of the Text

Design for Today and Tomorrow. The textbook has a unique approach that prepares students to design web pages that work today in addition to being ready to take advantage of new HTML5 coding techniques of the future. XHTML syntax is introduced but the focus is HTML5 syntax. New HTML5 elements are presented with an emphasis on coding web pages that work in both current and future browsers. Hands-On Practice solution files are available in both HTML5 syntax and (where applicable) XHTML syntax.

Well-Rounded Selection of Topics. This text includes both "hard" skills such as HTML5 and Cascading Style Sheets (Chapters 1–3 and 5–11) and "soft" skills such as web design (Chapter 4) and publishing to the Web (Chapter 12). This well-rounded foundation will help students as they pursue careers as web professionals. Students and instructors will find classes more interesting because they can discuss, integrate, and apply both hard and soft skills as students create web pages and websites. The topics in each chapter are introduced on concise two-page sections that are intended to provide quick overviews and timely practice with the topic.

Two-Page Topic Sections. Each topic in this text is introduced in a concise, two-page section. Many sections also include immediate hands-on practice of the new skill or concept. This approach is intended to appeal to your busy students—especially the millennial multi-taskers—who need to drill down to the important concepts right away.

Hands-On Practice. Web design is a skill, and skills are best learned by hands-on practice. This text emphasizes hands-on practice through practice exercises within the chapters, end-of-chapter exercises, and the development of a website through ongoing real-world case studies. The variety of exercises provides instructors with a choice of assignments for a particular course or semester.

Website Case Study. There is a case study that continues throughout most of the text (beginning at Chapter 2). The case study serves to reinforce skills discussed in each chapter. Sample solutions to the case study exercises are available on the Instructor Resource Center at http://www.pearsonhighered.com/irc.

Focus on Web Design. Every chapter offers an additional activity that explores web design topics related to the chapter. These activities can be used to reinforce, extend, and enhance the course topics.

 FAQs. In her web design courses, the author is frequently asked similar questions by students. They are included in the book and are marked with the identifying FAQ icon.

 Focus on Accessibility. Developing accessible websites is more important than ever, and this text is infused with accessibility techniques throughout. The special icon shown here makes accessibility information easy to find.

 Focus on Ethics. Ethics issues as related to web development are highlighted throughout the text with the special ethics icon shown here.

 Quick Tips. Quick tips, which provide useful background information, or help with productivity, are indicated with this Quick Tip icon.

 Explore Further. The special icon identifies enrichment topics along with web resources useful for delving deeper into a concept introduced in book.

Reference Materials. The appendixes offer reference material, including an XHTML reference, an HTML5 reference, a Cascading Style Sheets reference, and a WCAG 2.0 Quick Reference.

Supplemental Materials

Student Resources. Student files for web page hands-on practice exercises and the case study are available to all readers of this book at its companion website http://www.pearsonhighered.com/felke-morris. A complimentary access code for the companion website is available with a new copy of this book. Subscriptions may also be purchased online.

Instructor Resources. The following supplements are available to qualified instructors only. Visit the Pearson Instructor Resource Center (http://www.pearsonhighered.com/irc) or send an e-mail to computing@pearson.com for information on how to access them:

- Solutions to the end-of-chapter exercises
- Solutions for the case study assignments
- Test questions
- PowerPoint® presentations
- Sample syllabi

Author's Website. In addition to the publisher's companion website for this book, the author maintains a website at http://www.webdevbasics.net. This website contains additional resources, including a color chart, learning/review games, Adobe Flash® Tutorial, Adobe Fireworks® Tutorial, Adobe Photoshop® Tutorial, and a page for each chapter with examples, links, and updates. This website is not supported by the publisher.

XHTML and HTML5

There is a lot of buzz about HTML5, which will eventually be the next official standard version of HTML. This is an exciting time to be a web designer. However, even with all the promise of HTML5, web designers still have to create web pages for their clients that work in the browsers being used today.

This textbook takes a unique approach that bridges the gap between what works today and what will be done in the future. Are you currently using XHTML syntax instead of HTML5? You'll notice that in many cases, the web page code for XHTML and HTML5 is the same except for the Document Type Definition, html, meta tags, and stand-alone elements. To provide a well-rounded foundation in web page markup, both XHTML syntax and HTML5 syntax are introduced. However, the focus of this book is HTML5. New HTML5 elements are discussed, with emphasis on coding web pages that work in both current and future browsers. Hands-On Practice solution files are available in both HTML5 syntax and (when applicable) XHTML syntax. If you are coding web pages using XHTML syntax instead of HTML5 syntax, check the XHTML solutions located in the student file XHTMLfiles folder. Except where examples are HTML5 specific, students can complete the hands-on practice and case study activities using either XHTML or HTML5.

Acknowledgments

Very special thanks go to the people at Addison-Wesley, including Michael Hirsch, Matt Goldstein, Chelsea Bell, Heather McNally, and Jeffrey Holcomb. Thank you also to Philip Koplin and Dennis Free of Aptara Corp.

Most of all, I would like to thank my family, especially my wonderful husband, for patience, love, support, and encouragement. Of course, this wouldn't be complete without mentioning the dog, Sparky—who likes to make a cameo appearance in each book—his playful antics and quirky personality helped to brighten long hours spent at the computer.

About the Author

Dr. Terry Ann Felke-Morris is an associate professor at Harper College in Palatine, Illinois. She holds a Doctor of Education degree, a Master of Science degree in information systems, and numerous certifications, including Adobe Certified Dreamweaver 8 Developer, WOW Certified Associate Webmaster, Microsoft Certified Professional, Master CIW Designer, and CIW Certified Instructor.

Dr. Felke-Morris received the Blackboard Greenhouse Exemplary Online Course Award in 2006 for use of Internet technology in the academic environment. She was the recipient of two international awards in 2008: the Instructional Technology Council's Outstanding e-Learning Faculty Award for Excellence and the MERLOT Award for Exemplary Online Learning Resources—MERLOT Business Classics.

With more than 20 years of information technology experience in business and industry, Dr. Felke-Morris published her first website in 1996 and has been working with the Web ever since. A long-time promoter of web standards, she has been a member of the Web Standards Project Education Task Force. Dr. Felke-Morris is the author of the popular textbook *Web Development and Design Foundations with XHTML*, currently in its fifth edition. She was instrumental in developing the Web Development degree and certificate programs at Harper College and currently is the senior faculty member in that area. For more information about Dr. Terry Ann Felke-Morris, visit http://terrymorris.net.

Contents

CHAPTER 1

Internet and Web Basics

The Internet and the Web are parts of our daily lives. How did they begin? What networking protocols and programming languages work behind the scenes to display a web page? This chapter provides an introduction to some of these topics and is a foundation for the information that web developers need to know. This chapter also gets you started with your very first web page. You'll be introduced to Hypertext Markup Language (HTML), the language used to create web pages, eXtensible Hypertext Markup Language (XHTML), the most recent standardized version of HTML, and HTML5—the newest draft version of HTML.

You'll learn how to . . .

- Describe the evolution of the Internet and the Web
- Explain the need for web standards
- Describe universal design
- Identify benefits of accessible web design
- Identify reliable resources of information on the Web
- Identify ethical use of the Web

- Describe the purpose of web browsers and web servers
- Identify Internet protocols
- Define URIs and domain names
- Describe HTML, XHTML and HTML5
- Create your first web page
- Use the body, head, title, and meta elements
- Name, save, and test a web page

The Internet and the Web

The Internet

The **Internet**, the interconnected network of computer networks, seems to be everywhere today. It has become part of our lives. You can't watch television or listen to the radio without being urged to visit a website. Even newspapers and magazines have their place on the Internet.

The Birth of the Internet

The Internet began as a network to connect computers at research facilities and universities. Messages in this network would travel to their destination by multiple routes or paths. This would allow the network to function even if parts of it were broken or destroyed. The message would be rerouted through a functioning portion of the network while traveling to its destination. This network was developed by the Advanced Research Projects Agency (ARPA)—and the ARPAnet was born. Four computers (located at UCLA, Stanford Research Institute, University of California Santa Barbara, and the University of Utah) were connected by the end of 1969.

Growth of the Internet

As time went on, other networks, such as the National Science Foundation's NSFnet, were created and connected with the ARPAnet. Use of this interconnected network, or Internet, was originally limited to government, research, and educational purposes. The ban on commercial use of the Internet was lifted in 1991. The growth of the Internet continues—Internet World Stats reported over 1.9 billion users, about 28% of the world's population, on the Internet in 2010. Figure 1.1 shows the growth of Internet use by geographic area between 2000 and 2010.

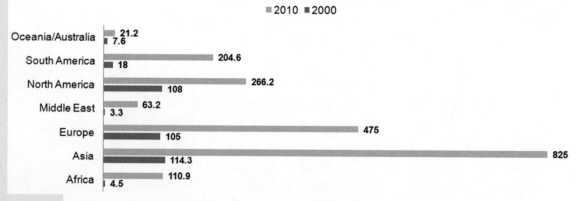

Millions of Internet Users by Geographic Area
■ 2010 ■ 2000

Geographic Area	2010	2000
Oceania/Australia	21.2	7.6
South America	204.6	18
North America	266.2	108
Middle East	63.2	3.3
Europe	475	105
Asia	825	114.3
Africa	110.9	4.5

FIGURE 1.1   Growth of Internet use.
Statistics from http://www.internetworldstats.com. Copyright © 2001–2010, Miniwatts Marketing Group. All rights reserved worldwide.

When the restriction on commercial use of the Internet was lifted, it set the stage for future electronic commerce: businesses were now welcome on the Internet. However, while businesses were no longer banned, the Internet was still text based and not easy to use. The next developments solved this issue.

The Birth of the Web

While working at CERN, a research facility in Switzerland, Tim Berners-Lee envisioned a means of communication for scientists by which they could easily "hyperlink" to another research paper or article and immediately view it. Berners-Lee created the **World Wide Web** to fulfill this need. In 1991 Berners-Lee posted the code in a newsgroup and made it freely available. This version of the World Wide Web used **Hypertext Transfer Protocol (HTTP)** to communicate between the client computer and the web server, used **Hypertext Markup Language (HTML)** to format the documents, and was text based.

The First Graphical Browser

In 1993, Mosaic, the first graphical web browser (shown in Figure 1.2), became available.

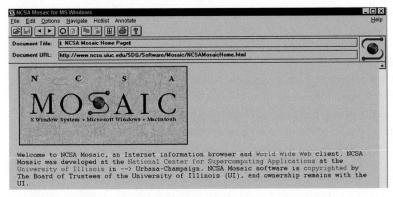

FIGURE 1.2   Mosaic: The first graphical browser.

Marc Andreessen and graduate students working at the National Center for Supercomputing Applications (NCSA) at the University of Illinois Urbana-Champaign developed Mosaic. Some individuals in this group later created another well-known web browser—Netscape Navigator—which is an ancestor of today's Mozilla Firefox browser.

Convergence of Technologies

By the early 1990s, personal computers with easy-to-use graphical operating systems (such as Microsoft's Windows, IBM's OS/2, and Apple's Macintosh OS) were increasingly available and affordable. Online service providers such as CompuServe, AOL, and Prodigy offered low-cost connections to the Internet. The convergence of available computer hardware, easy-to-use operating systems, low-cost Internet connectivity, the HTTP protocol and HTML language, and a graphical browser made information on the Internet much easier to access. The **World Wide Web**—the graphical user interface to information stored on computers running web servers connected to the Internet—had arrived!

Web Standards and Accessibility

You are probably aware that no single person or group runs the World Wide Web. However, the **World Wide Web Consortium** (http://www.w3.org), referred to as the W3C, takes a proactive role in developing recommendations and prototype technologies related to the Web. Topics that the W3C addresses include web architecture, standards for web design, and accessibility. In an effort to standardize web technologies, the W3C (logo shown in Figure 1.3) produces specifications called recommendations.

FIGURE 1.3 The W3C logo.

W3C Recommendations

The W3C Recommendations are created in working groups with input from many major corporations involved in building web technologies. These recommendations are not rules; they are guidelines. Major software companies that build web browsers, such as Microsoft, do not always follow the W3C Recommendations. This makes life difficult for web developers because not all browsers will display a web page in exactly the same way.

The good news is that there is a convergence toward the W3C Recommendations in new versions of major browsers. There are even organized groups, such as The Web Standards Project, http://webstandards.org, whose mission is to promote W3C Recommendations (often called Web standards) not only to the creators of browsers but also to web developers and designers. You'll follow W3C Recommendations as you code web pages in this book. Following the W3C Recommendations is the first step towards creating a website that is accessible.

Web Standards and Accessibility

The Web Accessibility Initiative (http://www.w3.org/WAI) referred to as the WAI, is a major area of work by the W3C. Since the Web has become an integral part of daily life, there is a need for all individuals to be able to access it.

The Web can present barriers to individuals with visual, auditory, physical, and neurological dis-.abilities. An **accessible** website provides accommodations that help individuals overcome these barriers. The WAI has developed recommendations for web content developers, web authoring tool developers, web browser developers, and developers of other user agents to facilitate use of the Web by those with special needs. See the WAI's Web Content Accessibility Guidelines (WCAG) at http://www.w3.org/WAI/WCAG20/glance/WCAG2-at-a-Glance.pdf for a quick overview.

Accessibility and the Law

The **Americans with Disabilities Act (ADA)** of 1990 is a federal civil rights law that prohibits discrimination against people with disabilities. The ADA requires that business, federal, and state services are accessible to individuals with disabilities. A 1996 Department of Justice ruling (http://www.usdoj.gov/crt/foia/cltr204.txt) indicated that ADA accessibility requirements apply to Internet resources.

Section 508 of the Federal Rehabilitation Act was amended in 1998 to require that U.S. government agencies give individuals with disabilities access to information technology that is comparable to the access available to others. This law requires developers creating information technology (including web pages) for use by the federal government to provide for accessibility. The Federal IT Accessibility Initiative (http://www.section508.gov) provides accessibility requirement resources for information technology developers.

In recent years, state governments have also begun to encourage and promote web accessibility. The Illinois Information Technology Accessibility Act (IITAA) guidelines are an example of this trend (see http://www.dhs.state.il.us/IITAA/IITAAWebImplementationGuidelines.html).

Putting It All Together: Universal Design for the Web

The Center for Universal Design defines **universal design** as "the design of products and environments to be usable by all people, to the greatest extent possible, without the need for adaptation or specialized design." Examples of universal design are all around us. The cutouts on curbs also benefit a person pushing a stroller or doing a little rollerblading (Figure 1.4). Doors that open automatically also benefit people carrying packages. A ramp is useful for a person dragging a rolling backpack or carry-on bag, and so on.

FIGURE 1.4 Inline skaters benefit from universal design.

Awareness of universal design by web developers has been steadily increasing. Forward-thinking web developers design with accessibility in mind because it is the right thing to do. Providing access for visitors with visual, auditory, and other challenges should be an integral part of web design rather than an afterthought.

Focus on Accessibility

A person with visual difficulties may not be able to use graphical navigation buttons and may use a screen reader device to provide an audible description of the web page. By making a few simple changes, such as providing text descriptions for the images and perhaps providing a text navigation area at the bottom of the page, web developers can make the page accessible. Often, providing for accessibility increases the usability of the website for all visitors.

Accessible websites, with alternate text for images, headings used in an organized manner, and captions or transcriptions for multimedia are more easily used not only by visitors with disabilities but also by visitors using a mobile browser. Finally, accessible websites may be more thoroughly indexed by search engines, which can be helpful in bringing new visitors to a site. As this text introduces web development and design techniques, corresponding web accessibility and usability issues are discussed.

Information on the Web

These days anyone can publish just about anything on the Web. In this section we'll explore how you can tell if the information you've found is reliable and also how you can use that information.

Reliability and Information on the Web

There are many websites—but which ones are reliable sources of information?

When visiting websites to find information it is important not to take everything at face value (Figure 1.5). Anyone can post anything on the Web! Choose your information sources wisely.

FIGURE 1.5 Who really updated that web page you are viewing?

First, evaluate the credibility of the website itself. Does it have its own domain name, such as http://mywebsite.com, or is it a free website consisting of just a folder of files hosted on a free web server?

The URL of a site hosted on a free web server usually includes part of the free web server's name and might begin with something such as http://mysite.tripod.com or http://www.angelfire.com/foldername/mysite. Information obtained from a website that has its own domain name will usually (but not always) be more reliable than information obtained from a free website.

Evaluate the type of domain name—is it a nonprofit organization (.org), a business (.com or .biz), an educational institution (.edu)? Businesses may provide information in a way that gives them an advantage, so be careful. Nonprofit organizations or schools will sometimes treat a subject more objectively.

Another item to look at is the date the web page was created or last updated. Although some information is timeless, very often a web page that has not been updated for several years is outdated and may not be the best source of information.

Ethical Use of Information on the Web

Focus on Ethics

This wonderful technology called the World Wide Web provides us with information, graphics, and music—all virtually free (after you pay your Internet service provider, of course). Let's consider the following issues relating to the ethical use of this information:

- Is it acceptable to copy someone's graphic to use on your website?

- Is it acceptable to copy someone's website design to use on your site or on a client's site?

- Is it acceptable to copy an essay that appears on a web page and use it or parts of it as your writing?

- Is it acceptable to insult someone on your website or link to another website in a derogatory manner?

The answer to all these questions is no. Using someone's graphic without permission is the same as stealing it. In fact, if you link to it you are actually using up some of their bandwidth and may be costing them money. Copying the website design of another person or company is also a form of stealing. Any text or graphic on a website is automatically copyrighted in the United States whether or not a copyright symbol appears on the site. Insulting a person or company on your website or linking to them in a derogatory manner could be considered a form of defamation.

Issues like these, related to intellectual property, copyright, and freedom of speech, are regularly discussed and decided in courts of law. Good web etiquette requires that you ask permission before using others' work, give credit for what you use as a student ("fair use" in the U.S. copyright law), and exercise your freedom of speech in a manner that is not harmful to others. The **World Intellectual Property Organization (WIPO)** is dedicated to protecting intellectual property rights internationally (see http://wipo.int).

What if you'd like to retain ownership but make it easy for others to use or adapt your work? Creative Commons (http://creativecommons.org) is a nonprofit organization that provides free services that allow authors and artists to register a type of a copyright license called a Creative Commons license. There are several licenses to choose from, depending on the rights you wish to grant. The Creative Commons license informs others exactly what they can and cannot do with your creative work. See http://meyerweb.com/eric/tools/color-blend for a web page licensed under a Creative Commons Attribution-ShareAlike 1.0 License with "Some Rights Reserved."

Web Browsers and Web Servers

Network Overview

A **network** consists of two or more computers connected for the purpose of communicating and sharing resources. Common components of a network are shown in Figure 1.6 and include the following:

- Server computer(s)
- Client workstation computer(s)
- Shared devices such as printers
- Networking devices (router and switch) and the media that connect them

FIGURE 1.6   Common components of a network.

The **clients** are the computer workstations used by individuals, such as a PC on a desk. The **server** receives requests from client computers for resources such as files. Computers used as servers are usually kept in a protected, secure area and are only accessed by network administrators. Networking devices such as hubs and switches provide network connections for computers, and routers direct information from one network to another. The **media** connecting the clients, servers, peripherals, and networking devices may consist of copper cables, fiber optic cables, or wireless technologies.

The Client/Server Model

The term **client/server** dates from the last millennium (the 1980s) and refers to personal computers joined by a network. Client/server can also describe a relationship between two computer programs—the client and the server. The client requests some type of service (such as a file or database access) from the server. The server fulfills the request and transmits the results to the client over a network. While both the client and the server programs can reside on the same computer, typically they run on different computers (Figure 1.7). It is common for a server to handle requests from multiple clients.

The Internet is a great example of client/server architecture at work. Consider the following scenario: An individual is at a computer using a web browser client to access the Internet. The individual uses the web browser to visit a website, say http://www.yahoo.com. The server is the web server program running on the computer with an IP address that corresponds to yahoo.com. It is contacted, locates the web page and related resources that were requested, and responds by sending them to the individual. In short, here's how to distinguish between web clients and web servers:

Browser Request

Server Response

Web Client　　　　　　　　**Web Server**

FIGURE 1.7 Web client and web server.

Web Client

- Connected to the Internet when needed
- Usually runs web browser (client) software such as Internet Explorer or Firefox
- Uses HTTP
- Requests web pages from a web server
- Receives web pages and associated files from a web server

Web Server

- Continually connected to the Internet
- Runs web server software (such as Apache or Microsoft Internet Information Server)
- Uses HTTP
- Receives a request for the web page
- Responds to the request and transmits the status code, web page, and associated files

When clients and servers exchange files, they often need to indicate the type of file that is being transferred; this is done through the use of a MIME type. **Multi-Purpose Internet Mail Extensions (MIME)** are rules that allow multimedia documents to be exchanged among many different computer systems. MIME was initially intended to extend the original Internet e-mail protocol, but it is also used by HTTP. MIME provides for the exchange of seven different media types on the Internet: audio, video, image, application, message, multipart, and text. MIME also uses subtypes to further describe the data. The MIME type of a web page is text/html. MIME types of gif and jpeg images are image/gif and image/jpeg, respectively.

A web server determines the MIME type of a file before it is transmitted to the web browser. The MIME type is sent along with the document. The web browser uses the MIME type to determine how to display the document.

How does information get transferred from the web server to the web browser? Clients (such as web browsers) and servers (such as a web server) exchange information through the use of communication protocols such as HTTP, TCP, and IP, which are introduced in the next section.

Internet Protocols

Protocols are rules that describe how clients and servers communicate with each other over a network. There is no single protocol that makes the Internet and the Web work—a number of protocols with specific functions are needed.

E-Mail Protocols

Most of us take e-mail for granted, but there are two servers involved in its smooth functioning—an incoming mail server and an outgoing mail server. When you send e-mail to others, **Simple Mail Transfer Protocol (SMTP)** is used. When you receive e-mail, **Post Office Protocol** (POP; currently **POP3**) and **Internet Message Access Protocol (IMAP)** can be used.

Hypertext Transfer Protocol

HTTP is a set of rules for exchanging files such as text, graphic images, sound, video, and other multimedia files on the Web. Web browsers and web servers usually use this protocol. When the user of a web browser requests a file by typing a website address or clicking a hyperlink, the browser builds an HTTP request and sends it to the server. The web server in the destination machine receives the request, does any necessary processing, and responds with the requested file and any associated media files.

File Transfer Protocol

File Transfer Protocol (FTP) is a set of rules that allow files to be exchanged between computers on the Internet. Unlike HTTP, which is used by web browsers to request web pages and their associated files in order to display a web page, FTP is used simply to move files from one computer to another. Web developers commonly use FTP to transfer web page files from their computers to web servers. FTP is also commonly used to download programs and files from other servers to individual computers.

Transmission Control Protocol/Internet Protocol

Transmission Control Protocol/Internet Protocol (TCP/IP) has been adopted as the official communication protocol of the Internet. TCP and IP have different functions that work together to ensure reliable communication over the Internet.

FIGURE 1.8 TCP packet.

TCP. The purpose of TCP is to ensure the integrity of network communication. TCP starts by breaking files and messages into individual units called **packets**. These packets (see Figure 1.8) contain information such as the destination, source, sequence number, and checksum values used to verify the integrity of the data.

TCP is used together with IP to transmit files efficiently over the Internet. IP takes over after TCP creates the packets, using IP addressing to send each packet over the Internet using the best path at the particular time. When the destination address is reached, TCP verifies the integrity of each packet using the checksum, requests a resend if a packet is damaged, and reassembles the file or message from the multiple packets.

IP. Working in harmony with TCP, IP is a set of rules that controls how data are sent between computers on the Internet. IP routes a packet to the correct destination address. Once sent, the packet gets successively forwarded to the next closest router (a hardware device designed to move network traffic) until it reaches its destination.

IP Addresses

Each device connected to the Internet has a unique numeric **IP address**. These addresses consist of a set of four groups of numbers, called octets. The current version of IP, IPv4, uses 32-bit (binary digit) addressing. This results in a decimal number in the format of xxx.xxx.xxx.xxx, where each xxx is a value from 0 to 255. The IP address may correspond to a domain name. The **Domain Name System (DNS)** associates these IP addresses with the text-based URLs and domain names you type into a web browser address box (more on this later). For example, at the time this was written the IP address of Google was 74.125.95.104.

You can enter this number in the address text box in a web browser (as shown in Figure 1.9), press Enter, and the Google home page will display. Of course, it's much easier to type "google.com," which is why domain names such as google.com were created in the first place! Since long strings of numbers are difficult for humans to remember, the Domain Name System was introduced as a way to associate text-based names with numeric IP addresses.

FIGURE 1.9 Entering an IP address in a web browser.

What is IPv6?

IPv6, Internet Protocol Version 6, is the most recent version of the Internet Protocol. IPv6 was designed as an evolutionary set of improvements to the current IPv4 and is backwardly compatible with it. Service providers and Internet users can update to IPv6 independently without having to coordinate with each other.

IPv6 provides for more Internet addresses because the IP address is lengthened from 32 bits to 128 bits. This means that there are potentially 2^{128} unique IP addresses possible, or 340,282,366,920,938,463,463,374,607,431,768,211,456. (Now there will be enough IP addresses for everyone's PC, notebook, cell phone, pager, PDA, automobile, toaster, and so on!)

Uniform Resource Identifiers and Domain Names

URIs and URLs

A Uniform Resource Identifier (URI) identifies a resource on the Internet. A **Uniform Resource Locator (URL)** is a type of URI that represents the network location of a resource such as a web page, a graphic file, or an MP3 file. The URL consists of the protocol, the domain name, and the hierarchical location of the file on the web server.

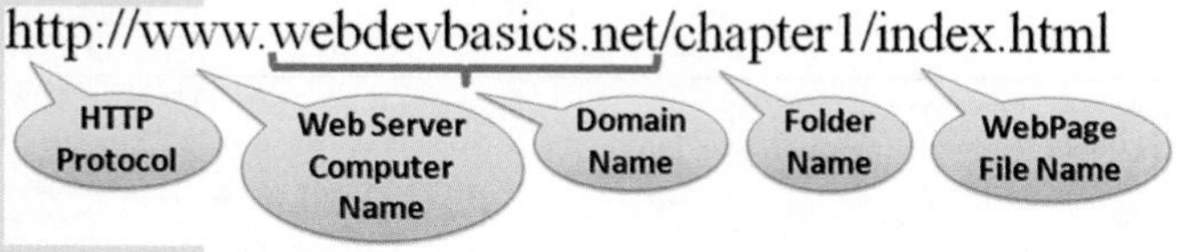

http://www.webdevbasics.net/chapter1/index.html

| HTTP Protocol | Web Server Computer Name | Domain Name | Folder Name | WebPage File Name |

FIGURE 1.10   URL describing a file within a folder.

The URL http://www.webdevbasics.net/chapter1/index.html, as shown in Figure 1.10, denotes the use of HTTP protocol and the web server named www at the domain name of webdevbasics.net. In this case, the root file (which is usually index.html or index.htm) of the chapter 1 directory will be displayed.

Domain Names

A **domain name** locates an organization or other entity on the Internet. The purpose of the **Domain Name System** (DNS) is to divide the Internet into logical groups and understandable names by identifying the exact address and type of the organization. The DNS associates the text-based domain names with the unique numeric IP address assigned to a device.

Let's consider the domain name www.yahoo.com. The .com is the top-level domain name. The portion yahoo.com is the domain name that is registered to Yahoo! and is considered a second-level domain name. The www is the name of the web server (sometimes called a **web host server**) at the yahoo.com domain. Taken all together, www.yahoo.com is considered to be a **Fully Qualified Domain Name (FQDN)**.

Top-Level Domain Names (TLDs). A **top-level domain (TLD)** identifies the rightmost part of the domain name. A TLD is either a generic top-level domain, such as com for commercial, or a country code top-level domain, such as fr for France. The Internet Assigned Numbers Authority (IANA) website has a complete list of country code TLDs (http://www.iana.org/cctld/cctld-whois.htm). The Internet Corporation for Assigned Names and Numbers (ICANN) administers the generic top-level domains shown in Table 1.1.

Generic TLD	Intended for Use By
.aero	Air-transport industry
.asia	Pan-Asia and Asia Pacific community
.biz	Businesses
.cat	Catalan linguistic and cultural community
.com	Commercial entities
.coop	Cooperative
.edu	Restricted to accredited degree-granting institutions of higher education
.gov	Restricted to government use
.info	Unrestricted use
.int	International organization (rarely used)
.jobs	Human resource management community
.mil	Restricted to military use
.mobi	Corresponds to a .com website—designed for easy access by mobile devices
.museum	Museums
.name	Individuals
.net	Entities associated with network support of the Internet, usually Internet service providers or telecommunication companies
.org	Nonprofit entities
.pro	Accountants, physicians, and lawyers
.tel	Contact information for individuals and businesses
.travel	Travel industry

TABLE 1.1 Top-Level Domains

The .com, .org, and .net TLD designations are currently used on the honor system, which means that an individual who owns a shoe store (not related to networking) can register shoes.net.

The DNS associates domain names with IP addresses. The following happens each time a new URL is typed into a web browser:

1. The DNS is accessed.
2. The corresponding IP address is obtained and returned to the web browser.
3. The web browser sends an HTTP request to the destination computer with the corresponding IP address.
4. The HTTP request is received by the web server.
5. The necessary files are located and sent by HTTP responses to the web browser.
6. The web browser renders and displays the web page and associated files.

The next time you wonder why it's taking so long to display a web page, think about all of the processing that goes on behind the scenes.

HTML Overview

Markup languages consist of sets of directions that tell the browser software (and other user agents such as mobile phones) how to display and manage a web document. These directions are usually called tags and perform functions such as displaying graphics, formatting text, and referencing hyperlinks.

The World Wide Web is composed of files containing Hypertext Markup Language (HTML) and other markup languages that describe web pages. Tim Berners-Lee developed HTML using Standard Generalized Markup Language (SGML). SGML prescribes a standard format for embedding descriptive markup within a document and for describing the structure of a document. SGML is not in itself a document language, but rather a description of how to specify one and create a document type definition (DTD). The W3C (http://w3c.org) sets the standards for HTML and its related languages. HTML (like the Web itself) is in a constant state of change.

What Is HTML?

HTML is the set of markup symbols or codes placed in a file that is intended for display on a web page. These markup symbols and codes identify structural elements such as paragraphs, headings, and lists. HTML can also be used to place media (such as graphics, video, and audio) on a web page and describe fill-in forms. The browser interprets the markup code and renders the page. HTML permits the platform-independent display of information across a network. No matter what type of computer a web page was created on, any browser running on any operating system can display the page.

Each individual markup code is referred to as an **element** or **tag**. Each tag has a purpose. Tags are enclosed in angle brackets, the < and > symbols. Most tags come in pairs: an opening tag and a closing tag. These tags act as containers and are sometimes referred to as container tags. For example, the text that is between the `<title>` and `</title>` tags on a web page would display in the title bar on the browser window.

Some tags are used alone and are not part of a pair. For example, a `<hr>` tag that displays a horizontal line on a web page is a stand-alone or self-contained tag and does not have a closing tag. You will become familiar with these as you use them. Most tags can be modified with **attributes** that further describe their purpose.

What is XHTML?

The most recent standardized version of HTML used today is actually **eXtensible HyperText Markup Language (XHTML)**. XHTML uses the tags and attributes of HTML 4 along with the more rigorous syntax of XML (Extensible Markup Language). HTML was originally developed to provide access to electronic documents via a web browser. Web browsers that evolved along with HTML were written to forgive coding errors, ignore syntax errors, and allow "sloppy" HTML code. Web browsers contain many program instructions that are designed to ignore mistakes such as missing ending tags and to guess how the developer meant the page to display. This is not a problem for a personal computer, which has relatively large processing power. However, this could be an issue for electronic devices with fewer resources, such as an Internet tablet or mobile phone.

The purpose of XHTML was to provide a foundation for device-independent web access. XHTML was developed by the W3C to be the reformulation of HTML as an application of XML. Tim Berners-Lee, the W3C director and inventor of the Web, stated in a press release (http://www.w3.org/2000/01/xhtml-pressrelease), "XHTML 1.0 connects the present Web to the future Web. It provides the bridge to page and site authors for entering the structured data, XML world, while still being able to maintain operability with user agents that support HTML4." XHTML combines the formatting strengths of HTML and the data structure and extensibility strengths of XML. Since XHTML was designed using XML, let's take a quick look at XML.

XML (eXtensible Markup Language) is the W3C standard method for creating new markup languages that will support the display of nontraditional content such as mathematical notation, as well as support newer display devices such as PDAs and mobile phones. XML can fulfill these diverse needs because it is an extensible language—it is designed to allow the definition of new tags or markup. The syntax of XML is very exacting so that the portable devices will not have to waste processing power guessing how the document should display but will be able to display information efficiently. XHTML, which combines the language of HTML with the syntax of XML, is a markup language that should adapt to future needs. An XML document must be well formed. A **well-formed** document is a document that adheres to the syntax rules of the language. The XHTML examples in the text will guide you in creating well-formed web pages.

HTML5—The Newest Version of HTML

As this was being written, the W3C's HTML Working Group (HTML WG) was busy creating a draft recommendation for HTML5, which is intended to be the successor to HTML4 and will replace XHTML. HTML5 incorporates features of both HTML and XHTML, adds new elements, provides new features such as form edits and native video, and is intended to be backward compatible.

It's possible to begin using the language right away! The newest versions of popular browsers, such as Internet Explorer 9, Firefox 4, Safari 5, Google Chrome, and Opera 10 already support some of the new features of HTML5. As you learn to design web pages you need to not only know what works today in current browsers and but also to get ready to use new HTML5 coding techniques. To meet this challenging goal, this book introduces both XHTML syntax and HTML5 syntax, presents coding web pages in HTML5 with backwards-compatible elements that work in current browsers, and also provides practice with HTML5's new features that will only work in the latest versions of browsers. Since HTML5 is in draft status and may change after this book is printed, consult http://www.w3.org/TR/html-markup for a current list of HTML5 elements.

Your First Web Page

No special software is needed to create a web page document—all you need is a text editor. The Notepad text editor is included with Microsoft Windows. TextEdit is distributed with the Mac OS X operating system (see http://support.apple.com/kb/TA20406 for configuration information). An alternative to using a simple text editor or word processor is to use a commercial web-authoring tool, such as Microsoft Expression Web or Adobe Dreamweaver. There are also many free or shareware editors available, including Notepad++, TextPad, and PageBreeze. Regardless of the tool you use, having a solid foundation in HTML will be useful. The examples in this text use Notepad.

Document Type Definition

Because multiple versions and types of HTML and XHTML exist, the W3C recommends identifying the type of markup language used in a web page document with a **Document Type Definition (DTD)**. The DTD identifies the version of HTML contained in your document. Browsers and HTML code validators can use the information in the DTD when processing the web page. The DTD statement, commonly called a doctype statement, is placed at the top of a web page document. XHTML is the current standard version of HTML and is supported by popular browsers. HTML5 is the newest version and is currently in draft status. You can choose to use either XHTML or HTML5 syntax as you work through this book. Except where specifically noted, the HTML5 syntax will display on commonly used browsers.

Your First XHTML Web Page

We'll use the XHTML 1.0 Transitional DTD—it's the least strict version of XHTML 1.0. The DTD for XHTML 1.0 Transitional is as follows:

```
<!DOCTYPE html PUBLIC "-//W3C//DTD XHTML 1.0 Transitional//EN"
"http://www.w3.org/TR/xhtml1/DTD/xhtml1-transitional.dtd">
```

The rest of your web page document will consist of HTML elements and text. After the DTD, each web page begins with an opening **<html>** tag and ends with a closing **</html>** tag. These tags indicate that the text between them is HTML formatted. It tells the browser how to interpret the document. Every single web page you create will include the html, head, title, meta, and body elements. A basic XHTML web page template (found in the student files at XHTMLfiles/chapter1/template.html) is as follows:

```
<!DOCTYPE html PUBLIC "-//W3C//DTD XHTML 1.0 Transitional//EN"
"http://www.w3.org/TR/xhtml1/DTD/xhtml1-transitional.dtd">
<html xmlns="http://www.w3.org/1999/xhtml" lang="en" xml:lang="en">
<head>
 <title>Page Title Goes Here</title>
 <meta http-equiv="Content-Type" content="text/html; charset=utf-8" />
</head>
<body>
 ... body text and more XHTML tags go here ...
</body>
</html>
```

With the exception of the specific page title, the first eight lines will usually be the same on every web page that you create. Review the code above and notice that the XHTML tags are lowercase. This conforms to XML syntax. Notice also that the DTD statement does not follow this syntax. The DTD statement indicates the markup language being used and has its own formatting—mixed case.

When using XHTML, the `<html>` tag also needs to describe the XML namespace (xmlns), which is the location of the documentation for the elements being used. This additional information is added to the `<html>` tag in the form of an **attribute**, which modifies or further describes the function of an element. The **xmlns** attribute points to the URL of the XHTML namespace used in the document, the standard http://www.w3.org/1999/xhtml. The optional **lang** and **xml:lang** attributes specify the spoken language of the document. For example, lang="en" xml:lang="en" indicate the English language. Search engines and screen readers may access these attributes.

Don't worry if the concept of specifying a DTD and the xmlns URL seem a bit overwhelming at first—these lines are reused over and over again in every web page. Once you create your web page template, you'll have these statements ready and waiting for all of your future pages.

Your First HTML5 Web Page

Now that you've seen an example of a web page using XHTML, let's focus on HTML5. The syntax is streamlined and easier to use. We will follow the coding style to use lowercase letters and place quotes around attribute values. A basic HTML5 web page template (also found in the student files at chapter1/template.html) is as follows:

```
<!DOCTYPE html>
<html lang="en">
<head>
 <title>Page Title Goes Here</title>
 <meta charset="utf-8">
</head>
<body>
 ... body text and more HTML tags go here ...
</body>
</html>
```

The next section will discuss the purpose of the head, title, meta, and body elements.

Head, Body, Title, and Meta Elements

There are two sections on a web page: the head and the body. The **head section**, sometimes called the header, contains information that describes the web page document. The **body section** contains the actual tags, text, images, and other objects that are displayed by the browser as a web page.

The Head Section

Elements that are located in the head section include the title of the web page, meta tags that describe the document (such as the character encoding used and information that may be accessed by search engines), and references to scripts and styles. Many of these do not show directly on the web page. The **head element** contains the head section, which begins with the **<head>** tag and ends with the **</head>** tag. You'll always code at least two other elements in the head section: a title element and a meta element.

The first element in the head section, the **title element,** configures the text that will appear in the title bar of the browser window. The text between the **<title>** and **</title>** tags is called the title of the web page and is accessed when web pages are bookmarked and printed. The title should be descriptive. If the web page is for a business or organization, the title should include the name of the organization or business.

The **meta element** describes a characteristic of a web page, such as the character encoding. Character encoding is the internal representation of letters, numbers, and symbols in a file such as a web page or other file that is stored on a computer and may be transmitted over the Internet. There are many different character-encoding sets. However, it is common practice to use a character-encoding set that is widely supported, such as utf-8, which is a form of Unicode. The meta tag is not used as a pair of opening and closing tags. It is considered to be a stand-alone **self-contained** tag (referred to as a **void element** in HTML5). The meta tag is coded differently in XHTML and HTML5. The XHTML meta tag has more detailed attributes and is coded with an ending />. The HTML5 meta tag is streamlined and only includes the charset attribute to indicate the character encoding.

XHTML Meta Tag:

```
<meta http-equiv="Content-Type" content="text/html; charset=utf-8" />
```

HTML5 Meta Tag:

```
<meta charset="utf-8">
```

The Body Section

The body section contains text and elements that display directly on the web page in the browser viewport. The purpose of the body section is to configure the contents of the web page. The **body element** contains the body section, which begins with the **<body>** tag and ends with the **</body>** tag. You will spend most of your time writing code in the body of a web page. If you type text in the body section, it will appear directly on the page.

HANDS-ON PRACTICE 1.1

Create your first HTML5 web page. Launch Notepad or another text editor. Either type in the following code or access the student files and select File > Open to edit the sample file located at chapter1/index.html:

```
<!DOCTYPE html>
<html lang="en">
<head>
<title>My First HTML5 Web Page</title>
<meta charset="utf-8">
</head>
<body>
Hello World
</body>
</html>
```

Notice that the first lines in the file contain the DTD. The HTML code begins with an opening <html> tag and ends with a closing </html> tag. The purpose of these tags is to indicate that the content between the tags makes up a web page. The head section is delimited by <head> and </head> tags and contains a pair of title tags with the words "My First HTML5 Web Page" in between along with a <meta> tag to indicate the character encoding. The body section is delimited by <body> and </body> tags. The words "Hello World" are typed on a line between the body tags. See Figure 1.11 for a screenshot of the code as it would appear in Notepad. You have just created the **source code** for a web page document.

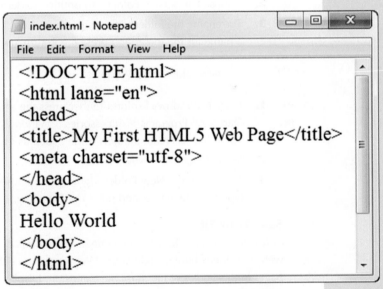

FIGURE 1.11 Your web page source code displayed in Notepad.

FAQ

Do I have to start each tag on its own line?

No, you are not required to start each tag on a separate line. A browser can display a page even if all the tags follow each other on one line with no spaces. Humans, however, find it easier to write and read web page code if line breaks and indentation (more on this later) are used.

Name, Save, and Test Your Web Page

File Management

You'll find it helpful to create folders to organize your files as you develop the web pages in this book and create your own websites. Use your operating system to create a new folder named chapter1 on your hard drive or a portable flash drive.

To create a new folder on a Mac:

1. Launch Finder and select the location where you'd like to create the new folder.
2. Choose File > New Folder. An untitled folder is created.
3. To rename the folder with a new name: select the folder and click on the current name. Type a name for the folder and press the Return key.

To create a new folder with Windows:

1. Launch Windows Explorer (either press the Windows key or select Start > All Programs > Accessories > Windows Explorer) and navigate to the location where you'd like to create the new folder, such as My Documents or your C: drive.
2. Select Organize > New Folder.
3. To rename the New Folder: right-click on it, select Rename from the context-sensitive menu, type the new name, and press the Enter key.

Save Your File

You will save your file with the name of index.html. A common file name for the home page of a website is index.html or index.htm. Web pages use either an .htm or .html file extension. The web pages in this book use the .html file extension. Display your file in Notepad or another text editor. Select File from the menu bar, and then select Save As. The Save As dialog box appears. Using Figure 1.12 as an example, type the file name. Click the Save button after you type the file name. Sample solutions for the exercises are available in the student files. If you would like, compare your work with the solution (chapter1/index.html) before you test your page.

FAQ

Why does my file have a .txt file extension?

In some older versions of Windows, Notepad will automatically append a .txt file extension. If this happens, type the name of the file within quotes, "index.html", and save your file again.

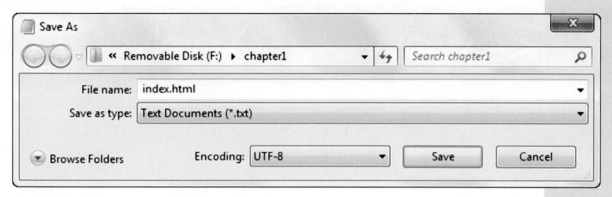

FIGURE 1.12 Save and name your file.

Test Your Page

There are two ways to test your page:

1. Launch Windows Explorer (Windows) or Finder (Mac). Navigate to your index.html file. Double-click index.html. The default browser will launch and will display your index.html page. Your page should look similar to the one shown in Figure 1.13.

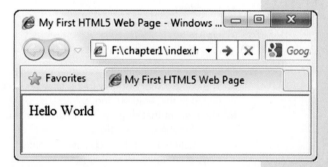

FIGURE 1.13 Web page displayed by Internet Explorer.

2. Launch a Browser. (If you are using Internet Explorer 8, select Tools, Menu Bar.) Select File, Open, Browse, My Computer, and then select your drive. Navigate to your index.html file. Double-click index.html and click OK. If you used Internet Explorer, your page should look similar to the one shown in Figure 1.13. A display of the page using Firefox is shown in Figure 1.14.

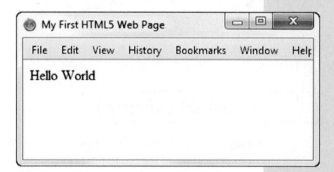

FIGURE 1.14 Web page displayed by Firefox.

Examine your page. Look carefully at the browser window. Notice how the title bar of the browser window contains the title text, "My First HTML5 Web Page." Some search engines need the text surrounded by the `<title>` and `</title>` tags to help determine relevance of keyword searches, so make certain that your pages contain descriptive titles. The `<title>` tag is also used when viewers bookmark your page or add it to their Favorites. An engaging and descriptive page title may entice a visitor to revisit your page. If your web page is for a company or an organization, it's a good idea to include the name of the company or organization in the title.

Review and Apply

Multiple Choice. Choose the best answer for each item.

1. What is a unique text-based Internet address corresponding to a computer's unique numeric IP address called?
   a. IP address
   b. domain name
   c. URL
   d. user name

2. Choose the true statement:
   a. The content that displays in the browser is contained in the head section.
   b. The content that displays in the browser is contained in the body section.
   c. Information about the web page is contained in the body section.
   d. All of the above are true.

3. The purpose of _____ is to ensure the integrity of the communication.
   a. IP
   b. TCP
   c. HTTP
   d. FTP

True or False. Choose the best answer for each question.

4. ____ Markup languages contain sets of directions that tell the browser software how to display and manage a web document.

5. ____ A domain name that ends in .net indicates that the website is for a networking company.

Fill in the Blank

6. _____ combines the formatting strengths of HTML 4.0 and the data structure and extensibility strengths of XML.

7. The newest version of HTML is _____.

8. _____ is the set of markup symbols or codes placed in a file intended for display on a web browser.

9. Web page documents typically use the ____ or ____ file extension.

10. The home page of a website is typically named _____ or _____.

Hands-On Exercise

A **blog**, or web log, is a journal that is available on the Web—it's a frequently updated page with a chronological list of ideas and links. Blog topics range from political journals to technical information to personal diaries. It's up to the person, called a blogger, who creates and maintains the blog.

Create a blog to document your learning experiences as you study web design. Visit one of the many sites that offer free blogs, such as http://blogspot.com or http://www.wordpress.com. Follow their instructions to establish your blog. Your blog could be a place to note websites that you find useful or interesting. You might report on websites that contain useful web design resources. You might describe sites that have interesting features, such as compelling graphics or easy-to-use navigation. Write a few sentences about the site that you find intriguing. After you begin to develop your sites, you could include the URLs and reasons for your design decisions. Share this blog with your fellow students and friends.

Web Research

1. The World Wide Web Consortium creates standards for the Web. Visit its site at
http://www.w3c.org and then answer the following questions:

   a. How did the W3C get started?

   b. Who can join the W3C? What does it cost to join?

   c. The W3C home page lists a number of technologies. Choose one that interests you, click its
   link, and read several of the associated pages. List three facts or issues you discover.

2. The World Organization of Webmasters (WOW) is a professional association dedicated to the
support of individuals and organizations that create and manage websites. Visit its site at
http://webprofessionals.org and answer the following questions:

   a. How can you join WOW? What does it cost to join?

   b. List one of the events that WOW participates in. Would you like to attend this event? Why
   or why not?

   c. List three ways that WOW can help you in your future career as a web developer.

Focus on Web Design

1. Visit a website referenced in this chapter that interests you. Print the home page or one other
pertinent page from the site. Write a one-page summary and your reaction to the site. Address
the following topics:

   a. What is the purpose of the site?

   b. Who is the intended audience?

   c. Do you think that the site reaches its intended audience? Why or why not?

   d. Is the site useful to you? Why or why not?

   e. List one interesting fact or issue that this site addresses.

   f. Would you encourage others to visit this site?

   g. How could this site be improved?

CHAPTER 2

Web Page Structural Basics

In the previous chapter you created your first web page using HTML5. You coded a web page and tested it in a browser. You used a Document Type Definition to identify the version of HTML being used along with the `<html>`, `<head>`, `<title>`, `<meta>`, and `<body>` tags. In this chapter you will continue your study of HTML and configure the structure and formatting of text on a web page using HTML elements. As you read this chapter, be sure to work through the examples. Coding a web page is a skill, and every skill improves with practice.

You'll learn how to . . .

- Configure the body of a web page with headings, paragraphs, divs, lists, and blockquotes
- Configure text with phrase elements
- Configure special entity characters, line breaks, and horizontal rules
- Test a web page for valid syntax

Heading Element

Heading elements are organized into six levels: h1 through h6. The text contained within a heading element is rendered as a "block" of text by the browser (referred to as block display) and appear with empty space (sometimes called "white space") above and below. The size of the text is largest for **<h1>** (called the heading 1 tag) and smallest for **<h6>** (called the heading 6 tag). Depending on the font being used (more on font sizes in Chapter 7), the text contained within **<h4>**, **<h5>**, and **<h6>** tags may be displayed smaller than the default text size. All text contained within heading tags is displayed with bold font weight.

FAQ

Why doesn't the heading tag go in the head section?

It's common for students to try to code the heading tags in the head section of the document, but someone doing this won't be happy with the way the browser displays the web page. Even though "heading tag" and "head section" sound similar, always code heading tags in the body section of the web page document.

Figure 2.1 shows a web page document with six levels of headings.

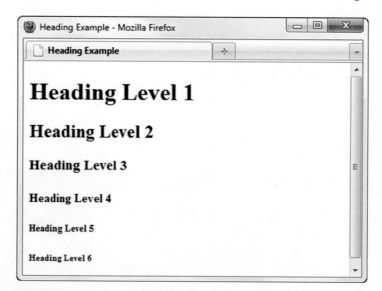

FIGURE 2.1   Sample heading.html.

HANDS-ON PRACTICE 2.1

To create the web page shown in Figure 2.1, launch Notepad or another text editor. Select File > Open to edit the HTML5 template file located at chapter1/template.html in the student files. Modify the title element and add heading tags to the body section as indicated by the following highlighted code:

```
<!DOCTYPE html>
<html lang="en">
<head>
<title>Heading Example</title>
<meta charset="utf-8">
</head>
<body>
<h1>Heading Level 1</h1>
<h2>Heading Level 2</h2>
<h3>Heading Level 3</h3>
<h4>Heading Level 4</h4>
<h5>Heading Level 5</h5>
<h6>Heading Level 6</h6>
</body>
</html>
```

Save the document as heading2.html on your hard drive or flash drive. Launch a browser such as Internet Explorer or Firefox to test your page. It should look similar to the page shown in Figure 2.1. You can compare your work with the HTML5 solution found in the student files (chapter2/heading.html) and the XHTML solution (XHTMLfiles/chapter2/heading.html). Notice that in this example, the code for both solutions is the same except for the Document Type Declaration, html, and meta tags. While this is true for many of the examples in this chapter, you'll see coding syntax differences as you work through the textbook. The XHTML and HTML5 solutions for each hands-on practice activity are provided in the student files.

■

More Heading Options in HTML5

You may have heard about the new HTML5 header element and hgroup element. They offer additional options for configuring headings, but they are only supported in newer browsers. We'll introduce these new elements in Chapter 8.

Quick Tip

Heading tags can help to make your pages more accessible and usable. It is good coding practice to use heading tags to outline the structure of your web page content. To indicate areas within a page hierarchically, code heading tags numerically as appropriate (h1, h2, h3, and so on) and include page content in block display elements such as paragraphs and lists. Visually challenged visitors who are using a screen reader can configure the software to display a list of the headings used on a page to focus on the topics that interest them. Your well-organized page will be more usable for every visitor to your site, including those who are visually challenged.

Paragraph Element

Paragraph elements are used to group sentences and sections of text together. Text that is contained by `<p>` and `</p>` tags will have a blank line above and below it.

Figure 2.2 shows a web page document with a paragraph after the first heading.

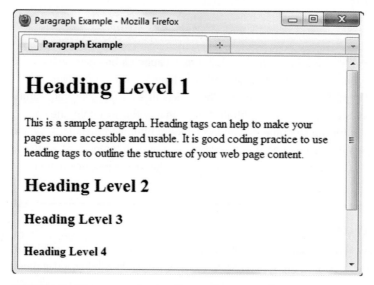

FIGURE 2.2   Web page using headings and a paragraph.

HANDS-ON PRACTICE 2.2 —————————————————

To create the web page shown in Figure 2.2, launch a text editor. Select File > Open to edit the file located at chapter2/heading.html in the student files. Use the following code as an example. Modify the page title and add a paragraph of text to your page below the line with the `<h1>` tags and above the line with the `<h2>` tags.

```
<!DOCTYPE html>
<html lang="en">
<head>
<title>Paragraph Example</title>
<meta charset="utf-8">
</head>
<body>
<h1>Heading Level 1</h1>
<p>This is a sample paragraph. Heading tags can help to make your
pages more accessible and usable. It is good coding practice to use
heading tags to outline the structure of your web page content.
</p>
<h2>Heading Level 2</h2>
<h3>Heading Level 3</h3>
<h4>Heading Level 4</h4>
<h5>Heading Level 5</h5>
<h6>Heading Level 6</h6>
</body>
</html>
```

Save the document as paragraph2.html on your hard drive or flash drive. Launch a browser to test your page. It should look similar to the page shown in Figure 2.2. You can compare your work with the solution found in the student files (chapter2/paragraph.html). Notice how the text in the paragraph wraps automatically as you resize your browser window.

Alignment

As you tested your web pages, you may have noticed that the headings and text begin near the left margin. This is called **left alignment** and is the default alignment for web pages. There are times when you want a paragraph or heading to be centered or right aligned (justified). The align attribute can be used for this. The purpose of an **attribute** is to modify the properties of an HTML element. In this case, the **align** attribute modifies the element's horizontal alignment (left, center, or right) on a web page. To center an element on a web page, use the attribute align="center". To right-justify an element on a web page, use the align="right" attribute. The default alignment is left. In XHTML syntax the align attribute can be used with a number of block display elements, including the paragraph (<p>) and heading (<h1> through <h6>) tags. The align attribute is **obsolete** in HTML5, which means that while it may be used in XHTML, the attribute has been removed from the W3C HTML5 draft specification. In Chapter 7 you'll learn how to configure alignment using a more modern approach with Cascading Style Sheets (CSS).

Quick Tip

When writing for the Web, avoid long paragraphs. People tend to skim web pages rather than read them word for word. Use heading tags to outline the page content along with short paragraphs (about three to five sentences) and lists (which you'll learn about later in the chapter).

Line Break and Horizontal Rule

The Line Break Element

The **line break element** causes the browser to advance to the next line before displaying the next element or text on a web page. The line break tag is not coded as a pair of opening and closing tags. It is considered to be a **stand-alone** or **self-contained** tag. In HTML5 syntax, the line break tag is coded as <br>. In XHTML (which follows XML syntax), the line break tag is coded as
 (the ending /> indicates a self-contained tag). Figure 2.3 shows a web page document with a line break after the first sentence in the paragraph.

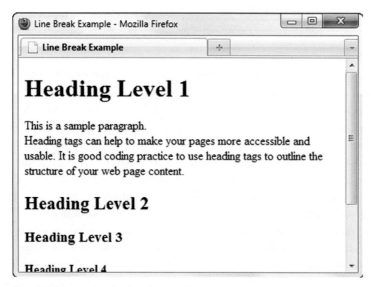

FIGURE 2.3 Notice the line break after the first sentence.

HANDS-ON PRACTICE 2.3 ——————————————————

To create the web page shown in Figure 2.3, launch a text editor. Select File > Open to edit the file located at chapter2/paragraph.html in the student files. Modify the text contained between the title tags to be "Line Break Example". Place your cursor after the first sentence in the paragraph (after "This is a sample paragraph."). Press the Enter key. Save your file. Test your page in a browser and notice that even though your source code showed the "This is a sample paragraph." sentence on its own line, the browser did not render it that way. A line break tag is needed to configure the browser to display the second sentence on a new line. The file uses HTML5 syntax. Edit the file in a text editor and add a <br> tag after the first sentence in the paragraph as shown in the following code snippet.

```
<body>
<h1>Heading Level 1</h1>
<p>This is a sample paragraph. <br> Heading tags can help to make
your pages more accessible and usable. It is good coding practice to
use heading tags to outline the structure of your web page content.
</p>
<h2>Heading Level 2</h2>
<h3>Heading Level 3</h3>
<h4>Heading Level 4</h4>
<h5>Heading Level 5</h5>
<h6>Heading Level 6</h6>
</body>
```

Save your file as linebreak2.html. Launch a browser to test your page. It should look similar to the page shown in Figure 2.3. You can compare your work with the solution found in the student files (Chapter2/linebreak.html).

The Horizontal Rule Element

Web designers often use visual elements such as lines and borders to separate or define areas on web pages. A horizontal rule or line visually separates areas of a page and configures a horizontal line across a web page. Since the horizontal rule element does not contain any text, it is coded as a stand-alone tag and not in a pair of opening and closing tags. XHTML syntax for the horizontal rule is **<hr />**. HTML5 syntax for the horizontal rule is **<hr>** and the element has a new semantic meaning—it indicates a thematic break. Horizontal rules are centered within their container element (in this case the web page body) by default.

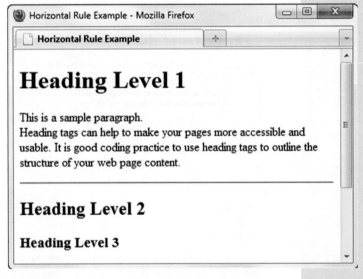

Figure 2.4 shows a web page document (also found in the student files at chapter2/hr.html) with a horizontal rule after the paragraph. In Chapter 7 you'll learn how to configure lines and borders on web page elements with Cascading Style Sheets (CSS).

FIGURE 2.4 The horizontal line is below the paragraph.

Quick Tip

When you are tempted to use a horizontal rule on a web page, consider whether it is really needed. Usually, just leaving extra blank space (referred to as "white space") on the page will serve to separate the content. Note: The term white space is borrowed from the print industry—since paper is white, extra blank space is known as white space.

Blockquote Element

Besides organizing text in paragraphs and headings, sometimes you need to add a quotation to a web page. The **<blockquote>** tag is used to display a block of quoted text in a special way—indented from both the left and right margins. A block of indented text begins with a **<blockquote>** tag and ends with a **</blockquote>** tag.

Figure 2.5 shows a web page document with a heading, a paragraph, and a blockquote.

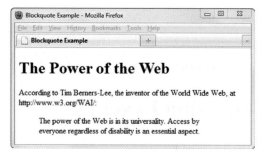

FIGURE 2.5   The text within the blockquote element is indented.

Quick Tip

You've probably noticed how convenient the <blockquote> tag could be if you needed to indent an area of text on a web page. You may have wondered whether it would be OK to use the <blockquote> anytime you'd like to indent text or whether the blockquote element is reserved only for long quotations. The semantically correct use of the <blockquote> tag is to use it only when displaying large blocks of quoted text within a web page. Why should you be concerned about semantics? Consider the future of the Semantic Web, described in *Scientific American* as "A new form of Web content that is meaningful to computers [that] will unleash a revolution of new possibilities." Using HTML in a semantic, structural manner is one step toward the Semantic Web. So, avoid using a <blockquote> just to indent text. You'll learn modern techniques to configure margins and padding on elements later in this book.

HANDS-ON PRACTICE 2.4 ———————————————————

To create the web page shown in Figure 2.5, launch a text editor. Select File > Open to edit the template file located at chapter1/template.html in the student files. Modify the title element. Add a heading tag, a paragraph tag, and a blockquote tag to the body section as indicated by the following highlighted code.

```
<!DOCTYPE html>
<html lang="en">
<head>
<title>Blockquote Example</title>
<meta charset="utf-8">
</head>
<body>
<h1>The Power of the Web</h1>
<p>According to Tim Berners-Lee, the inventor of the World Wide Web,
at http://www.w3.org/WAI/:</p>
<blockquote>
The power of the Web is in its universality. Access by everyone
regardless of disability is an essential aspect.
</blockquote>
</body>
</html>
```

Save the document as blockquote2.html on your hard drive or flash drive. Launch a browser such as Internet Explorer or Firefox to test your page. It should look similar to the page shown in Figure 2.5. You can compare your work with the solution found in the student files (chapter2/blockquote.html).

———————————————————————————————— ■

Why does my web page still look the same?

Often, students make changes to a web page but get frustrated because their browser shows an older version of the page. The following troubleshooting tips are helpful when you know you modified your web page but the changes do not show up in the browser:

1. Make sure that you save your web page file after you make the changes.

2. Verify the location that you are saving your file to—the hard drive, a particular folder.

3. Verify the location that your browser is requesting the file from—the hard drive, a particular folder.

4. Be sure to click the Refresh or Reload button in your browser.

Phrase Elements

Phrase elements, sometimes referred to as **logical style elements**, indicate the context and meaning of the text between the container tags. It is up to each browser to interpret that style. Phrase elements are displayed right in line with the text (referred to as inline display) and can apply to either a section of text or even a single character of text. For example, the **<strong>** element indicates that the text associated with it has strong importance and should be displayed in a "strong" manner in relation to normal text on the page. Table 2.1 lists common phrase elements and examples of their use. Notice that some tags, such as <cite> and <dfn>, result in the same type of display (italics) as the <em> tag in today's browsers. These tags semantically describe the text as a citation or definition, but the physical display is usually italics in both cases.

Element	Example	Usage
<abbr>	WIPO	Identifies text as an abbreviation, configures the title attribute
<b>	**bold** text	Text that has no extra importance but is styled in bold font
<cite>	*cite* text	Identifies a citation or reference; usually displayed in italics
<code>	code text	Identifies program code samples; usually a fixed-space font
<dfn>	*dfn* text	Identifies a definition of a word or term; usually displayed in italics
<em>	*emphasized* text	Causes text to be emphasized; usually displayed in italics
<i>	*italicized* text	Text that has no extra importance but is styled in italics
<kbd>	kbd text	Identifies user text to be typed; usually a fixed-space font
<mark>	mark text	Text that is highlighted in order to be easily referenced (HTML5 only)
<samp>	samp text	Shows program sample output; usually a fixed-space font
<small>	small text	Legal disclaimers and notices ("fine print") displayed in small font-size
<strong>	**strong** text	Strong importance; usually displayed in bold
<sub>	$_{sub}$text	Displays a subscript as small text below the baseline
<sup>	^{sup}text	Displays a superscript as small text above the baseline
<var>	*var* text	Identifies and displays a variable output; usually displayed in italics

TABLE 2.1 Phrase Elements

Note that all phrase elements are container tags—an opening and a closing tag should be used. As shown in Table 2.1, the **<strong>** element indicates that the text associated with it has "strong" importance. Usually the browser (or other user agent) will display <strong> text in bold font type. A screen reader, such as JAWS or Window-Eyes, might interpret <strong> text to indicate that the text should be more strongly spoken. In the following line the phone number is displayed with strong importance:

Call for a free quote for your web development needs: **888.555.5555**

The code is

```
<p>Call for a free quote for your web development needs:
<strong>888.555.5555</strong></p>
```

Notice that the opening <strong> and closing <strong> tags are contained within the paragraph tags (<p> and </p>). This code is properly nested and is considered to be **well formed**. When improperly nested, the <p> and <strong> tag pairs overlap each other instead of being nested within each other. Improperly nested code will not pass validation testing (see the HTML Syntax Validation section later in this chapter) and may cause display issues.

Figure 2.6 shows a web page document (also found in the student files at chapter2/em.html) that uses the <em> tag to display the emphasized phrase "Access by everyone" in italics.

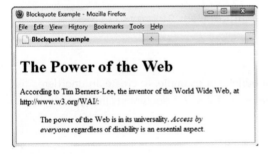

FIGURE 2.6 The <em> tag in action.

The code snippet is

```
<blockquote>
The power of the Web is in its universality.
<em>Access by everyone</em> regardless of disability is an essential
aspect.
</blockquote>
```

Unordered List

Unordered lists display a bullet before each entry in the list. This bullet can be one of several types: disc (the default), square, and circle. See Figure 2.7 for a sample unordered list.

Popular Web Servers

- Apache Web Server
- Microsoft IIS
- Oracle iPlanet Web Server

FIGURE 2.7 Sample unordered list.

Unordered lists begin with a **`<ul>`** tag and end with a **`</ul>`** tag. Each list item begins with an **`<li>`** tag and ends with an **`</li>`** tag. The code to configure the heading and unordered list shown in Figure 2.7 is

```
<h1>Popular Web Servers</h1>
<ul>
    <li>Apache Web Server</li>
    <li>Microsoft IIS</li>
    <li>Oracle iPlanet Web Server</li>
</ul>
```

The type Attribute

The **`type`** attribute can be used to change the type of bullet. For example, to create an unordered list organized with square bullets, use `<ul type="square">`. Table 2.2 documents the type attribute and its values for unordered lists.

Value	Example
disc (the default)	•
square	■
circle	○

TABLE 2.2 The `type` Attribute for Unordered Lists

HTML5 and the Unordered List Element

The type attribute is widely used in unordered lists and is valid in XHTML. However, be aware that the type attribute on the `<ul>` tag is considered obsolete in HTML5 because it is decorative and does not convey meaning. No worries—you'll learn how to configure the list markers in an unordered list in Chapter 6.

HANDS-ON PRACTICE 2.5

In this Hands-On Practice you will use a heading and an unordered list on the same page. To create the web page shown in Figure 2.8, launch a text editor. Select File > Open to edit the template file located at chapter1/template.html in the student files. Modify the title element and add h1, ul, and li tags to the body section as indicated by the following highlighted code:

```
<!DOCTYPE html>
<html lang="en">
<head>
<title>Heading and List</title>
<meta charset="utf-8">
</head>
<body>
<h1>Popular Web Servers</h1>
<ul>
    <li>Apache Web Server</li>
    <li>Microsoft IIS</li>
    <li>Oracle iPlanet Web Server</li>
</ul>
</body>
</html>
```

Save your file as ul2.html. Launch a browser and test your page. It should look similar to the page shown in Figure 2.8. You can compare your work with the solution in the student files (chapter2/ul.html).

Take a few minutes to experiment with the type attribute. Configure the unordered list to use square bullets. Save your file as ul3.html. Test your page in a browser. You can compare your work with the solution in the student files (chapter2/ulsquare.html).

FIGURE 2.8 An unordered list.

Can I use images as the "bullets" in unordered lists?

Yes, you can. In Chapter 6 you will learn to use Cascading Style Sheets (CSS) to configure the list markers ("bullets") in an unordered list to display images and shapes.

Ordered List

Ordered lists use a numbering or lettering system to itemize the information contained in the list. An ordered list can be organized by the use of numerals (the default), uppercase letters, lowercase letters, uppercase Roman numerals, and lowercase Roman numerals. See Figure 2.9 for a sample ordered list.

Popular Web Servers

1. Apache Web Server
2. Microsoft IIS
3. Oracle iPlanet Web Server

FIGURE 2.9   Sample ordered list.

Ordered lists begin with an **\<ol>** tag and end with an **\</ol>** tag. Each list item begins with an **\<li>** tag and ends with an **\</li>** tag. The code to configure the heading and ordered list shown in Figure 2.9 follows:

```
<h1>Popular Web Servers</h1>
<ol>
    <li>Apache Web Server</li>
    <li>Microsoft IIS</li>
    <li>Oracle iPlanet Web Server</li>
</ol>
```

The `type` Attribute

The `type` attribute configures the symbol used for ordering the list. For example, to create an ordered list organized by uppercase letters, use `<ol type="A">`. Table 2.3 documents the type attribute and its values for ordered lists.

Value	Symbol
1	Numerals (the default)
A	Uppercase letters
a	Lowercase letters
I	Roman numerals
i	Lowercase Roman numerals

TABLE 2.3   The `type` Attribute for Ordered Lists

HTML5 and the Ordered List Element

Even though unordered lists and ordered lists are similar, HTML5 treats their type attribute differently. In HTML5, the type attribute is obsolete for use with unordered lists. However, the type attribute is valid when used with ordered lists because the sequencing provides information. Another handy attribute that can still be used is the **start attribute**, which you can set to an integer value to begin the list at a number other than 1 (for example, `start="10"`). Configure the new HTML5 **reversed attribute** (set `reversed="reversed"`) to indicate that a list is in descending order.

HANDS-ON PRACTICE 2.6

In this Hands-On Practice you will use a heading and an ordered list on the same page. To create the web page shown in Figure 2.10, launch a text editor. Select File > Open to edit the template file located at chapter1/template.html in the student files. Modify the title element and add h1, h2, ol, and li tags to the body section as indicated by the following highlighted code:

```
<!DOCTYPE html>
<html lang="en">
<head>
<title>Heading and List</title>
<meta charset="utf-8">
</head>
<body>
<h1>Popular Web Servers</h1>
<ol>
    <li>Apache Web Server</li>
    <li>Microsoft IIS</li>
    <li>Oracle iPlanet Web Server</li>
</ol>
</body>
</html>
```

Save your file as ol2.html. Launch a browser and test your page. It should look similar to the page shown in Figure 2.10. You can compare your work with the solution in the student files (chapter2/ol.html).

FIGURE 2.10   An ordered list.

Take a few minutes to experiment with the `type` attribute. Configure the ordered list to use uppercase letters instead of numerals. Save your file as ol3.html. Test your page in a browser. You can compare your work with the solution in the student files (chapter2/ola.html).

Description List

Description lists (called **definition lists** in XHTML) help to organize terms and their descriptions. The terms stand out, and their descriptions can be as long as needed to convey your message. Each term begins on its own line at the margin. Each description begins on its own line and is indented. Description lists are also handy for organizing Frequently Asked Questions (FAQs) and their answers. The questions and answers are offset with indentation. Any type of information that consists of a number of corresponding terms and longer descriptions is well suited to being organized in a description list. See Figure 2.11 for an example of a web page that uses a description list.

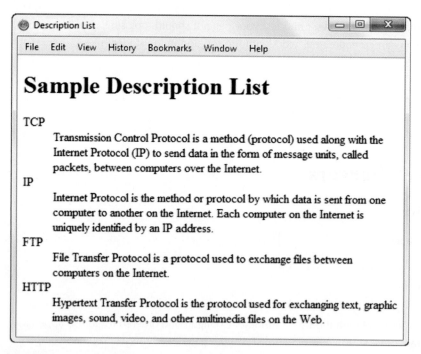

FIGURE 2.11   A description list.

Description lists begin with the **<dl>** tag and end with the **</dl>** tag. Each term or name in the list begins with the **<dt>** tag and ends with the **</dt>** tag. Each term description begins with the **<dd>** tag and ends with the **</dd>** tag.

HANDS-ON PRACTICE 2.7

In this Hands-On Practice you will use a heading and a description list on the same page. To create the web page shown in Figure 2.11, launch a text editor. Select File > Open to edit the template file located at chapter1/template.html in the student files. Modify the title element and add h1, dl, dd, and dt tags to the body section as indicated by the following highlighted code:

```
<!DOCTYPE html>
<html lang="en">
<head>
<title>Description List</title>
<meta charset="utf-8">
</head>
<body>
<h1>Sample Description List</h1>
<dl>
  <dt>TCP</dt>
    <dd>Transmission Control Protocol is a method (protocol) used along
with the Internet Protocol (IP) to send data in the form of message
units, called packets, between computers over the Internet.</dd>
  <dt>IP</dt>
    <dd>Internet Protocol is the method or protocol by which data is
sent from one computer to another on the Internet. Each computer on
the Internet is uniquely identified by an IP address.</dd>
  <dt>FTP</dt>
    <dd>File Transfer Protocol is a protocol used to exchange files
between computers on the Internet.</dd>
  <dt>HTTP</dt>
    <dd>Hypertext Transfer Protocol is the protocol used for
exchanging text, graphic images, sound, video, and other multimedia
files on the Web.</dd>
</dl>
</body>
</html>
```

Save your file as description2.html. Launch a browser and test your page. It should look similar to the page shown in Figure 2.11. Don't worry if the word wrap is a little different—the important formatting is that each <dt> term should be on its own line and the corresponding <dd> description should be indented under it. Try resizing your browser window and notice how the word wrap on the description text changes. You can compare your work with the solution in the student files (chapter2/description.html).

Why is the web page code in the Hands-On Practice examples indented?

Actually, it doesn't matter to the browser if web page code is indented, but humans find it easier to read and maintain code when it is logically indented. Review the description list created in Hands-On Practice 2.7. Notice how the <dt> and <dd> tags were indented. This makes it easier for you or another web developer to understand the source code in the future. There is no "rule" as to how many spaces to indent, although your instructor or the organization you work for may have a standard. Consistent indentation helps to create more easily maintainable web pages.

Special Entity Characters

In order to use special characters such as quotation marks, the greater-than sign (>), the less-than sign (<), and the copyright symbol (©) in your web page document, you need to use special characters, sometimes called entity characters. For example, if you wanted to include a copyright line on your page as follows:

© Copyright 2012 My Company. All rights reserved.

You would use the special character **©** to display the copyright symbol, as shown in the code in the following example:

```
&copy; Copyright 2012 My Company. All rights reserved.
```

Another useful special character is ** **, which stands for nonbreaking space. You may have noticed that web browsers treat multiple spaces as a single space. If you need a small number of spaces in your text, you may use   multiple times to indicate multiple blank spaces. This is acceptable if you simply need to tweak the position of an element a little. If you find that your web pages contain many   special characters in a row, you should use a different method to align elements, such as configuring the margin or padding with Cascading Style Sheets (see Chapter 7).

See Table 2.4 and the textbook website at http://webdevbasics.net/chapter2.html for a description of more special characters and their codes.

Character	Entity Name	Code
"	Quotation mark	"
©	Copyright symbol	©
&	Ampersand	&
Empty space	Nonbreaking space	
'	Apostrophe	’
-	Long dash	—
|	Vertical Bar	|

TABLE 2.4 Common Special Characters

HANDS-ON PRACTICE 2.8

Figure 2.12 shows the web page you will create in this Hands-On Practice. Launch a text editor. Select File > Open to edit the template file located at chapter1/template.html in the student files. Modify the title of the web page by changing the text between the `<title>` and `</title>` tags to Web Design Steps.

The sample page shown in Figure 2.12 contains a heading, an unordered list, and copyright information.

Configure the heading Web Design Steps as a level 1 heading (`<h1>`) as follows:

```
<h1>Web Design Steps</h1>
```

Now create the unordered list. The first line of each bulleted item is the title of the web design step. In the sample, each step title should be strong or stand out from the rest of the text. The code for the beginning of the unordered list is

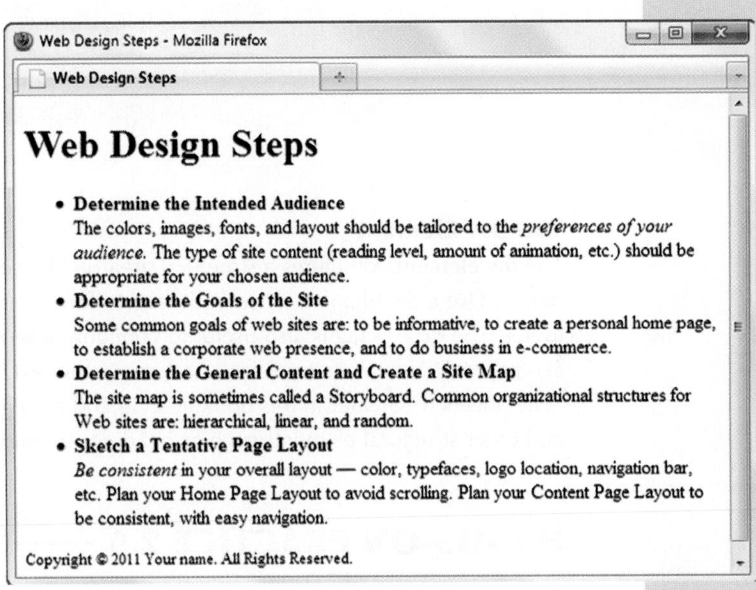

FIGURE 2.12 Sample design.html.

```
<ul>
<li><strong>Determine the
Intended Audience</strong><br>
The colors, images, fonts, and
layout should be tailored to the <em>preferences of your audience.
</em> The type of site content (reading level, amount of animation,
etc.) should be appropriate for your chosen audience.</li>
```

Edit your design.html file and code the entire ordered list. Remember to code the closing `</ul>` tag at the end of the list. Don't worry if your text wraps a little differently—your screen resolution or browser window size may be different.

Finally, configure the copyright information with the small element. Use the special character `&copy;` for the copyright symbol. The code for the copyright line is

```
<p><small>Copyright &copy; 2011 Your name. All Rights
Reserved.</small></p>
```

How did you do? Compare your work to the sample in the student files (chapter2/design.html).

Div Element

The Div Element

The **div element** configures a structural area or "division" on a web page with a line break above and below. Use a div element when you need to format an area of a web page such as a logo or page footer. The `<div>` tag is also useful to configure a section that contains block display elements, such as `<p>`, `<ul>`, `<blockquote>`, and even other `<div>` elements within it. You'll use Cascading Style Sheets (CSS) later in this book to style and configure the color, text typeface, and layout of divs and other structural elements such as headings, paragraphs, and lists.

HANDS-ON PRACTICE 2.9

In this Hands-On Practice you will practice using the div element as you edit the Trillium Media Design home page, shown in Figure 2.13. Launch a text editor and open the starter.html file from the chapter2 folder in the student files. Save your page as div2.html.

FIGURE 2.13   This page uses the div element.

View the source code. The code from the body section is as follows:

```
<body>
    <h1>Trillium Media Design</h1>
    <p>Home  :Services  Contact</p>
    <h2>New Media and Web Design</h2>
    <p>Trillium Media Design will bring your company&rsquo;'s Web
presence to the next level. We offer a comprehensive range of
services.</p>
    <h2>Meeting Your Business Needs</h2>
    <p>Our expert designers are creative and eager to work with you.
Take advantage of the power of Web 2.0!</p>
    <p><small>Copyright &copy; 2012 Your Name Here</small></p>
</body>
```

Review the code and notice that the navigation information and the copyright information are configured in paragraph tags, even though they are not really paragraphs (or even sentences). Both a paragraph element and a div element configure text in a block with empty space above and below. However, when the text is not a true paragraph in meaning, a div element is the better choice. Modify the code and replace the paragraph tags that contain the navigation and copyright information with div tags as follows:

```
<body>
    <h1>Trillium Media Design</h1>
    <div>Home  :Services  Contact</div>
    <h2>New Media and Web Design</h2>
    <p>Trillium Media Design will bring your company&rsquo;s Web
presence to the next level. We offer a comprehensive range of
services.</p>
    <h2>Meeting Your Business Needs</h2>
    <p>Our expert designers are creative and eager to work with you.
Take advantage of the power of Web 2.0!</p>
    <div><small>Copyright &copy; 2012 Your Name Here</small></div>
</body>
```

Save your file and display it in a browser. It should look about the same. However, it's improved "under the hood"—the div elements are a better semantic choice than paragraph elements to configure content areas that are not actually paragraphs, such as the navigation and copyright areas. The student files contain a sample solution at chapter2/div.html. As you continue to develop web pages you'll find that div elements are very handy for configuring areas on web pages.

 FAQ

Are there new structural elements in HTML5 that configure areas on web pages?

Yes, one of the characteristics of HTML5 is an emphasis on semantics. While the div element is useful, it is also quite generic. HTML5 offers a variety of special-purpose structural elements, including section, article, heading, nav, aside, and footer. You'll explore these elements in Chapter 8.

HTML Syntax Validation

The W3C has a free Markup Validation Service available at http://validator.w3.org that will check your code for syntax errors and validate your XHTML or HTML5 web pages. HTML validation provides students with quick self-assessment—you can prove that your code uses correct syntax. In the working world, HTML validation serves as a quality assurance tool. Invalid code may cause browsers to render the pages slower than otherwise.

HANDS-ON PRACTICE 2.10

In this Hands-On Practice you will use the W3C Markup Validation Service to validate a web page file. This example uses the page completed in Hands-On Practice 2.8 (student files chapter2/design.html). Locate design.html and open it in a text editor, such as Notepad. We will add an error to the design. html page. Delete the first closing `</strong>` tag. This modification should generate several error messages.

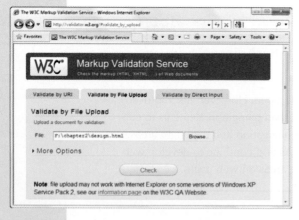

Next, attempt to validate the design.html file. Launch a browser and visit the W3C Markup Validation Service file upload page at http://validator.w3.org/#validate_by_upload. Click the Browse button and select the chapter2/design.html file from your computer. Click the Check button to upload the file to the W3C site (Figure 2.14).

FIGURE 2.14 Validate your page.

An error page will display. Notice the "Errors found while checking this document" message. You can view the errors by scrolling down the page, as shown in Figure 2.15.

Notice that the message indicates line 12, which is the first line after the missing closing `</strong>` tag. HTML error messages often point to a line that follows the error.

The text of the message "End tag for li seen, but there were unclosed elements" lets you know that something is wrong. It's up to you to figure out what it is. A good place to start is to check your container tags and make sure they are in pairs. In this case, that is the problem. You can scroll down to view the other errors. However, since multiple error messages are often displayed after a single error occurs, it's a good idea to fix one item at a time and then revalidate.

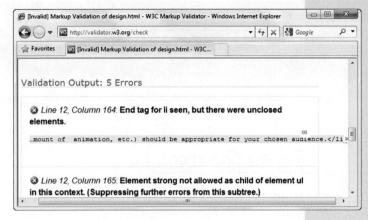

FIGURE 2.15   The error indicates line 12.

Edit the design.html file in a text editor and add the missing `</strong>` tag. Save the file. Launch a browser and visit http://validator.w3.org/#validate_by_upload. Select your file, select More Options, and verify the Show Source and Verbose Output check boxes are checked. Click the Revalidate button to begin the validation.

Your display should be similar to that shown in Figure 2.16. Notice the "This document was successfully checked as HTML5" message. This means that your page passed the validation test. Congratulations, your design.html page is valid! You may also notice a warning message which you can overlook that indicates the HTML5 conformance checker is in experimental status. It's a good practice to validate your web pages. However, when validating code, use common sense. Since web browsers still do not completely follow W3C recommendations, there will be situations, such as when adding multimedia to a web page, when HTML code configured to work reliably across a variety of browsers and platforms will not pass validation.

FIGURE 2.16   The page has passed the validation test.

In addition to the W3C validation service, there are other tools that you can use to check the syntax of your code. Explore the HTML5 validator at http://html5.validator.nu and the HTML5 "lint" tool at http://lint.brihten.com/html.

CHAPTER 2

Review and Apply

Review Questions

Multiple Choice. Choose the best answer for each item.

1. Which tag pair configures a structural area on a web page?
   a. `<area> </area>`
   b. `<div> </div>`
   c. `<cite> </cite>`
   d. `<strong> </strong>`

2. Which tag pair is used to create the largest heading?
   a. `<h1> </h1>`
   b. `<h9> </h9>`
   c. `<h type="largest"> </h>`
   d. `<h6> </h6>`

3. Which tag configures the following text or element to display on a new line?
   a. `<new line>`
   b. `<nl>`
   c. `<br>`
   d. `<line>`

4. Which tag pair configures a paragraph?
   a. `<para> </para>`
   b. `<paragraph> </paragraph>`
   c. `<p> </p>`
   d. `<body> </body>`

5. What is the default alignment for headings and paragraphs?
   a. center
   b. left
   c. right
   d. wherever you type them in the source code

6. Which type of XHTML list will automatically number the items for you?
   a. numbered list
   b. ordered list
   c. unordered list
   d. description list

7. Which tag pair is the best choice to emphasize text with bold font on a web page?
   a. `<b> </b>`
   b. `<strong> </strong>`
   c. `<em> </em>`
   d. `<bold> </bold>`

8. Which tag configures a horizontal line on a web page?
   a. `<br>`
   b. `<hl>`
   c. `<hr>`
   d. `<line>`

9. Which tag pair contains the items in an ordered or unordered list?
   a. `<item> </item>`
   b. `<li> </li>`
   c. `<dd> </dd>`
   d. all of the above

10. Which statement is true?
    a. The W3C Markup Validation Service describes how to fix the errors in your web page.
    b. The W3C Markup Validation Service lists syntax errors in a web page.
    c. The W3C Markup Validation Service is only available to W3C members.
    d. None of the above statements are true

Hands-On Exercises

1. Write the markup language code to display your name in the largest-size heading element.

2. Write the markup language code for an unordered list to display the days of the week.

3. Write the markup language code for an ordered list that uses uppercase letters to order the items. This ordered list will display the following: Spring, Summer, Fall, and Winter.

4. Think of a favorite quote by someone you admire. Write the XHTML code to display the person's name in a heading and the quote in a blockquote.

5. Modify the following code snippet to indicate that the bolded text has strong importance.

```
<p>A diagram of the organization of a website is called a <b>site
map</b> or <b>storyboard</b>. Creating the <b>site map</b> is one
of the initial steps in developing a website.</p>
```

Focus on Web Design

Markup language code alone does not make a web page—design is very important. Access the Web and find two web pages—one that is appealing to you and one that is unappealing to you. Print each page. Create a web page that answers the following questions for each of your examples.

a. What is the URL of the website?

b. Is the page appealing or unappealing? List three reasons for your answer.

c. If the page is unappealing, what would you do to improve it?

d. Would you encourage others to visit this site? Why or why not?

Case Study

PACIFIC TRAILS RESORT

This case study continues throughout most of the text. This chapter introduces the Pacific Trails Resort website scenario, presents the site map, and directs you to create the home page for the site. Melanie Bowie is the owner of Pacific Trails Resort, located right on the California North Coast. The resort offers a quiet getaway with luxury camping in yurts along with an upscale lodge for dining and visiting with fellow guests. The target audience for Pacific Trails Resort is couples who enjoy nature and hiking. Melanie would like a website that emphasizes the uniqueness of the location and accommodations. She would like the website to include a home page, a page about the special yurt accommodations, a reservations page with a contact form, and a page to describe the activities available at the resort.

A site map for the Pacific Trails Resort website is shown in Figure 2.17. The site map describes the architecture of the website—a Home page with three main content pages: Yurts, Activities, and Reservations.

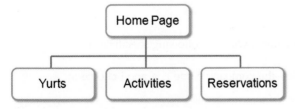

FIGURE 2.17 Pacific Trails Resort site map.

Figure 2.18 displays a wireframe sketch of the page layout for the Pacific Trails Resort website. The wireframe contains a site logo, a navigation area, a content area, and a footer area for copyright information.

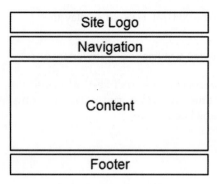

FIGURE 2.18 Pacific Trails Resort
wireframe page layout.

Your task in this case study is to create the Home page for the Pacific Trails Resort website. The file
name of the Home page file is index.html. Follow the instructions in the Hands-On Practice Case Study.

Step 1: Create a folder called pacific to contain your Pacific Trails Resort website files.

Step 2: *The Home Page.* You will use a text editor to create the Home page for the Pacific
Trails Resort website. The Home page is shown in Figure 2.19.

FIGURE 2.19 Pacific Trails Resort index.html.

Launch a text editor and create a web page document with the following specifications:

1. **Web Page Title:** Use a descriptive page title—the company name is a good choice for a
business website.

2. **Wireframe Logo Area:** Use <h1> for the Pacific Trails Resort logo.

3. **Wireframe Navigation Area:** Place the following text within a div with bold text (use the
<strong> logical style element). Add extra blank spaces between the words with the
  special character as needed:
   Home   Yurts   Activities   Reservations

4. **Wireframe Content Area:**

   a. Place the following within an h2 element: Enjoy Nature in Luxury
   b. Place the following content in a paragraph: Pacific Trails Resort offers a special lodging experience on the California North Coast. Relax in serenity with panoramic views of the Pacific Ocean.
   c. Place the following content in an unordered list:
   Private yurts with decks overlooking the ocean
   Activities lodge with fireplace and gift shop
   Nightly fine dining at the Overlook Cafe
   Heated outdoor pool and whirlpool
   Guided hiking tours of the redwoods
   d. Contact information:
   Place the address and phone number information within a div below the unordered list. Use line break tags as needed.
   Pacific Trails Resort
   12010 Pacific Trails Road
   Zephyr, CA 95555
   888-555-5555

5. **Wireframe Footer Area:**

   Configure the copyright and e-mail address information within a div. Also configure small text size (use the `<small>` element) and italics font style (use the `<i>` phrase element). The copyright information is
   Copyright © 2011 Pacific Trails Resort
   Place your name in the format yourfirstname@yourlastname.com on a new line under the copyright information.

The web page in Figure 2.19 may seem a little sparse, but don't worry. As you gain experience and learn to use more advanced techniques, your pages will look more professional. White space (blank space) on the page can be added with `<br>` tags where needed. Your page does not need to look exactly the same as the sample. Your goal at this point should be to practice and get comfortable using HTML. Save your file in the pacific folder and name it index.html.

CHAPTER 3

Hyperlink Basics

Now that you have had some experience coding a web page, you are ready to explore what makes the World Wide Web a web of interconnected information—hyperlinks. In this chapter you will learn how to configure the anchor element to connect web pages to each other with hyperlinks.

You'll learn how to . . .

- Use the anchor element to link from page to page
- Configure absolute, relative, and e-mail hyperlinks
- Configure relative hyperlinks to web pages in folders within a website
- Configure a hyperlink to a named fragment internal to a web page

Anchor Element

Use the **anchor element** to specify a **hyperlink**, often referred to as a *link*, to another web page or file that you want to display. Each anchor element begins with an <a> tag and ends with an </a> tag. The opening and closing anchor tags surround the text to click to perform the hyperlink. Use the **href** attribute to configure the hyperlink reference, which identifies the name and location of the file to access.

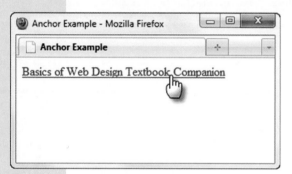

FIGURE 3.1 Sample hyperlink.

Figure 3.1 shows a web page document with an anchor tag that configures a hyperlink to this book's website, http://webdevbasics.net.

The code for the anchor tag in Figure 3.1 is

```
<a href="http://webdevbasics.net">Basics of
Web Design Textbook Companion</a>
```

Notice that the href value is the URL for the website and will display the home page. The text that is typed between the two anchor tags displays on the web page as a hyperlink and is underlined by most browsers. When you move the mouse over a hyperlink, the cursor changes to a pointing hand, as shown in Figure 3.1.

HANDS-ON PRACTICE 3.1 ─────────────

To create the web page shown in Figure 3.1, launch a text editor. Select File > Open to edit the template file located at chapter1/template.html in the student files. Modify the title element and add heading tags to the body section as indicated by the following highlighted code:

```
<!DOCTYPE html>
<html lang="en">
<head>
<title>Anchor Example</title>
<meta charset="utf-8">
</head>
<body>
<a href="http://webdevbasics.net">Basics of Web Design Textbook Companion</a>
</body>
</html>
```

Save the document as anchor2.html on your hard drive or flash drive. Launch a browser such as Internet Explorer or Firefox to test your page. It should look similar to the page shown in Figure 3.1. You can compare your work with the solution found in the student files (chapter3/anchor.html).

Targeting Hyperlinks

You may have noticed in Hands-On Practice 3.1 that when a visitor clicks on a hyperlink, the new web page will automatically open in the same browser window. You can configure the target attribute on an anchor tag with `target="_blank"` to open a hyperlink in a new browser window or browser tab. Note that you cannot control whether the web page opens in a new window or opens in a new tab—that is dependent on your visitor's browser configuration.

HANDS-ON PRACTICE 3.2

Let's experiment with the target attribute. Launch a text editor. Select File > Open to edit the anchor2.html file you created in Hands-On Practice 3.1. Modify the anchor tag to use the target attribute. Your new anchor tag is

```
<a href= "http://webdevbasics.net" target="_blank">Basics of Web
Design Textbook Companion</a>
```

Save the document as target2.html on your hard drive or flash drive. Launch a browser such as Internet Explorer or Firefox to test your page. It should still look similar to the page shown in Figure 3.1. However, when you click the hyperlink, the web page will open in a new browser window or new browser tab. You can compare your work with the solution found in the student files (chapter3/target.html).

Block Anchor

It's typical to use anchor tags to configure phrases or even just a single word as a hyperlink. HTML5 provides a new function for the anchor tag—the block anchor. A block anchor can configure one or more elements (even those that display as a block, such as a div, h1, or paragraph) as a hyperlink. See an example in the student files (chapter3/block.html).

FAQ

Can images be hyperlinks?

Yes. Although we'll concentrate on text hyperlinks in this chapter, it is also possible to configure an image as a hyperlink. You'll get practice with image links in Chapter 6.

Absolute and Relative Hyperlinks

Absolute Hyperlinks

An **absolute hyperlink** indicates the absolute location of the resource on the Web. Use absolute hyperlinks when you need to link to resources on other websites. The href value for an absolute hyperlink to the home page of a website includes the http:// protocol and the domain name. The following hyperlink is an absolute hyperlink to the home page of this book's website:

```
<a href="http://webdevbasics.net">Basics of Web Design Textbook
Companion</a>
```

Note that if we wanted to access a web page other than the home page on the book's website, we could also include a specific folder name and file name. For example, the following anchor tag configures an absolute hyperlink for a file named index.html located in a folder named chapter3 on this book's website.

```
<a href="http://webdevbasics.net/chapter3/index.html">Basics of Web
Design Chapter 3</a>
```

Relative Hyperlinks

When you need to link to web pages within your site, use a relative hyperlink. The href value for a relative hyperlink does not begin with the http:// and does not include a domain name. For a relative hyperlink, the href value will only contain the file name or file name and folder of the web page you want to display. The hyperlink location is relative to the page currently being displayed. For example, if you

FAQ

What if my relative hyperlink doesn't work?

Check the following:

- Did you save files in the specified folder?
- Did you save the files with the names as requested? Use Windows Explorer, My Computer, or Finder (Mac users) to verify the actual names of the files you saved.
- Did you type the file names correctly in the anchor tag's href property? Check for typographical errors.
- When you place your mouse over a link, the file name of a relative link will display in the status bar in the lower edge of the browser window. Verify that this is the correct file name.

On many operating systems, such as UNIX or Linux, the use of uppercase and lowercase in file names matters—make sure that the file name and the reference to it are in the same case. It's a good practice to always use lowercase for file names used on the Web.

were coding a home page (index.html) for the website shown in Figure 3.2 and wanted to link to a page named contact.html located in the same folder as index.html, you would use the following code sample:

```
<a href="contact.html">Contact Us</a>
```

More on Relative Hyperlinks

There are times when you need to link to files in other folders on your website. Let's consider the example of a website for a dog groomer that highlights services and products. The web developer for this site created separate folders called services and products in order to organize the site. See the folder and file listing shown in Figure 3.2.

📁 groomer
index.html
contact.html
📁 images
📁 products
collars.html
shampoo.html
📁 services
bathing.html
daycare.html

FIGURE 3.2 The dog groomer site contains the images, products, and services folders.

Relative Hyperlink Examples

- To review, when linking to a file in the same folder or directory, the value of the href is the name of the file. For example, to link to the contact.html page from the home page (index.html), code the anchor element as follows:

```
<a href="contact.html">Contact</a>
```

- When linking to a folder located within the current directory, use both the folder name and the file name in the relative link. For example, to link to the collars.html page in the products folder from the home page (index.html), code the anchor element as follows:

```
<a href="products/collars.html">Collars</a>
```

- In Figure 3.2 the collars.html page is located in a subfolder of the groomer folder. The home page for the site, index.html, is located in the groomer folder. When linking to a file that is up one directory level from the current page use " . . /" notation. To link to the home page for the site from the collars.html page, code the anchor element as follows:

```
<a href="../index.html">Home</a>
```

- When linking to a file that is in a folder on the same level as the current folder, the href value will use the " . . /" notation to indicate moving up one level and then down to the chosen folder. For example, to link to the bathing.html page in the services folder from the collars.html page in the products folder, code the anchor element as follows:

```
<a href="../services/bathing.html">Dog Bathing</a>
```

Don't worry if the use of " . . /" notation and linking to files in different folders seems new and different. In most of the exercises in this book you'll code either absolute hyperlinks to other websites or relative hyperlinks to files in the same folder. You'll get some practice coding hyperlinks in the next section.

Practice with Hyperlinks

The best way to learn how to code web pages is by actually doing it! Let's create three pages in a sample website to practice using the anchor tag to configure hyperlinks.

HANDS-ON PRACTICE 3.3

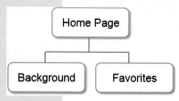

FIGURE 3.3 Site map.

1. Create a new folder. Name your folder "mypractice". This site is an example of a personal website. It will contain a home page called index.html and two content pages called background.html and favorites.html. A sample site map (see Figure 3.3) shows the organization of the site—a home page (index.html) with navigation hyperlinks to two pages (background.html and favorites.html).

2. Now create the home page for your mypractice website, as shown in Figure 3.4.

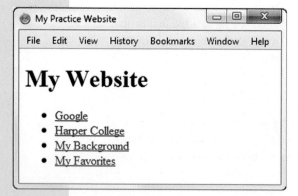

FIGURE 3.4 Sample index.html displayed in the Apple Safari browser.

Launch a text editor. Select File > Open to edit the template file located at chapter1/template.html in the student files. Modify the title element and configure the following:

- A "My Website" heading—use <h1> tags
- An unordered list with:
- An absolute link to your favorite search engine
- An absolute link to the website of your school
- A relative link to background.html
- A relative link to favorites.html

The body section of your web page will be similar to the following code sample:

```
<body>
<h1>My Website</h1>
  <ul>
    <li><a href="http://google.com">Google</a></li>
    <li><a href="http://harpercollege.edu">Harper College</a></li>
    <li><a href="background.html">My Background</a></li>
    <li><a href="favorites.html">My Favorites</a></li>
  </ul>
</body>
```

Save your page as index.html in the mypractice folder.
Display your page in a browser. It should look similar
to the page shown in Figure 3.4. Compare your work
to the sample (chapter3/practice/index.html) in the
student files.

Test your page by clicking each link. When you click the
absolute links to your favorite search engine and your
school you should see those pages displayed if you are
connected to the Internet. The relative links should not
work yet—let's create the Background page in Step 3.

3. Create the background.html page, as shown in Figure 3.5.

Let's work efficiently and build on the previous page.
Launch a text editor and open the index.html file. Select

FIGURE 3.5 Sample background.html.

File > Save As to save the file with the name background.html in the mypractice folder. In
order to create a consistent logo for the site, do not change the h1 heading area. Replace the
rest of the web page content with the following:

- A subheading of My Background—use <h2> tags
- A paragraph that contains one or two sentences about your background
- A navigation bar configured with a div that contains relative hyperlinks to the Home
  page (index.html), the Background page (background.html), and the Favorites page
  (favorites.html). As shown in Figure 3.5, you'll need to add a blank space between each
  anchor element.

The body section of your web page will be similar to the following code sample:

```
<body>
<h1>My Website</h1>
   <h2>My Background</h2>
      <p>As a college student majoring in Web Design, I'm interested in
         developing my skills in design principles, XHTML, and CSS.</p>
      <div><a href="index.html">Home</a>
      <a href="background.html">Background</a>
      <a href="favorites.html">Favorites</a></div>
</body>
```

Save your file. Now, test your index.html page again. This time when you click the
Background hyperlink your browser should display your new page. Click the Home hyperlink on your background.html page to redisplay your home page. Don't worry if these
hyperlinks don't work perfectly the first time. If you have problems, carefully examine the
source code of the pages and verify the existence and location of the files using Windows
Explorer or the Mac Finder.

4. Using Step 3 above as a guide, create the Favorites page (favorites.html) and include
   an unordered list of your favorite topics. See an example in the student files
   (chapter3/practice/favorites.html).

E-Mail Hyperlinks

The anchor tag can also be used to create e-mail hyperlinks. An e-mail hyperlink will automatically launch the default mail program configured for the browser. It is similar to an external hyperlink with the following two exceptions:

- It uses mailto: instead of http://.
- It launches the default e-mail application for the visitor's browser with your e-mail address as the recipient.

For example, to create an e-mail hyperlink to the e-mail address help@webdevbasics.net, code the following:

```
<a href="mailto:help@webdevbasics.net">help@webdevbasics.net</a>
```

It is good practice to place the e-mail address both on the web page and within the anchor tag. Not everyone has an e-mail program configured with his or her browser. By placing the e-mail address in both places, you increase usability for all of your visitors.

Quick Tip

Free web-based e-mail is offered by many providers, such as Yahoo!, Google, Hotmail, and so on. Create one or more free e-mail accounts to use when communicating with new websites or signing up for free services such as newsletters. This will help to organize your e-mail into those you need to access and respond to right away (such as school, work, or personal messages) and those you can get to at your convenience.

HANDS-ON PRACTICE 3.4 ———————

In this Hands-On Practice you will modify the home page of the website you created in Hands-On Practice 3.3 and add an e-mail link to the page footer area. Launch a text editor and open the index.html file from your mypractice folder. This example uses the index.html file found in the student files in the chapter3/practice folder.

Configure a paragraph that contains the text "Contact:" and an e-mail hyperlink at the bottom of the page as shown in Figure 3.6. Use your e-mail address as the href value.

FIGURE 3.6 An e-mail hyperlink has been added to the home page.

Save and test the page in a browser. The browser display should look similar to the page shown in Figure 3.6. Compare your work with the sample in the student files (chapter3/practice2/index.html). Modify the favorites.html and background.html files in a similar manner. Sample solutions are located in the student files (chapter3/practice2 folder).

Won't displaying my actual e-mail address on a web page increase spam?

Yes and no. While it's possible that some unethical spammers may harvest web pages for e-mail addresses, the chances are that your e-mail application's built-in spam filter will prevent your inbox from being flooded with messages.

When you configure an easily readable e-mail hyperlink you increase the usability of your website for your visitors in the following situations:

- The visitor may be at a public computer with no e-mail application configured. When the e-mail hyperlinked is clicked, this situation usually causes an error message to display. The visitor will have difficulty contacting you in this manner.

- The visitor may be at a private computer but prefer not to use the e-mail application (and address) that is configured by default to work with the browser. Perhaps he or she shares the computer with others, or perhaps he or she wishes to preserve the privacy of the default e-mail address

If you prominently displayed your actual e-mail address, in both of these situations the visitor can still access your e-mail address and use it to contact you (in either their e-mail application or via a web-based e-mail system such as Google's Gmail). The result is a more usable website for your visitors.

Fragment Identifiers

By now you should be comfortable with hyperlinks. You may have noticed that hyperlinks cause the browser to display the top of the web page. Sometimes it is helpful to link to an exact position on a web page. Internal hyperlinks and fragment identifiers are used for this function.

Linking to Fragment Identifiers

There are times when you need to provide the capability to link to a specific portion of a web page. You can accomplish this by coding a hyperlink to a **fragment identifier** (sometimes called a named fragment or fragment id), which is simply an HTML element with an id attribute. An **id** attribute serves to uniquely identify an element on a web page, just as your drivers' license id servers to uniquely identify you.

Lists of frequently asked questions (FAQs) often use fragment identifiers to jump to a specific part of the page and display the answer to a question. Other applications of fragment identifiers include hyperlinks that skip to the content of a page or skip back to the top of the page.

There are two components to your coding when using fragment identifiers:

1. The tag that identifies the **named fragment** of a web page. The tag must be assigned to an id. For example, `<div id="content">`.
2. The anchor tag that links to the named fragment on a web page.

Focus on Accessibility

An example of using a fragment identifier to increase the accessibility of a web page is the "Skip to Content" (also called "Skip Navigation") hyperlink, which provides a way for web page visitors who may be using keyboard-only access to skip repetitive navigation links (see Figure 3.7).

Quick Tip

Legacy Alert. Older web pages may use the name attribute and refer to named anchors rather than fragment identifiers. This coding technique is obsolete and not valid in HTML5. Named anchors used the name attribute to identify or name the fragment. For example, `<a name="content" id="content"></a>`.

Fragment Identifier Example: Skip to Content

When the visitor activates the "skip to content" hyperlink (by either clicking on it or tabbing to it and pressing the Enter key), the browser links to the fragment identifier and shifts focus to the content area of the page. Coding a hyperlink to a named fragment is accomplished in two steps:

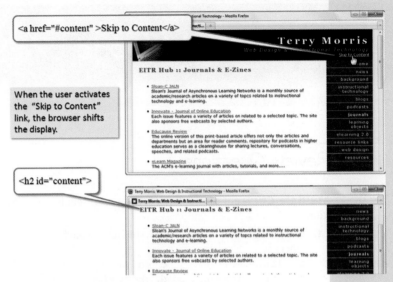

1. **Establish the Target.** Create the "skip to content" fragment identifier by configuring an element that begins the page content with an id, for example,

```
<h2 id="content">
```

2. **Reference the Target.** At the point of the page where you want to place a hyperlink to the content, code an anchor element. Use the href attribute and place a # symbol (called a **hash mark**) before the name of the fragment identifier. The code for a hyperlink to the named fragment "content" is

FIGURE 3.7 The "skip to content" link in action.

```
<a href="#content">Skip to Content</a>
```

The hash mark indicates that the browser should search for an id on the same page. If you forget to type the hash mark, the browser will not look on the same web page; it will look for an external file. A named fragment can be configured anywhere in the body of a web page document.

Fragment Identifiers in Action

Locate the chapter3/favorites.html file in the student files. Figure 3.8 shows a partial screenshot of this web page. Examine the source code and notice that the top portion of the page contains an unordered list with categories of interest (such as Hobbies, XHTML, CSS, and Professional Organizations) that correspond to the text displayed in the `<h2>` elements below. Display the page in a browser and explore clicking on the links in the unordered list to move the browser focus to the associated named fragment. Launch a text editor and open the chapter3/starter1.html file in the student files if you'd like to practice coding named fragments.

There may be times when you need to link to a named fragment on another web page. To accomplish this, place a "#" followed by the fragment identifier id value after the file name in the anchor tag. So, to link to the "Hobbies" heading (given that it is a named fragment called "hobbies") from any other page on the same website, you could use the following code:

FIGURE 3.8 Practice with fragment identifiers.

```
<a href="favorites.html#hobbies">Hobbies</a>
```

CHAPTER 3
Review and Apply

Multiple Choice. Choose the best answer for each item.

1. Which tag is used to hyperlink web pages to each other?
   a. `<link>` tag
   b. `<hyperlink>` tag
   c. `<a>` tag
   d. `<body>` tag

2. When do you need to use a domain name in a hyperlink?
   a. always
   b. when linking to a web page file on the same site
   c. when linking to a web page file on an external site
   d. never

3. What does an e-mail link do?
   a. automatically sends you an e-mail message with the visitor's e-mail address as the reply-to field
   b. launches the default e-mail application for the visitor's browser with your e-mail address as the recipient
   c. displays your e-mail address so that the visitor can send you a message later
   d. links to your mail server

4. How would you configure a hyperlink from the index.html file to another file named products.html that is located in the same folder?
   a. `<a target="products.html">Products</a>`
   b. `<a href="products.html">Products</a>`
   c. `<a name="products.html">Products</a>`
   d. `<a>Products</a>`

5. Which attribute can be applied to an anchor tag to open a link in a new browser window?
   a. window
   b. target
   c. rel
   d. media

6. Which of the following attributes defines a fragment identifier in a page?
   a. id
   b. identifier
   c. fragment
   d. bookmark

7. How would you link to the named fragment #jobs on the page employ.html from the home page of the site?
   a. `<a href="employ.html#jobs">Employment Opportunities</a>`
   b. `<a name="employ.html#jobs">Employment Opportunities</a>`
   c. `<a link="employ.html#jobs">Employment Opportunities</a>`
   d. none of the above

8. When should you code an absolute hyperlink?
   a. always; the W3C prefers absolute hyperlinks
   b. when linking to a web page that is external to your website
   c. when linking to a web page that is internal to your website
   d. never; the W3C has deprecated absolute hyperlinks

9. When should you code a relative hyperlink?
   a. always; the W3C prefers relative hyperlinks
   b. when linking to a web page that is external to your website
   c. when linking to a web page that is internal to your website
   d. never; the W3C has deprecated relative hyperlinks

10. Which attribute identifies the name and location of the file to access when a hyperlink is clicked?
    a. window
    b. href
    c. rel
    d. media

1. Describe when to use an absolute hyperlink. Is the http protocol used in the href value?

2. Describe when to use a relative hyperlink. Is the http protocol used in the href value?

3. Write the code to create an absolute hyperlink to a website whose domain name is google.com.

4. Write the code to create a relative hyperlink to a web page named services.html.

5. Create a web page about your favorite musical group. Include the name of the group, the individuals in the group, a hyperlink to the group's website, your favorite three (or fewer if the group is new) CD releases, and a brief review of each CD. Use an unordered list to organize the names of the individuals. Use a definition list for the names of the CDs and your reviews. Save the page as band.html. Open your file in a text editor and print the source code for the page. Display your page in a browser and print the page. Hand in both printouts to your instructor.

Focus on Web Design

You've learned how to configure anchor tags to create hyperlinks in this chapter, including how to specify both the text description of the link and the file to display. Visit the website of your school and create a web page that provides the following items.

a. What is the URL of the website?

b. Locate three example hyperlinks. For each example, report on the text of the hyperlink and whether you believe it is helpful and descriptive.

c. Share any suggestions that you have to improve the text used in the hyperlinks.

Case Study

PACIFIC TRAILS RESORT ——————————————

This case study continues throughout most of the book. In this chapter's case study you will use the existing Pacific Trails website (Chapter 2) as a starting point. You will add hyperlinks to the home page and create another page for the website.

Refer to Chapter 2 for the Pacific Trails Resort site map (Figure 2.17) and the wireframe (Figure 2.18). Note the navigation area in the wireframe. You have two tasks in this case study:

- Configure navigation hyperlinks and an e-mail hyperlink on the home page (index.html)
- Configure a second page named yurts.html.

Step 1: Create a folder called ch3pacific to contain your Pacific Trails Resort website files. Copy the index.html file from the Chapter 2 Case Study pacific folder.

Step 2: *The Home Page.* Launch a text editor and open the home page, index.html.

- You will update the index.html page and code anchor tags to configure the text in the navigation area as hyperlinks. See Table 3.1, which lists the text and corresponding href value.

Text	href Value
Home	index.html
Yurts	yurts.html
Activities	activities.html
Reservations	reservations.html

TABLE 3.1 Navigation for the Pacific Trails Resort Website

Next, you'll update the page footer area. Configure the text yourfirstname@yourlastname.com to be an e-mail hyperlink. Figure 3.9 shows the Home page after the hyperlinks have been configured.

FIGURE 3.9 Pacific Trails Resort index.html with hyperlinks.

Step 3: *The Yurts Page.* Create the Yurts page shown in Figure 3.10. A productivity technique is to create new pages based on existing pages so you can benefit from your previous work. Your new Yurts page will use the index.html page as a starting point. Open the index.html page for the Pacific Trails Resort website in a text editor. Select File > Save As and save the file with the new name of yurts.html in the ch3pacific folder.

FIGURE 3.10 The new Yurts page.

Now you are ready to edit the yurts.html file.

- Modify the page title. Change the text contained between the `<title>` and `</title>` tags to Pacific Trails Resort :: Yurts.
- Replace the text contained within the `<h2>` tags with The Yurts at Pacific Trails.
- Delete the paragraph, the unordered list, and the contact information. Do not delete the logo, navigation, or page footer areas of the page.
- The Yurts page contains a list with questions and answers. Add this content to the page using a definition list. Use the `<dt>` element to contain each question. Configure the question to display in bold text (use the `<strong>` element). Use the `<dd>` element to contain the answer to the question. The questions and answers are as follows:

What is a yurt?

Our luxury yurts are permanent structures four feet off the ground. Each yurt has canvas walls, a wooden floor, and a roof dome that can be opened.

How are the yurts furnished?

Each yurt is furnished with a queen-size bed with down quilt and gas-fired stove. The luxury camping experience also includes electricity and a sink with hot and cold running water. Shower and restroom facilities are located in the lodge.

What should I bring?

Bring a sense of adventure and some time to relax! Most guests also pack comfortable walking shoes and plan to dress for changing weather with layers of clothing.

Save your page and test it in a browser. Test the hyperlink from the yurts.html page to index.html. Test the hyperlink from the index.html page to yurts.html. If your links do not work, review your work with close attention to these details:

- Verify that you have saved the pages with the correct names in the correct folder.
- Verify your spelling of the page names in the anchor tags.
- After you make changes, test again.

CHAPTER 4

Web Design Basics

As a website visitor, you have probably found that certain websites are appealing and easy to use, while others seem awkward or just plain annoying. What separates the good from the bad? This chapter discusses recommended website design practices. The topics include site organization, site navigation, page design, text design, graphic design, and accessibility considerations.

You'll learn how to . . .

- Describe the most common types of website organization
- Describe principles of visual design
- Design for your target audience
- Create clear, easy-to-use navigation
- Improve the readability of the text on your web pages

- Use graphics appropriately on web pages
- Apply the concept of universal design to web pages
- Describe web page layout design techniques
- Apply best practices of web design

Design for Your Target Audience

Whatever your personal preferences, your website should appeal to your **target audience**—the people who will use your site. Your intended target audience may be specific, such as kids, college students, young couples, or seniors, or you may intend your site to appeal to everyone. The purpose and goals of your visitors will vary—they may be casually seeking information, performing research for school or work, comparison shopping, job hunting, and so on. The design of a website should appeal to and meet the needs of the target audience.

For example, NASA's website, http://www.nasa.gov, as shown in Figure 4.1, features compelling graphics and has a different look and feel from the text-based, link-intensive website of the Bureau of Labor Statistics, http://www.bls.gov (Figure 4.2).

FIGURE 4.1   The compelling graphic draws you in.

The first site engages you, draws you in, and invites exploration. The second site provides you with a wide range of choices so that you can quickly get down to work. Keep your target audience in mind as you explore the web design practices in this chapter.

FIGURE 4.2 This text-intensive website immediately offers numerous choices.

Browser-Friendly

Just because your web page looks great in your favorite browser doesn't automatically mean that all browsers will render it well. Determine the browser most likely to be used by your target audience. A good source of browser statistics is Net Market Share (http://marketshare.hitslink.com). Develop the site so that it looks great in your target audience's most popular browser and looks acceptable (degrades gracefully) in other browsers.

Always try to test your pages with the most popular versions of browsers on both PC and Mac operating systems. At the time of this writing, these are Internet Explorer 8, Firefox 3, Safari, Opera 10, and Google's Chrome browser. Many web page components, including default text size and default margin size, are different among browsers, browser versions, and operating systems.

Screen Resolution

Your website visitors will use a variety of screen resolutions. The most commonly used screen resolutions are currently 1024×768, 1280×800, and 1280×1024. Design your pages to avoid horizontal scrolling at these resolutions. Depending on your target audience, you still may have some visitors using 800×600 screen resolution. Be aware that mobile devices have low screen resolution, such as 240×320 or 320×480. One method of creating a page that looks good in multiple screen resolutions is to center the page content with balanced left and right margins (see Chapter 7).

Focus on Accessibility

Which screen resolution is everyone using?

A recent survey by Net Market Share (http://marketshare.hitslink.com/report.aspx?qprid=17) reported that 1024×768 is currently the most popular screen resolution. Of visitors surveyed, about 22 percent use 1024×768, 17 percent use 1280×800, 11 percent use 1280×1024, 8 percent use 1440×900, 5 percent use 1680×1050, and 2 percent use 800×600.

Website Organization

How will visitors move around your site? How will they find what they need? This is largely determined by the website's organization or architecture. There are three common types of website organization:

- Hierarchical
- Linear
- Random (sometimes called Web organization)

A diagram of the organization of a website is called a **site map**. Creating the site map is one of the initial steps in developing a website.

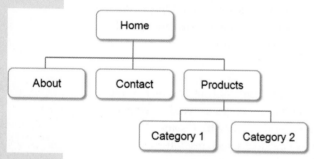

FIGURE 4.3 Hierarchical site organization.

Hierarchical Organization

Most websites use **hierarchical organization**. A site map for hierarchical organization, such as the one shown in Figure 4.3, is characterized by a clearly defined home page with links to major site sections. Web pages within sections are placed as needed. The home page plus the first level of pages in a hierarchical site map typically indicates the hyperlinks on the main navigation bar of each web page.

It is important to be aware of pitfalls of hierarchical organization. Figure 4.4 shows a site design that is too shallow—there could be too many major site sections.

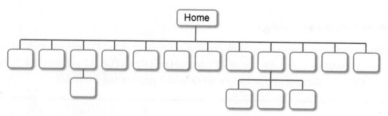

FIGURE 4.4 This site design uses a shallow hierarchy.

Another design pitfall is designing a site that is too deep. Figure 4.5 shows an example of this. The interface design "three-click rule" says that a web page visitor should be able to get to any page on your site with a maximum of three hyperlinks. In other words, a visitor who cannot get what he or she wants in three mouse clicks will begin to feel frustrated and may leave your site. This rule may be very difficult to satisfy on a large site, but in general, the goal is to organize your site so that your visitors can easily navigate from page to page within the site structure.

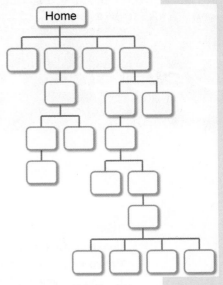

FIGURE 4.5 This site design uses a deep hierarchy.

Linear Organization

Linear organization, shown in Figure 4.6, is useful when the purpose of a website or series of pages within a site is to provide a tutorial, tour, or presentation that needs to be viewed sequentially.

FIGURE 4.6 Linear site organization.

In linear organization, the pages are viewed one after another. Some websites use hierarchical organization in general but with linear organization in a few small areas.

Random Organization

Random organization (sometimes called Web organization) offers no clear path through the site, as shown in Figure 4.7. There is often no clear home page and no discernible structure. Random organization is not as common as hierarchical or linear organization and is usually found only on artistic sites or sites that strive to be especially different and original. This type of organization is typically not used for commercial websites.

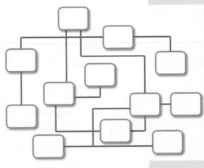

FIGURE 4.7 Random site organization.

What's a good way to organize my site map?

Sometimes it is difficult to begin creating a site map for a website. Some design teams meet in a room with a blank wall and a package of large Post-it Notes. They write the titles of topics and subtopics needed on the site on the Post-it Notes. They arrange the notes on the wall and discuss until the site structure becomes clear and there is consensus within the group. If you are not working in a group, you can try this on your own and then discuss the way you have chosen to organize the website with a friend or fellow student.

Principles of Visual Design

There are four visual design principles that you can apply to the design of just about anything: repetition, contrast, proximity, and alignment. Whether you are designing a web page, a button, a logo, a CD cover, a brochure, or a software interface, the design principles of repetition, contrast, proximity, and alignment will help to create the "look and feel" of your project and will determine whether your message is effectively communicated.

Repetition: Repeat Visual Elements Throughout the Design

When applying the principle of **repetition**, the web designer repeats one or more elements throughout the page. The repeating aspect ties the work together. Figure 4.8 displays the home page of the State of Tennessee website (http://www.tn.gov). The page design demonstrates the use of repetition in a variety of design components, including shape, color, font, and images.

- The main navigation links on the left side of the page are the same rectangular shape. Notice how background color is used within the repetition of the navigation rectangles to differentiate the type of link—blue indicates target audience, medium gray indicates site section, and light gray indicates "housekeeping" (site map, contact page, etc.).
- The gray colors are also repeated in the Governor's section in the lower middle of the page and in the bottom border of the right sidebar category headings.
- The use of only two font typefaces on the page also demonstrates repetition and helps to create a cohesive look. Page headings are configured with Verdana font. Other page content uses Arial font.
- The large rectangular visual element in the middle of the page engages the visitor and incorporates repetition of three thumbnail images. The services area also utilizes several thumbnail images.

Whether it is color, shape, font, or image, repetition of elements helps to unify a design.

Contrast: Add Visual Excitement and Draw Attention

To apply the principle of **contrast**, emphasize the differences between page elements in order to make the design interesting and direct attention. There should be good contrast between the background color and the text color on a web page. If there is too little contrast, the text will be difficult to read. Notice how the navigation area in Figure 4.8 uses text color with good contrast (either light text with the blue and medium gray background or dark text with the light gray background). The main content areas use dark text on a medium or light background to provide good visual contrast and easy reading.

FIGURE 4.8 The design principles of repetition, contrast, proximity, and alignment are well used on this site.

Proximity: Group Related Items

When designers apply the principle of **proximity**, related items are placed physically close together. Unrelated items should have space separating them. The placing of interface items close together gives visual clues to the logical organization of the information or functionality. In Figure 4.8, the vertical navigation links are all placed in close proximity to each other. This creates a visual group on the page and makes the navigation easier to use. Notice the proximity of the options in the Governor's section, services options, and right-sidebar links. Proximity is used well on this page to group related elements.

Alignment: Align Elements to Create Visual Unity

Another principle that helps to create a cohesive web page is **alignment**. When applying this principle, the designer organizes the page so that each element placed has some alignment (vertical or horizontal) with another element on the page. The page shown in Figure 4.8 also applies this principle. Notice how the page components are vertically aligned in columns. Examine the services area (Driver Online Services, Renew Health License, Annual Report Filing) and observe the alignment of the thumbnail images, headings, and text.

Repetition, contrast, proximity, and alignment are four visual design principles that can greatly improve your web page designs. If you apply these principles effectively, your web pages will look more professional and you will communicate your message more clearly. Keep these principles in mind as you design and build web pages.

Design to Provide for Accessibility

In Chapter 1 you were introduced to the concept of **universal design**. The Center for Universal Design defines universal design as "the design of products and environments to be usable by all people, to the greatest extent possible, without the need for adaptation or specialized design."

Who Benefits from Universal Design and Increased Accessibility?

Consider the following scenarios:

- Maria, a young woman in her twenties with physical challenges who cannot manipulate a mouse and who uses a keyboard with much effort—Accessible web pages designed to function without a mouse will help Maria access content.

- Leotis, a college student who is deaf and wants to be a web developer—Captions for audio/video content and transcripts will provide Leotis access to content.

- Jim, a middle-aged man who has a dial-up Internet connection and is using the Web for personal enjoyment—Alternate text for images and transcripts for multimedia will provide Jim improved access to content.

- Nadine, a mature woman with age-related macular degeneration who has difficulty reading small print—Web pages designed so that text can be enlarged in the browser will make it easier for Nadine to read.

- Karen, a college student using a smart phone to access the Web—Accessible content organized with headings and lists will make it easier for Karen to surf the Web on a mobile device.

- Prakesh, a man in his thirties who is legally blind and needs access to the Web to do his job—Web pages designed to be accessible (which are organized with headings and lists, display descriptive text for hyperlinks, provide alternate text descriptions for images, and are usable without a mouse) will help Prakesh access content.

All of these individuals benefit from web pages designed with accessibility in mind. A web page that is designed to be accessible is typically more usable for all—even a person who has no physical challenges and is using a broadband connection benefits from the improved presentation and organization of a well-designed web page (Figure 4.9).

Accessible Design Can Benefit Search Engine Listing

Search engine programs (commonly referred to as bots or spiders) walk the Web and follow hyperlinks on websites. An accessible website with descriptive page titles that is well organized with headings, lists, descriptive text for hyperlinks, and alternate text for images is more visible to search engine robots and may result in better ranking.

FIGURE 4.9 Everyone benefits from an accessible web page.

Legal Requirements

The Internet and World Wide Web are such a pervasive part of our culture that accessibility is mandated by laws in the United States. Section 508 of the Rehabilitation Act requires electronic and information technology, including web pages, used by federal agencies to be accessible to people with disabilities. The accessibility recommendations presented in this text are intended to satisfy the Section 508 standards and the W3C Web Accessibility Initiative guidelines. At the time this was written the Section 508 standards were undergoing revision; see http://www.access-board.gov for current information.

Accessibility Is the Right Thing to Do

The federal government is promoting accessibility by law, and the private sector is following its lead. The W3C is also active in this cause and has created the Web Accessibility Initiative (WAI) to create guidelines and standards applicable to web content developers, authoring-tool developers, and browser developers. You can access WAI's Web Content Accessibility Guidelines 2.0 (WCAG 2.0) at http://www.w3.org/TR/WCAG20/Overview. The following four principles are essential to conformance with WCAG 2.0—**P**erceivable, **O**perable, **U**nderstandable, and **R**obust—referred to by the acronym POUR.

1. Content must be **P**erceivable. Perceivable content is easy to see or hear. Any graphic or multimedia content should be available in a text format, such as text descriptions for images, closed captions for videos, and transcripts for audio.

2. Interface components in the content must be **O**perable. Operable content has navigation forms, or other interactive features that can be used or operated with either a mouse or keyboard. Multimedia content should be designed to avoid flashing, which may cause a seizure.

3. Content and controls must be **U**nderstandable. Understandable content is easy to read, organized in a consistent manner, and provides helpful error messages when appropriate.

4. Content should be **R**obust enough to work with current and future user agents, including assistive technologies. Robust content is written to follow W3C Recommendations and should be compatible with multiple operating systems, browsers, and assistive technologies such as screen reader applications.

The WCAG 2.0 Quick Reference in the Appendix contains a more detailed list of guidelines for designing accessible web pages. As you work through this book you'll learn to include accessibility features as you create practice pages. You've already discovered the importance of the title tag, heading tags, and descriptive text for hyperlinks in Chapters 2 and 3. You're already well on your way to creating accessible web pages!

Use of Text

Writing for the Web

Long-winded sentences and explanations are often found in academic textbooks and romance novels, but they really are not appropriate on a web page. Long blocks of text and long paragraphs are difficult to read on the Web.

- Use the text equivalent of sound bytes—short sentences and phrases.
- Be concise.
- Organize the page content with headings and subheadings.
- Keep in mind that bulleted lists stand out on the page and are easily read.

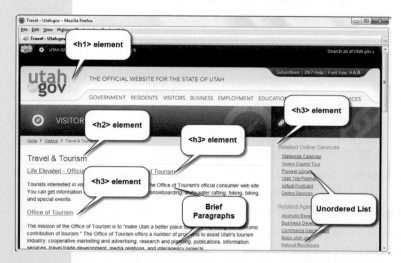

FIGURE 4.10 The State of Utah website content is well organized with headings.

The State of Utah Travel & Tourism web page shown in Figure 4.10 provides an example of using headings, brief paragraphs, and unordered lists to organize web page content so that it is easy to read and visitors can quickly find what they need.

Text Design Considerations

You may be wondering how to know whether a web page is easy to read. Readable text is crucial to providing content of value for your web page visitors. Carefully consider the font typeface, size, weight, and color when you select fonts for your web pages. You'll learn to configure fonts on web pages in Chapter 7. The following are some suggestions that will help increase the readability of your pages:

- *Use Common Fonts*

    Use common font typefaces such as Arial, Verdana, or Times New Roman. Remember that the web page visitor must have the font installed on his or her computer in order for that particular font to appear. Your page may look great with Gill Sans Ultra Bold Condensed, but if your visitor doesn't have the font, the browser's default font will be displayed. Explore the list of "web-safe" fonts at http://www.ampsoft.net/webdesign-l/WindowsMacFonts.html.

- *Carefully Choose Font Typeface*

  Serif fonts, such as Times New Roman, were originally developed for printing text on paper, not for displaying text on a computer monitor. Research shows that sans serif fonts, such as Arial and Verdana, are easier to read than serif fonts when displayed on a computer screen (see http://www.alexpoole.info/academic/literaturereview.html or http://www.wilsonweb.com/wmt6/html-email-fonts.htm for details).

- *Check Font Size*

  Be aware that fonts display smaller on a Mac than on a PC. Even within the PC platform, the default font size displayed by browsers may not be the same. Consider creating prototype pages of your font size settings to test on a variety of browsers and screen resolution settings.

- *Check Font Weight*

  Bold (use the `<strong>` element) or *emphasize* (use the `<em>` element to configure italics) important text. However, be careful not to bold everything—that has the same effect as bolding nothing.

- *Check Font Color for Contrast*

  Use appropriate color combinations. Newbie web designers sometimes choose color combinations for web pages that they would never dream of using in their wardrobe. An easy way to choose colors that contrast well and look good together is to select colors from an image or logo that you will use for your site. Make sure that your page background color properly contrasts with your text and hyperlink colors.

- *Check Line Length*

  Be aware of line length—use white space and multiple columns if possible. Look ahead to Figure 4.27 for examples of text placement on a web page.

- *Check Alignment*

  A paragraph of centered text is more difficult to read than left-aligned text.

- *Carefully Choose Text in Hyperlinks*

  Hyperlink keywords or descriptive phrases—do not hyperlink entire sentences. Avoid the use of the words "click here" in hyperlinks—users know what to do by now.

- *Check Spelling and Grammar*

  Unfortunately, many websites contain misspelled words. Most web-authoring tools have built-in spell checkers; consider using this feature.

Finally, be sure that you proofread and test your site thoroughly. It's very helpful if you can find web developer buddies—you check their sites, and they check yours. It's always easier to see someone else's mistake than your own.

Web Color Palette

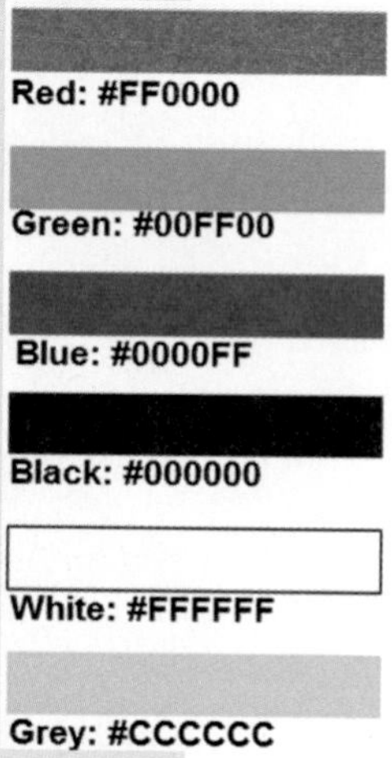

Computer monitors display color as a combination of different intensities of red, green, and blue, also known as **RGB color**. RGB intensity values are numeric from 0 to 255.

Each RGB color has three values, one each for red, green, and blue. These are always listed in the same order (red, green, blue) and specify the numerical value of each color (see examples in Figure 4.11). You will usually use hexadecimal color values to specify RGB color on web pages.

Hexadecimal Color Values

Hexadecimal is the name for the base 16 numbering system, which uses the characters 0, 1, 2, 3, 4, 5, 6, 7, 8, 9, A, B, C, D, E, and F to specify numeric values.

Hexadecimal color values specify RGB color with numeric value pairs ranging from 00 to FF (0 to 255 in base 10). Each pair is associated with the amount of red, green, and blue displayed. Using this notation, one would specify the color red as #FF0000 and the color blue as #0000FF. The # symbol signifies that the value is hexadecimal. You can use either uppercase or lowercase letters in hexadecimal color values; #FF0000 and #ff0000 both configure the color red.

Red: #FF0000

Green: #00FF00

Blue: #0000FF

Black: #000000

White: #FFFFFF

Grey: #CCCCCC

FIGURE 4.11 Sample colors.

Don't worry—you won't need to do calculations to work with web colors. Just become familiar with the numbering scheme. See Figure 4.12 for an excerpt from the textbook companion website at http://webdevbasics.net/color.

#FFFFFF	#FFFFCC	#FFFF99	#FFFF66	#FFFF33	#FFFF00
#FFCCFF	#FFCCCC	#FFCC99	#FFCC66	#FFCC33	#FFCC00
#FF99FF	#FF99CC	#FF9999	#FF9966	#FF9933	#FF9900
#FF66FF	#FF66CC	#FF6699	#FF6666	#FF6633	#FF6600
#FF33FF	#FF33CC	#FF3399	#FF3366	#FF3333	#FF3300
#FF00FF	#FF00CC	#FF0099	#FF0066	#FF0033	#FF0000

FIGURE 4.12 Partial color chart.

Web-Safe Colors

It is easy to tell whether a color is a web-safe color—check the hexadecimal color values.

Web-Safe Hexadecimal Values

00, 33, 66, 99, CC, FF

Look at the color chart at the end of the book (also shown at http://webdevbasics.net/color). Note that all the colors listed follow this numbering scheme—they comprise the Web Safe Color Palette.

Must I use only web-safe colors?

No, you are free to choose any color, as long as you check that there is adequate contrast between your text and background colors—you want your visitors to be able to read the content on your site! Back in the day of eight-bit color it was very important to use web-safe colors. Today, it is less important since most video drivers support millions of colors.

Accessibility and Color

Everyone who visits your website may not be able to see or distinguish between colors. Keep in mind that you'll need to convey information even if color cannot be viewed. According to VisCheck (http://vischeck.com/vischeck), one out of twenty people experiences some type of color perception deficiency.

Color choices can be crucial. For example, red text on a blue background, as shown in Figure 4.13, is usually difficult for everyone to read. Also avoid using red, green, brown, gray, or purple next to each other. White, black, and shades of blue and yellow are easier for most people to differentiate.

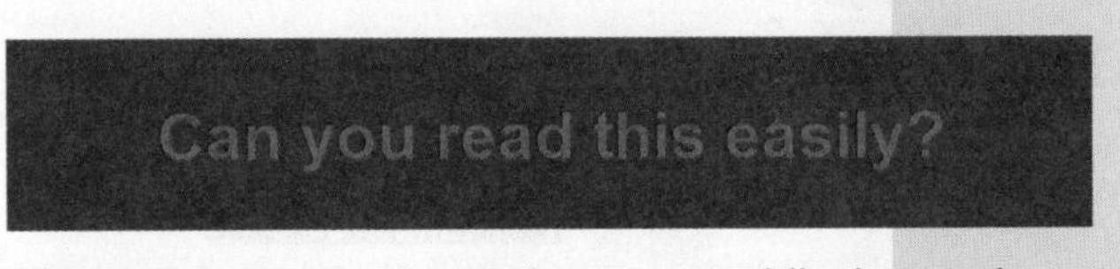

Can you read this easily?

FIGURE 4.13 Some color combinations are difficult to read.

More About Color

Check out the following websites for some color ideas. Then continue with the next section for more tips on choosing colors for your web pages.

- http://www.colorschemedesigner.com
- http://www.colorjack.com
- http://www.colorsontheweb.com/colorwizard.asp

Use of Color

The first section in this chapter focused on the importance of designing for your target audience. In this section, we consider how to use color to appeal to a target audience.

FIGURE 4.14 A typical site for children at http://usmint.gov/kids.

Appealing to Children and Preteens

Younger audiences, such as children and preteens, prefer bright, lively colors. The U.S. Mint's Site for Kids home page, shown in Figure 4.14, features bright graphics, lots of color, and interactivity.

Appealing to Young Adults

Individuals in their late teens and early twenties generally prefer dark background colors with occasional use of bright contrast, music, and dynamic navigation. Figure 4.15 shows http://underatedrock.com, a website designed by Michael Martin for this age group. Note how it has a completely different look and feel from the site designed for children.

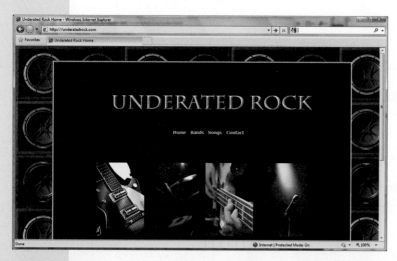

FIGURE 4.15 Many teens and young adults find dark sites appealing.

Appealing to Everybody

If your goal is to appeal to everyone, follow the example of the popular Amazon.com and eBay.com websites in their use of color. These sites use a neutral white background with splashes of color to add interest and highlight page areas. Use of white as a background color was also reported by Jakob Nielsen and Marie Tahir in *Homepage Usability: 50 Websites Deconstructed*, a book that analyzed 50 top websites. According to this study, 84 percent of the sites used white as the background color, and 72 percent used black as the text color. This maximized the contrast between text and background—providing maximum ease of reading.

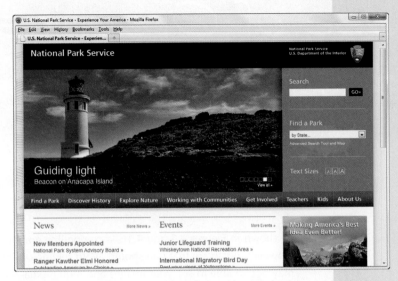

FIGURE 4.16   A compelling graphic along with white background for the content area.

You'll also notice that websites targeting "everyone" often include compelling visual graphics. The National Park Service home page (http://www.nps.gov), shown in Figure 4.16, engages the visitor with color and graphics while providing the main content on a white background for maximum contrast.

Appealing to Older Adults

For an older target audience, light backgrounds, well-defined images, and large text are appropriate. The screenshot of the National Institutes of Health Senior Health site (http://nihseniorhealth.gov) shown in Figure 4.17 is an example of a web page intended for the 55-and-older age group.

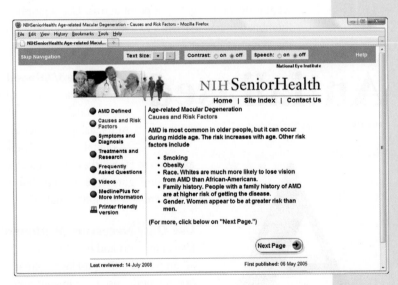

FIGURE 4.17   A site designed specifically for the 55-and-older age group.

Use of Graphics and Multimedia

As shown in Figures 4.1 and 4.16, a compelling graphic can be an engaging element on a web page. However, be aware that you should avoid relying on images to convey meaning. Some individuals may not be able to see your images and multimedia—they may be accessing your site with a mobile device or using an assistive technology such as a screen reader to visit your page. You may need to include text descriptions of important concepts or key points that a graphic image or multimedia file conveys. In this section, you'll explore recommended techniques for use of graphics and multimedia on web pages.

File Size and Dimension Matter

Keep both the file size and the dimensions of images as small as possible. Try to display only exactly what is needed to get your point across. Use a graphic application to crop an image or create a thumbnail image that links to a larger version of the image. You'll learn how to optimize a photo for the Web in Chapter 6.

Antialiased

FIGURE 4.18   Antialiased text.

Antialiased/Aliased Text Considerations

Refer back to Figure 4.14 and notice how easy it is to read the text in the coin navigation images—the text in each coin is **antialiased text**. Antialiasing introduces intermediate colors to smooth jagged edges in digital images. Graphic applications such as Adobe Photoshop and Adobe Fireworks can be used to create antialiased text images. The graphic shown in Figure 4.18 was created using antialiasing. Figure 4.19 displays an image created without antialiasing; note the jagged edges.

Use Only Necessary Multimedia

Use animation and multimedia only if it will add value to your site. Don't include an animated GIF or a Flash animation (see Chapter 11) just because you have one. Limit the use of animated items. Only use animation if it makes the page more effective. Consider limiting how long an animation plays.

FIGURE 4.19   This graphic has a jagged look and was not saved using antialiasing.

In general, younger audiences find animation more appealing than older audiences. The U.S. Mint's Site for Kids (Figure 4.14) is geared to children and uses lots of animation. This would be too much animation for a website targeted to adult shoppers. However, a well-done navigation animation or an animation that describes a product or service could be appealing to almost any target group. Adobe Flash is frequently used on the Web to add visual interest and interactivity to web pages, as shown on the Library of Congress page in Figure 4.20. You'll configure a Flash animation on a web page in Chapter 11.

FIGURE 4.20   The Flash slideshow adds visual interest to the text-based home page of http://www.loc.gov.

Provide Alternate Text

Focus on Accessibility

Each image on your web page should be configured with alternate text. See Chapter 6 for a discussion of configuring images on web pages. Alternate text may be displayed by mobile devices, displayed briefly when an image is slow to load, and displayed when a browser is configured to not show images. Alternate text is also read aloud when a person with a disability uses a screen reader to access your website. In Figure 4.21, the Firefox Web Developer extension was used to display the alt text for an image on the National Park Service website (http://nps.gov).

FIGURE 4.21   The alt text is displayed above the image by the Web Developer Extension for Firefox.

Navigation Design

Ease of Navigation

Sometimes web developers are so close to their sites that they can't see the forest for the trees. A new visitor will wander onto the site and not know what to click or how to find the information he or she seeks. Clearly labeled navigation on each page is helpful—it should be in the same location on each page for maximum usability.

FIGURE 4.22   Horizontal text-based navigation is used at http://www.dot.gov.

Navigation Bars

Clear **navigation bars**, either graphic or text based, make it obvious to website users where they are and where they can go next. It's quite common for site-wide navigation to be located in either a horizontal navigation bar placed under the logo (see Figure 4.22) or in a vertical navigation bar on the left side of the page. Less common is a vertical navigation bar on the right side of the page—this area can be cut off at lower screen resolutions.

Breadcrumb Navigation

Jakob Nielsen, a well-known usability and web design professional, favors what he calls a **breadcrumb trail** for larger sites, which indicates the path of web pages a visitor has viewed during the current session. Figure 4.23 shows a page with a well-organized main navigation area below the logo area in addition to the breadcrumb trail navigation at the top of the main content area that indicates the pages the visitor has viewed in this visit: Home → Albuquerque Green → Take Action → In Your Community. Visitors can easily retrace their steps or jump back to a previously viewed page. The left side of this page also contains a vertical navigation bar with links for the Albuquerque Green section. As this demonstrates, it's common for a website to use more than one type of navigation.

FIGURE 4.23   Visitors can follow the "breadcrumbs" to retrace their steps through http://www.cabq.gov.

Using Graphics for Navigation

Sometimes graphics are used to provide navigation, as in the web page shown in Figure 4.24. The "text" for the navigation is actually stored in image files.

FIGURE 4.24 The navigation hyperlinks are images on links on http://www.fruitsandveggiesmatter.gov.

Focus on Accessibility

Even though image hyperlinks instead of text hyperlinks provide the main navigation of the site, the web page in Figure 4.24 demonstrates two techniques that provide for accessibility:

- Each image element is configured with an alternate text description (see Chapter 6).
- The page is configured with text hyperlinks in the footer section.

Dynamic Navigation

The City of Fresno website (http://www.fresno.gov) has a dynamic navigation menu. In Figure 4.25 "For Visitors" has been selected, causing the vertical menu to appear. This type of navigation on a large, complex site keeps the visitor from feeling overwhelmed by choices.

FIGURE 4.25 Dynamic navigation with HTML, CSS, and JavaScript.

Site Map

Even with clear and consistent navigation, visitors sometimes may lose their way on large websites. A site map provides an outline of the organization of the website with hyperlinks to each major page. This can help visitors find another route to get to the information they seek, as shown in the Ready.gov website in Figure 4.26.

Site Search Feature

Note the search feature in the upper right corner of the web page in Figure 4.26. The site search feature helps visitors find information that is not apparent from the navigation or the site map.

FIGURE 4.26 This large site offers a site search and a site map to visitors.

Wireframes and Page Layout

A **wireframe** is a sketch or blueprint of a web page that shows the structure (but not the detailed design) of basic page elements such as the logo, navigation, content, and footer. Wireframes are used as part of the design process to experiment with various page layouts, develop the structure and navigation of the site, and provide a basis for communication among project members. Note that the exact content (text, images, logo, and navigation) does not need to be placed in the wireframe diagram. Figure 4.27 depicts a diagram of a web page with a logo, navigation area, content area (with headings, subheadings, images, paragraphs, and unordered lists), and a footer area.

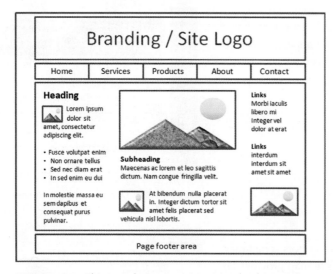

FIGURE 4.27 This page layout uses images and columns of varied widths.

In Chapter 8 you'll learn how to use Cascading Style Sheets (CSS) to configure web pages with multiple columns. Sometimes the page layout for the home page is different from the page layout used for the content pages. Even when this is the case, a consistent logo and color scheme will produce a more cohesive website.

Page Layout Design Techniques

Now that you have been introduced to page layout, it's time to consider three popular techniques of web page layout design: ice, jello, and liquid.

Ice Design

The **ice design** technique is sometimes referred to as a solid or fixed design. The page hugs the left margin and has a fixed width. The Federal Student Aid page (http://studentaid.ed.gov) shown in Figure 4.28 is an example of ice design. This page is formatted with a fixed width. Other sites that use this technique include http://www.cabelas.com and http://www.league.org.

FIGURE 4.28 This page is configured with a fixed width and demonstrates ice design.

Jello Design

The **jello design** technique configures content that is centered and may be of a fixed width or a percentage width, such as 80 percent. Regardless of the screen resolution, the content is centered in the page with even margins on both sides. The Department of Energy site (http://energy.gov), as shown in Figure 4.29, uses jello design. Other sites using this technique include http://www.pbs.org and http://www.officedepot.com.

FIGURE 4.29 The left and right margins are balanced on this page using jello design.

Liquid Design

The **liquid design** technique results in a fluid web page with content that takes up 100 percent of the browser window regardless of the screen resolution. There is no empty margin on the left or right—the multicolumn content will flow to fill whatever size of window is used to display it. A disadvantage of this page layout is that at high screen resolutions the lines of text may extend quite far across the browser screen and become more difficult to read. Figure 4.30 shows a page from the State of Illinois site at http://www.illinois.gov/tech. Other sites using this technique include http://www.amazon.com and http://moodle.org.

FIGURE 4.30 This page uses liquid design to adjust content to fill the browser window.

Websites designed using ice, jello, and liquid techniques can be found throughout the Web. Ice designs using a fixed-width layout provide the web developer the most control over the page configuration but result in pages with large empty areas when viewed at higher screen resolutions. Liquid designs may become less readable when viewed at high screen resolutions due to the page stretching to fill a wider area than originally intended by the developer. Jello designs are often used because the web pages are typically most pleasing to view on a variety of screen resolutions.

More Design Considerations

Load Time

The last thing you want to happen is for your visitors to leave your page before it has even finished loading! Make sure your pages load as quickly as possible. Web usability expert Jakob Nielsen reports that visitors will often leave a page after waiting more than 10 seconds. It takes just less than 9 seconds at 56Kbps for a browser to display a web page and associated files of 60KB. It's a good practice to try to limit the total file size of a website's home page and all of its associated images and media files to less than 60KB. However, it's common to go over this recommended limit for content pages when you're sure your visitors will be interested enough to wait to see what your site is presenting.

According to a recent study by the PEW Internet and American Life Project, the percentage of U.S. Internet users with a broadband (cable, DSL, and so on) connection at home or at work is rising. Sixty-five percent of adult Americans have access to broadband at home. Even with the trend of increasing bandwidth available to your visitors, keep in mind that 35 percent of households do not have broadband Internet access. Visit http://www.pewinternet.org for the most up-to-date statistics.

The chart shown in Figure 4.31 compares file sizes and connection speed download times, and was created using the calculator at http://www.t1shopper.com/tools/calculate/downloadcalculator.php.

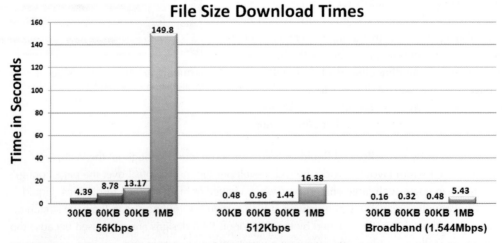

FIGURE 4.31 File size download times and Internet connection speeds.

One method to help determine whether the load time of your page is acceptable is to view the size of your website files in Windows Explorer. Calculate the total file size of your web page plus all of its associated images and media. If the total file size for a single page and of its associated files is greater than 60KB and it is likely that your target audience may not be using broadband access, take a closer look at your design. Consider whether you really need to use all the images to convey your message. Perhaps the images can be better optimized for the Web or the content of the page should be divided into multiple pages. This is a time for some decision making! Popular web-authoring tools such as Microsoft Expression Web and Adobe Dreamweaver will calculate load time at various transmission speeds.

Perceived Load Time

Perceived load time is the amount of time a web page visitor is aware of waiting while your page is loading. Since visitors often leave a website if a page takes too long to load, it is important to shorten their perception of waiting. A common technique is to shorten the perceived loading time by breaking the long page into multiple smaller pages. This might even aid in the organization of your website.

Web pages containing large graphics may appear to load very slowly. **Image slicing** is a graphic editing technique that divides large images into several smaller image files. Since each small graphic displays as it loads, the perceived load time is shorter than it is for a single large graphic. Even though the total download time is about the same, the visitor sees the browser window changing and perceives the wait as being shorter. Adobe Photoshop and Adobe Fireworks are two graphic editing applications that can be used to slice images.

Above the Fold

Placing important information **above the fold** is a technique borrowed from the newspaper industry. When newspapers are placed on counters and in vending machines waiting to be sold, the portion above the fold in the page is viewable. Publishers noticed that more papers were sold when the most important, attention-getting information was placed in this location. You may use this technique to attract and keep visitors on your web pages. Arrange interesting content above the fold—the area the visitor sees before scrolling down the page. At the most popular screen resolution of 1024×768, the amount of screen viewable above the fold (after accounting for browser menus and controls) is about 600 pixels.

Adequate White Space

The term **white space** is also borrowed from the publishing industry. Placing blank or white space (because paper is usually white) in areas around blocks of text increases the readability of the page. Placing white space around graphics helps them to stand out. Allow for some blank space between blocks of text and images. How much is adequate? It depends—experiment until the page is likely to look appealing to your target audience.

Horizontal Scrolling

In order to make it easy for visitors to view and use your web pages, avoid creating pages that are too wide to be displayed in the browser window. These pages require the user to scroll horizontally. Cameron Moll (http://www.cameronmoll.com/archives/001220.html) suggests that the optimal web page width for display at 1024×768 screen resolution is 960 pixels. Be mindful that many of your web page visitors will not maximize their browser viewport.

Web Design Best Practices Checklist

Use Table 4.1 as a guide to help you create easy-to-read, usable, and accessible web pages.

Page Layout Criteria

☐ 1. Consistent site header/logo

☐ 2. Consistent navigation area

☐ 3. Informative page title that includes the company/organization/site name

☐ 4. Page footer area—copyright, last update, contact email address

☐ 5. Good use of basic design principles: repetition, contrast, proximity, and alignment

☐ 6. Displays without horizontal scrolling at 1024×768 and higher resolutions

☐ 7. Balance of text/graphics/white space on page

☐ 8. Repetitive information (header/logo and navigation) takes up no more than one fourth to one third of the browser window at 1024×768 resolution

☐ 9. Home page has compelling information before scrolling at 1024×768 resolution

☐ 10. Home page downloads within 10 seconds on dial-up connection

Navigation Criteria

☐ 1. Main navigation links are clearly and consistently labeled

☐ 2. Navigation is easy for the target audience to use

☐ 3. When the main navigation consists of images and/or multimedia, the page footer area contains plain text hyperlinks (accessibility)

☐ 4. Navigational aids, such as site map, skip to content link, or breadcrumbs, are used

Color and Graphics Criteria

☐ 1. Use of different colors is limited to a maximum of three or four plus neutrals

☐ 2. Color is used consistently

☐ 3. Background and text colors have good contrast

☐ 4. Color is not used alone to convey meaning (accessibility)

☐ 5. Use of color and graphics enhances rather than distracts from the site

☐ 6. Graphics are optimized and do not slow download significantly

☐ 7. Each graphic used serves a clear purpose

☐ 8. Image tags use the alt attribute to configure alternate text (accessibility)

☐ 9. Animated images do not distract from the site and either do not loop endlessly

TABLE 4.1 Web Design Best Practices Checklist.

Multimedia Criteria

- ☐ 1. Each audio/video/Flash file used serves a clear purpose
- ☐ 2. The audio/video/Flash files used enhance rather than distract from the site
- ☐ 3. Captions or transcripts are provided for each audio or video file used (accessibility)
- ☐ 4. Download times for audio or video files are indicated
- ☐ 5. Hyperlinks are provided to downloads for media plug-ins

Content Presentation Criteria

- ☐ 1. Common fonts such as Arial or Times New Roman are used
- ☐ 2. Techniques of writing for the Web are applied: headings, subheadings, bulleted lists, short sentences in brief paragraphs, use of white space
- ☐ 3. Fonts, font sizes, and font colors are consistently used
- ☐ 4. Content provides meaningful, useful information
- ☐ 5. Content is organized in a consistent manner
- ☐ 6. Information is easy to find (minimal clicks)
- ☐ 7. Timeliness: The date of the last revision and/or copyright date is accurate
- ☐ 8. Content is free of typographical and grammatical errors
- ☐ 9. Avoids the use of "Click here" when writing text for hyperlinks
- ☐ 10. Hyperlinks use a consistent set of colors to indicate visited/nonvisited status
- ☐ 11. Alternate text equivalent of content is provided for graphics and media (accessibility)

Functionality Criteria

- ☐ 1. All internal hyperlinks work
- ☐ 2. All external hyperlinks work
- ☐ 3. All forms function as expected
- ☐ 4. No error messages are generated by the pages

Additional Accessibility Criteria

- ☐ 1. Use attributes designed to improve accessibility such as alt, longdesc, title, and summary where appropriate
- ☐ 2. To assist screen readers, the html element's lang and xml:lang attributes indicate the spoken language of the page

Browser Compatibility Criteria

- ☐ 1. Displays on current versions of Internet Explorer (8+)
- ☐ 2. Displays on current versions of Firefox (3+)
- ☐ 3. Displays on current versions of Safari (both Mac and Windows)
- ☐ 4. Displays on current versions of Google Chrome
- ☐ 5. Displays on current versions of Opera (10+)

CHAPTER 4
Review and Apply

Review Questions

1. Which of the following would a consistent website design *not* have?
   a. a similar navigation area on each content page
   b. the same fonts on each content page
   c. a different background color on each page
   d. the same logo in the same location on each content page

2. Which of the following are the three most common methods of organizing websites?
   a. horizontal, vertical, and diagonal
   b. hierarchical, linear, and random
   c. accessible, readable, maintainable
   d. none of the above

3. Which of the following is not a web design recommended practice?
   a. design your site to be easy to navigate
   b. colorful pages appeal to everyone
   c. design your pages to load quickly
   d. limit the use of animated items

4. Which are the four principles of the Web Content Accessibility Guidelines?
   a. contrast, repetition, alignment, proximity
   b. perceivable, operable, understandable, robust
   c. accessible, readable, maintainable, reliable
   d. hierarchical, linear, random, sequential

5. Which of the following is a sketch or blueprint of a web page that shows the structure (but not the detailed design) of basic page elements?
   a. drawing   c. site map
   b. HTML code   d. wireframe

6. Which of the following is influenced by the intended or target audience of a site?
   a. the amount of color used on the site
   b. the font size and styles used on the site
   c. the overall look and feel for the site
   d. all of the above

7. Which of the following recommended design practices applies to a website that uses images for its main site navigation?
   a. provide alternative text for the images
   b. place text links at the bottom of the page
   c. both a and b
   d. no special considerations are needed

8. Which of the following is known as white space?
   a. the empty screen area around blocks of text and images
   b. the background color of white used for a page
   c. both a and b
   d. none of the above

9. Which of the following should you do when creating text hyperlinks?
   a. create the entire sentence as a hyperlink
   b. include the words "click here" in your text
   c. use a key phrase as a hyperlink
   d. none of the above

10. Which of the following is the design technique used to create pages that stretch to fill the browser window?
    a. ice   c. jello
    b. liquid   d. none of the above

Hands-On Exercise

Website Design Evaluation. In this chapter you've explored web page design, including navigation design techniques and the design principles of contrast, repetition, alignment, and proximity. In this Hands-On Exercise, you'll review and evaluate screenshots of web pages.

A. Review Figure 4.32 and complete the following information.

    a. Indicate the type(s) of navigation evident.

    b. Describe how the design principles of contrast, repetition, alignment, and proximity are applied. Be specific.

    c. Complete the Web Design Best Practices Checklist (see Table 4.1).

FIGURE 4.32   The ARM Climate Research Facility website at http://www.arm.gov.

B. Review Figure 4.33 and complete the following information.

    a. Indicate the type(s) of navigation evident.

    b. Describe how the design principles of contrast, repetition, alignment, and proximity are applied. Be specific.

    c. Complete the Web Design Best Practices Checklist (see Table 4.1).

FIGURE 4.33 Telework.gov at http://www.telework.gov.

Focus on Web Design

Choose two sites that are similar in nature or have a similar target audience, such as the following:

- http://amazon.com and http://bn.com
- http://chicagobears.com and http://greenbaypackers.com
- http://cnn.com and http://msnbc.com

1. Describe how the two sites that you chose to review exhibit the design principles of repetition, contrast, alignment, and proximity.

2. Describe how the two sites that you chose to review exhibit web design best practices. How would you improve these sites? Recommend three improvements for each site.

Web Project Case Study

The purpose of this Web Project Case Study is to design a website using recommended design practices. Your website might be about a favorite hobby or subject, your family, a church or club you belong to, a company that a friend owns, the company you work for, and so on. Your website will contain a home page and at least six (but no more than ten) content pages. The Web Project Case Study provides an outline for a semester-long project in which you design, create, and publish an original website.

PROJECT MILESTONES

- Web Project Topic Approval (must be approved before moving on to other milestones)
- Web Project Planning Analysis Sheet
- Web Project Site Map
- Web Project Page Layout Design
- Web Project Update 1
- Web Project Update 2
- Publish and Present Project

1. **Web Project Topic Approval.** The topic of your website must be approved by your instructor. Write a one-page paper with a discussion of the following items:

   - What is the name and purpose of the site?
     List the website name and the reasons you are creating the site.
   - What do you want the site to accomplish?
     Explain the goal you have for the site. Describe what needs to happen for you to consider your site a success.
   - Who is your target audience?
     Describe your target audience by age, gender, socioeconomic characteristics, and so on.
   - What opportunity or issue is your site addressing?
     Note: Your site might be addressing the opportunity of providing information about a topic to others, creating an initial web presence for a company, and so on.
   - What type of content might be included in your site?
     Describe the type of text, graphics, and media you will need for the site.
   - List at least two related or similar sites found on the Web.

2. **Web Project Planning Analysis Sheet.** Write a one-page paper with a discussion of the following items. Include the following headings:

   Website Goal
   > List the website name and describe the goal of your site in one or two sentences.

   What results do I want to see?
   > List the working title of each page on your site. A suggested project scope is seven to eleven pages.

What information do I need?

List the sources of the content (facts, text, graphics, sounds, video*) for the web pages you listed. While you should write the text content yourself, you may use outside sources for royalty-free images and multimedia. Review copyright considerations (see Chapter 6).*

3. **Web Project Site Map.** Use the drawing features of a word processing program, a graphic application, or paper and pencil to create a site map of your website that shows the hierarchy of pages and relationships between pages. Unless otherwise directed by your instructor, use the style for a site map shown in Figure 4.3.

4. **Web Project Page Layout Design.** Use the drawing features of a word processing program, a graphic application, or paper and pencil to create wireframe page layouts for the home page and content pages of your site. Unless otherwise directed by your instructor, use the style for page layout composition shown in Figure 4.27. Indicate where the logo, navigation, text, and images will be located. Do not worry about exact wording or exact images.

5. **Project Update Meeting 1.** You should have at least three pages of your website completed by this time. If you have not done so already, your instructor will help you to publish your pages to the Web (see Chapter 10 for information about FTP). Unless prior arrangements to meet are made, the Project Update Meeting will be held during class lab time. Bring the following items to discuss with your instructor:

   - The URL of your website
   - Source files of your web pages and images
   - Site map (revise as needed)

6. **Project Update Meeting 2.** You should have at least six pages of your website completed by this time. They should be published to the Web. Unless prior arrangements to meet are made, the Project Update Meeting will be held during class lab time. Prepare the following items to discuss with your instructor:

   - The URL of your website
   - Source files of your web pages and images
   - Site map (revise as needed)

7. **Publish and Present Project.** Finish publishing your project to your website. Be prepared to show your website to the class, explaining project goal, target audience, use of color, and any challenges you faced (and how you overcame them) while you completed the project.

CHAPTER 5

Cascading Style Sheets Basics

Now that you have experience with configuring the structure and information on a web page with HTML, let's explore **Cascading Style Sheets (CSS)**. Web designers use CSS to separate the presentation style of a web page from the information on the web page. CSS is used to configure text, color, and page layout.

CSS first became a W3C Recommendation in 1996. Additional properties for positioning web page elements were introduced to the language with CSS level 2 (CSS2) in 1998. CSS continues to evolve, with proposals for CSS level 3 (CSS3) properties to support features such as embedding fonts, rounded corners, and transparency. This chapter introduces you to the use of CSS on the Web as you explore configuring color on web pages.

You'll learn how to . . .

- Describe the purpose of Cascading Style Sheets
- List advantages of using Cascading Style Sheets
- Configure color on web pages with Cascading Style Sheets
- Configure inline styles
- Configure embedded style sheets
- Configure external style sheets
- Configure web page areas with element name, class, id, and contextual selectors
- Test your Cascading Style Sheets for valid syntax

Cascading Style Sheets Overview

For years, style sheets have been used in desktop publishing to apply typographical styles and spacing instructions to printed media. CSS provides this functionality (and much more) for web designers. CSS allows web designers to apply typographical styles (typeface, font size, and so on), color, and page layout instructions to a web page.

FIGURE 5.1 The CSS Zen Garden home page at http://csszengarden.com.

The CSS Zen Garden (http://www.csszengarden.com) exemplifies the power and flexibility of CSS (Figure 5.1). Visit this site for an example of CSS in action. Notice how the content looks dramatically different depending on the design (configured with CSS style rules) that you select. Although the designs on CSS Zen Garden are created by CSS masters, at some point these designers were just like you—starting out with CSS basics.

CSS is a flexible, cross-platform, standards-based language developed by the W3C (see http://www.w3.org/Style). Be aware that even though CSS has been in use for many years, it is still considered an emerging technology, and different browsers do not support it in exactly the same way. We concentrate on aspects of CSS that are well supported by popular browsers.

Advantages of Cascading Style Sheets

There are several advantages to using CSS (see Figure 5.2):

- **Typography and page layout can be better controlled.** These features include font size, line spacing, letter spacing, indents, margins, and element positioning.
- **Style is separate from structure.** The format of the text and colors used on the page can be configured and stored separately from the body section of the web page document.

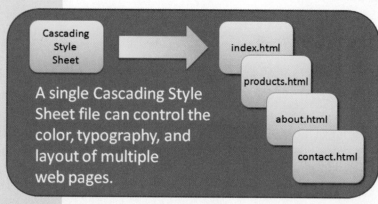

A single Cascading Style Sheet file can control the color, typography, and layout of multiple web pages.

FIGURE 5.2 The power of a single CSS file.

- **Styles can be stored.** You can store styles in a separate document and associate them with the web page. When the styles are modified, the web page code remains intact. This means that if your client decides to change the background color from red to white, you only need to change one file that contains the styles, instead of each web page document.
- **Documents are potentially smaller.** The formatting is separate from the document; therefore, the actual documents should be smaller.
- **Site maintenance is easier.** Again, if the styles need to be changed, it's possible to complete the modifications by changing only the style sheet file.

You may be wondering whether there are any disadvantages. In fact, there is one large disadvantage—CSS technology is not yet uniformly supported by browsers. This disadvantage should be less of an issue in the future as browsers improve their compliance with W3C standards. At the time this was written modern browsers had begun to support new CSS3 features such as rounded corners and color transparency—although not always in the same way! In this book we'll focus on aspects of CSS that are well supported by modern browsers.

Methods of Configuring Cascading Style Sheets

Web designers use four methods to incorporate CSS technology in a website: inline, embedded, external, and imported.

- **Inline styles** are coded in the body of the web page as an attribute of an HTML tag. The style only applies to the specific element that contains it as an attribute.
- **Embedded styles** are defined in the head section of a web page. These style instructions apply to the entire web page document.
- **External styles** are coded in a separate text file, called an external style sheet. This text file is associated with a web page by coding a link element in the head section.
- **Imported styles** are similar to external styles in that they can connect styles coded in a separate text file with a web page document. An external style sheet can be imported into embedded styles or into another external style sheet by using the @import directive.

The "Cascade" in Cascading Style Sheets

Figure 5.3 shows the "cascade" (**rules of precedence**) that applies the styles in order from outermost (external styles) to innermost (HTML attributes coded on the page). This allows the site-wide styles to be configured with an external style sheet file but overridden when needed by more granular, page-specific styles (such as embedded or inline styles).

You'll learn to configure inline styles, embedded styles, and external styles in this chapter.

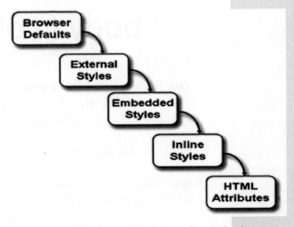

FIGURE 5.3 The "cascade" of Cascading Style Sheets.

CSS Selectors and Declarations

Style Rule Basics

Style sheets are composed of **rules** that describe the styling to be applied. Each **rule** has two parts: a **selector** and a **declaration**.

- **CSS Style Rule Selector**
  The selector can be an HTML element name, a class name, or an id name. In this section we'll focus on applying styles to element name selectors. You'll work with class selectors and id selectors later in this chapter.

- **CSS Style Rule Declaration**
  The declaration indicates the CSS property you are setting (such as color) and the value you are assigning to the property.

For example, the CSS rule shown in Figure 5.4 would set the color of the text used on a web page to blue. The selector is the body tag, and the declaration sets the color property to the value of blue.

FIGURE 5.4   Using CSS to set the text color to blue.

The background-color Property

The CSS property to configure the background color of an element is `background-color`. The following style rule will configure the background color of a web page to be yellow:

```
body { background-color: yellow }
```

Notice how the declaration is enclosed within braces and how the colon symbol (:) separates the declaration property and the declaration value.

The color Property

The CSS property to configure the text color of an element is `color`. The following CSS style rule will configure the text color of a web page to be blue:

```
body { color: blue }
```

Configure Background and Text Color

To configure more than one property for a selector, use a semicolon (;) to separate the declarations as follows (see Figure 5.5):

```
body { color: blue; background-color: yellow; }
```

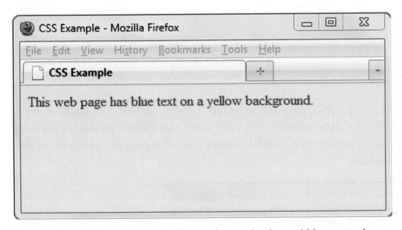

FIGURE 5.5 A web page with yellow background color and blue text color.

You might be asking how you would know what properties and values are allowed to be used. See the CSS Cheat Sheet in the Appendix for a detailed list of CSS properties. This chapter introduces you to the CSS properties commonly used to configure color, shown in Table 5.1.

Property	Description	Value
background-color	Background color of an element	Any valid color value
color	Foreground (text) color of an element	Any valid color value

TABLE 5.1 CSS Properties Used in This Chapter

You'll learn more about configuring color with CSS in the next section.

CSS Syntax for Color Values

The previous section used color names to configure color with CSS. You can find a list of color names and numerical color values on the textbook's companion website at http://webdevbasics.net/color. However, there are a limited number of color names, and they may not be supported by all browsers.

For more flexibility and control, use a numerical color value, such as the hexadecimal color values introduced in Chapter 4 (Web Color Palette section). The Web Safe Color Palette, located at the end of the book, and on the companion website (http://webdevbasics.net/color) provides examples of the colors created by hexadecimal values.

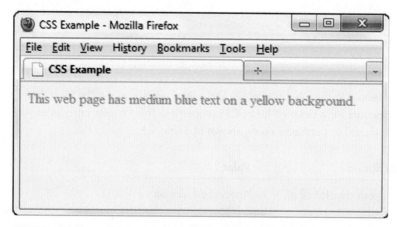

FIGURE 5.6   The color was configured using hexadecimal color values.

A style rule to configure the web page displayed in Figure 5.6 with medium blue text (#3399CC) on a soft yellow background (#FFFFCC) is

```
body { color: #3399CC; background-color: #FFFFCC; }
```

The spaces in these declarations are optional. The ending semicolon (;) is also optional but useful in case you need to add additional style rules at a later time. The following code samples are also valid:

EXAMPLE 1:

```
body {color:#3399CC;background-color:#FFFFCC}
```

EXAMPLE 2:

```
body {
color: #3399CC;
background-color: #FFFFCC;
}
```

CSS syntax allows you to configure colors in a number of ways:

- color name
- hexadecimal color value
- hexadecimal shorthand color value
- decimal color value (RGB triplet)

Table 5.2 shows CSS syntax examples that configure a paragraph with red text.

CSS Syntax	Color Type
p { color: red }	Color name
p { color: #FF0000 }	Hexadecimal color value
p { color: #F00 }	Shorthand hexadecimal (one character for each hexadecimal pair—only used with web-safe colors)
p { color: rgb(255,0,0) }	Decimal color value (RGB triplet)

TABLE 5.2 Syntax to Configure a Paragraph with Red Text

Are there other methods to configure color with CSS?

Yes, the CSS3 Color Module (currently in proposed recommendation status) provides a way for web designers to configure not only color, but also the transparency of the color with RGBA (Red, Green, Blue, Alpha). Also new to CSS3 is HSLA (Hue, Saturation, Lightness, Alpha) color, the opacity property, and CSS gradient backgrounds. You'll explore these techniques in Chapter 7.

Inline CSS with the style Attribute

Recall that there are four methods for configuring CSS: inline, embedded, external, and imported. In this section we focus on inline CSS using the `style` attribute.

The `style` Attribute

Inline styles are coded as an attribute on an HTML tag using the **style** attribute. The value of the **style** attribute is set to the style rule declaration that you need to configure. Recall that a declaration consists of a property and a value. Each property is separated from its value with a colon (:). The following code will set the text color of an <h1> tag to a shade of red:

```
<h1 style="color:#cc0000">This is displayed as a red heading</h1>
```

If there is more than one property, they are separated by a semicolon (;). The following code configures the heading with a red text color and a gray background color:

```
<h1 style="color:#cc0000;background-color:#cccccc;">
This is displayed as a red heading on a gray background</h1>
```

HANDS-ON PRACTICE 5.1 ─────────────────────────────────────

In this Hands-On Practice you will configure a web page with inline styles. The inline styles will specify the following:

- Global body tag styles for an off-white background with teal text. These styles will be inherited by other elements by default.

  ```
  <body style="background-color:#F5F5F5;color:#008080;">
  ```

- Styles for an h1 element with a teal background with off-white text. This will override the global styles configured on the body element.

  ```
  <h1 style="background-color:#008080;color:#F5F5F5;">
  ```

A sample is shown in Figure 5.7. Launch a text editor. Select File > Open to edit the template file located at chapter1/template.html in the student files. Modify the title element and add heading tag, paragraph tags, style attributes, and text to the body section as indicated by the following highlighted code:

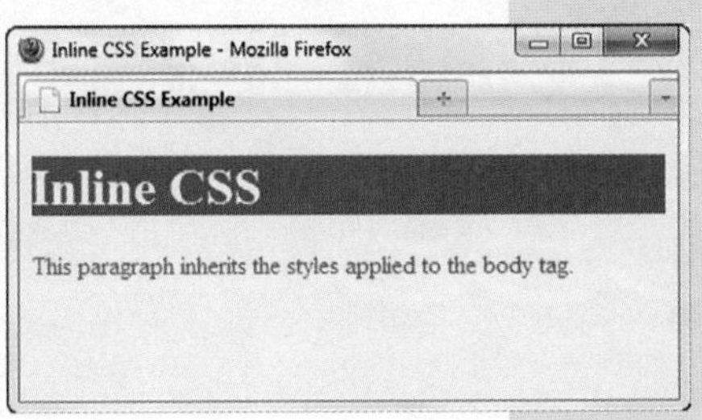

```
<!DOCTYPE html>
<html lang="en">
<head>
<title>Inline CSS Example</title>
<meta charset="utf-8">
</head>
<body style="background-color:#F5F5F5;color:#008080;">
    <h1 style="background-color:#008080;color:#F5F5F5;">Inline CSS</h1>
    <p>This paragraph inherits the styles applied to the body tag.</p>
</body>
</html>
```

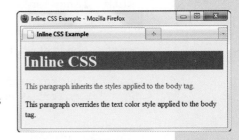

FIGURE 5.7 Web page using inline styles.

Save the document as inline2.html on your hard drive or flash drive. Launch a browser such as Internet Explorer or Firefox to test your page. It should look similar to the page shown in Figure 5.7. Note that the inline styles applied to the body tag are inherited by other elements on the page (such as the paragraph) unless more-specific styles are specified (such as those coded on the <h1> tag. You can compare your work with the solution found in the student files (chapter5/inline.html).

Let's continue and add another paragraph with the text color configured to be dark gray.

```
<p style="color:#333333"> This paragraph overrides the text color style
applied to the body tag.</p>
```

Save the document as inline3.html. It should look similar to the page shown in Figure 5.8. You can compare your work with the solution found in the student files (chapter5/inlinep.html).

Note that the inline styles applied to second paragraph override the global styles applied to the body of the web page. What if you had ten paragraphs that needed to be configured in this manner? You'd have to code an inline style on *each* of the ten paragraph tags. This would add quite a bit of redundant code to the page. For this reason, inline styles are not the most efficient way to use CSS. In the next section you'll learn how to configure embedded styles, which can apply to the entire web page document.

FIGURE 5.8 The second paragraph's inline styles override the global styles configured on the body tag.

Quick Tip

While inline styles can sometimes be useful, you'll find that you won't use this technique much in practice—it's inefficient, adds extra code to the web page document, and is inconvenient to maintain. However, inline styles can be quite handy in some circumstances, such as when you post an article to a content management system or blog and need to tweak the site-wide styles a bit to help get your point across.

Configure Embedded CSS

The Style Element

Embedded styles apply to the entire document and are placed within a `<style>` element located in the head section of a web page. The opening `<style>` tag begins the area with embedded style rules, and the closing `</style>` tag ends the area containing embedded style rules. When using XHTML syntax, the `<style>` tag requires a **type** attribute that should have the value of `"text/css"` to indicate the CSS MIME type. HTML5 syntax does not require the type attribute.

FIGURE 5.9 Web page using embedded styles.

The web page in Figure 5.9 uses embedded styles to set the text color and background color of the web page document with the `body` element selector. See the example in the student files at chapter5/embed.html.

```
<!DOCTYPE html>
<html lang="en">
<head>
<title>Embedded Styles</title>
<meta charset="utf-8">
<style>
body { background-color: #CCFFFF;
       color: #000033;
}
</style>
</head>
<body>
  <h1>Embedded CSS</h1>
  <p>This page uses embedded styles.</p>
</body>
</html>
```

Notice the way the style rules were coded with each rule on its own line. This makes the styles more readable and easier to maintain than one long row of text. The styles are in effect for the entire web page document because they were applied to the `<body>` tag using the `body` element selector.

HANDS-ON PRACTICE 5.2

Launch a text editor and open the starter.html file from the chapter5 folder in the student files. Save your page as embedded2.html and test it in a browser. Your page should look similar to the one shown in Figure 5.10.

Open the file in a text editor and view the source code. Notice that the web page code uses the `<h1>`, `<h2>`, `<div>`, `<p>`, `<ul>`, and `<li>` elements. In this Hands-On Practice you'll code embedded styles to configure selected background and text colors. You'll use the `body` element selector to configure the default background color (#E6E6FA) and default text color (#191970) for the entire page. You'll also use the `h1` and `h2` element selectors to configure different background and text colors for the heading areas.

Edit the embedded.html file in a text editor and add the following code below the `<title>` element in the head section of the web page:

FIGURE 5.10 The web page without any styles.

```
<style>
body { background-color: #E6E6FA; color: #191970; }
h1 { background-color: #191970; color: #E6E6FA; }
h2 { background-color: #AEAED4; color: #191970; }
</style>
```

Save and test your file in a browser. Figure 5.11 displays the web page along with color swatches. A monochromatic color scheme was chosen. Notice how the repetition of a limited number of colors adds interest and unifies the design of the web page.

View the source code for your page and review the CSS and HTML code. An example of this web page is in the student files at chapter5/embedded.html. Note that all the styles were located in a single place on the web page. Since embedded styles are coded in a specific location, they are easier to maintain over time than inline styles. Also notice that you only needed to code the styles for the h2 element selector once (in the head section) and *both* of the `<h2>` elements applied the h2 style. This is more efficient than coding the same inline style on each `<h2>` element.

FIGURE 5.11 The web page after embedded styles are configured.

However, it's uncommon for a website to have only one page. Repeating the CSS in the head section of each web page file is inefficient and difficult to maintain. In the next section, you'll use a more efficient approach—configuring an external style sheet.

Configure External CSS

The flexibility and power of CSS are best utilized when the CSS is external to the web page document. An external style sheet is a text file with a .css file extension that contains CSS style rules. The external style sheet file is associated with a web page using the link element. This provides a way for multiple web pages to be associated with the same external style sheet file. The external style sheet file does not contain any HTML tags—it only contains CSS style rules.

The advantage of external CSS is that styles are configured in a single file. This means that when styles need to be modified only one file needs to be changed, instead of multiple web pages. On large sites this can save a web developer much time and increase productivity. Let's get some practice with this useful technique.

The Link Element

The **link element** associates an external style sheet with a web page. It is placed in the head section of the page and is a stand-alone, void tag. In HTML5 syntax, the link element is coded as <link>. When using XHTML syntax, the link element is coded as <link />. Three attributes are used with the link element: rel, href, and type.

- The value of the **rel** attribute is "stylesheet".
- The value of the **href** attribute is the name of the style sheet file.
- The value of the **type** attribute is "text/css", which is the MIME type for CSS. The type attribute is optional in HTML5 and required in XHTML.

Code the following in the head section of a web page to associate the document with the external style sheet named color.css:

```
<link rel="stylesheet" href="color.css">
```

HANDS-ON PRACTICE 5.3 ————————————————

Let's practice using external styles. First, you'll create an external style sheet. Next, you'll configure a web page to be associated with the external style sheet.

Create an External Style Sheet. Launch a text editor and type in the style rules to set the `background-color` of a page to blue and the text color to white. Save the file as color.css. The code is as follows:

```
body { background-color: #0000FF;
       color: #FFFFFF; }
```

Figure 5.12 shows the external color.css style sheet displayed in Notepad. Notice that there is no HTML in this file. HTML tags are not coded within an external style sheet. Only CSS rules (selectors, properties, and values) are coded in an external style sheet.

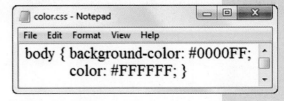

FIGURE 5.12 The external style sheet color.css.

Configure the Web Page. To create the web page shown in Figure 5.13, launch a text editor. Select File > Open to edit the template file located at chapter1/template.html in the student files. Modify the title element, add a link tag to the head section, and add a paragraph to the body section as indicated by the following highlighted code:

```
<!DOCTYPE html>
<html lang="en">
<head>
<title>External Styles</title>
<meta charset="utf-8">
<link rel="stylesheet" href="color.css">
</head>
<body>
<p>This web page uses an external style sheet.</p>
</body>
</html>
```

Save your file as external2.html. Launch a browser and test your page. It should look similar to the page shown in Figure 5.13. You can compare your work with the solution in the student files (chapter5/external.html).

The color.css style sheet can be associated with any number of web pages. If you ever need to change the style of formatting, you only need to change a single file (color.css) instead of multiple files (all of the web pages). As mentioned earlier, this technique can boost productivity on a large site. This is a simple example, but the advantage of having only a single file to update is significant for both small and large websites.

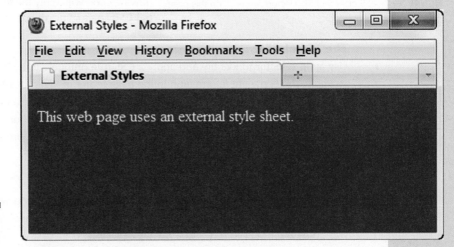

FIGURE 5.13 This page is associated with an external style sheet.

CSS Class, Id, and Contextual Selectors

FIGURE 5.14   CSS class and id selectors are used on this page.

The Class Selector

Use a CSS **class selector** when you need to apply a CSS declaration to a certain set of elements on a web page and not necessarily tie the style to a particular element. See Figure 5.14 and notice that the last two items in the unordered list are displayed in a different color than the others—this is an example of using a class. When setting a style for a class, configure the class name as the selector. Place a dot or period (.) in front of the class name in the style sheet. The following code configures a class called `feature` in a style sheet with a foreground (text) color set to red: `.feature { color: #FF0000; }`

The styles set in the new class can be applied to any element you wish. You do this by using the class attribute, such as `class="feature"`. Do not write the dot in front of the class value in the opening tag where the class is being applied. The following code will apply the feature class styles to a `<li>` element:
`<li class="feature">Usability Studies</li>`

The Id Selector

Use an **id selector** to identify and apply a CSS rule uniquely to a *single area* on a web page. For example, the copyright information in the page footer in Figure 5.14 displays with a dark gray color (#333333). This could have been configured with a class. However, because the page will have only one footer area, an id is more appropriate. When setting a style for an id, place a hash mark (#) in front of the id name in the style sheet. The following code will configure an id called footer in a style sheet:

`#footer { color: #333333; }`

The styles set in the footer id can be applied to any element you wish by using the id attribute, `id="footer"`. Do not write the # in front of the id value in the opening tag. The following code will apply the footer id styles to a div tag:

`<div id="footer">This paragraph will be displayed using styles configured in the footer id.</div>`

Using CSS with an id selector is similar to using CSS with a class selector. Use an id selector to configure a single element on a web page. Use a class selector to configure one or more elements on a web page.

The Contextual Selector

Use a **contextual selector** when you want to specify an element with the context of its container (parent) element. Contextual selectors are sometimes referred to as descendent selectors. To configure a contextual selector, list the container selector (which can be an element selector, class, or id) followed by the specific selector you are styling.

For example, to specify a green text color for anchor tags located *within* the footer id declared earlier, code the following style rule:

```
#footer a { color: #00ff00; }
```

You'll get practice with contextual selectors in Chapters 7 and 8.

HANDS-ON PRACTICE 5.4

In this Hands-On Practice you will modify the Trillium Media Design page while you practice configuring a class and an id. Launch a text editor and open embedded.html (found in the student files at chapter5/embedded.html). Save the file as classid.html.

Configure the CSS. Code CSS to configure a class named feature and an id named footer.

1. Create a class named feature that configures red (#FF0000) text. Add the following code to the embedded styles in the head section of the web page:
   ```
   .feature { color: #FF0000; }
   ```
2. Create an id named footer that configures dark gray text. Add the following code to the embedded styles in the head section of the web page:
   ```
   #footer { color: #666666; }
   ```

Configure the HTML. Associate HTML elements with the class and id you just created,

1. Modify the last two `<li>` tags in the unordered list. Add a class attribute that associates the `<li>` with the feature class as follows:
   ```
   <li class="feature">Usability Testing</li>
   <li class="feature">Search Engine Optimization</li>
   ```
2. Modify the opening div tag of the footer area. Add an id attribute that associates the div with the id class:
   ```
   <div id="footer">Copyright &copy; 2012 Your Name Here</div>
   ```

Save your classid.html file and test it in a browser. Your page should look similar to the image shown in Figure 5.14. Notice how the class and id styles are applied. The student files contain a sample solution at chapter5/classy.html.

Quick Tip

For maximum compatibility choose your class and id names carefully. Always begin with a letter. Do not use any blank spaces. Feel free to use numerals, the dash character, and the underscore character in addition to letters. See the following URLs for lists of commonly used class and id names: http://code.google.com/webstats/2005-12/classes.html and http://dev.opera.com/articles/view/mama-common-attributes.

Span Element

The Span Element

The inline **`<span>` element** defines a section on a web page that is not physically separated from other areas by line breaks. Use the `<span>` tag when you need to format an area that is contained within another, such as within a `<p>`, `<blockquote>`, or `<div>` element.

HANDS-ON PRACTICE 5.5

In this Hands-On Practice you will experiment with div and span elements in the Trillium Media Design home page. Launch a text editor and open the starter.html file from the chapter5 folder in the student files. Save your page as span2.html and test it in a browser. Your page should look similar to the one shown in Figure 5.10.

Open span2.html in a text editor and view the source code. In this Hands-On Practice you'll code embedded styles to configure selected background and text colors. You'll also add `<span>` tags to the web page. When you are finished with the first part of this Hands-On Practice, your web page will be similar to Figure 5.15.

Part 1
Configure the Embedded Styles. Edit span2.html in a text editor and add embedded styles below the `<title>` element in the head section of the web page. You will configure styles for the body, h1, and h2 element selectors, an id named nav, and a class named `companyname`. The code is

FIGURE 5.15 This page uses the div and span elements.

```
<style>
body { background-color: #FFFFFF;
       color: #191970; }
h1 { background-color: #191970;
     color: #E6E6FA; }
h2 { color: #6A6AA7; }
#nav { background-color: #E2E2EF;   }
.companyname { color: #6A6AA7; }
</style>
```

Configure the Navigation Area. View the source code of span2.html and notice the div element that contains the navigation area. You've already created an id named nav in the CSS. Assign the div to the id named nav. The code is

```
<div id="nav"><a href="index.html">Home</a> <a href=
"services.html">Services</a> <a href="contact.html">Contact</a></div>
```

Configure the Company Name. View Figure 5.15 and notice that the company name, Trillium Media Design, is displayed in a different color than the other text within the first paragraph. You've already created a class named companyname in the CSS. You'll use a span to apply this formatting. Find the text "Trillium Medium Design" in the first paragraph. Configure a span element to contain this text. Assign the span to the class named companyname. A sample code excerpt is

```
<p><span class="companyname">Trillium Media Design</span> will bring
```

Save your file and test in a browser. Your page should look similar to the one shown in Figure 5.15. The student files contain a sample solution at chapter5/span.html.

Part 2

As you review your web page and Figure 5.15, notice the empty space between the h1 element and the navigation area div element—the empty space is the margin between these two block-level elements. The margin is one of the components of the CSS box model with which you'll work in Chapter 7. One technique that will cause the browser to collapse this empty space is to configure the margin between the elements. Add the following style to the h1 element selector in the embedded CSS: margin-bottom: 0;

Save the file and launch in a browser. Your web page should now be similar to Figure 5.16. Notice how the display of the h1 and navigation area has changed. The student files contain a sample solution at chapter5/rework.html.

FIGURE 5.16 The new logo header area.

Practice with CSS

HANDS-ON PRACTICE 5.6

In this Hands-On Practice you'll continue to gain experience using external style sheets as you modify the Trillium Media Design website to use an external style sheet. You'll create the external style sheet file named trillium.css, modify the home page (index.html) to use external styles instead of embedded styles, and associate a second web page with the trillium.css style sheet.

A version of the Trillium home page is in the student files. Launch a browser and open the file at chapter5/span.html. The display should be the same as the web page shown in Figure 5.15 from Hands-On Practice 5.5.

Now that you've seen what you're working with, let's begin. Launch a text editor and open the chapter5/span.html file. Save the file as index.html in a folder named trillium.

FIGURE 5.17 The external style sheet named trillium.css.

Convert the Embedded CSS to External CSS

Edit the index.html file and select the CSS rules (all the lines of code between, but not including, the `<style>` and `</style>` tags). Use Edit > Copy or press the Ctrl+C keys to copy the CSS code to the clipboard. You will place the CSS in a new file. Launch a text editor, select File > New to create a new file, paste the CSS style rules (use Edit > Paste or press the Ctrl+V keys), and save the file as trillium.css in the trillium folder. See Figure 5.17 for a screenshot of the new trillium.css file in the Notepad text editor. Notice that there are no HTML elements in trillium. css—not even the `<style>` element. The file contains CSS rules only.

Associate the Web Page with the External CSS File

Next, edit the index.html file in a text editor. Delete the CSS code you just copied. Delete the closing `</style>` tag. Replace the opening `<style>` tag with a `<link>` element to associate the style sheet named trillium.css. The `<link>` element code follows:

```
<link href="trillium.css" rel="stylesheet">
```

Save the file and test in a browser. Your web page should look just like the one shown in Figure 5.15. Although it looks the same, the difference is in the code—the page now uses external instead of embedded CSS.

Now, for the fun part—you'll associate a second page with the style sheet. The student files contain a services.html page for Trillium at chapter5/services.html. When you display this page in a browser it should look similar to the one shown in Figure 5.18. Notice that although the structure of the page is similar to the home page, the styling of the text and colors is absent.

Launch a text editor to edit the services.html file. Code a `<link>` element to associate the services.html web page with the trillium.css external style sheet. Place the following code in the head section above the closing `</head>` tag:

```
<link href="trillium.css" rel="stylesheet">
```

Save your file in the trillium folder and test in a browser. Your page should look similar to Figure 5.19—the CSS rules have been applied!

If you click the Home and Services hyperlinks, you can move back and forth between the index.html and services.html pages in the browser. The student files contain a sample solution in the chapter5/trillium folder.

Notice that when using an external style sheet, if the style rule declarations need to be changed in the future, you'll typically only have to modify *one* file—the external style sheet. Think about how this can improve productivity on a site with many pages. Instead of modifying potentially hundreds of pages to make a color or font change, only a single file—the CSS external style sheet—needs to be updated. Becoming comfortable with CSS will be important as you develop your skills and increase your technical expertise.

FIGURE 5.18 The services.html page is not yet associated with a style sheet.

FIGURE 5.19 The services.html page has been associated with trillium.css.

FAQ

My CSS doesn't work; what can I do?

Coding CSS is a detail-oriented process. There are several common errors that can cause the browser not to apply CSS correctly to a web page. With a careful review of your code and the following tips, you should get your CSS working:

- Verify that you are using the colon ":" and semicolon ";" symbols in the right spots—they are easy to confuse. The : symbol should separate the properties from their values. The ; symbol should be placed between each property:value configuration.
- Check that you are not using = signs instead of : between each property and its value.
- Verify that the { and } symbols are properly placed around the style rules for each selector.
- Check the syntax of your selectors, their properties, and property values for correct usage.
- If part of your CSS works and part doesn't, read through the CSS and check to determine the first rule that is not applied. Often the error is in the rule above the rule that is not applied.
- Use a program to check your CSS code. The W3C's CSS validator at http://jigsaw.w3.org/css-validator can help you find syntax errors. See the next section for an overview of how to use this tool to validate your CSS.

CSS Syntax Validation

The W3C has a free Markup Validation Service (http://jigsaw.w3.org/css-validator) that will validate your CSS code and check it for syntax errors. CSS validation provides students with quick self-assessment—you can prove that your code uses correct syntax. In the working world, CSS validation serves as a quality assurance tool. Invalid code may cause browsers to render the pages slower than otherwise.

HANDS-ON PRACTICE 5.7

In this Hands-On Practice you will use the W3C CSS Validation Service to validate an external CSS style sheet. This example uses the color.css file completed in Hands-On Practice 5.3 (student files chapter5/color.css). Locate color.css and open it in a text editor. We will add an error to the color.css file. Find the body element selector style rule and delete the first "r" in the `background-color` property. Remove the # from the `color` property value. Save the file.

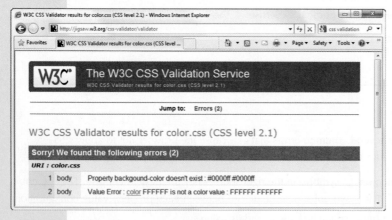

Next, attempt to validate the color.css file. Visit the W3C CSS Validation Service page at http://jigsaw.w3.org/css-validator and select the "by File Upload" tab. Click the Browse button and select the color.css file from your computer. Click the Check button. Your display should be similar to that shown in Figure 5.20. Notice that two errors were found. The selector is listed, followed by the reason an error was noted.

FIGURE 5.20 The validation results indicate errors.

Notice that the first message in Figure 5.20 indicates that the "backgound-color" property does not exist. This is a clue to check the syntax of the property name. Edit color.css and correct the error. Test and revalidate your page. Your browser should now look similar to the one shown in Figure 5.21 and report only one error.

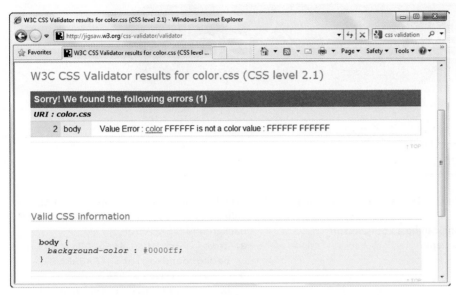

FIGURE 5.21 The valid CSS is displayed below the errors (and warnings, if any).

The error reminds you that FFFFFF is not a color value and expects you to already know that you need to add a "#" character to code a valid color value, #FFFFFF. Notice how any valid CSS rules are displayed below the error messages. Correct the color value, save the file, and test again.

Your results should look similar to those shown in Figure 5.22. There are no errors listed. The Valid CSS Information contains all the CSS style rules in color.css. This means that your file passed the CSS validation test. Congratulations, your color.css file is valid CSS syntax! It's a good practice to validate your CSS style rules. The CSS validator can help you to identify code that needs to be corrected quickly and indicate which style rules a browser is likely to consider valid. Validating CSS is one of the many productivity techniques that web developers commonly use.

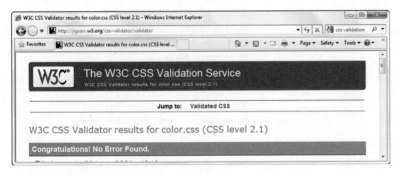

FIGURE 5.22 The CSS is valid!

CHAPTER 5

Review and Apply

Review Questions

Multiple Choice. Choose the best answer for each item.

1. Which of the following can be a CSS selector?
   a. an HTML element name
   b. a class name
   c. an id name
   d. all of the above

2. Which of the following is the CSS property used to set the background color?
   a. bgcolor   **c.** color
   b. background-color   **d.** none of the above

3. Which type of CSS is coded in the body of the web page as an attribute of an HTML tag?
   a. embedded   **c.** external
   b. inline   **d.** imported

4. Which of the following describe two components of CSS rules?
   a. selectors and declarations
   b. properties and declarations
   c. selectors and attributes
   d. none of the above

5. Which of the following associates a web page with an external style sheet?
   a. `<style rel="external" href="style.css">`
   b. `<style src="style.css">`
   c. `<link rel="stylesheet" href="style.css">`
   d. `<link rel="stylesheet" src="style.css">`

6. Which of the following configures a CSS class called news with red text (#FF0000) and light gray background (#EAEAEA)?
   a. `news {  color: #FF0000; background-color: #EAEAEA; }`
   b. `.news { color: #FF0000; background-color: #EAEAEA; }`
   c. `.news { text: #FF0000; background-color: #EAEAEA;  }`
   d. `#news { color: #FF0000; background-color: #EAEAEA; }`

7. An External Style Sheet uses the _____ file extension.
   a. ess   **c.** htm
   b. css   **d.** No file extension is necessary

8. Where do you place the code to associate a web page with an external style sheet?
   a. in the external style sheet
   b. in the DOCTYPE of the web page document
   c. in the body section of the web page document
   d. in the head section of the web page document

9. Which of the following configures a background color of #FFF8DC for a web page using CSS?
   a. `body { background-color: #FFF8DC; }`
   b. `document { background: #FFF8DC; }`
   c. `body {bgcolor: #FFF8DC;}`
   d. none of the above

10. Which tag configures a block display area or division on a page?
    a. `<div>`   **c.** `<division>`
    b. `<span>`   **d.** `<head>`

Hands-On Exercises

Practice with External Style Sheets. In this exercise you will create two external style sheet files and a web page. You will experiment with linking the web page to the external style sheets and note how the display of the page is changed.

   a. Create an external style sheet (call it format1.css) to format as follows: document background color of white, document text color of #000099.

   b. Create an external style sheet (call it format2.css) to format as follows: document background color of yellow, document text color of green.

c. Create a web page about your favorite movie that displays the movie name in an `<h1>` tag, a description of the movie in a paragraph, and an unordered (bulleted) list of the main actors and actresses in the movie. The page should also have a hyperlink to a website about the movie. Place an e-mail link to yourself on the web page. This page should be associated with the format1.css file. Save the page as moviecss1.html. Be sure to test your page in more than one browser.

d. Modify the moviecss1.html page to be associated with the format2.css external style sheet instead of the format1.css file. Save the page as moviecss2.html and test it in a browser. Notice how different the page looks!

Focus on Web Design

In this chapter you learned how to configure color with CSS. In this activity you will design a color scheme, code an external CSS file for the color scheme, and code an example web page that applies the styles you configured. Use any of the following sites to help you get started with color and web design ideas:

Psychology of Color

- http://www.infoplease.com/spot/colors1.html
- http://iit.bloomu.edu/vthc/Design/psychology.htm
- http://www.1stwebdesigner.com/design/color-psychology-website-design
- http://www.my-photoshop.com/bydesign/id-tutorials/color-psychology.html

Color Theory

- http://www.colormatters.com/colortheory.html
- http://colortheory.liquisoft.com
- http://www.digital-web.com/articles/color_theory_for_the_colorblind

Color Scheme Generators

- http://meyerweb.com/eric/tools/color-blend
- http://colorschemer.com/schemes
- http://www.colr.org
- http://colorsontheweb.com/colorwizard.asp
- http://kuler.adobe.com
- http://colorschemedesigner.com

You have the following tasks:

a. Design a color scheme. List three hexadecimal color values in addition to white (#FFFFFF) or black (#000000) in your design.

b. Describe the process you went through as you selected the colors. Describe why you chose these colors. What type of website would they be appropriate for? List the URLs of any resources you used.

c. Create an external CSS file name color1.css that configures text color and background color selections for the document, h1 element selector, p element selector, and `footer` class using the colors you have chosen.

d. Create a web page named color1.html that shows examples of the CSS style rules.

PACIFIC TRAILS RESORT CASE STUDY

#000033

#3399CC

#90C7E3

#666666

FIGURE 5.23 New Pacific Trails Resort home page with color swatches.

In this chapter's case study you will use the existing Pacific Trails (Chapter 3) website as a starting point while you create a new version of the website that uses an external style sheet to configure color (see Figure 5.23).

Step 1: Create a folder called ch5pacific to contain your Pacific Trails Resort website files. Copy the index.html and yurts.html files from the Chapter 3 Case Study ch3pacific folder.

Step 2: The External Style Sheet. Launch a text editor. You will create an external style sheet named pacific.css. A sample wireframe is shown in Figure 5.24.

```
h1

nav id

content id

   contact id

footer id
```

FIGURE 5.24 The wireframe for the Pacific Trails Resort home page.

Code the CSS to configure the following:

- Global styles for the document (use the body element selector) with background color white (#FFFFFF) and text color dark gray (#666666)
- Style rules for the h1 element selector that configure background color (#000033) and text color (#FFFFFF)
- Styles for an id named nav that configure sky blue background color (#90C7E3)
- Styles for the h2 element selector that configure medium blue text color (#3399CC)
- Styles for the dt element selector that configure dark blue text color (#000033)
- Styles for a class named resort that configure dark blue text color (#000033)

Save the file as pacific.css in the ch5pacific folder. Check your syntax with the CSS validator at http://jigsaw.w3.org/css-validator. Correct and retest if necessary.

Step 3: The Home Page. Launch a text editor and open the home page, index.html.
   a. Associate the pacific.css external style sheet. Add a `<link>` element in the head section to associate the web page with the pacific.css external style sheet file.
   b. Assign the div that contains the navigation hyperlinks to the nav id. When you are done, your code should be similar to the following example:

```
<div id="nav"><strong><a href="index.html">Home</a>   
<a href="yurts.html">Yurts</a>   
<a href="activities.html">Activities</a>   
<a href="reservations.html">Reservations</a></strong>
</div>
```

c. Configure a div element assigned to the id named content that contains the home page content area. The opening content div tag should be placed on a blank line below the closing tag for the nav div. The closing content div tag should be placed on a blank line above the closing body tag. We'll configure this div in a future case study.

d. Find the company name ("Pacific Trails Resort") in the first paragraph below the h2. Configure a span that contains this text. Assign the span tag to the resort class.

e. Look for the company name ("Pacific Trails Resort") directly above the street address. Configure a span that contains this text. Assign the span tag to the resort class.

f. Configure the div that contains the address and phone information to an id named contact. We'll configure this id in a future case study.

g. Configure the div that contains the copyright and e-mail address information to an id named footer. We'll configure this id in a future case study.

Save and test your index.html page in a browser. It should be similar to the page shown in Figure 5.25, and you'll notice that the styles you configured in the external CSS file are applied!

Step 4: The Yurts Page. Launch a text editor and open the yurts.html file. An example of the new version of the web page is shown in Figure 5.26.

a. Add a `<link>` element in the head section to associate the web page with the pacific.css external style sheet file.

b. Refer to Step 2 and configure the nav, content, and footer divs. Save and test your new yurts.html page. It should look similar to the one shown in Figure 5.26.

Step 5: Update the CSS. You may notice an empty space between the h1 element and the nav div. The empty space is the margin between these two block display elements. Refer back to Hands-On Practice 5.5 (Part 2), and recall that a technique to cause the browser to collapse this empty space is to configure the margin. To set the bottom margin of the h1 element to 0, add the following style to the h1 element selector in the pacific.css file: `margin-bottom: 0;`

Save the pacific.css file. Launch a browser and test your index.html and yurts.html pages. The gap between the h1 element and the nav div should be gone. Your home page should now display similar to Figure 5.23. Click the navigation link to display the yurts.html page—it should also render with the new styling from the pacific.css external style sheet.

FIGURE 5.25 First version of the new index.html page.

FIGURE 5.26 First version of the new yurts.html page.

CHAPTER 6

Web Graphics Styling Basics

A key component of a compelling website is the use of interesting and appropriate graphics. This chapter introduces you to working with visual elements on web pages.

When you include images on your website, it is important to remember that not all web users are able to view them. Some users may have vision problems and need assistive technology such as a screen reader application that reads the web page to them. In addition, search engines send out spiders and robots to walk the web and catalog pages for their indexes and databases; such programs do not access your images. Some of your visitors may be using a mobile device that may not display your images. As a web designer, strive to create pages that are enhanced by graphical elements but that are usable without them.

You'll learn how to . . .

- Describe types of graphics used on the Web
- Optimize a photo for the Web
- Apply the image element to add graphics to web pages
- Configure images as backgrounds on web pages
- Configure images as hyperlinks
- Configure bullets in unordered lists with images
- Configure multiple background images with CSS3

Web Graphics

Graphics can make web pages compelling and engaging. This section discusses types and features of graphic files used on the Web: **GIF**, **JPEG**, and **PNG**.

FIGURE 6.1   This logo is a GIF.

Graphic Interchange Format (GIF) Images

GIF images are best used for flat line drawings containing mostly solid tones and simple images such as clip art. The maximum number of colors in a GIF file is 256.

GIF images have a .gif file extension. Figure 6.1 shows a logo image created in GIF format. **Lossless compression** is used when a GIF is saved. This means that nothing in the original image is lost and that the compressed image, when rendered by a browser, will contain the same pixels as the original. An **animated GIF** consists of several images or frames, each of which is slightly different. When the frames flash on the screen in order, the image appears animated.

FIGURE 6.2   Comparison of transparent and nontransparent GIFs.

The format GIF89A used by GIF images supports image **transparency**. In a graphics application, such as the open-source GIMP, one color (typically the background color) of the image can be set to be transparent. The background color (or background image) of the web page shows through the transparent area in the image. Figure 6.2 displays two GIF images on a blue texture background.

To avoid slow-loading web pages, graphic files should be optimized for the Web. Image **optimization** is the process of creating an image with the lowest file size that still renders a good-quality image—balancing image quality and file size. GIF images are typically optimized by reducing the number of colors in the image using a graphics application such as Adobe Photoshop.

Joint Photographic Experts Group (JPEG) Images

JPEG images are best used for photographs. In contrast to a GIF image, a JPEG image can contain 16.7 million colors. However, JPEG images cannot be made transparent and they cannot be animated. JPEG images usually have a .jpg or .jpeg file extension. JPEG images are saved using **lossy compression**. This means that some pixels in the original image are lost or removed from the compressed file. When a browser renders the compressed image, the display is similar to but not exactly the same as the original image.

There are trade-offs between the quality of the image and the amount of compression. An image with less compression will have higher quality and result in a larger file size. An image with more compression will have lower quality and result in a smaller file size.

When you take a photo with a digital camera, the file size is too large for optimal display on a web page. Figure 6.3 shows an optimized version of a digital photo with an original file size of 250KB. The image was optimized using a graphics application set to 80 percent quality, is now only 55KB, and displays well on a web page.

FIGURE 6.3 JPEG saved at 80 percent quality (55KB file size) displays well on a web page.

Figure 6.4 was saved with 20 percent quality and is only 19KB, but its quality is unacceptable. The quality of the image degrades as the file size decreases. The square blockiness you see in Figure 6.4 is called **pixelation** and should be avoided.

FIGURE 6.4 JPEG saved at 20 percent quality (19KB file size).

Another technique used with web graphics is to display a small version of the image, called a **thumbnail image**. Often the thumbnail is configured as an image hyperlink to display the larger image. Figure 6.5 shows a thumbnail image.

FIGURE 6.5 This small thumbnail image is only 5KB.

Portable Network Graphic (PNG) Images

PNG images combine the best of GIF and JPEG images and will be a replacement for GIF in the future. PNG graphics can support millions of colors, support variable transparency levels, and use lossless compression. PNG images also support interlacing.

Image Type	Extension	Compression	Transparency	Animation	Colors
GIF	.gif	Lossless	Yes	Yes	256
JPEG	.jpg or .jpeg	Lossy	No	No	Millions
PNG	.png	Lossless	Yes	No	Millions

TABLE 6.1 Overview of Image File Types

Image Element

The image element configures graphics on a web page. These graphics can be photographs, banners, company logos, navigation buttons—you are limited only by your creativity and imagination. The image element is not coded as a pair of opening and closing tags. It is considered to be a stand-alone or void element. Use `<img/>` for XHTML syntax and `<img>` for HTML5 syntax. The following code example configures an image named logo.gif, which is located in the same folder as the web page:

```
<img src="logo.gif" height="200" width="500" alt="My Company Name">
```

The **src attribute** specifies the file name of the image. The **alt attribute** provides a text replacement, typically a text description, of the image. The browser reserves the correct amount of space for your image if you use the height and width attributes with values either equal to or approximately the size of the image. Table 6.2 lists `<img>` tag attributes and their values. Commonly used attributes are shown in bold.

Attribute	Value
align	right, left (default), top, middle, bottom; (obsolete)
alt	Text phrase that describes the image
border	Image border size in pixels; use border="0" to prevent the border of an image hyperlink from being displayed; (obsolete)
height	Height of image in pixels
hspace	Amount of space that is blank to the left and right of the image in pixels; (obsolete)
id	Text name, alphanumeric, beginning with a letter, no spaces—the value must be unique and not used for other id values on the same web page document
name	Text name, alphanumeric, beginning with a letter, no spaces—this attribute names the image so that it can be easily accessed by client-side scripting languages such as JavaScript; (obsolete)
src	The URL or file name of the image
title	A text phrase containing advisory information about the image—typically more descriptive than the alt text
vspace	Amount of space that is blank above and below the image in pixels; (obsolete)
width	Width of image in pixels

TABLE 6.2 Attributes of the `<img />` Tag

Review Table 6.2 and notice that several attributes are marked as obsolete. Although obsolete in HTML5, they are still valid in XHTML so you'll see them coded in existing web pages. As you work through this book, you'll learn to use CSS to recreate the functions of these now-obsolete attributes.

HANDS-ON PRACTICE 6.1

In this Hands-On Practice you will place a logo graphic on a web page. Create a new folder called trilliumch6. The graphic used in this Hands-On Practice is located in the student files chapter6/starters folder. Save trilliumbanner.jpg file in a folder named trilliumch6. A starter version of the Trillium Media Design Home page is ready for you in the student files. Save the chapter6/starter.html file to your trilliumch6 folder. Launch a browser to display the starter.html web page—notice that a monochromatic green color scheme has been configured with CSS. When you are finished with this Hands-On Practice, your page will look similar to the one shown in Figure 6.6—with a logo banner.

Launch a text editor and open the starter.html file. Notice that the h1 selector in the CSS has been configured with a height of 86px which is the same as the height of the logo graphic.

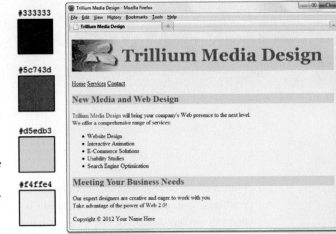

FIGURE 6.6   Color swatches are shown at the left of the new Trillium Home page with a logo banner.

Configure the graphic as follows:

> Delete the text contained between the `<h1>` opening and closing tags. Code an `<img>` element to display trilliumbanner.jpg in this area. Remember to include the src, alt, height, and width attributes. Sample code follows:

```
<img src="trilliumbanner.jpg" alt="Trillium Media Design" width="700"
height="86">
```

Save your page as index.html in the trilliumch6 folder. Launch a browser and test your page. It should look similar to the one shown in Figure 6.6. *Note*: If the image did not display on your web page, verify that you have saved the trilliumbanner.jpg file in the trilliumch6 folder and that you have spelled the file name correctly in the `<img>` tag. The student files contain a sample solution in the chapter6/trillium folder. Isn't it interesting how just one image can add visual interest to a web page? ∎

Focus on Accessibility

Use the alt attribute to provide accessibility. Recall from Chapter 1 that Section 508 of the Rehabilitation Act requires the use of accessibility features for new information technology (including websites) associated with the federal government. The alt attribute configures an alternative text description of the image. This alt text is used by the browser in two ways. The browser will show the alt text in the image area before the graphic is downloaded and displayed. Some browsers will also show the alt text as a tool tip whenever the web page visitor places a mouse over the image area.

Standard browsers such as Internet Explorer and Mozilla Firefox are not the only type of application or user agent that can access your website. Major search engines run programs called spiders or robots; these programs index and categorize websites. They cannot process images, but some process the value of the alt attributes in image tags. Applications such as screen readers will read the text in the alt attribute out loud. A mobile browser may display the alt text instead of the image.

Optimize a Photo for the Web

Photos taken with a digital camera are too large—both in their dimensions and file size—to display well on a web page. **Image optimization** is the process of creating an image with the lowest file size that still renders a good-quality image—balancing image quality and file size. Adobe Photoshop and Adobe Fireworks are often used by web professionals to optimize images for the Web. GIMP (available at http://gimp.org) is a popular open source image editor that supports multiple platforms.

HANDS-ON PRACTICE 6.2

In this Hands-On Practice you will optimize a photo for use on a web page using the free open-source GIMP application. There are versions of GIMP for Windows, Mac, and Linux operating systems. The graphic used in this Hands-On Practice is located in the student files chapter6/starters folder. Save the island.jpg file in a folder named optimize. If you view the optimize folder in Windows Explorer or the Mac Finder, you'll notice that the file size is quite large, as shown in Figure 6.7.

FIGURE 6.7 The original photograph is too large for display on a web page.

Step 1: Visit http://gimp.org, download the GIMP installation file to your hard drive, and run the installation program. Respond to the installation prompts, and in less than 5 minutes, you'll have a free image editor installed on your computer!

Step 2: Launch GIMP (be patient, GIMP takes about a minute to start up the first time you use it) and you should see the application as shown in Figure 6.8 with three separate panels—the GNU Image Manipulation Program main panel (this is where your image will display later), the Toolbox panel, and the Layers, Channels, Paths panel. We'll concentrate on using the main panel in this Hands-On Practice.

FIGURE 6.8 The GIMP application after launch.

Step 3: Let's open the island.jpg file. Select File > Open. Navigate to the island.jpg file and click Open. You should now see part of the island.jpg photo in the GNU Image Manipulation Program main panel. Note that the dimensions of the file are too large for the entire photo to display in most monitors.

Resize the photo. Select Image > Scale Image. The Scale Image dialog box displays, as shown in Figure 6.9. Change the width to be 640 and the height to be 480. Click Scale.

Compress the photo. Select File > Save As. The Save As dialog box displays. Change the name of the image to myisland.jpg and navigate to the new folder you created named optimize. Click Save.

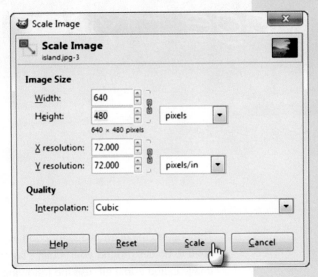

FIGURE 6.9 The Scale Image dialog box.

The Save as JPEG dialog box displays (shown in Figure 6.10). Select the checkbox for "Show preview in image window" and as you move the Quality slider bar notice that the file size of the image is displayed. Set the Quality to about 54—the estimated file size should be just about 40KB. Click Save.

GIMP will now display your resized and compressed image. You may notice that GIMP offers many editing features. If you are interested in learning more about this application, access the GIMP User Manual at http://docs.gimp.org/2.6/en.

FIGURE 6.10 The Save as JPEG dialog box.

Step 4: Display the optimized image on a web page. Launch a text editor. Select File > Open to edit the template file located at chapter1/template.html in the student files. Modify the title element. Add an image tag to the body section to display the myisland.jpg image as follows:

```
<img src="myisland.jpg" alt="Tropical Island" height="480" width="640">
```

Save the file as index.html in the optimize folder. Launch a browser to test your page. It should look similar to the page shown in Figure 6.11. You can compare your work with the solution found in the student files (chapter6/optimize/index.html).

FIGURE 6.11 The image is optimized for web page display.

Image Hyperlinks

The code to make an image function as a hyperlink is very easy. To create an **image link** all you need to do is surround your `<img>` tag with anchor tags. For example, to place a link around an image called home.gif, use the following code:

```
<a href="index.html"><img src="home.gif" height="19" width="85"
alt="Home"></a>
```

When an image is used as a hyperlink, the default is to show a blue outline (border) around the image. If you would prefer not to display this outline, you could use the `border="0"` attribute in your image tag as follows:

```
<a href="index.html"><img src="home.gif" height="19" width="85"
alt="Home" border="0"></a>
```

A more modern approach is to use CSS to configure the border on the img element selector. The next Hands-On Practice will demonstrate this technique as you add image hyperlinks to a web page.

HANDS-ON PRACTICE 6.3 ————————————————————————

You will add image links to the Trillium Media Design Home page in this Hands-On Practice. You should already have the index.html and trilliumbanner.jpg files in your trilliumch6 folder. The graphics used in this Hands-On Practice are located in the student files in the chapter6/starters folder. Save the home.gif, services.gif, and contact.gif files to your trilliumch6 folder. View Figure 6.12 to see how your page should look after you are done with this Hands-On Practice.

Let's get started. Launch a text editor and open index.html. Notice that the anchor tags are already coded—you'll just need to convert the text links to image links!

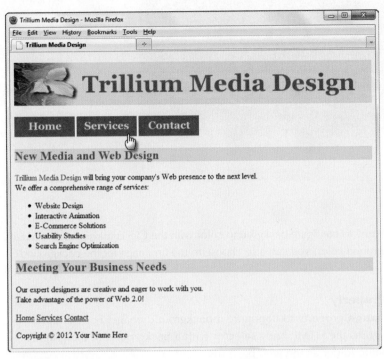

FIGURE 6.12 The new Trillium Home page navigation with image links.

1. Whenever the main navigation consists of media, such as an image, some individuals may not be able to see the images (or may have images turned off in their browser). To provide navigation that is accessible to all, configure a set of plain text navigation links in the page footer area. Copy the `<div>` element containing the navigation area to the lower portion of the page and paste it above the page footer.

2. Now, focus on the top navigation area. Replace the text contained between each pair of anchor tags with an image element. Use home.gif for the link to index.html, services.gif for the link to services.html, and contact.gif for the link to contact.html. A sample follows:

```
<a href="index.html"><img src="home.gif" alt="Home" width="120"
height="40"></a>
```

3. You'll work with borders in Chapter 7, but here's a quick preview. To eliminate the borders on the image hyperlinks, create a new style rule in the embedded CSS that configures no border for the img element selector. The code follows:

```
img   { border-style: none; }
```

4. Save your page as index.html. Launch a browser and test your page. It should look similar to the one shown in Figure 6.12.

The student files contain a sample solution in the chapter6/trillium2 folder.

Configure Background Images

Back in Chapter 5 you learned how to configure background color with the CSS `background-color` property. In addition to a background color, you can also choose to use an image for the background of an element.

The background-image Property

Use the CSS **background-image** property to configure a background image. For example, the following CSS code configures the HTML body selector with a background of the graphic texture1.png located in the same folder as the web page file:

```
body { background-image: url(texture1.png); }
```

Using Both Background Color and a Background Image

You can configure both a background color and a background image. The background color (specified by the background-color property) will display first. Next, the image specified as the background will be displayed as it is loaded by the browser.

By coding both a background color and a background image you provide your visitor with a more pleasing visual experience. If the background image does not load for some reason, the background color will still have the expected contrast with your text color. If the background image is smaller than the web browser window and the web page is configured with CSS to not automatically tile (repeat), the page background color will display in areas not covered by the background image. The CSS for a page with both a background color and a background image is as follows:

```
body { background-color: #99cccc;
       background-image: url(background.jpg); }
```

Browser Display of a Background Image

You may think that a graphic created to be the background of a web page would always be about the size of the browser window viewport. However, often the dimensions of the background image are much smaller than the typical viewport. The shape of a background image is typically either a long, thin rectangle or a small rectangular block. Unless otherwise specified in a style rule, browsers repeat, or tile, these images to cover the page background, as shown in Figures 6.13 and 6.14. The images have small file sizes so that they download as quickly as possible.

Background Image

Web Page with Background Image

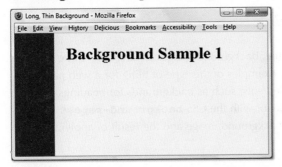

FIGURE 6.13   A long, thin background image tiles down the page.

Background Image

Web Page with Background Image

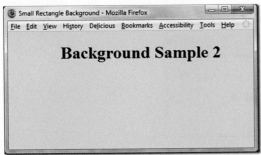

FIGURE 6.14   A small rectangular background is repeated to fill the web page window.

What if my images don't display?

The following are common reasons for an image to not display on a web page:

- Is your image *really* in the website folder? Use Windows Explorer or the Mac Finder to double-check.
- Did you code the HTML and CSS correctly? Perform W3C CSS and HTML validation testing to find syntax errors that could prevent the image from displaying.
- Does your image have the exact file name that you have used in the CSS or HTML code? Attention to detail and consistency will be very helpful here.

Position Background Images

The background-repeat Property

The default behavior of a browser is to repeat, or tile, background images to cover the entire element's background. Figures 6.13 and 6.14 display examples of this type of tiling for a web page background. This behavior also applies to other elements, such as backgrounds for headings, paragraphs, and so on. You can change this tiling behavior with the CSS **background-repeat** property. Figure 6.15 provides examples of the actual background image and the result of applying various background-repeat property values.

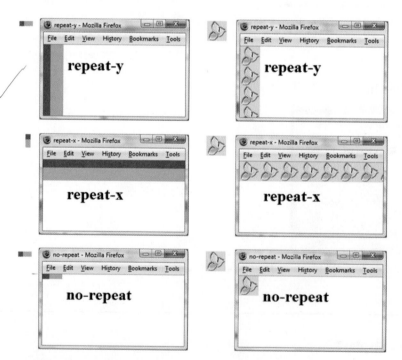

FIGURE 6.15   Examples of the CSS background-repeat property.

Positioning the Background Image

You can specify other locations for the background image besides the default top left location using the **background-position** property. Table 6.3 lists CSS properties related to background images and background color. In Figure 6.16, the background image has been placed on the right side of the element using the style rule

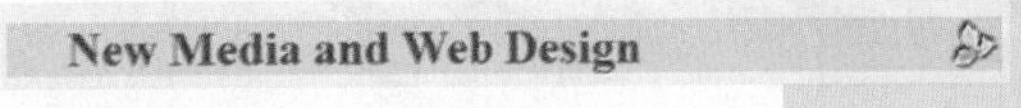

```
h2 { background-image: url(trilliumbg.gif); background-position: right;
     background-repeat: no-repeat; }
```

FIGURE 6.16 The flower background image was configured to display on the right side with CSS.

Property	Description	Value
background-color	Background color of an element	Any valid color value Example: `background-color: #cccccc;`
background-image	Background image of an element	The url keyword with parentheses surrounding the file name or path for the image Example: `background-image: url(logo.gif);`
background-position	Position of the background image	Two percentages, pixel values, or position values: (left, top, center, bottom, right) The first value indicates horizontal position. The second value indicates vertical position. If only one value is provided, the second value defaults to center. Example: `background-position: right, bottom;`
background-repeat	Controls how the background image will be repeated within the element	repeat, repeat-y, repeat-x, no-repeat Example: `background-repeat: no-repeat;`
background-attachment	Configures whether the background image scrolls with the page or is fixed in place	fixed, scroll (default) Example: `background-attachment: fixed;`
background-size	Configures the size of the background image. This CSS3 property is not supported in all browsers.	Two percentages, pixel values, or auto. The first value indicates width. The second value indicates height. If only one value is provided, the second value defaults to auto.
background-origin	Configures the background positioning area. This CSS3 property is not supported in all browsers.	padding-box, border-box, or content-box
background-clip	Configures the background painting area. This CSS3 property is not supported in all browsers.	padding-box, border-box, or content-box

TABLE 6.3   CSS Properties for Background

Practice with Background Images

HANDS-ON PRACTICE 6.4 ————————————————

Let's practice using a background image. In this Hands-On Practice you will configure the h2 element selector with a background image that does not repeat. Obtain the trilliumbg.gif image from the student files in the chapter6/starters folder. Save the image in your trilliumch6 folder. You'll update the index. html file from the previous Hands-On Practice (shown in Figure 6.12). When you are completed with this exercise your page should look similar to the one shown in Figure 6.17.

FIGURE 6.17 The background image in the `<h2>` areas is configured with background-repeat: no-repeat.

Launch a text editor and open index.html.

1. Modify the style rule for the h2 element selector and configure the `background-image` and `background-repeat` properties. Set the background image to be trilliumbg.gif. Set the background to not repeat. The h2 element selector style rules are

   ```
   h2   {   background-color:  #d5edb3;
            color:  #5c743d;
            background-image:  url(trilliumbg.gif);
            background-repeat:  no-repeat;
   }
   ```

2. Save your page as index.html. Launch a browser and test your page. You may notice that the text in the h2 element is displayed over the background image. In this case, the page would look more appealing if there was more space, or padding, before the beginning of the text displayed by the h2 elements. A quick way to adjust this is to code the   nonbreaking space special character (refer back to Chapter 2) about five times just after each opening <h2> tag. However, a more modern technique is to use the CSS padding-left property (there will be more on this in Chapter 7) to add empty space within the left side of the element. Add the following declaration to the h2 element selector to add empty space before the text:

```
padding-left: 30px;
```

3. Save and test your page again. It should look similar to the one shown in Figure 6.17. The student files contain a sample solution in the chapter6/trillium3 folder.

What if my images are in their own folder?

It's a good idea to organize your website by placing all your images in a folder separate from your web pages. Notice that the CircleSoft website shown in Figure 6.18 has a folder called images, which contains GIF and JPEG files. To refer to these files in code, you also need to refer to the images folder. The following are some examples:

- The CSS code to configure the background.gif file from the images folder as the page background is as follows:

```
body { background-image: url(images/background.gif); }
```

- To configure a web page to display the logo.jpg file from the images folder, use the following code:

```
<img src="images/logo.jpg" alt="CircleSoft" width="588" height="120">
```

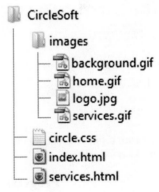

FIGURE 6.18 A folder named "images" contains the graphic files.

A **sprite** is an image file that contains multiple small graphics that are configured as background images for various web page elements using the CSS background-image, background-repeat, and background-position properties. The single image saves download time because the browser only needs to make one http request for the combined image instead of many requests for the individual smaller images. See http://css-tricks.com/css-sprites for more information on CSS Sprites.

CSS3 Multiple Background Images

FIGURE 6.19. The Safari browser displays multiple background images.

Now that you are familiar with background images, let's explore applying multiple background images to a web page. Although the CSS3 Backgrounds and Borders module is still in working draft status, current versions of most popular web browsers support the use of multiple background images.

Figure 6.19 shows a web page with two background images configured on the body selector: a green gradient image that repeats across the entire browser viewport and a flower image that displays once in the right footer area. Use the **CSS3 background property** to configure multiple background images. Each image declaration is separated by a comma. You can optionally add property values to indicate the image's position and whether the image repeats. The `background` property uses a short-hand notation—just list the values that are needed for relevant properties such as `background-position` and `background-repeat`.

Progressive Enhancement

Multiple background images are currently supported by recent versions of Firefox, Chrome, Safari, and Opera. Although supported in Internet Explorer 9, multiple background images are not supported by earlier versions of Internet Explorer. You'll use the technique of **progressive enhancement**, which is defined by web developer and HTML5 evangelist Christian Heilmann as "Starting with a baseline of usable functionality, then increasing the richness of the user experience step by step by testing for support for enhancements before applying them." In other words, start with a web page that displays well in most browsers and then add new design techniques, such as multiple background images, in a way that enhances the display for visitors using browsers that support the new technique.

FIGURE 6.20. Progressive enhancement in action. Although only one background image displays, the web page has a similar display to Figure 6.19.

To provide for progressive enhancement when using multiple background images, first configure a separate `background-image` property with a single image (rendered by nonsupporting browsers) before the `background` property with multiple images (rendered by supporting browsers and ignored by nonsupporting browsers). Figure 6.20 shows the page displayed in Internet Explorer 8, which rendered the standard `background-image` property.

HANDS-ON PRACTICE 6.5

Let's practice configuring multiple background images. In this Hands-On Practice you will configure the body element selector to display multiple background images on the web page. Obtain the trilliumgradient.png and the trilliumfoot.gif images from the student files in the chapter6/starters folder. Save the images in your trilliumch6 folder. You'll update the index.html file from the previous Hands-On Practice (shown in Figure 6.17). Launch a text editor and open index.html.

1. Modify the style rule for the body element selector. Configure the `background-image` property to display trilliumgradient.png. This style rule will be applied by browsers that do not support multiple background images. Configure a `background` property to display both the trilliumgradient.png image and the trilliumfoot.gif image. The trilliumfoot.gif image should not repeat and should be displayed in the lower right corner. The body selector style rules are as follows:

```
body { background-color: #f4ffe4; color: #333333;
       background-image: url(trilliumgradient.png);
       background: url(trilliumfoot.gif) no-repeat bottom right,
                   url(trilliumgradient.png);}
```

2. Save your page as index.html. Launch a browser and test your page. It will look different, depending on which browser you use—similar to either Figure 6.19 (a browser that supports multiple background images) or Figure 6.20 (a browser that does not support multiple background images). Note: The W3C CSS validator currently defaults to CSS level 2.1, but the background property is part of CSS level 3 (CSS3). You need to choose the appropriate CSS level when validating. Visit http://jigsaw.w3.org/css-validator and select "CSS level 3" for the Profile value.

3. There is usually more than one way to design a web page. Let's consider the placement of the flower image in the footer area of the web page. Why not configure the gradient image as the body selector background and the flower image as the #footer background? This will provide for a similar display on all currently popular browsers. Let's try this out. Edit the index.html file. Remove the background property from the body selector. A code sample is

```
body { background-color: #f4ffe4; color: #333333;
       background-image: url(trilliumgradient.png);}
```

Next, configure the trilliumfoot.gif image as the background for the #footer selector. Configure a height value that will be larger enough to display the image. The code is

```
#footer { background-image: url(trilliumfoot.gif);
          background-repeat: no-repeat;
          background-position: bottom right;
          height: 90px; }
```

4. Save your page as index2.html. Launch a browser and test your page. It should look similar to Figure 6.19 on all popular modern browsers. See the chapter6/trillium4 folder in the student files for solutions to this Hands-On Practice.

The Favorites Icon

Ever wonder about the small icon you sometimes see in the address bar or tab of a browser? That's a favorites icon, usually referred to as a favicon, which is a square image (either 16×16 pixels or 32×32 pixels) associated with a web page. The favicon, shown in Figure 6.21, may display in the browser address bar, tab, or the favorites/bookmarks list. You can create a favicon in a graphics application, such as Adobe Fireworks, or at a number of websites, including http://favicon.cc, http://www.favicongenerator.com, and http://www.freefavicon.com.

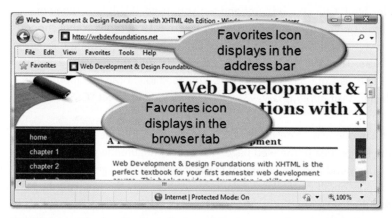

FIGURE 6.21 The favorites icon displays in the browser tab and address bar.

Configuring a Favorites Icon

While earlier versions of Internet Explorer (such as versions 5 and 6) expected the file to be named favicon.ico and to reside in the root directory of the web server, a more modern approach is to associate the favicon.ico file with a web page using the link element. Recall that in Chapter 5 you coded the `<link>` tag in the head section of a web page to associate an external style sheet file with a web page file. You can also use the `<link>` tag to associate a favorites icon with a web page. Three attributes are used to associate a web page with a favorites icon: `rel`, `href`, and `type`. The value of the `rel` attribute is `icon`. The value of the `href` attribute is the name of the image file. The value of the `type` attribute describes the MIME type of the image—which defaults to `image/x-icon` for .ico files. The code to associate a favorites icon named favicon.ico to a web page is as follows:

```
<link rel="icon" href="favicon.ico" type="image/x-icon">
```

Note that to be compatible with Internet Explorer and follow Microsoft's proprietary syntax, you'll also need to code a second link tag:

```
<link rel="shortcut icon" href="favicon.ico" type="image/x-icon">
```

Be aware that Internet Explorer's support of the favorites icon is somewhat "buggy." You may need to publish your files to the Web (see Chapter 12) in order for the favicon to display in even current versions of Internet Explorer. Other browsers, such as Firefox, display favicons more reliably and also support GIF and PNG image formats.

HANDS-ON PRACTICE 6.6

Let's practice using a favorites icon. Obtain the favicon.ico file from the student files in the chapter6/starters folder. In this exercise you will use your files from Hands-On Practice 6.4 (see the student files chapter6/trillium3 folder) as a starting point.

1. Launch a text editor and open index.html. Add the following link tags to the head section of the web page:

    ```
    <link rel="icon" href="favicon.ico" type="image/x-icon">
    <link rel="shortcut icon" href="favicon.ico" type="image/x-icon">
    ```

2. Save your page as index.html. Launch the Firefox browser and test your page. You should notice the small trillium flower in the Firefox browser tab as shown in Figure 6.22. The student files contain a sample solution in the chapter6/trillium5 folder.

FIGURE 6.22 The favorites icon displays in the Firefox browser location and tab.

Configure List Markers with CSS

The default display for an unordered list is to show a disc marker (often referred to as a bullet) in front of each list item. The default display for an ordered list is to show a decimal number in front of each list item. Use the `list-style-type` property to configure the marker for an unordered or ordered list. See Table 6.4 for common property values.

Property	Description	Value	List Marker Display
list-style-type	Configures the style of the list marker	none	No list markers display
		disc	Circle ("bullet")
		circle	Open circle
		square	Square
		decimal	Decimal numbers
		upper-alpha	Uppercase letters
		lower-alpha	Lowercase letters
		lower-roman	Lowercase Roman numerals
list-style-image	Image replacement for the list marker	The url keyword with parentheses surrounding the file name or path for the image	The image displays in front of each list item
list-style-position	Configures placement of markers	inside	Markers are indented, text wraps under the markers
		outside (default)	Markers have default placement

TABLE 6.4 CSS Properties for Ordered and Unordered List Markers

The property `list-style-type: none` prevents the browser from displaying the list markers (you'll see a use for this when configuring navigation hyperlinks in Chapter 8). Figure 6.23 shows an unordered list configured with square markers using the following CSS:

```
ul { list-style-type: square; }
```

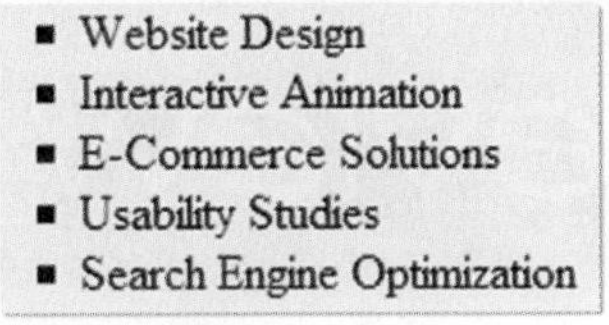

- Website Design
- Interactive Animation
- E-Commerce Solutions
- Usability Studies
- Search Engine Optimization

FIGURE 6.23 The unordered list markers are square.

Figure 6.24 shows an ordered list configured with uppercase letter markers using the following CSS:

```
ol { list-style-type: upper-alpha; }
```

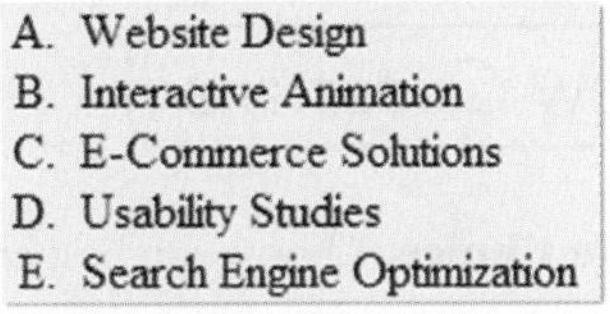

A. Website Design
B. Interactive Animation
C. E-Commerce Solutions
D. Usability Studies
E. Search Engine Optimization

FIGURE 6.24 The ordered list markers use uppercase letters.

Configure an Image as a List Marker

Use the `list-style-image` property to configure an image as the marker in an unordered or ordered list. In Figure 6.25 an image named trillium.gif was configured to replace the list markers using the following CSS:

```
ul {list-style-image: url(trillium.gif); }
```

✿ Website Design
✿ Interactive Animation
✿ E-Commerce Solutions
✿ Usability Studies
✿ Search Engine Optimization

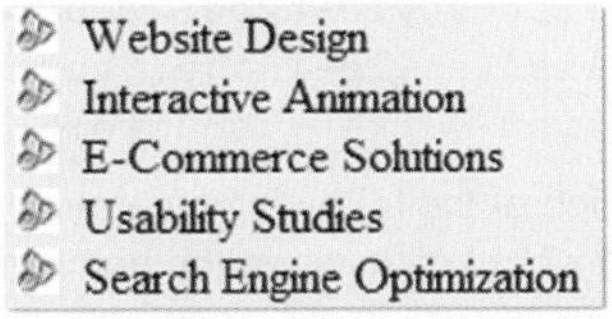

FIGURE 6.25 The list markers are replaced with an image.

HANDS-ON PRACTICE 6.7 ⎯⎯⎯⎯⎯⎯⎯⎯⎯⎯⎯⎯⎯⎯

In this Hands-On Practice you'll replace the list markers on the Trillium Media Design home page with an image. Obtain the trillium.gif file from the student files in the chapter6/starters folder. In this exercise you will use your files from Hands-On Practice 6.5 (see the student files chapter6/trillium5 folder) as a starting point.

1. Launch a text editor and open index.html. Add the following style rule to the embedded CSS in the head section to configure the ul element selector with the `list-style-image` property:

   ```
   ul { list-style-image: url(trillium.gif); }
   ```

2. Save your page as index.html. Launch in a browser and test your page. You should notice the small trillium flower before each item in the unordered list as shown in Figure 6.25. The student files contain a sample solution in the chapter6/trillium6 folder.

CHAPTER 6

Review and Apply

Review Questions

Multiple Choice. Choose the best answer for each item.

1. Which property and value are used to configure an unordered list item with a square list marker?
   a. `list-bullet: none;`
   b. `list-style-type: square;`
   c. `list-style-image: square;`
   d. `list-marker: square;`

2. Which of the following creates an image link to the index.html page when the home.gif graphic is clicked?
   a. `<a href="index.html" src="home.gif" alt="Home"></a>`
   b. `<a href="index.html"><img src="home.gif" alt="Home"></a>`
   c. `<img src="home.gif" href="index.html" alt="Home">`
   d. `<a src="home.gif"><img src="home.gif" alt="Home"></a>`

3. Why should you include height and width attributes on an `<img>` tag?
   a. They are required attributes and must always be included.
   b. They help the browser render the page faster because it reserves the appropriate space for the image.
   c. They help the browser display the image in its own window.
   d. none of the above

4. Which attribute specifies text that is available to browsers and other user agents that do not support graphics?
   a. `alt`   **c.** `src`
   b. `text`   **d.** none of the above

5. What is the term used to describe a square icon that is associated with a web page and is displayed in the browser address bar or tab?
   a. background   **c.** favicon
   b. bookmark icon   **d.** logo

6. Which of the following graphic types is best suited to photographs?
   a. GIF   **c.** BMP
   b. photo   **d.** JPEG

7. Which of the following configures a graphic to repeat vertically down the side of a web page?
   a. `background-repeat: repeat-x;`
   b. `background-repeat:repeat;`
   c. `valign="left"`
   d. `background-repeat: repeat-y;`

8. Which CSS property configures the background image of an element?
   a. `background-color`   **c.** `favicon`
   b. `bgcolor`   **d.** `background-image`

9. What is the process of creating an image with the lowest file size that still renders a good-quality image—balancing image quality and file size?
   a. progressive enhancement   **c.** usability
   b. optimization   **d.** image validation

10. What is the process of ensuring that web pages which are coded with new or advanced techniques still are usable in browsers that do not support the new techniques.
    a. validation   **c.** valid enhancement
    b. progressive enhancement   **d.** optimization

Hands-On Exercises

1. Write the code to place an image called primelogo.gif on a web page. The image is 100 pixels high by 650 pixels wide.

2. Write the code to create an image hyperlink. The image is called schaumburgthumb.jpg. It is 100 pixels high by 150 pixels wide. The image should link to a larger image called schaumburg.jpg. There should be no border on the image.

3. Write the code to create a `<div>` containing three images used as navigation links. Table 6.5 provides information about the images and their associated links.

Image Name	Link Page Name	Image Height	Image Width
homebtn.gif	index.html	50	200
productsbtn.gif	products.html	50	200
orderbtn.gif	order.html	50	200

TABLE 6.5

4. Experiment with background images.

   a. Locate the twocolor.gif file in the student files chapter6/starters folder. Design a web page that uses this file as a background image that repeats down the left side of the browser window. Save your file as bg1.html

   b. Locate the twocolor1.gif file in the student files chapter6/starters folder. Design a web page that uses this file as a background image that repeats across the top of the browser window. Save your file as bg2.html

5. Design a new web page named movie6.html about your favorite movie. Configure a background color for the page and either background images or background colors for at least two sections of the page. Search the Web for a photo of a scene from the movie, an actress in the movie, or an actor in the movie. Include the following information on your web page:

- Title of the movie
- Director or producer
- Leading actor
- Leading actress
- Rating (R, PG-13, PG, G, NR)
- A brief description of the movie
- An absolute link to a review about the movie

Focus on Web Design

Providing access to the Web for all people is an important issue. Visit the W3C's Web Accessibility Initiative and explore their WCAG 2.0 Quick Reference at http://w3.org/WAI/WCAG20/quickref (the textbook's website at http://webdevbasics.net/chapter6.html has an updated link if needed). View additional pages at the W3C's site as necessary. Explore the checkpoints that are related to the use of color and images on web pages. Create a web page that uses color, uses images, and includes the information that you discovered.

PACIFIC TRAILS RESORT CASE STUDY

In this chapter's case study you will use the existing Pacific Trails (Chapter 5) website as a starting point to create a new version of the website that incorporates images.

Step 1: Create a folder called ch6pacific to contain your Pacific Trails Resort website files. Copy the index.html, yurts.html, and pacific.css files from the Chapter 5 Case Study ch5pacific folder. Copy the following files from the chapter6/casestudystarters folder in the student files and save them in your ch6pacific folder: coast.jpg, favicon.ico, sunset.jpg, trail.jpg, and yurt.jpg.

Step 2:   The Logo Image. Launch a text editor and open the pacific.css external style sheet file. Add the CSS to configure the h1 element selector to display the background image named sunset.jpg on the right without any repeats. Save your pacific.css file.

Test your index.html page in a browser and notice that the logo header area will seem a bit crowded. To fix this, add some extra space with the CSS padding property (see Chapter 7) and add the declaration shown below to the h1 element selector:

```
padding: 10px;
```

Save the file. Check your syntax with the CSS validator (http://jigsaw.w3.org/css-validator). Correct and retest if necessary.

Step 3:   The Home Page. Launch a text editor and open the home page, index.html. Add an <img> tag on a new line below the h2 element. Configure the <img> tag to display the coast.jpg image. Configure the alt, height, and width attributes for the image. Add extra space under the address/ phone area using a few line break tags. Save and test your page in a browser. It should look similar to Figure 6.26.

Step 4:   The Yurts Page. Launch a text editor and open the yurts.html file. You will modify this file to display the yurt.jpg image below the h2 element and configure it in a similar manner as you configured the coast.jpg image on the home page. Save and test your new yurts.html page. It should look similar to the one shown in Figure 6.27.

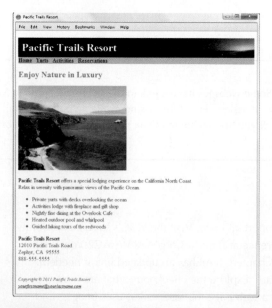

FIGURE 6.26 Pacific Trails Resort home page.

FIGURE 6.27 Pacific Trails Resort yurts page.

Step 5:   The Activities Page. Launch a text editor, open the yurts.html document, and save the file as activities.html—this is the start of your new activities page. Modify the page title area as appropriate. Change the h2 text to be "Activities at Pacific Trails." Modify the `<img>` tag to display the trail.jpg image. Delete the description list. Configure the following text using h3 tags for the headings and paragraph tags for the sentences.

Hiking
Pacific Trails Resort has 5 miles of hiking trails and is adjacent to a state park. Go it alone or join one of our guided hikes.

Kayaking
Ocean kayaks are available for guest use.

Bird Watching
While anytime is a good time for bird watching at Pacific Trails, we offer guided birdwatching trips at sunrise several times a week.

Save your activities.html file.

Next, configure CSS for the activities page. Open the pacific.css file in a text editor and add a style rule to configure the h3 element selector with #000033 text color. Save the file.

Launch a browser and test your new activities.html page. It should look similar to Figure 6.28.

FIGURE 6.28   New Pacific Trails Resort activities page.

What if I don't know the height and width of an image?

Most graphics applications can display the height and width of an image. If you have a graphics application such as Adobe Photoshop or Adobe Fireworks handy, launch the application and open the image. These applications include options that will display the properties of the image, such as height and width.

If you don't have a graphics application available, you can determine the dimensions of an image using a browser. Display the image on a web page. Right-click on the image to display the context-sensitive menu. Select properties and view the dimensions (height and width) of the image. (*Warning*: if the height and width are specified on the web page, those values will be displayed even if the image's actual height and width are different.)

CHAPTER 7

More CSS Basics

You'll add to your CSS skill set in this chapter. In addition to configuring text with CSS, you'll be introduced to the CSS box model and the associated properties, including margin, border, and padding. You'll also explore new CSS3 properties to round corners, apply shadow, and configure color with opacity.

You'll learn how to . . .

- Configure text typeface, size, weight, and style with CSS
- Align and indent text with CSS
- Describe and apply the CSS box model
- Configure width and height with CSS
- Configure margin, border, and padding with CSS

- Center web page content with CSS
- Apply shadows with CSS3
- Configure rounded corners with CSS3
- Configure opacity, RGBA color, and gradients with CSS3

Fonts with CSS

The font-family Property

The `font-family` property configures font typefaces. A web browser displays text using the fonts that have been installed on the user's computer. When a font is specified that is not installed on your web visitor's computer, the default font is substituted. Times New Roman is the default font displayed by most web browsers. Table 7.1 shows font family categories and some common font typefaces.

Font Family Category	Font Family Description	Font Typeface Examples
serif	Serif fonts have small embellishments on the end of letter strokes; often used for headings.	Times New Roman, Georgia, Palatino
sans-serif	Sans-serif fonts do not have serifs; often used for web page text.	Arial, Tahoma, Helvetica, Verdana
monospace	Fixed-width font; often used for code samples.	Courier New, Lucida Console
cursive	Hand-written style; use with caution; may be difficult to read on a web page.	Lucida Handwriting, Brush Script, Comic Sans MS
fantasy	Exaggerated style; use with caution; sometimes used for headings; may be difficult to read on a web page.	Jokerman, Impact, Papyrus

TABLE 7.1 Common Fonts

Not every computer has the same fonts installed. See http://www.ampsoft.net/webdesign-l/WindowsMacFonts.html for a list of "web-safe" fonts. Create a built-in backup plan by listing multiple fonts and categories for the value of the `font-family` property. The browser will attempt to use the fonts in the order listed. The following CSS configures the p element selector to display text in Arial (if installed) or Helvetica (if installed) or the default installed sans-serif font.

```
p { font-family: Arial, Helvetica, sans-serif; }
```

HANDS-ON PRACTICE 7.1 ——————————————

In this Hands-On Practice you will configure the `font-family` property. Create a new folder called trilliumch7. A starter version of the Trillium Media Design Home page is ready for you in the student files. Save the chapter7/starter.html file to your trilliumch7 folder. Copy the following files from the chapter7/starters folder to your trilliumch7 folder: contact.gif, home.gif, services.gif, and trilliumbanner.jpg.

Launch a browser to display the starter.html web page—notice that the default browser font (typically Times New Roman) is used. When you are finished with this Hands-On Practice, your page will look similar to the one shown in Figure 7.1.

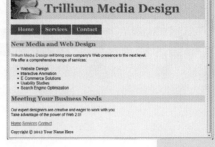

Launch a text editor and open the starter.html file. Configure the embedded CSS as follows:

FIGURE 7.1 The new Trillium home page.

1. Configure the body element selector to set global styles to use a sans-serif font typeface, such as Arial or Helvetica. An example is

```
body { background-color:#f4ffe4;
       color:#333333;
       font-family: Arial, Helvetica, sans-serif; }
```

2. Configure h2 elements to use a serif font typeface, such as Georgia or Times New Roman. An example is shown as follows. Notice that "Times New Roman" is enclosed within quotation marks because the font name is more than a single word:

```
h2 { background-color:#d5edb3;
     color:#5c743d;
     font-family: Georgia, "Times New Roman", serif; }
```

3. Configure the footer id to use a serif font typeface, such as Georgia or Times New Roman. An example is

```
#footer { font-family: Georgia, "Times New Roman", serif; }
```

Save your page as index.html in the trilliumch7 folder. Launch a browser and test your page. It should look similar to the one shown in Figure 7.1. A sample solution is in the chapter7/trillium folder.

FAQ

I've heard about "embedding" fonts to use special fonts on a web page—what's that all about?

Still in draft form and not yet an official standard, CSS3 introduces @font-face, which can be used to "embed" fonts within web pages, although you actually provide the location of the font and the browser downloads it. For example, if you own the rights to freely distribute the font named MyAwesomeFont and it is stored in a file named myawesomefont.otf in the same folder as your web page, the CSS to make it available to your web page visitors is

```
@font-face { font-family: 'MyAwesomeFont';
             src: url('myawesomefont.otf');  }
```

Current browsers support @font-face, but there are file size and copyright issues to consider, You may have purchased a font, but you need to check your license to determine whether you also have the right to freely distribute the font. See the textbook's website at http://webdevbasics.net/chapter7.html and http://nimbupani.com/font-in-your-face.html for more information about @font-face.

Keep in mind that if you just need a nonstandard font for a logo area or for an image on a web page, there's an easy solution. You are free to use any font that's available to you when you create an image with a graphics application.

Text Properties with CSS

CSS provides you with lots of options for configuring the text on your web pages. In this section, you'll explore the `font-size`, `font-weight`, `font-style`, and `line-height` properties.

The font-size Property

The `font-size` property sets the size of the font. Table 7.2 lists a wide variety of text and numeric values— there are almost too many choices available. See the notes in Table 7.2 for recommended use.

Value Category	Values	Notes
Text Value	xx-small, x-small, small, medium (default), large, x-large, xx-large	Scales well when text is resized in browser; limited options for text size.
Pixel Unit (px)	Numeric value with unit, such as 10 px	Pixel-perfect display depends on screen resolution; may not scale in every browser when text is resized.
Point Unit (pt)	Numeric value with unit such as 10 pt	Use to configure print version of web page (see Chapter 8); may not scale in every browser when text is resized.
Em Unit (em)	Numeric value with unit, such as .75 em	Recommended by W3C; scales well when text is resized in browser; many options for text size.
Percentage Value	Numeric value with percentage, such as 75%	Recommended by W3C; scales well when text is resized in browser; many options for text size.

TABLE 7.2 Configuring Font Size

The **em unit** is a relative font unit that has its roots in the print industry back in the day when printers set type manually with blocks of characters. An em unit is the width of a square block of type (typically the uppercase M) for a particular font and type size. On web pages, an em unit corresponds to the width of the font and size used in the parent element (typically the body element). With this in mind, the size of an em unit is relative to the font typeface and default size. Percentage values work in a similar manner to em units. For example, `font-size: 100%` and `font-size: 1em` should render the same in a browser. To compare font sizes on your computer—launch a browser and view chapter7/fonts.html in the student files.

The `font-weight` Property

The `font-weight` property configures the boldness of the text. Configuring the CSS rule `font-weight: bold;` has an effect similar to the <b> or <strong> XHTML element.

The `font-style` Property

The `font-style` property typically is used to configure text displayed in italics. Valid values for `font-style` are normal (the default), italic, and oblique. The CSS `font-style: italic;` has the same visual effect in the browser as an <i> or <em> XHTML element.

The `line-height` Property

The `line-height` property modifies the default height of a line of text and is often configured using a percentage value. For example, code `line-height: 200%;` configures text to appear double spaced.

HANDS-ON PRACTICE 7.2 ——————————

Let's try out those new CSS properties. You should already have the index.html, home.gif, services.gif, contact.gif, and trilliumbanner.jpg files in your trilliumch7 folder. Launch a text editor and open the index html file. You'll code additional CSS style rules to configure the text on the page. When complete, your web page will look similar to the one shown in Figure 7.2.

Launch a text editor and open the index.html file. Configure the embedded CSS as follows:

1. Configure the p element selector to add some extra space between the lines of text in the paragraph with the `line-height` property as follows:

    ```
    p    { line-height: 120%;   }
    ```

FIGURE 7.2 CSS configures the text on the web page.

2. Configure the li and p element selectors to display font smaller than the default. Note that you can list multiple selectors separated by commas in a style rule.

    ```
    li, p { font-size: 90%:   }
    ```

3. Add a style rule to the company name class to display the text in bold font.

    ```
    .companyname { color: #5c743d; font-weight: bold; }
    ```

4. Add style rules to the footer id to configure small text (use .80 em) that is in italics.

    ```
    #footer { font-family: Georgia, "Times New Roman", serif;
              font-size: .80em; font-style: italic;   }
    ```

    Save your page as index.html in the trilliumch7 folder. Launch a browser and test your page. A sample solution is in the chapter7/trillium2 folder.

■

Align and Indent Text with CSS

HTML elements are left-aligned by default—they begin at the left margin. In this section you'll work with CSS properties to align and indent text.

The `text-align` Property

The CSS `text-align` property configures the alignment of text and inline elements within block elements such as headings, paragraphs, and divs. Table 7.3 lists the values for the `text-align` property.

Property	Common Values
text-align	left (default), center, right, justify

TABLE 7.3   The `text-align` Property

The following CSS code sample configures an h1 element to have centered text:

```
h1 { text-align: center; }
```

Quick Tip

While it can be quite effective to center the text displayed in web page headings, be careful about centering text in paragraphs. According to WebAIM (http://www.webaim.org/techniques/textlayout), studies have shown that centered text is more difficult to read than left-aligned text.

The text-indent Property

The CSS `text-indent` property configures the indentation of the first line of text within an element. The value can be numeric (such as a px, pt, or em unit) or a percentage. The following CSS code sample configures the first line of all paragraphs to be indented:

```
p { text-indent: 5em; }
```

HANDS-ON PRACTICE 7.3

You'll work with `text-align` and `text-indent` properties in this Hands-On Practice. You should already have the index.html, home.gif, services.gif, contact.gif, and trilliumbanner.jpg files in your trilliumch7 folder.

Launch a text editor and open index.html. You'll code additional CSS style rules to configure the text on the page. When complete, your web page will look similar to the one shown in Figure 7.3.

FIGURE 7.3 CSS has been used to indent paragraphs and center the footer.

Configure the embedded CSS as follows:

1. Add a new style rule to the p selector to indent the text on the first line (use the value 3em) as follows:

```
p   { line-height: 120%;
      text-indent: 3em; }
```

2. Add a style rule to the footer id to configure center alignment.

```
#footer { font-family: "Times New Roman", Georgia, serif;
          font-size: .80em;
          font-style: italic;
          text-align: center; }
```

Save your page as index.html in the trilliumch7 folder. Launch a browser and test your page. It should look similar to the one shown in Figure 7.3. A sample solution is in the chapter7/trillium3 folder.

Is there a way to place a comment within CSS?

Yes. An easy way to add a comment to CSS is to type "/*" before your comment and "*/" after your comment. For example,

```
/* Configure Footer */
#footer {  font-size: .80em; font-style: italic;   text-align: center; }
```

Width and Height with CSS

FIGURE 7.4   The web page is set to 80% width.

The `width` Property

The `width` property configures the width of an element's content in the browser viewport with either a numeric value unit (such as 100px or 20em) or percentage (such as 80%, as shown in Figure 7.4) of the parent element. The width of an element displayed in the browser viewport includes the width of the element's content, padding, border, and margin—it is not the same as the value of the width property, which only configures the width of the actual content.

The `min-width` Property

The `min-width` property sets the minimum width of an element's content in the browser viewport with either a numeric value unit (such as 100px or 20em) or percentage (such as 75%) of the parent element. This minimum width value can prevent content jumping around when a browser is resized. Scrollbars appear if the browser viewport is resized below the minimum width (see Figures 7.5 and 7.6).

FIGURE 7.5   As the browser is resized, the text wraps.

FIGURE 7.6   The min-width property avoids display issues.

The `max-width` Property

The `max-width` property sets the maximum width of an element's content in the browser viewport with either a numeric value unit (such as 900px) or percentage (such as 60%) of the parent element. This maximum width value can reduce the possibility of text stretching across large expanses of the screen by a high-resolution monitor.

The `height` Property

The `height` property configures the height of an element's content in the browser viewport with either a numeric value unit (such as 900px) or percentage (such as 60%) of the parent element. Figure 7.7 shows a web page with an h1 area with no `height` property configured. Notice how part of the background image is truncated, or cut off. In Figure 7.8, the h1 area is configured with the `height` property. Notice the improved display of the background image.

FIGURE 7.7 The background image is truncated.

FIGURE 7.8 The height property value corresponds to the height of the background image.

HANDS-ON PRACTICE 7.4

You'll work with the height and width properties in this Hands-On Practice. When complete, your web page will look similar to the one shown in Figure 7.4.

You should already have the index.html, home.gif, services.gif, and contact.gif files in your trilliumch7 folder. Obtain the trilliumlogo.jpg file from the chapter7/starters folder. Launch a text editor and open the index.html file.

1. Edit the embedded CSS to configure the document to take up 80% of the browser window but with a minimum width of 600px. Add the following style rules to the body element selector:

    ```
    width: 80%; min-width: 600px;
    ```

2. Configure the h1 element selector to display the trilliumlogo.jpg image once (with no repeating) in the background and be 86px in height (the height of the background image), indent the text 140px, and use 250% line height. Add the following declarations to the h1 element selector:

    ```
    background-image: url(trilliumlogo.jpg);
    background-repeat: no-repeat; text-indent: 140px;
    height: 86px; line-height: 250%;
    ```

3. Next, edit the HTML in the index.html file. Remove the image tag for the trilliumbanner.jpg file from the h1 area and replace it with the following text: Trillium Media Design. Save your page as index.html in the trilliumch7 folder. Launch a browser and test your page. A sample solution is in the chapter7/trillium4 folder.

The Box Model

Each element in a document is considered to be a rectangular box. As shown in Figure 7.9, this box consists of a content area surrounded by padding, a border, and margins. This is known as the box model.

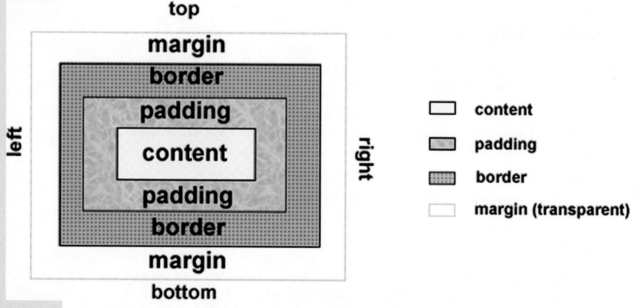

FIGURE 7.9 The CSS box model.

Content

The content area can consist of a combination of text and web page elements such as images, paragraphs, headings, lists, and so on. The visible width of the element on a web page is the total of the content width, the padding width, and the border width. However, the `width` property only configures the actual width of the content—not including any padding, border, or margin.

Padding

The padding area is between the content and the border. The default padding value is zero. When the background of an element is configured, the background is applied to both the padding and the content areas.

Border

The border area is between the padding and the margin. The default border has a value of 0 and does not display.

Margin

The margin determines the empty space between the element and any adjacent elements. The margin is always transparent—the background color of the web page or container element (such as a div) shows in this area. The solid line in Figure 7.9 that contains the margin area does not display on a web page. Browsers often have default margin values set for the web page document and for certain elements such as paragraphs, headings, forms, and so on. Use the margin property to override the default browser values.

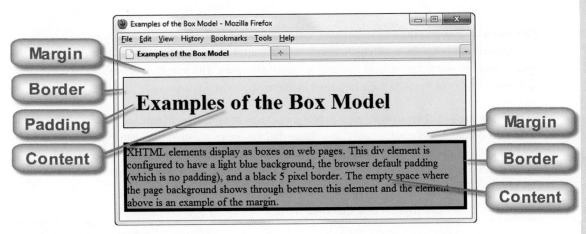

FIGURE 7.10 Examples of the box model.

The Box Model in Action

The web page shown in Figure 7.10 (student files chapter7/box.html) depicts the box model in action with an h1 and a div element.

- The h1 element is configured to have a light blue background, 20 pixels of padding (the space between the content and the border), and a black, 1-pixel border.
- The empty space where the white web page background shows through is the margin. When two vertical margins meet (such as between the h1 element and the div element), the browser collapses the margin size to be the larger of the two margin values instead of applying both margins.
- The div element has a medium-blue background, the browser default padding (which is no padding), and a black, 5-pixel border.

You will get more practice using the box model in this chapter. Feel free to experiment with the box model and the chapter7/box.html file.

Margin and Padding with CSS

The `margin` Property

Use the `margin` property to configure margins on all sides of an element. The margin determines the empty space between the element and any adjacent elements. The margin is always transparent—the background color of the web page or parent element shows in this area.

To configure the size of the margin, use a numeric value (px or em). To eliminate the margin, configure it to 0 (with no unit). Use the value "auto" to indicate that the browser should calculate the margin (more on this later in the chapter). You can also configure individual settings for `margin-top`, `margin-right`, `margin-bottom`, and `margin-left`. Table 7.4 shows CSS properties that configure margin.

Property	Description and Common Values
margin	Shorthand notation to configure the margin surrounding an element
	A numeric value (px or em) or percentage; for example: `margin: 10px;` if you set a value to 0, omit the unit
	The value `"auto"` is used to cause the browser to automatically calculate the margin for the element.
	Two numeric values (px or em) or percentages; the first value configures the top margin and bottom margin, the second value configures the left margin and right margin; for example: `margin: 20px 10px;`
	Three numeric values (px or em) or percentage; the first value configures the top margin, the second value configures the left margin and right margin, and the third value configures the bottom margin
	Four numeric values (px or em) or percentages; the values configure the margins in the following order: `margin-top, margin-right, margin-bottom, margin-left`
margin-bottom	Bottom margin; a numeric value (px or em), percentage, or `auto`
margin-left	Left margin; a numeric value (px or em), percentage, or `auto`
margin-right	Right margin; a numeric value (px or em), percentage, or `auto`
margin-top	Top margin; a numeric value (px or em), percentage, or `auto`

TABLE 7.4 Configuring `margin` with CSS

The `padding` Property

The `padding` **property** configures empty space between the content of the HTML element (such as text) and the border. By default, the padding is set to 0. If you configure a background color or background image for an element, it is applied to both the padding and the content areas. See Table 7.5 for CSS properties that configure padding.

Property	Description and Common Values
padding	Shorthand notation to configure the amount of padding—the empty space between the element's content and its border
	A numeric value (px or em) or percentage; for example: `padding: 10px;` if you set a value to 0, omit the unit
	Two numeric values (px or em) or percentages; the first value configures the top padding and bottom padding, the second value configures the left padding and right padding; for example: `padding: 20px 10px;`
	Three numeric values (px or em) or percentage; the first value configures the top padding, the second value configures the left padding and right padding, and the third value configures the bottom padding
	Four numeric values (px or em) or percentages; the values configure the padding in the following order: `padding-top`, `padding-right`, `padding-bottom`, `padding-left`
padding-bottom	Empty space between the content and bottom border; a numeric value (px or em) or percentage
padding-left	Empty space between the content and left border; a numeric value (px or em) or percentage
padding-right	Empty space between the content and right border; a numeric value (px or em) or percentage
padding-top	Empty space between the content and top border; a numeric value (px or em) or percentage

TABLE 7.5 Configuring padding with CSS

The web page shown in Figure 7.11 demonstrates use of the margin and padding properties. The example is in the student files at chapter7/box2.html.

The CSS is shown below:

```
body { background-color: #FFFFFF; }
h1   { background-color: #D1ECFF;
       padding-left: 60px; }
#box { background-color: #74C0FF;
       margin-left: 60px;
       padding: 5px 10px; }
```

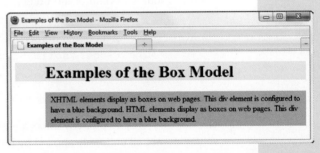

FIGURE 7.11 Margin and padding have been configured.

Borders with CSS

The `border` property configures the border, or boundary, around an element. By default, the border has a width set to 0 and does not display. See Table 7.6 for commonly used CSS properties that configure border.

Property	Description and Common Values
border	Shorthand notation to configure the `border-width`, `border-style`, and `border-color` of an element; the values for `border-width`, `border-style`, and `border-color` separated by spaces; for example, `border: 1px solid #000000;`
border-bottom	Bottom border; the values for `border-width`, `border-style`, and `border-color` separated by spaces
border-left	Left border; the values for `border-width`, `border-style`, and `border-color` separated by spaces
border-right	Right border; the values for `border-width`, `border-style`, and `border-color` separated by spaces
border-top	Top border; the values for `border-width`, `border-style`, and `border-color` separated by spaces
border-width	Width of the border; a numeric pixel value (such as 1px) or the values `thin`, `medium`, `thick`
border-style	Style of the border; `none`, `inset`, `outset`, `double`, `groove`, `ridge`, `solid`, `dashed`, `dotted`
border-color	Color of the border; a valid color value

TABLE 7.6 Configuring `border` with CSS

The `border-style` property offers a variety of formatting options. Be aware that these property values are not all uniformly applied by browsers. Figure 7.12 shows how Firefox 3 and Internet Explorer 8 render various border-style values.

The CSS to configure the borders shown in Figure 7.12 uses a `border-width` of 3 pixels, `border-color` of #000033, and the value indicated for the `border-style` property. For example, the style rule to configure the dashed border is

```
.dashedborder { border-width: 3px;
                border-style: dashed;
                border-color: #000033; }
```

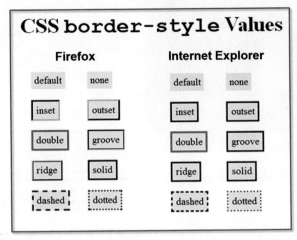

FIGURE 7.12 Not all `border-style` values are rendered the same way by popular browsers.

A shorthand notation allows you to configure all the border properties in one style rule by listing the values of border-width, border-style, and border-color. An example is

```
.dashedborder { border: 3px dashed #000033 }
```

HANDS-ON PRACTICE 7.5

You'll work with the height and width properties in this Hands-On Practice. When complete, your web page will look similar to the one shown in Figure 7.13. You will use the box2.html file in the chapter7 folder of the student files as a starter file. Launch a text editor and open the box2.html file. Configure the embedded CSS as follows:

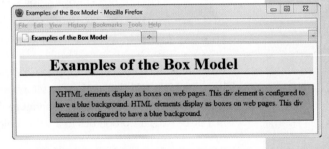

FIGURE 7.13 The border property has been configured.

1. Configure the h1 to display a 3-pixel ridged bottom border in a dark gray color. Add the following style rule to the h1 element selector:

   ```
   border-bottom: 3px ridge #330000;
   ```

2. Configure the #box id to display a 1-pixel solid black border. Add the following style rule to the #box selector:

   ```
   border: 1px solid #000000;
   ```

3. Save your page as boxborder.html. Launch a browser and test your page. Compare your work with the sample solution at chapter7/box3.html.

CSS3 Rounded Corners

Now that you have worked with borders and the box model, you may have begun to notice a lot of rectangles on your web pages! Still in draft form and not yet an official standard, CSS3 introduces the `border-radius` property, which can be used to create rounded corners and soften up those rectangles.

There is a complication when using this technique, though—developers of browser rendering engines, such as **WebKit** (used by Safari and Google Chrome) and **Gecko** (used by Firefox and other Mozilla-based browsers), have developed their own proprietary properties to implement rounded corners. In addition, Internet Explorer 9 is the first version of IE to support the `border-radius` property. So, you need to code three different style declarations to round those corners:

- `-webkit-border-radius` (for WebKit browsers)
- `-moz-border-radius` (for Gecko browsers)
- `border-radius` (W3C Draft Syntax)

Eventually all browsers will support CSS3 and the `border-radius` property, so code this property last in the list. CSS declarations to set a border with rounded corners are show below. If you would like a visible border to display, configure the border property. Then set the value of the three `border-radius` properties to a value below 20px for best results.

```
border: 1px solid #000000;
-webkit-border-radius: 15px;
-moz-border-radius: 15px;
border-radius: 15px;
```

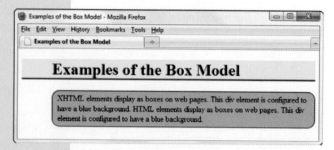

FIGURE 7.14 Rounded corners were configured with CSS.

See Figure 7.14 (chapter7/box4.html in the student files) for an example of this code in action. With progressive enhancement in mind, note that your visitors using older versions of Internet Explorer will see right-angle rather than rounded corners. However, the functionality and usability of the web page will not be affected.

Be aware that when you code the nonstandard properties, your CSS will not pass W3C validation. Keep in mind that another approach to getting a rounded look is to create a rounded rectangle background image with a graphics application. However, once CSS3 becomes a well-supported standard, the box model will be easy to "round out" and is a much more efficient way to accomplish rounded corners.

HANDS-ON PRACTICE 7.6

You'll configure a logo header area that uses a background image and rounded borders in this Hands-On Practice. When complete, your web page will look similar to the one shown in Figure 7.15.

1. Create a new folder called borderch7. Copy the lighthouselogo.jpg and the background.jpg files in the chapter7/starters folder to your borderch7 folder. A starter file is ready for you in the student files. Save the chapter7/starter1.html file to your borderch7 folder. Launch a browser to display the starter1.html web page shown in Figure 7.16.

FIGURE 7.15 The web page with the logo area configured.

2. Launch a text editor and open the starter1.html file. Save the file as index.html. Edit the embedded CSS and add the following style declarations to the h1 selector that will configure the lighthouselogo.jpg image as a background image that does not repeat: height set to 100px, width set to 700px, font size set to 3em, 150px of left padding, 20px of top padding, no top margin, and a solid dark blue border (#000033) with a border radius of 15px. The style declarations are as follows:

```
h1 {background-image: url(lighthouselogo.jpg);
    background-repeat: no-repeat;
    height: 100px; width: 700px; font-size: 3em;
    padding-left: 150px; padding-top: 30px;
    margin-top: 0; border: 1px solid #000033;
    -webkit-border-radius: 15px;
    -moz-border-radius: 15px;
    border-radius: 15px;     }
```

FIGURE 7.16 The starter1.html file.

3. Save the file. When you test your index.html file in a browser, it should look similar to the one shown in Figure 7.15 if you are using a browser that supports rounded corners. Otherwise the logo will have right-angle corners, but the web page will still be usable. Compare your work with the solution in the student files (chapter7/lighthouse/index.html).

After I added the new properties, my CSS no longer passes W3C Validation. What should I do?

Well, since you are using the browser proprietary properties -webkit-border-radius and -moz-border-radius in addition to the CSS3 border-radius property, your CSS code will not pass validation, but your pages will display in modern browsers with the visual aesthetic you envisioned. In this case it's a deliberate decision to choose the visual display over the use of absolutely correct syntax. In time, all browsers will support the border-radius property, you'll be able to remove the proprietary code, and your CSS will pass W3C CSS Level 3 validation testing.

Center Page Content with CSS

You learned how to center text on a web page earlier in this chapter—but what about centering the entire web page itself? A popular page layout design that is easy to accomplish with just a few lines of CSS is to center the entire content of a web page within a browser viewport. The key is to configure a div element that contains or "wraps" the entire page content. The HTML is

```
<body>
<div id="wrapper">
. . . page content goes here . . .
</div>
</body>
```

Next, configure CSS style rules for this container. Set the width property to an appropriate value. Set the margin-left and margin-right CSS properties to the value auto. This tells the browser to automatically divide the amount of space available for the left and right margins. The CSS is

```
#wrapper { width: 700px;
           margin-left: auto;
           margin-right: auto; }
```

You'll practice this technique in the next Hands-On Practice.

HANDS-ON PRACTICE 7.7

FIGURE 7.17 The web page is centered with CSS.

You'll center a web page in this Hands-On Practice. When complete, your web page will look similar to the one shown in Figure 7.17.

Create a new folder called centerch7. A starter file is ready for you in the student files. Save the chapter7/starter.html file to your centerch7 folder. Rename the file index.html. Copy the following files from the chapter7/starters folder to your centerch7 folder: trilliumbanner.jpg, contact.gif, home.gif, and services.gif.

Launch a browser to display the starter.html web page—notice that the web page stretches to fill the entire browser window. You will modify the CSS and HTML to configure the page content to be centered.

Launch a text editor and open the index.html file.

1. Edit the embedded CSS and configure a new selector, an id named container. Add style declarations for the width, min-width, margin-left, and margin-right properties as follows:

```
#container { margin-left:   auto;
             margin-right:  auto;
             width: 80%;
             min-width: 700px;
}
```

2. Edit the HTML. Configure a div element assigned to the id container that "wraps" or contains the code within the body section. Code an opening <div> tag on a new line after the opening body tag. Code the closing div tag on a new line before the closing body tag. Save the file. When you test your index.html file in a browser, it should look similar to the one shown in Figure 7.17. The student files contain a sample solution in the chapter7/trillium5 folder. ■

A common design practice is to configure the background color of the wrapper or container to be a light, neutral color that provides good contrast with text. Figure 7.18 (found in the student files, chapter7/lighthouse/lcenter.html) shows a web page with a background image along with centered page content (in a div assigned to the container id) with a neutral background. The example uses shorthand notation to set all margins for #container to the value auto. The CSS is as follows:

FIGURE 7.18 The centered #container has a neutral background.

```
#container { margin: auto;
             background-color: #ffffff;
             width: 800px;
             padding: 20px; }
```

CSS3 Box Shadow and Text Shadow

FIGURE 7.19 Shadow properties add dimension.

The CSS3 shadow properties **box-shadow** and **text-shadow** add depth and dimension to the visual display of a web page, as shown in Figure 7.19.

CSS3 Box Shadow

Still in draft form and not yet an official standard, CSS3 introduces the box-shadow property, which can be used to create a shadow effect on the box model. The developers of the WebKit and Gecko browser rendering engines have introduced their own proprietary properties. You'll need to code three style declarations to create a shadow and provide four values for each:

- Numeric pixel value for the shadow's horizontal offset:
  Positive value configures a shadow on the right.
  Negative value configures a shadow on the left.
- Numeric pixel value for the shadow's vertical offset:
  Positive value configures a shadow below.
  Negative value configures a shadow above.
- Numeric pixel value for the blur radius:
  Higher values configure more blur. 0 configures a sharp shadow.
- Valid color value

Here's an example:

```
-webkit-box-shadow: 5px 5px 5px #828282;
-moz-box-shadow: 5px 5px 5px #828282;
box-shadow: 5px 5px 5px #828282;
```

Eventually all browsers will support CSS3 and the official box-shadow property, so code this property last in the list. Note that if you include the nonstandard properties, your CSS will not pass W3C validation.

CSS3 Text Shadow

The CSS3 `text-shadow` **property** is supported by most recent versions of modern browsers, except for Internet Explorer 9. The property requires four values:

- Numeric pixel value for the shadow's horizontal offset:
  Positive value configures a shadow on the right. Negative value configures a shadow on the left.
- Numeric pixel value for the shadow's vertical offset:
  Positive value configures a shadow below. Negative value configures a shadow below.
- Numerical pixel value for the blur radius:
  Higher values configure more blur. 0 configures a sharp shadow.
- Valid color value

Here's an example: `text-shadow: 3px 3px 3px #666;`

HANDS-ON PRACTICE 7.8

You'll configure `text-shadow` and `box-shadow` in this Hands-On Practice. When complete, your web page will look similar to the one shown in Figure 7.19. Create a new folder called shadowch7. Copy the lighthouselogo.jpg and the background.jpg files from the chapter7/starters folder to your shadowch7 folder. Launch a text editor and open the chapter7/lighthouse/lcenter.html file (shown in Figure 7.18). Save the file in your shadowch7 folder with the name index.html.

1. Edit the embedded CSS and add the following style declarations to the #container selector to configure a box shadow:

   ```
   -webkit-box-shadow: 5px 5px 5px #1e1e1e;
   -moz-box-shadow: 5px 5px 5px #1e1e1e;
   box-shadow: 5px 5px 5px #1e1e1e;
   ```

2. Add the following style declaration to the h1selector to configure a dark gray text shadow:

   ```
   text-shadow: 3px 3px 3px #666;
   ```

3. Add the following style declaration to the h2 selector to configure a light gray text shadow with no blur: `text-shadow: 1px 1px 0 #ccc;`

4. Save the file. When you test your index.html file in a browser, it should look similar to the one shown in Figure 7.19 if you are using a browser that supports the `box-shadow` and `text-shadow` properties. Otherwise the shadows will not display, but the web page will still be usable. See the student files for a solution (chapter7/lighthouse/shadow.html).

Explore Further

Browser support changes with each new browser version. There is no substitute for thoroughly testing your web pages. However, several resources are available with support lists. The following websites provide this information:

- http://westciv.com/wiki/Experimental_CSS_compatibility_table
- http://www.findmebyip.com/litmus
- http://www.quirksmode.org/css/contents.html

CSS3 Opacity

The CSS3 **opacity** property configures the transparency of the background color. Opacity values range from 0 (which is completely transparent) to 1 (which is completely opaque and has no transparency). See Figure 7.20 for an example of using the opacity property to configure an h1 element that is 60% opaque.

FIGURE 7.20 The background of the h1 area is transparent.

HANDS-ON PRACTICE 7.9

In this Hands-On Practice you'll work with the opacity property as you configure the web page shown in Figure 7.20.

1. Create a new folder called opacitych7. Copy fall.jpg file from the chapter7/starters folder to your opacitych7 folder. Launch a text editor and open the chapter1/template.html file. Save it in your opacitych7 folder with the name index.html. Change the page title to "Fall Nature Hikes".

2. Let's create the structure of the web page with a div that contains an h1 element. Add the following code to your web page in the body section:

```
<div id="content">
<h1>Fall Nature Hikes</h1>
</div>
```

3. Now, add style tags to the head section and configure the embedded CSS. You'll create an id named content to display the fall.jpg as a background image that does not repeat. The content id also has a width of 640 pixels, a height of 480 pixels, auto margins (which will center the object in the browser viewport), and 20 pixels of top padding. The code is

```
#content { background-image: url(fall.jpg);
          background-repeat: no-repeat;
          margin: auto;
          width:640px;
          height: 480px;
          padding-top: 20px; }
```

4. Now configure the h1 selector to have opacity set to .60, font size set to 4em, 10 pixels of padding, and a 40-pixel left margin. Sample code is

```
h1 {background-color: #FFFFFF;
    opacity: 0.6;
    font-size: 4em;
    padding: 10px;
    margin-left: 40px; }
```

5. Save the file. When you test your index.html file in a browser that supports opacity (such as Chrome, Firefox, Safari, or Internet Explorer 9), it should look similar to the page shown in Figure 7.20. See the student files for a solution (chapter7/opacity/index.html).

6. Figure 7.21 shows the web page displayed in Internet Explorer 8, which does not support the opacity property. Notice that the visual aesthetic is not exactly the same, but the page is still usable. While Internet Explorer 9 supports opacity, earlier versions support the proprietary `filter` property with an opacity level configured between 1 (transparent) and 100 (opaque). A sample is found in the student files (chapter7/opacity/opacityie. html). The CSS for the filter property is

```
filter: alpha(opacity=60);
```

FIGURE 7.21 Internet Explorer 8 does not support the opacity property and displays an opaque background color.

CSS3 RGBA Color

CSS3 supports new syntax for the color property that configures transparent color, called **RGBA color**. Four values are required: red color, green color, blue color, and alpha (transparency). RGBA color does not use hexadecimal color values. Instead, decimal color values are configured—see the partial color chart in Figure 7.22 and the Web Safe Color Palette at the end of the book for examples.

The values for red, green, and blue must be decimal values from 0 to 255. The alpha value must be a number between 0 (transparent) and 1 (opaque). Figure 7.23 shows a web page with the text configured to be slightly transparent.

#FFFFFF
rgb (255, 255, 255)
	#FFFFCC
	rgb(255, 255, 204)
		#FFFF99
		rgb(255,255,153)
			#FFFF66
			rgb(255,255,102)

#FFFF33
rgb(255,255,51)
	#FFFF00
	rgb(255,255,0)
		#FFCCFF
		rgb(255, 204, 255)
			#FFCCCC
			rgb(255,204,204)

#FFCC99
rgb(255,204,153)
	#FFCC66
	rgb(255,204,102)
		#FFCC33
		rgb(255,204,51)
			#FFCC00
			rgb(255,204,0)

#FF99FF
rgb(255,153,255)
	#FF99CC
	rgb(255,153,204)
		#FF9999
		rgb(255,153,153)
			#FF9966
			rgb(255,153,102)

FIGURE 7.22 Hexadecimal and RGB decimal color values.

FIGURE 7.23 CSS3 RGBA color configures the transparent text.

HANDS-ON PRACTICE 7.10

In this Hands-On Practice you'll configure transparent text as you configure the web page shown in Figure 7.23.

1. Launch a text editor and open the file you created in the previous Hands-On Practice (also located in the student files, chapter7/opacity/index.html). Save the file with the name rgba.html.

2. Delete the current style declarations for the h1 selector. You will create new style rules for the h1 selector to configure 10 pixels of right padding and right-aligned sans-serif white text that is 80% opaque with a font size of 5em. Since not all browsers support RBGA color, you'll configure the color property twice. The first instance will be the standard color value that is supported by all modern browsers; the second instance will configure the RGBA color. Older browsers will not understand the RGBA color and will ignore it. Newer browsers will "see" both of the color style declarations and will apply them in the order they are coded, so the result will be transparent color. The CSS for the h1 selector is

```
h1 { color: #ffffff;
     color: rgba(255, 255, 255, 0.8);
     font-family: Verdana, Helvetica, sans-serif;
     font-size: 5em;
     padding-right: 10px;
     text-align: right; }
```

3. Save the file. When you test your rgba.html file in a browser that supports RGBA color (such as Chrome, Firefox, Safari, or Internet Explorer 9), it should look similar to the page shown in Figure 7.23. See the student files for a solution (chapter7/opacity/rgba.html). If you are using a nonsupporting browser such as Internet Explorer 8 (or earlier), you'll see white text instead of transparent text. While Internet Explorer 9 supports RGBA color, earlier versions support the proprietary filter property; an example is in the student files (chapter7/opacity/rbgaie.html).

Quick Tip

There is another new method to configure color when using CSS3, called HSLA color. The letters in HSLA stand for hue, saturation, lightness, and alpha. It's a different way of thinking about color than the RGB that web designers typically use. HSLA color is not yet supported on all browsers. Check out the following resources for more information:

- http://www.w3.org/TR/2003/CR-css3-color-20030514/#hsla-color
- http://www.useragentman.com/blog/2010/08/28/coding-colors-easily-using-css3-hsl-notation
- http://css-tricks.com/yay-for-hsla

CSS3 Gradients

CSS3 provides a method to configure color as a **gradient**, which is a smooth blending of shades from one color to another color. A CSS3 gradient background color is defined purely with CSS—No image file is needed! This provides flexibility for web designers along with a savings in the bandwidth required to serve out gradient background image files.

Sound great? Yes, it does, but there is a catch—The WebKit and Gecko browser rendering engines use their own proprietary coding syntax to process CSS gradients. The W3C has added gradient support to the CSS Image Value and Replaced Content Module (in draft status) but at the time this was written, this syntax had not yet been adopted by browsers. This section will provide an example of a CSS3 gradient along with links to resources for further study.

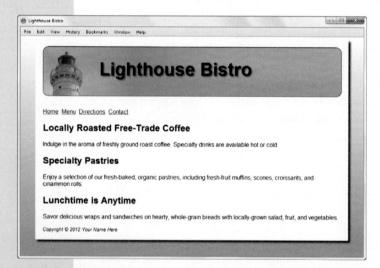

FIGURE 7.24   The gradient in the background was configured with CSS3 without an image file.

Figure 7.19 displays a web page with a JPG gradient background image that was configured in a graphics application. The web page shown in Figure 7.24 (available in the student files, chapter7/lighthouse/gradient.html) does not use a JPG for the background—CSS3 gradient properties recreated the look of the linear gradient image.

CSS3 Gradients and Progressive Enhancement

It's very important to keep progressive enhancement in mind when using CSS3 gradients. Configure a "fallback" `background-color` property or `background-image` property, which will be rendered by browsers that do not support CSS3 gradients. In Figure 7.24 the background color was configured to be same value as the ending gradient color.

Configuring CSS3 Gradients

Code four style declarations to configure a gradient background:

- `-webkit-gradient` (for Webkit browsers)
- `-moz-linear-gradient` (for Gecko browsers)
- `filter` (for Internet Explorer)
- `linear-gradient` (W3C draft syntax)

Configure the gradient as the value of the `background-image` property (except for Internet Explorer, which uses its `filter` property). The following CSS code first configures a background color (for nonsupporting browsers) and then configures a linear gradient that blends from white (#FFFFFF) to a medium blue (#8FA5CE):

```
background-color: #8FA5CE;
background-image: -webkit-gradient(linear, left top, left bottom,
    from(#FFFFFF), to(#8FA5CE));
background-image: -moz-linear-gradient(top, #FFFFFF, #8FA5CE);
filter: progid:DXImageTransform.Microsoft.gradient
    (startColorstr=#FFFFFFFF, endColorstr=#FF8FA5CE);
background-image: linear-gradient(#FFFFFF, #8FA5CE);
```

W3C Syntax

The W3C syntax uses different functions for linear (`linear-gradient`) and radial (`radial-gradient`) gradients. The basic format for a two-color linear gradient lists the value for each color (in this example, #FFFFFF and #8FA5CE):

```
background-image: linear-gradient(#FFFFFF, #8FA5CE);
```

As shown in the code samples, the syntax for configuring gradients varies by browser engine. It is expected that eventually all browsers will support W3C syntax CSS3 and `linear-gradient`, so code this declaration last in the list. Recall that the browser proprietary CSS syntax in this section is nonstandard. Your CSS code will not pass W3C validation when you use these properties. For more information on the syntax described above, visit the corresponding websites:

- **Webkit**: http://webkit.org/blog/175/introducing-css-gradients
- **Mozilla**: http://developer.mozilla.org/en/CSS/-moz-linear-gradient
- **Internet Explorer**: http://msdn.microsoft.com/en-us/library/ms532997(VS.85,loband).aspx

Explore Further

Visit the following resources to delve deeper into CSS3 gradients:

- http://robertnyman.com/2010/02/15/css-gradients-for-all-web-browsers-without-using-images
- https://developer.mozilla.org/en/Using_gradients
- http://net.tutsplus.com/tutorials/html-css-techniques/quick-tip-understanding-css3-gradients

Experiment with generating CSS3 gradient code at http://www.westciv.com/tools/gradients and http://gradients.glrzad.com, and http://www.westciv.com/tools/gradients.

CHAPTER 7

Review and Apply

Review Questions

Multiple Choice. Choose the best answer for each item.

1. Which CSS property will configure the font typeface?
   a. font-face   c. font-family
   b. face   d. size

2. Which CSS property will configure bold text?
   a. font-face   c. font-weight
   b. font-style   d. font-size

3. Which CSS property will configure italic text?
   a. font-face   c. font-weight
   b. font-style   d. font-size

4. Which configures a class called news with red text, large font, and Arial or a sans-serif font using CSS?
   a. news { color: red;
              font-size: large;
              font-family: Arial, sans-serif;}
   b. .news { color: red;
               font-size: large;
               font-family: Arial, sans-serif;}
   c. .news { text: red;
               font-size: large;
               font-family: Arial, sans-serif;}
   d. #news { text: red;
               font-size: large;
               font-family: Arial, sans-serif;}

5. Which of the following, from outermost to innermost, are components of the box model?
   a. margin, border, padding, content
   b. content, padding, border, margin
   c. content, margin, padding, border
   d. margin, padding, border, content

6. Which of the following is the CSS property that configures a drop shadow effect on text
   a. box-shadow   c. drop-shadow
   b. text-shadow   d. shadow

7. Which of the following will configure padding that is 15 pixels on the top, 0 pixels on the left and right, and 5 pixels on the bottom?
   a. padding: 0px 5px 0px 15px;
   b. padding: top-15, left-0, right-0, bottom-5;
   c. padding: 15px 0 5px 0;
   d. padding: 0 0 15px 5px;

8. Which of the following is used along with the width property to configure centered page content?
   a. margin-left: auto; margin-right: auto
   b. margin: top-15, left-0, right-0, bottom-5;
   c. margin: 15px 0 5px 0;
   d. margin: 20px;

9. Which CSS property will center text within an element?
   a. center   c. align
   b. text-align   d. text-center

10. Which of the following will configure a border that is 5 pixels wide, the color #330000, and a solid line?
    a. border: 5px solid #330000;
    b. border-style: solid 5px;
    c. border: 5px, solid, #330000;
    d. border: 5px line #330000;

Hands-On Exercises

1. Write the CSS code for an external style sheet file named mystyle.css that configures the text to be brown, 1.2 em in size, and in Arial, Verdana, or a sans-serif font.

2. Write the XHTML and CSS code for an embedded style sheet that configures a class called new, which has bold and italic text.

3. Write the CSS for a class named footer with the following characteristics: a light-blue background color, Arial or sans-serif font, dark-blue text color, 10 pixels of padding, and a narrow, dashed border in a dark-blue color.

4. Write the CSS for an id named notice that is configured with width set to 80% and centered.

5. Write the CSS to configure a class that will produce a headline with a dotted line underneath it. Choose a color that you like for the text and dotted line.

6. Write the CSS to configure an h1 selector with drop shadow text, a 50% transparent background color, and sans-serif font that is 4em in size.

7. Write the CSS to configure an id named section with small, red, Arial font, a white background, a width of 80%, and a drop shadow.

Focus on Web Design

This chapter expanded your capabilities to use CSS to configure web pages. Use a search engine to search for CSS resources. The following resources can help you get started:

- http://www.w3.org/Style/CSS
- http://positioniseverything.net
- http://www.dezwozhere.com/links.html

Create a web page that provides a list of at least five CSS resources on the Web. For each CSS resource provide the URL, website name, and a brief description. Your web page content should take up 80% of the browser viewport and be centered. Use at least five CSS properties from this chapter to configure the color and text. Place your name in the e-mail address at the bottom of the web page.

PACIFIC TRAILS RESORT CASE STUDY

In this chapter's case study you will use the existing Pacific Trails (Chapter 6) website as a starting point to create a new version of the website. The new design is a centered page layout that takes up 80% of the browser viewport. You'll use CSS to configure the new page layout, a background image, and other styles, including font and padding. Figure 7.25 displays a wireframe with the wrapper div, which contains the other web page elements.

FIGURE 7.25 The wrapper div contains the other page elements.

HANDS-ON PRACTICE CASE STUDY

Step 1: Create a folder called ch7pacific to contain your Pacific Trails Resort website files. Copy the files from the Chapter 6 Case Study ch6pacific folder. Copy the background.jpg file from the chapter7/starters folder in the student files into your ch7pacific folder.

Step 2:   Configure the CSS. Launch a text editor and open the pacific.css external style sheet file.

- **The body Element Selector.** Add a declaration to display a background image named background.jpg. Add a style rule to use Arial, Helvetica, or sans-serif font typeface.
- **The wrapper id Selector.** Add a new selector for an id named wrapper. Configure the wrapper id to be centered (see Hands-On Practice 7.7) with a width of 80%, white background color (#FFFFFF), and a minimum width of 960 pixels.
- **The nav id Selector:** Add a declaration to display 20 pixels of padding on the left side and 5 pixels of padding on the top, bottom, and right sides. Add a declaration to display bold text.
- **The content id Selector.** Add a new selector for an id named content and configure this with 0 padding on the top and 20 pixels of padding the right, bottom, and left sides.
- **The h1, h2, and h3 Element Selectors.** Add a declaration to each of these selectors to display Georgia, Times New Roman, or serif font typeface.
- **The resort class Selector.** Add a declaration to display bold text.
- **Left-align the image in the content id.** View Figure 7.26 and notice that the large image in the content area is displayed alongside the text. An outdated technique (valid in XHTML syntax but not in HTML5 syntax) to accomplish this layout would be to code the `align="left"` attribute on the img tag. The modern approach is to use CSS to float the image on the left side of its container (the content id). You'll explore the CSS float property in Chapter 8, but let's try it out in this case study. Use the following contextual selector to configure img elements within the content id to display on the left and have 20 pixels of padding on the right side. The sample code is

```
#content img {float: left; padding-right: 20px; }
```

- **Configure unordered lists in the content id.** Use the following contextual selector to configure ul elements *within the content id* to display list markers inside the element. The sample code is

```
#content ul {list-style-position: inside; }
```

- **The contact id Selector.** Add new selector for an id named address with a declaration to configure text with 90% font size.
- **The footer id Selector.** Add a new selector for an id named footer. Configure the footer id to use 75% size, italic font in the Georgia, Times New Roman, Times, or serif font typeface.

Save the pacific.css file.

Step 3:   Edit the Home Page. Launch a text editor and open the index.html file. Code div tags to add a wrapper div that contains the content of the web page. Use Hands-On Practice 7.7 as a guide. Remove the tags for the strong element, the i element, and the small element—they are no longer needed since CSS is now used to configure the text. Save the file.

Step 4:   Edit the Activities Page. Launch a text editor and open the activities.html file. Code div tags to add a wrapper div that contains the content of the web page. Use Hands-On Practice 7.7 as a guide. Remove the tags for the strong element, the i element, and the small element—they are no longer needed since CSS is now used to configure the text. Save the file.

Step 5:   Edit the Yurts Page. Launch a text editor and open the yurts.html file. Code div tags to add a wrapper div that contains the content of the web page. Use Hands-On Practice 7.7 as a guide. The Yurts page currently uses a definition list. Rework the page content so that the web page uses h3 and paragraph elements instead of the definition list. Remove the tags for the strong element, the i element, and the small element—they are no longer needed since CSS is now used to configure the text. Save the file.

Test your web pages in a browser. Your home page should be similar to the example in Figure 7.26. Isn't it amazing what a little CSS can do?

Step 6: **Experiment with CSS3.** Launch a text editor and open the pacific.css file. Apply a shadow effect the to the wrapper id. Add the following styles to the wrapper selector:

FIGURE 7.26 The new Pacific Trails home page with centered layout.

```
-webkit-box-shadow: 5px 5px 5px #000033;
-moz-box-shadow: 5px 5px 5px #000033;
box-shadow: 5px 5px 5px #000033;
```

Apply a text-shadow effect to the level 2 headings. Add the following declaration to the h2 selector:

```
text-shadow: 1px 1px 1px #ccc;
```

Save the file. Launch a modern browser such as Safari, Google Chrome, or Firefox and test the home page (index.html). Figure 7.27 shows a screen capture of the page displayed in the Safari browser. Note that the CSS will no longer pass W3C CSS validation testing since it now contains nonstandard properties.

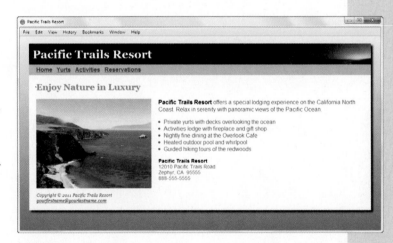

FIGURE 7.27 The Pacific Trails home page with a shadow effect.

CHAPTER 8

Page Layout Basics

You've already configured centered page layout with CSS; we'll add to your toolbox of CSS page layout techniques in this chapter. You'll explore floating and positioning elements with CSS. You'll be introduced to using CSS to add interactivity to hyperlinks with pseudo-classes. You will practice using new HTML5 elements that structure web page content. You'll also learn to configure web pages for printing and for the mobile web.

You'll learn how to . . .

- Configure float with CSS
- Configure relative and absolute positioning with CSS
- Create two-column page layouts with CSS
- Configure navigation in unordered lists and style with CSS
- Add interactivity to hyperlinks with CSS pseudo-classes

- Configure web pages with HTML5 structural elements, including figure, figcaption, section, header, hgroup, nav, aside, and footer
- Configure web pages for printing with CSS
- Configure web pages for mobile devices with CSS

Normal Flow

Browsers render your web page code line by line in the order it appears in the .html document. This processing is called normal flow. **Normal flow** displays the elements on the page in the order they appear in the web page source code.

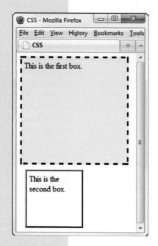

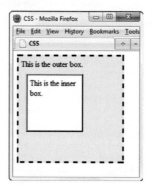

FIGURE 8.1 Two div elements.   **FIGURE 8.2** Nested elements.

Figures 8.1 and 8.2 each display two div elements that contain text content. Let's take a closer look. Figure 8.1 shows a screenshot of two div elements placed one after another on a web page. In Figure 8.2 the boxes are nested inside each other. In both cases, the browser used normal flow (the default) and displayed the elements in the order that they appeared in the source code. As you've worked through the exercises in the previous chapters, you created web pages that the browser rendered using normal flow.

You'll practice this a bit more in the next Hands-On Practice, then later in the chapter you'll experiment with CSS positioning and float to configure the flow, or placement, of elements on a web page.

HANDS-ON PRACTICE 8.1 ———————————

You will explore the box model and normal flow in this Hands-On Practice as you work with the web pages shown in Figures 8.1 and 8.2.

Practice with Normal Flow
Launch a text editor and open the chapter8/starter1.html file from the student files. Save the file with the name box1.html. Edit the body of the web page and add the following code to configure two div elements:

```
<div class="div1">
This is the first box.
</div>
<div class="div2">
This is the second box.
</div>
```

Now let's add embedded CSS in the head section to configure the "boxes." Add a new style rule for a class named div1 to configure a light blue background, dashed border, width of 200, height of 200, and 5 pixels of padding. The code is

```
.div1 { width: 200px;
        height: 200px;
        background-color: #D1ECFF;
        border: 3px dashed #000000;
        padding: 5px; }
```

Create a style rule for a class named div2 to configure a width and height of 100, white background color, ridged border, 10 pixel margin, and 5 pixels of padding. The code is

```
.div2 { width: 100px;
        height: 100px;
        background-color: #ffffff;
        border: 3px ridge #000000;
        padding: 5px;
        margin: 10px; }
```

Save the file. Launch a browser and test your page. It should look similar to the one shown in Figure 8.1. The student files contain a sample solution at chapter8/box1.html.

Practice with Normal Flow and Nested Elements

Launch a text editor and open the box1.html file from the student files (chapter8/box1.html). Save the file with the name box2.html. Edit the code. Delete the content from the body section of the web page. Add the following code to configure two div elements—one nested inside the other:

```
<div class="div1">
This is the outer box.
   <div class="div2">
   This is the inner box.
   </div>
</div>
```

Save the file. Launch a browser and test your page. It should look similar to the one shown in Figure 8.2. Notice how the browser renders the nested div elements—the second box is nested within the first box because it is coded inside the first div element in the web page source code. This is an example of normal flow. The student files contain a sample solution at chapter8/box2.html.

A Look Ahead—CSS Layout Properties

You've seen how normal flow causes the browser to render the elements in the order that they appear in the HTML source code. When using CSS for page layout there are situations in which you will want to specify the location of an element on the page—either the absolute pixel location, the location relative to where the element would normally display, or floating on the page. The CSS properties that configure the placement of elements on a web page are discussed in the following sections.

Relative and Absolute Positioning

You've seen how normal flow causes the browser to render the elements in the order that they appear in the HTML source code. When using CSS for page layout there are situations when you may want more control over the position of an element. This section introduces relative and absolute positioning.

Relative Positioning

Use **relative positioning** to change the location of an element slightly, relative to where it would otherwise appear in normal flow. Configure relative positioning with the `position: relative;` property along with one or more of the following offset properties: `left`, `right`, `top`, `bottom`. Table 8.1 lists CSS position and offset properties.

Property	Value	Purpose
position	static	Default value; the element is rendered in normal flow
	relative	Configures the location of an element relative to where it would otherwise render in normal flow
	absolute	Configures the location of an element outside of normal flow precisely in its container element
	fixed	Configures the location of an element within the browser viewport; the element does not move when the page is scrolled
left	Numeric value or percentage	The position of the element offset from the left side of the container element
right	Numeric value or percentage	The position of the element offset from the right side of the container element
top	Numeric value or percentage	The position of the element offset from the top of the container element
bottom	Numeric value or percentage	The position of the element offset from the bottom of the container element

TABLE 8.1 CSS Properties for Relative and Absolute Positioning

Figure 8.3 shows a web page (see the student files chapter8/relative.html) that uses relative positioning along with the `left` property to configure the placement of an element in relation to the normal flow. In this case, the container element is the body of the web page.

The result is that the content of the element is rendered as being offset or shifted by 30 pixels from the left where it would normally be placed at the browser's left margin. Notice also how the padding and background-color properties configure the heading element.

The CSS is

```
#myContent { position: relative;
             left: 30px;
             font-family: Arial, sans-serif; }
h1 { background-color: #cccccc;
     padding: 5px;
     color: #000000; }
```

The HTML source code follows:

```
<h1>Relative Positioning</h1>
<div id="myContent">
<p>This paragraph uses CSS relative
positioning to be placed 30 pixels
in from the left side.</p>
</div>
```

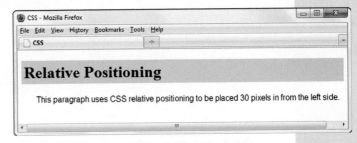

FIGURE 8.3 The paragraph is configured using relative positioning.

Absolute Positioning

Use **absolute positioning** to specify the location of an element outside of normal flow precisely in its container element. Configure absolute positioning with the `position: absolute;` property along with one or more of the following offset properties: `left`, `right`, `top`, `bottom`. Table 8.1 lists CSS position and offset properties.

Figure 8.4 depicts a web page that configures a div element using absolute positioning to display the content 200 pixels in from the left margin and 100 pixels down from the top of its container element, which is the body of the document. Padding and background-color are used to configure the heading element. An example is in the student files, chapter8/absolute.html).

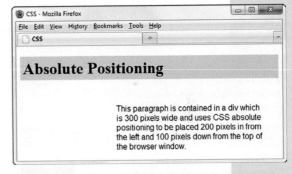

FIGURE 8.4 The div element is configured using absolute positioning.

The CSS is

```
#content { position: absolute;
           left: 200px;
           top: 100px;
           font-family: Arial, sans-serif;
           width: 300px; }
h1 { background-color: #cccccc;
     padding: 5px;
     color: #000000; }
```

The HTML source code is

```
<h1>Absolute Positioning</h1>
<div id="content">
<p>This paragraph is contained in a div configured to be 300 pixels
wide and uses CSS absolute positioning to be placed 200 pixels in from
the left and 100 pixels down from the top of the browser window.</p>
</div>
```

Float

The `float` Property

Elements that seem to float on the right or left side of either the browser window or another element are often configured using the `float` property. The browser renders these elements using normal flow and then shifts them to either the right or left as far as possible within their container (usually either the browser viewport or a div element).

- Use `float: right;` to float the element on the right side of the container.
- Use `float: left;` to float the element on the left side of the container.
- Specify a width for a floated element unless the element already has an implicit width—such as an img element.
- Other elements and web page content will flow around the floated element.
- Only block-level elements (such as divs, paragraphs, and images) can be configured to float.

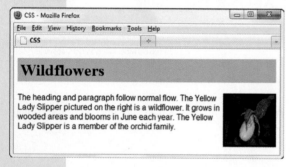

FIGURE 8.5   The image is configured to float.

Figure 8.5 shows a web page with an image configured with `float: right;` to float on the right side of the browser viewport (see the student files, chapter8/float.html). When floating an image, the margin property is useful to configure empty space between the image and text on the page.

View Figure 8.5 and notice how the image stays on the right side of the browser viewport. An id called yls was created that applies the `float`, `margin`, and `border` properties. The attribute `id="yls"` was placed on the image tag. The CSS is

```
h1 { background-color: #A8C682;
     padding: 5px;
     color: #000000; }
p { font-family: Arial, sans-serif; }
#yls { float: right;
       margin: 0 0 5px 5px;
       border: 1px solid #000000; }
```

The HTML source code is

```
<h1>Wildflowers</h1>
<img id="yls" src="yls.jpg" alt="Yellow Lady Slipper" height="100" width="100">
<p>The heading and paragraph follow normal flow. The Yellow Lady Slipper pictured
on the right is a wildflower. It grows in wooded areas and blooms in June each
year. The Yellow Lady Slipper is a member of the orchid family.</p>
```

HANDS-ON PRACTICE 8.2

In this Hands-On Practice you'll practice using the CSS float property as you configure the web page shown in Figure 8.6.

Create a folder named ch8float. Copy the starter2.html and yls.jpg files from the chapter8 folder in the student files into your ch8float folder. Launch a text editor and open the starter2.html file. Notice the order of the images and paragraphs. Notice that there is no CSS to float the image. Display starter2.html in a browser. The browser renders the page using normal flow and displays the elements in the order they are coded.

Let's add CSS to float the image. Save the file with the name floatyls.html. With floatyls.html open in a text editor, modify the code as follows:

FIGURE 8.6 The CSS float property left-aligns the image.

1. Add a style rule for a class name float that configures float, margin, and border properties:

```
.float {  float: left;
          margin-right: 10px;
          border: 3px ridge #000000; }
```

2. Assign the image element to the class named float (use `class="float"`).

Save the file. Launch a browser and test your page. It should look similar to the web page shown in Figure 8.6. The student files contain a sample solution at chapter8/floatyls.html.

The Floated Element and Normal Flow

Take a moment to examine your file in a browser (see Figure 8.6) and consider how the browser rendered the page. The div element is configured with a light background color to demonstrate how floated elements are rendered outside of normal flow. Observe that the floated image and the first paragraph are contained within the div element. The h2 element follows the div. If all the elements were rendered using normal flow, the area with the light background color would contain both the child elements of the div: the image and the first paragraph. In addition, the h2 element would be placed on its own line under the div element.

However, once the image is placed vertically on the page, it is floated *outside of normal flow*—that's why the light background color only appears behind the first paragraph and why the h2 element's text begins immediately after the first paragraph and appears next to the floated image.

Clear a Float

The `clear` Property

The `clear` property is often used to terminate, or "clear," a float. You can set the value of the clear property to `left`, `right`, or `both`—depending on the type of float you need to clear.

FIGURE 8.7 The float needs to be cleared to improve the display.

Review Figure 8.7 and the code sample in the student files at chapter8/floatyls.html. Notice that although the div element contains both an image and the first paragraph, the light background color of the div only displays behind the screen area occupied by the first paragraph—it stops a bit earlier than expected. Clearing the float will help take care of this display issue.

Clearing a Float with a Line Break

A common technique to clear a float within a container element is to add a line break element configured with the `clear` property. See the example in the student files at chapter8/floatylsclear1.html.

Observe that a CSS class is configured to clear the left float:

```
.clearleft   { clear: left; }
```

Also, a line break tag assigned to the `clearleft` class is coded before the closing `</div>` tag. The code snippet for the div element is

```
<div>
<img class="float" src="yls.jpg" alt="Yellow Lady Slipper"
height="100" width="100">
<p>The Yellow Lady Slipper grows in wooded areas and blooms in June
each year. The flower is a member of the orchid family.</p>
<br class="clearleft">
</div>
```

Figure 8.8 displays a screen shot of this page. Note that the light background color of the div element extends farther down the page and the h2 element's text begins on its own line under the image.

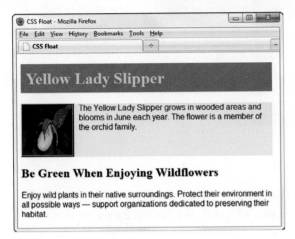

FIGURE 8.8 The clear property is applied to a line break tag.

If you are not concerned about the light background color display, another option is to omit the line break tag and instead apply the `clearleft` class to the h2 element. This does not change the display of the light background color, but it does force the h2 element's text to begin on its own line, as shown in Figure 8.9 (see the student files at chapter8/floatylsclear2.html).

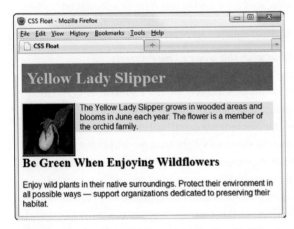

FIGURE 8.9 The clear property is applied to the h2 element.

Overflow

The `overflow` Property

The `overflow` property is often used to clear a float, although its intended purpose is to configure how content should display if it is too large for the area allocated. See Table 8.2 for a list of commonly used values for the overflow property.

Value	Purpose
visible	Default value; the content is displayed, and if it's too large, the content will "overflow" outside the area allocated to it
hidden	The content is clipped to fit the room allocated to the element in the browser viewport
auto	The content fills the area allocated to it and, if needed, scroll bars are displayed to allow access to the remaining content
scroll	The content is rendered in the area allocated to it and scroll bars are displayed

TABLE 8.2 The `overflow` Property

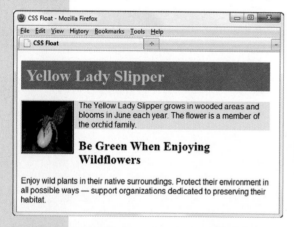

FIGURE 8.10 The display can be improved by clearing the float with overflow.

Clearing a Float with the `overflow` Property

Review Figure 8.10 and the code sample in the student files at chapter8/floatyls.html. Observe the div element, which contains the floated image and first paragraph on the page. Notice that although the div element contains both an image and the first paragraph, the div element's light background color does not extend as far as expected; it is only visible in the area occupied by the first paragraph. You can use the `overflow` property assigned to the container element to resolve this display issue and clear the float. In this case we'll apply the `overflow` and `width` properties to the div element selector. The CSS to configure the div in this manner is

```
div { background-color: #F3F1BF;
       overflow: auto;
       width: 100%; }
```

This CSS is all that is needed to be added to the code to clear the float and cause the web page to display similar to Figure 8.11 (found in student files chapter8/floatylsoverflow.html).

The `clear` Property Versus the `overflow` Property

Notice that Figure 8.11 (using the `overflow` property) and Figure 8.8 (applying the `clear` property to a line break tag) result in a similar web page display. You may be wondering about which CSS property (`clear` or `overflow`) is the best to use when you need to clear a float.

Although the `clear` property is widely used, in this example it is more efficient to apply the `overflow` property to the container element (for example, a div element). This will clear the float, avoid adding an extra line break tag, and ensure that the container element expands to enclose the entire floated element. You'll get more practice with the `float`, `clear`, and `overflow` properties as you continue working through the book. Floating elements is a key technique in designing multicolumn page layouts with CSS.

FIGURE 8.11 The overflow property is applied to the div element selector.

Configuring Scrollbars with the overflow Property

The web page in Figure 8.12 demonstrates the use of `overflow: auto;` to automatically display scroll bars if the content exceeds the space allocated to it. In this case, the div that contains the paragraph and the floated image was configured with a width of 300px and a height of 100px.

See the example web page in the student files at chapter8/floatylsscroll.html. The CSS for the div is shown below:

```
div { background-color: #F3F1BF;
      overflow: scroll;
      width: 300px;
      height: 100px;
}
```

FIGURE 8.12 The browser displays scrollbars

Why aren't we using external styles?

Since we are only creating sample pages to practice new coding techniques, it is practical to work with a single file. However, if this were an actual website, you would be using an external style sheet for maximum productivity and efficiency.

CSS Two-Column Page Layout

A common design for a web page is a two-column layout. This is accomplished with CSS by configuring one of the columns to float on the web page. This section introduces you to two formats of the two-column page layout.

wrapper

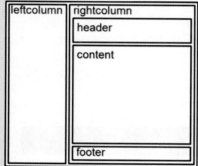

FIGURE 8.13 The wireframe for a two-column layout with left navigation.

Two Column with Left Navigation

See Figure 8.13 for a wireframe of a web page that has two columns. The left column will contain navigation. The HTML template for the page layout is

```
<div id="wrapper">
    <div id="leftcolumn">
    </div>
    <div id="rightcolumn">
        <div id="header">
        </div>
        <div id="content">
        </div>
        <div id="footer">
        </div>
    </div>
</div>
```

The web page shown in Figure 8.14 implements the two columns with left navigation layout. An example is in the student files, chapter8/twocolumn1.html. The key to this layout is that the left column is coded to float to the left with the `float` property. The browser renders the other content on the page using normal flow.

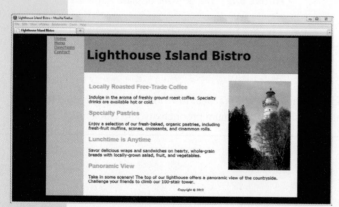

FIGURE 8.14 A two-column page layout with left navigation.

- The wrapper is centered and takes up 80% of the web page width. This area is assigned a medium-blue background color that will display behind the left column:

```
#wrapper { width: 80%;
          margin-left: auto;
          margin-right: auto;
          background-color: #b3c7e6; }
```

- The left column is assigned a fixed width configured to float to the left. Since no background color is configured, the background color of the container element (the wrapper div) displays:

```
#leftcolumn { float: left; width: 150px; }
```

- The right column is assigned a margin on the left that is equal to or greater than the width of the left column. This margin creates the look of two columns (often called "faux" columns). A white background color is assigned to the right column, which overrides the background color configured in the wrapper:

```
#rightcolumn { margin-left: 155px; background-color: #ffffff; }
```

Two Column with Top Logo Header and Left Navigation

See Figure 8.15 for a wireframe of a web page with that has a top logo header spanning two columns with a navigation area in the left column. The HTML template for the page layout is

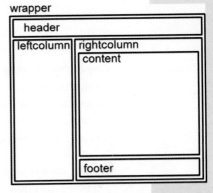

```
<div id="wrapper">
    <div id="header">
    </div>
    <div id="leftcolumn">
    </div>
    <div id="rightcolumn">
        <div id="content">
        </div>
        <div id="footer">
        </div>
    </div>
</div>
```

FIGURE 8.15 The wireframe for a two-column layout with a top logo area.

The web page shown in Figure 8.16 implements the two columns with top logo layout. An example is in the student files, chapter8/twocolumn2.html. The CSS that configures the wrapper, leftcolumn, and rightcolumn areas is the same as for the web page shown in Figure 8.14. However, notice that the location of the div assigned to the header id is different. It is now coded as the first div element within the wrapper and displays before the left and right columns.

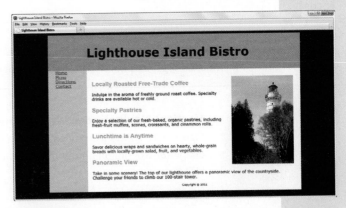

FIGURE 8.16 A two-column page layout with a top logo and left navigation.

Do I have to use a wrapper?

No, you are not required to use a wrapper or container for a web page layout. However, it does make it easier to get the two-column look because the background color of the wrapper div will display behind any of its child elements that do not have their own background color configured.

Not Yet Ready for Prime Time

There is one more aspect of the two-column layout web page design before it is ready for "prime time." The navigation area is a list of hyperlinks. In order to more closely semantically describe the navigation area, the hyperlinks should be configured in an unordered list. In the next section you'll learn techniques to configure horizontal and vertical navigation hyperlinks in unordered lists.

Hyperlinks in an Unordered List

One of the advantages of using CSS for page layout involves the use of semantically correct code. Writing semantically correct code means using the markup tag that most accurately reflects the purpose of the content. Using the various levels of heading tags for content headings and subheadings or placing paragraphs of text within paragraph tags (rather than using line breaks) are examples of writing semantically correct code. This type of coding is a step in the direction to support the Semantic Web.

Leading Web developers such as Eric Meyer, Mark Newhouse, Jeffrey Zeldman, and others have promoted the idea of using unordered lists to configure navigation menus. After all, a navigation menu is a list of hyperlinks. Recall from Chapter 6 that you can configure an unordered list to omit the display of the list markers, or even display an image instead of a standard list marker.

Focus on Accessibility

Configuring navigation with a list also helps to provide for accessibility. Screen reader applications offer easy keyboard access and verbal cues for information organized in lists, such as the number of items in the list.

- Home
- Menu
- Directions
- Contact

FIGURE 8.17
Navigation in an unordered list.

Vertical Navigation with an Unordered List

Figure 8.17 shows the navigation area of a web page (found in the student files chapter8/twocolumn3.html) that uses an unordered list to organize the navigation links. The HTML is

```
<ul>
    <li><a href="index.html">Home</a></li>
    <li><a href="menu.html">Menu</a></li>
    <li><a href="directions.html">Directions</a></li>
    <li><a href="contact.html">Contact</a></li>
</ul>
```

Home
Menu
Directions
Contact

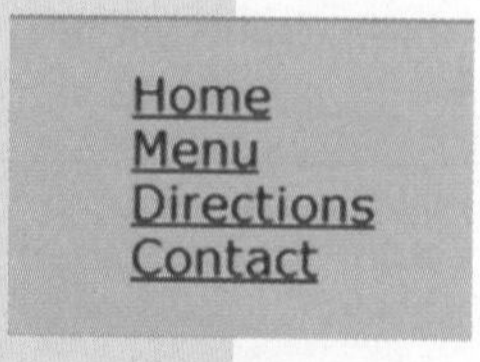

FIGURE 8.18 The list markers have been eliminated with CSS.

Configure with CSS

OK, so now that we're semantically correct, how about improving the visual aesthetic? Let's use CSS to eliminate the list marker (refer back to Chapter 6). We also need to make sure that our special styles only apply to the unordered lists in the navigation area (within the leftcolumn id) so we'll use a contextual selector. The CSS to configure the list in Figure 8.18 is

```
#leftcolumn ul { list-style-type: none; }
```

Remove the Underline with the CSS text-decoration Property

The `text-decoration` property modifies the display of text in the browser. This property is most often used to eliminate the underline from the navigation hyperlinks with:

```
text-decoration: none;
```

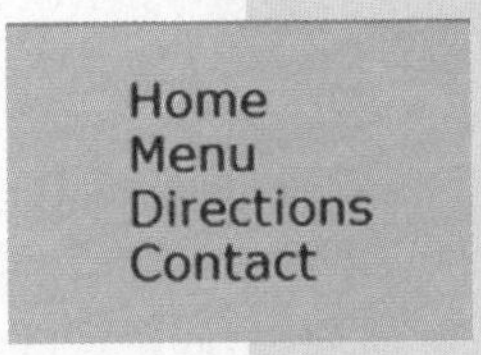

The CSS to configure the list in Figure 8.19 (also found in twocolumn4.html) that eliminates the underline on the hyperlinks in the navigation area (within the leftcolumn id) is

```
#leftcolumn a { text-decoration: none; }
```

Home
Menu
Directions
Contact

FIGURE 8.19 The CSS property text-decoration has been applied.

Horizontal Navigation with an Unordered List

You may be wondering how to use an unordered list for a horizontal navigation menu. The answer is CSS! List items are block elements. They need to be configured as inline elements to display in a single line. The CSS `display` property can configure this. See Table 8.3 for a list of commonly used values.

Value	Purpose
none	The element will not display
inline	The element will display as an inline element
block	The element will display as a block element with a margin above and below

TABLE 8.3 The display Property

Figure 8.20 shows the navigation area of a web page (found in the student files chapter8/navigation.html) with a horizontal navigation area organized by an unordered list. The HTML is

Home   Menu   Directions   Contact

FIGURE 8.20 Navigation in an unordered list.

```
<div id="nav">
 <ul>
    <li><a href="index.html">Home</a></li>
    <li><a href="menu.html">Menu</a></li>
    <li><a href="directions.html">Directions</a></li>
    <li><a href="contact.html">Contact</a></li>
 </ul>
</div>
```

Configure with CSS

The following CSS was applied in this example:

- To eliminate the list marker, apply `list-style-type: none;` to the ul element selector:

  ```
  #nav ul { list-style-type: none; }
  ```

- To render the list items horizontally instead of vertically, apply `display: inline;` to the li element selector:

  ```
  #nav li { display: inline;    }
  ```

- To eliminate the underline from the hyperlinks, apply `text-decoration: none;` to the a selector. Also, to add some space between the hyperlinks, apply `padding-right` to the a element selector:

  ```
  #nav a { text-decoration: none; padding-right: 10px; }
  ```

CSS Interactivity with Pseudo-classes

Have you ever visited a website and found that the text hyperlinks changed color when you moved the mouse pointer over them? Often, this is accomplished using a CSS **pseudo-class**, which can be used to apply a special effect to a selector. The five pseudo-classes that can be applied to the anchor element are shown in Table 8.4.

Pseudo-Class	When Applied
:link	Default state for a hyperlink that has not been clicked (visited)
:visited	Default state for a visited hyperlink
:focus	Triggered when the hyperlink has keyboard focus
:hover	Triggered when the mouse moves over the hyperlink
:active	Triggered when the hyperlink is actually clicked

TABLE 8.4 Commonly Used CSS Pseudo-Classes

Notice the order in which the pseudo-classes are listed in Table 8.4. Anchor element pseudo-classes *must be coded in this order* (although it's OK to omit one or more of those listed). If you code the pseudo-classes in a different order, the styles will not be reliably applied. It's common practice to configure the focus and active pseudo-classes with the same styles.

To apply a pseudo-class, write it after the selector. The following code sample will configure text hyperlinks to be red initially. The sample also uses the :hover pseudo-class to configure the hyperlinks to change their appearance when the visitor places the mouse pointer over them so that the underline disappears and the color changes.

1. Text hyperlinks are underlined by default.

🖨 <u>Print This Page</u>

2. The hover pseudo-class is triggered by the mouse. The browser no longer displays the underline below the hyperlink.

🖨 Print This Page

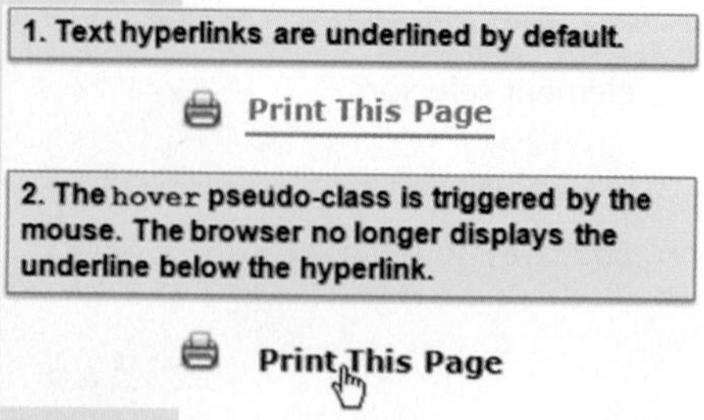

FIGURE 8.21 Using the hover pseudo-class.

```
a:link { color: #ff0000; }
a:hover { text-decoration: none;
        color: #000066; }
```

Figure 8.21 shows part of a web page that uses a similar technique. Note the position of the mouse pointer over the Print This Page hyperlink—the text color has changed and has no underline. Most modern browsers support CSS pseudo-classes.

HANDS-ON PRACTICE 8.3

You will use pseudo-classes to create interactive hyperlinks in this Hands-On Practice. Create a folder named ch8hover. Copy the lighthouseisland.jpg, lighthouselogo.jpg, and starter3.html files from the chapter8 folder in the student files into your ch8hover folder. Display the web page in a browser. It should look similar to Figure 8.22—notice that the navigation area needs to be configured. Launch a text editor and open the starter3.html file. Save the file as index.html in your ch8hover folder.

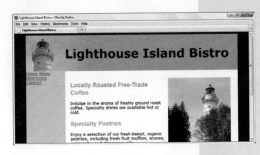

FIGURE 8.22 The navigation area needs to be styled in this two-column page layout.

1. Review the code for this page, which uses a two-column layout. Examine the `leftcolumn` id and modify the code to configure the navigation in an unordered list.

```
<ul>
  <li><a href="index.html">Home</a></li>
  <li><a href="menu.html">Menu</a></li>
  <li><a href="directions.html">Directions</a></li>
  <li><a href="contact.html">Contact</a></li>
</ul>
```

2. Let's add CSS to the embedded styles to configure the unordered list elements in the leftcolumn id: eliminate the list marker, set the padding to 10 pixels.

```
#leftcolumn ul { list-style-type: none; padding: 10px; }
```

3. Next, configure basic interactivity with pseudo-classes.

   - Configure the anchor tags in the `leftcolumn` id to have 10 pixels of padding, use bold font, and display no underline.

     ```
     #leftcolumn a { text-decoration: none; padding: 10px;
                     font-weight: bold; }
     ```

   - Use pseudo-classes to configure anchor tags in the `leftcolumn` id to display white (#ffffff) text for unvisited hyperlinks, light-gray (#eaeaea) text for visited hyperlinks, and dark blue (#000066) text when the mouse hovers over hyperlinks:

     ```
     #leftcolumn a:link { color: #ffffff; }
     #leftcolumn a:visited { color: #eaeaea; }
     #leftcolumn a:hover { color: #0000066; }
     ```

Save your page and test in a browser. Move your mouse over the navigation area and notice the text color change. Your page should look similar to Figure 8.23. A sample is found in the student files (chapter8/hover/index.html).

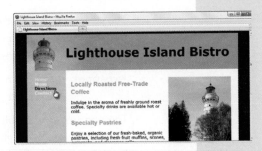

FIGURE 8.23 CSS pseudo-classes add interactivity to the navigation.

Practice with CSS Two-Column Layout

HANDS-ON PRACTICE 8.4

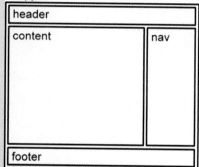

FIGURE 8.24 The wireframe for a two-column layout with a top logo area.

In this Hands-On Practice you'll create a new version of the Lighthouse Island Bistro home page with a top header section spanning two columns, content in the left column, navigation in the right column, and a footer section below the two columns. See Figure 8.24 for the wireframe. You will configure the CSS in an external style sheet. Create a new folder named ch8practice. Copy the starter4.html, lighthouseisland.jpg, and lighthouselogo.jpg files from the chapter8 folder in the student files into your ch8practice folder.

1. Launch a text editor and open the starter4.html file. Save the file as index.html. Add a link element to the head section of the web page that associates this file with an external style sheet named lighthouse.css. A code sample is

```
<link href="lighthouse.css" rel="stylesheet">
```

2. Save the index.html file. Launch a text editor and create a new file named lighthouse.css in your ch8practice folder. Configure the CSS for the wireframe sections as follows:

- The body element selector: very dark blue background (#00005D) and Verdana, Arial, or the default sans-serif font typeface

```
body { background-color: #00005D; font-family: Verdana, Arial, sans-serif; }
```

- The wrapper id: centered, take up 80% of the browser viewport, a minimum width of 850px, display text in a dark-blue color (#000066), and display a medium-blue (#B3C7E6) background color (*this color will display behind the nav section*)

```
#wrapper { margin: 0 auto;  width: 80%; min-width: 850px;
          background-color: #B3C7E6; color: #000066; }
```

- The header id: slate blue (#869DC7) background color, very dark blue (#00005D) text color, 150% font size, top, right, and bottom padding of 10px, 155 pixels of left padding, and the lighthouselogo.jpg background image

```
#header { background-color: #869DC7; color: #00005D; font-size: 150%;
         padding: 10px 10px 10px 155px; background-repeat: no-repeat;
         background-image: url(lighthouselogo.jpg); }
```

- The `nav` id: float on the right, width of 150px, display bold text, letter spacing of 0.1 em

```
#nav { float: right; width: 150px; font-weight: bold; letter-spacing: 0.1em; }
```

- The `content` id: white background color (#FFFFFF), black text color (#000000), 10 pixels of padding on the top and bottom, and 20 pixels of padding on the left and right and overflow set to auto.

```
#content { background-color: #ffffff; color: #000000; padding: 10px 20px; overflow: auto; }
```

- The `footer` id: 70% font size, centered text, 10 pixels of padding, a slate blue background color (#869DC7) and clear set to both.

```
#footer { font-size: 70%; text-align: center; padding: 10px;
          background-color: #869DC7; clear: both;}
```

Save the file and display it in a browser. Your display should be similar to Figure 8.25.

3. Continue editing the lighthouse.css file to style the h2 element selector and floating image. Configure the h2 element selector with slate blue text color (#869DC7) and Arial or sans-serif font typeface. Configure the `floatright` id to float on the right side with 10 pixels of margin.

```
h2 { color: #869DC7; font-family: Arial, sans-serif; }
#floatright { float: right; margin: 10px; }
```

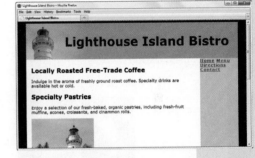

FIGURE 8.25 The home page with major page sections configured using CSS.

4. Continue editing the lighthouse.css file and configure the navigation bar.

- The `ul` selector: eliminate list markers, set zero margin and zero padding:

```
#nav ul { list-style-type: none; margin: 0; padding: 0; }
```

- The a element selector: no underline, 20 pixels padding, medium-blue background color (#B3C7E6), and 1 pixel solid white bottom border. Use display: block; to allow the web page visitor to click anywhere in the anchor "button" to activate the hyperlink.

```
#nav a { text-decoration: none;  padding: 20px; display: block;
         background-color: #B3C7E6;  border-bottom: 1px solid #FFFFFF;}
```

- Configure the `:link`, `:visited`, and `:hover` pseudo-classes as follows:

```
#nav a:link { color: #FFFFFF; }
#nav a:visited { color: #EAEAEA;   }
#nav a:hover { color: #EAEAEA;
               background-color: #869DC7; }
```

Save your files. Display your index.html page in a browser. Move your mouse over the navigation area and notice the interactivity, as shown in Figure 8.26. A sample solution is in the chapter8/practice/index.html file.

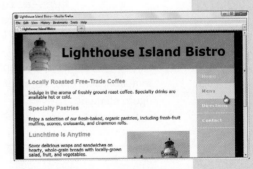

FIGURE 8.26 CSS pseudo-classes add interactivity to the page.

Caption a Figure

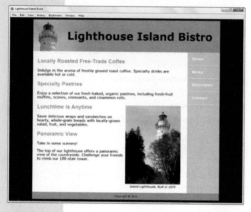

FIGURE 8.27   A figure with a centered caption.

This section presents two methods to configure a common design pattern—an image with a centered caption—shown in Figure 8.27. The first method can be used both with XHTML and HTML5 syntax. The second method implements new HTML5 elements and requires a modern browser that supports HTML5 (such as Safari, Firefox, Chrome, Opera, or Internet Explorer 9).

Method 1: Configure with a Div Element

The first technique is supported by all commonly used browsers. The image element and text caption are contained within a div element. The HTML code is

```
<div class="figure">
<img src="lighthouseisland.jpg" width="250"
height="355" alt="Lighthouse Island"><br>
Island Lighthouse, Built in 1870
</div>
```

The div is assigned to a class named figure that is configured as follows: float to the right, 260 pixels in width, 10-pixel margin, and display small italic text that is centered. The CSS is

```
.figure {float: right;
        width: 260px;
        margin: 10px;
        text-align: center;
        font-size: .8em;
        font-style: italic;  }
```

Access the student files (chapter8/caption/caption1.html) to view an example of this coding technique in action. The class name of figure was chosen to correspond with the name of the new HTML5 figure element.

Method 2: Configure with New HTML5 Elements

Looking ahead to the future, the second technique requires a modern browser that supports HTML5 (such as Safari, Firefox, Chrome, or Internet Explorer 9). The new HTML5 figure and figcaption elements are utilized in this coding technique.

- **The Figure Element.** The block display figure element contains a unit of content that is self-contained, such as an image, along with one optional figcaption element.
- **The Figcaption Element.** The figcaption element provides a caption for a figure.

An example in the student files (chapter8/caption/caption2.html) configures a text caption centered below the image. The HTML code is

```
<figure>
  <img src="lighthouseisland.jpg" width="250"
  height="355" alt="Lighthouse Island">
  <figcaption>
  Island Lighthouse, Built in 1870
  </figcaption>
</figure>
```

CSS is needed to configure the display. The figure HTML selector is set as follows: float to the right, 260 pixels in width, and 10-pixel margin. The figcaption HTML selector is set to block display (with empty space above and below) and to render small, italic, centered text. The CSS is

```
figure { float: right;
         width: 260px;
         margin: 10px; }
figcaption { text-align: center;
             font-size: .8em;
             font-style: italic;
             display: block; }
```

You might be wondering why these new HTML5 elements are needed when the same visual aesthetic can be configured using a div element as a container. The reason is semantics. The div element is useful but very generic in nature. When the figure and figcaption elements are used, the structure of the content is well defined. However, if you are designing pages for commercial websites, hold off on using the new figure and figcaption elements until browser support of HTML5 is more widespread.

HTML5 Structural Elements

HTML5 introduces a number of semantic structural elements that can be used to configure areas on a web page. These new block display elements are not intended to completely replace the div element but are intended to be used along with div and other elements to structure web page documents in a more meaningful manner that indicates the purpose of the structural areas. You'll explore four of these new elements in this section.

- **The Header Element.** The header element contains the headings of either a web page document or an area in the document such as a section or article. The header element will typically contain one or more heading level elements (h1 through h6) and, optionally, the hgroup element. Standard HTML4 and XHTML coding practice is to use only one h1 element on a web page and configure the heading level elements in outline format. Outlining is different in HTML5. Instead of a heading level outline, the outline is also configured by sections and heading levels within each section. Explore an HTML5 outliner at http://gsnedders.html5.org/outliner.

- **The Hgroup Element.** The hgroup element groups heading level tags and is useful if the logo header area of a web page contains both the website name and a **tagline** [a phrase that identifies and captures the essence of a business; e.g., the tagline of L. L. Bean (http://www.llbean.com) is "GUARANTEED. You Have Our Word"]. When there is more than one heading level element in an hgroup, only the first heading element is placed in the page outline.

- **The Nav Element.** The nav element contains a section of navigation links.

- **The Footer Element.** The footer element contains the footer content of a web page, section, article, paragraph, or even the blockquote element.

Remember that these new HTML5 elements are not supported by all browsers. However, you can begin to practice with them today.

HANDS-ON PRACTICE 8.5

In this Hands-On Practice you'll begin with the two-column Lighthouse Island Bistro home page (shown in Figure 8.27) and modify it to use HTML5 structural elements. You'll also add a tagline to the header area. Create a new folder named ch8structure. Copy the caption2.html, lighthouseisland.jpg, and lighthouselogo.jpg files from the student files (chapter8/caption folder).

1. Launch a text editor, and open the caption2.html file. Save the file as index.html. Examine the source code, and notice that the HTML5 figure and figcaption elements are already in place. Replace the div assigned to the header id with the new HTML5 header element that

contains an hgroup. Also add the tagline "the best coffee on the coast" with an h2 element. The new code is

```
<header>
  <hgroup>
    <h1>Lighthouse Island Bistro</h1>
    <h2>the best coffee on the coast</h2>
  </hgroup>
</header> <!-- end of header -->
```

2. Replace the opening and closing tags for the div assigned to the nav id with the new HTML5 nav element. Replace the opening and closing tags for the div assigned to the footer id with the footer element.

3. Edit the embedded CSS to use HTML element selectors for the header, nav, and footer elements. Replace the #header selector with the HTML header selector. Replace all instances of the #nav selector with the HTML nav selector. Replace the #footer selector with the HTML footer selector.

4. Configure CSS for the h1 and h2 elements in the header. Use contextual HTML selectors. Set the h1 bottom margin to 0. Set the h2 with 20 pixels of right padding, a top margin of 0, and .80em italic, right-aligned, #00005D color text. The CSS is

```
header h1 { margin-bottom: 0; }
header h2 { margin-top: 0; padding-right: 20px;
            font-size: .80em; font-style: italic;
            text-align: right; color: #00005D; }
```

5. How will current browsers "understand" the HTML5 code? One technique that you can experiment with is to use CSS to configure new element selectors as block display elements. At the time this was written, all modern browsers (except Internet Explorer version 8 and earlier) correctly applied this style declaration. Add the following CSS:

```
header, nav, footer { display: block; }
```

6. Save your file. Display your index.html page in a modern browser. It should look similar to the page shown in Figure 8.28. A sample solution is in the student files at chapter8/structure/structure.html.

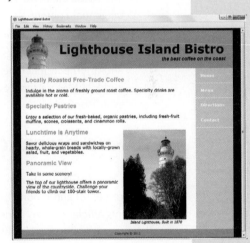

FIGURE 8.28 The HTML5 header, hgroup, nav, and footer elements were used on this web page.

As you completed this Hands-On Practice, you might have noticed that some of the id names used for standard page areas, such as header, nav, and footer, were also names of new HTML5 structural elements. This is a great way to prepare for HTML5, even if you are still coding XHTML! Become accustomed to the new HTML5 element names by configuring divs with these names as id or class values. Then, later, when it's time to always code in HTML5 syntax, you've got a head start!

More HTML5 Structural Elements

The HTML5 Gallery at http://html5gallery.com contains many examples of how HTML5 is being used on the Web today. Now that you've worked with the HTML5 header, hgroup, nav, and footer elements, we'll explore the HTML5 section, article, aside, and time elements.

- **The Section Element.** The section element contains a "section" of a document, such as a chapter or topic. A section element is block display and might contain header, footer, article, aside, div, and other elements needed to display the content. Sections can contain other section elements.

- **The Article Element.** The article element contains an independent entry, such as a blog posting, comment, or e-zine article that could stand on its own. An article element is block display and might contain header, footer, section, aside, div, and other elements needed to display the content.

- **The Aside Element.** The aside element is block display and contains a sidebar, a note, or other tangential content.

- **The Time Element.** The time element represents a date or a time and could be useful to date articles or blog postings. An optional datetime attribute can be used to specify a calendar date and/or time in machine-readable format. Use YYYY-MM-DD for a date. Use a 24-hour clock and HH:MM for time. See http://www.w3.org/TR/html-markup/time.html for additional datetime syntax options.

HANDS-ON PRACTICE 8.6

In this Hands-On Practice you'll begin with the HTML5 Lighthouse Island Bistro home page (shown in Figure 8.28) and modify the content to use a blog format that is structured with the new HTML5 elements article, header, aside, and time. Create a new folder named ch8blog. Copy the structure.html, lighthouseisland.jpg, and lighthouselogo.jpg files from the student files (chapter8/structure folder).

1. Launch a text editor and open the structure.html file. Save the file as index.html. Examine the source code and delete the text and elements that are contained with the content div. Use the article, header, aside, and time elements to create a blog posting for the home page. Replace the content div with the following code:

```
<h2>Bistro Blog</h2>
  <section>
    <article>
        <header><h1>Valentine Wrap</h1></header>
        <time datetime="2011-02-01">February 2, 2011</time>
        <aside>Watch for the March Madness Wrap next month!</aside>
        <p>The February special sandwich is the Valentine Wrap &mdash; heart-healthy
organic chicken with roasted red peppers on a whole wheat wrap.</p>
    </article>
    <article>
        <header><h1>New Coffee of the Day Promotion</h1></header>
        <time datetime="2011-01-11">January 11, 2011</time>
        <p>Enjoy the best coffee on the coast in the comfort of your home. We will
feature a different flavor of our gourmet, locally roasted coffee each day with
free bistro tastings and a discount on one-pound bags.</p>
    </article>
  </section>
```

2. The aside element contains content that is tangential to the main content. Configure CSS to display the aside element on the right (use float) in a light gray rectangle about 120 pixels wide, a 10-pixel left margin, 5 pixels of padding, a 5px box shadow, and 80% font size.

3. If you save and test your page, you may be surprised with the way the article headings display. That's because the browser is applying the CSS for the web page header to the article headers, too. We'll need to code CSS declarations specifically for the article headings. Use a contextual selector. Add the following new CSS code:

```
article header { background-color: #FFFFFF;
                 background-image: none;
                 font-size: 60%;
                 padding: 0; }
```

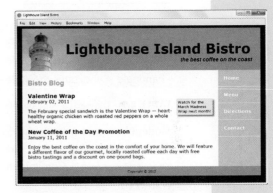

4. Save your file. Display your index.html page in a modern browser. It should look similar to the page shown in Figure 8.29. A sample solution is in the student files at chapter8/blog/blog.html.

FIGURE 8.29 The section, article, and aside HTML5 elements were used on this page.

Quick Tip

Internet Explorer 9 and current versions of Safari, Chrome, Firefox, and Opera offer good support of HTML5 structural elements. The issue is that many people still use earlier versions of browsers. For the best chance at compatibility, code using either HTML5 or XHTML syntax and avoid using the new HTML5 elements. Instead, use the new element names as class or id names. In this way you'll become used to the new element names. See chapter8/blog/blogall.html for an example of this technique. As time goes by and older browsers are used less and less, and you'll be all set!

CSS for Print

Even though the "paperless society" has been talked about for decades, the fact is that many people still love paper, and you can expect your web pages to be printed. CSS offers you some control over what gets printed and how the printouts are configured. This is easy to do using external style sheets. Create one external style sheet with the configurations for browser display and a second external style sheet with the special printing configurations. Associate both of the external style sheets to the web page using two link elements. The link elements will use a new attribute, called **media**, with values described in Table 8.5.

Value	Purpose
screen	The default value; indicates the style sheet that configures typical browser viewport display on a color computer screen
print	Indicates the style sheet that configures the printed formatting
handheld	Indicates the style sheet that configures display on handheld mobile devices

TABLE 8.5   The media Attribute

Modern browsers will use the correct style sheet depending on whether they are rendering a screen display or preparing to print a document. Configure the link element for your browser display with `media="screen"`. Configure the link element for your printout with `media="print"`. An example of the HTML is

```
<link rel="stylesheet" href="lighthouse.css" media="screen">
<link rel="stylesheet" href="lighthouseprint.css" media="print">
```

Often `display: none;` is used in the print style sheet to prevent banner ads, navigation, or other extraneous areas from appearing on the printout. Another common practice is to configure the font sizes on the print style sheet to use pt units—this will better control the text on the printout. You can also use styles to configure areas in the document, such as detailed contact info, that are only printed out and do not appear in the browser window. Figure 8.30 shows the print preview of the content page you created in Hands-On Practice 8.4 (see Figure 8.26). Notice that the print preview includes the navigation area. Figure 8.31 displays a version of the page that uses CSS to configure the text in the header and content areas and to prevent the navigation area from printing.

FIGURE 8.30 Print preview of the page displayed in Figure 8.26.

FIGURE 8.31 Print preview using CSS to remove the navigation from the printout.

HANDS-ON PRACTICE 8.7

In this Hands-On Practice you will code special styles to use when printing a web page. We will use the index.html and lighthouse.css files that you created in Hands-On Practice 8.4 as a starting point. Create a new folder named ch8print. Copy the index.html, lighthouse.css, lighthouseisland.jpg, and lighthouselogo.jpg files from the chapter8/practice folder in the student files into your ch8print folder.

1. Launch a text editor and open the index.html file. This page is associated with an external style sheet called lighthouse.css. The styles in lighthouse.css should be used when the web page is displayed on a computer screen. Modify the link element and add the `media` attribute with the value of `screen`. Code a new link element to associate an external style sheet called lightouseprint.css for printing (`media="print"`). The code is

   ```
   <link rel="stylesheet" href="lighthouse.css" media="screen">
   <link rel="stylesheet" href="lighthouseprint.css" media="print">
   ```

   Save the file.

2. Launch a text editor and open lighthouse.css. Since you want to keep most of the styles for printing, you will start by creating a new version of the external style sheet. Save lighthouse.css with the name of lighthouseprint.css in the ch8print folder. You will modify three areas on this style sheet: the header id, the content id, and the nav id configuration.

   • Modify the `header` id to print using black text in 20-point font size, with no background color:

   ```
   #header { color: #000000; font-size: 20pt; }
   ```

   • Modify the `content` id to print using a serif typeface in a 12-point font size:

   ```
   #content { font-family: "Times New Roman", serif; font-size: 12pt; }
   #nav { display: none; }
   ```

   Save your file in the ch8print folder.

3. Test your work. Display your index.html file in a browser. Select Print > Preview. Your display should look similar to the page shown in Figure 8.31. The header and content font sizes have been configured. The navigation does not display. The student files contain a copy of index.html and lighthouseprint.css in the chapter8/print folder.

CSS for the Mobile Web

Access to the Web from cell phones, smartphones, and Internet tablets makes it possible to always be online. The research firm eMarketer.com predicts significant growth for mobile web access, with a projected 134.3 million mobile Internet users by 2013. With this growth in mind, it's becoming more important to design web pages that are accessible and usable for your mobile visitors. There are a few schools of thought on the best way to accomplish this, including developing a new mobile site with a .mobi TLD (see Chapter 1 to review TLDs), creating a separate website hosted within your current domain targeted for mobile users, using CSS to create a style sheet to configure your current website for display on mobile devices, and using new CSS3 media queries.

You can create a separate style sheet to configure the display on handheld devices, just as you configured a separate style sheet to control the printed format of a web page. Associate the style sheet with your web page using the media attribute (media="handheld") on the link element. An example is

FIGURE 8.32 http://disability.gov displayed in a mobile browser.

```
<link href="mobile.css" rel="stylesheet" media="handheld">
```

Now that you know how to associate a handheld style sheet with a web page, what's the best way to configure the page? Compare the regular browser display of the Disabilityinfo.gov site in Figure 8.33 with the handheld display in Figure 8.32—there's quite a difference!

FIGURE 8.33 The browser display of http://disability.gov.

Mobile Device Design Considerations

Small screen size. Common mobile phone screen sizes include 240 × 260 pixels, 320 × 240 pixels, 320 × 480 pixels, and 640 × 960 pixels (iPhone 4). Even on one of the large phones, that's not a lot of pixels to work with! Also, not every mobile device (such as iPhones) will honor the media="handheld" attribute. CSS3 offers the ability to perform media queries (see http://w3.org/TR/CSS3/media-queries) in which media query properties are listed for the browser to verify and, if met, render the specified style sheet. For example, the code below targets devices with screens less than 400 pixels wide:

```
<link media="screen and (max-width: 480px)"
href="mobile.css" rel="stylesheet">
```

Low bandwidth (slow connection speed). Although the use of faster 3G and 4G networks is becoming more widespread, many mobile users experience slow connection speeds. Images usually take up quite a bit of bandwidth on a typical website. Depending on the service plan, some mobile web visitors may be paying per kilobyte. Be aware of this and eliminate unnecessary images.

Font, color, and media issues. Mobile devices may have very limited font support. Configure font size using ems or percentages. Include generic font family names in your stylesheet. Mobile devices may have very limited color support. Choose colors carefully to maximize contrast. Many mobile devices do not support Adobe Flash media.

Awkward controls, limited processor and memory. While smartphones with touch controls are becoming more popular, many mobile users will not have access to mouse-like controls. Provide keyboard access to assist these users. Although mobile device processing speed and available memory are improving, they still cannot compare to the resources of a desktop computer. While this won't be an issue for the websites you create now, be mindful of this issue in the future as you continue to develop your skills and create web applications.

Mobile Design Checklist

- Be aware of the small screen size and bandwidth issues.
- Configure nonessential content, such as sidebar content, to not display (use `display: none;`).
- Consider replacing background images with graphics optimized for small screen display.
- Provide descriptive alt text for images.
- Use a single-column page layout.
- Choose colors to maximize contrast.

 Explore Further

Explore the following resources to find out more about designing for the mobile Web: http://www.w3.org/TR/mobile-bp, http://css-tricks.com/css-media-queries, http://aralbalkan.com/3331, and http://developer.practicalecommerce.com/articles/2343-CSS-Media-Queries-For-Mobile-Designs.

Review and Apply

Review Questions

Multiple Choice. Choose the best answer for each item.

1. Which of the following causes an element not to display either in the browser window or on a printed page?
   - **a.** `display: block;`
   - **b.** `display: 0px;`
   - **c.** `display: none;`
   - **d.** this cannot be done with CSS

2. Which of the following is the attribute used to indicate whether the style sheet is for printing, screen display, or for mobile devices?
   - **a.** `rel`   **c.** `media`
   - **b.** `type`   **d.** `content`

3. Which of the following properties can be used to clear a float?
   - **a.** `float` or `clear`
   - **b.** `clear` or `overflow`
   - **c.** `position` or `clear`
   - **d.** `overflow` or `float`

4. Which of the following is an HTML5 element used to indicate tangential content?
   - **a.** `header`   **c.** `nav`
   - **b.** `sidebar`   **d.** `aside`

5. Which of the following pseudo-classes is the default state for a hyperlink that has already been clicked?
   - **a.** `:hover`   **c.** `:onclick`
   - **b.** `:link`   **d.** `:visited`

6. Which of the following is used to change the location of an element slightly in relation to where it would otherwise appear on the page?
   - **a.** relative positioning
   - **b.** the float property
   - **c.** absolute positioning
   - **d.** this cannot be done with CSS

7. Which of the following configures a class called nav to float to the left?
   - **a.** `.nav { left: float; }`
   - **b.** `.nav { float: left; }`
   - **c.** `.nav { float-left: 200px; }`
   - **d.** none of the above

8. Which of the following is the rendering flow used by a browser by default?
   - **a.** XHTML flow   **c.** browser flow
   - **b.** normal display   **d.** normal flow

9. Which of the following is an example of using a contextual selector to configure the anchor tags within the .nav class?
   - **a.** `nav. a`
   - **b.** `a nav.`
   - **c.** `.nav a`
   - **d.** this cannot be done with CSS

10. Which of the following is used along with the left, right, and/or top property to configure the position of an element precisely outside of normal flow?
    - **a.** `position: relative;`
    - **b.** `position: absolute;`
    - **c.** `position: float;`
    - **d.** `absolute: position;`

Hands-On Exercises

1. Write the XHTML to associate a web page with an external style sheet named myprint.css to configure a printout.

2. Write the CSS for an id with the following attributes: float to the left of the page, light-beige background, Verdana or sans-serif large font, and 20 pixels of padding.

3. Write the CSS for an id that will be absolutely positioned on a page 20 pixels from the top and 40 pixels from the right. This area should have a light-gray background and a solid border.

4. Write the CSS for a class that is relatively positioned. This class should appear 15 pixels in from the left. Configure the class to have a light-green background.

5. Create a web page about your favorite hobby, movie, or music group. Include the following HTML5 elements: header, nav, figure, figcaption, article, and footer. Configure the text, color, and layout with CSS.

Focus on Web Design

There is still much for you to learn about CSS. A great place to learn about web technology is on the Web itself. Use a search engine to search for CSS page layout tutorials. Choose a tutorial that is easy to read. Select a section that discusses a CSS technique that was not covered in this chapter. Create a web page that uses this new technique. Consider how the suggested page layout follows (or does not follow) principles of design such as contrast, repetition, alignment, and proximity (refer back to Chapter 4). The web page should provide the URL of your tutorial, the name of the website, a description of the new technique you discovered, and a discussion of how the technique follows (or does not follow) principles of design.

PACIFIC TRAILS RESORT CASE STUDY

In this chapter's case study you will use the Pacific Trails existing website (Chapter 7) as a starting point to create a new version of the website that uses a two-column page layout. Figure 8.34 displays a wireframe with the new layout.

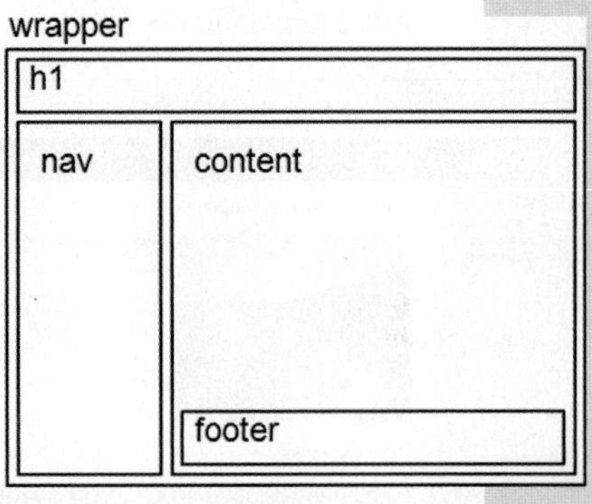

Step 1: Create a folder called ch8pacific to contain your Pacific Trails Resort website files. Copy the files from the Chapter 7 Case Study ch7pacific folder.

Step 2: Configure the CSS. Launch a text editor and open the pacific.css external style sheet file.

FIGURE 8.34 Pacific Trails two-column page layout.

- **The wrapper id Selector.** Change the background color from white (#FFFFFF) to blue (#90C7E3).

- **The `nav` id Selector.** This is the area that will float on the page. Remove the background color property—the nav area will pick up the background color of the wrapper id. Modify the padding property and add the float and width properties as follows:

```
#nav { padding: 20px 5px 5px 20px;
       font-weight: bold;
       float: left;
       width: 175px; }
```

- **The `content` id Selector.** Configure a white (#FFFFFF) background, 175 pixels of left margin (this value corresponds to the width of the floated navigation area), and update the padding values:

```
#content { padding: 1px 20px 20px 30px;
           background-color:#ffffff;
           margin-left: 175px;   }
```

- **Configure the Navigation Area.** Use contextual selectors to configure the unordered list and anchor elements *within the nav id.*
  - **Style the Unordered List.** Configure the `ul` element selector with no list markers, zero margin, zero left padding, and 1.2 em font size:

    ```
    #nav ul { list-style-type: none;
              margin: 0;
              padding-left: 0;
              font-size: 1.2em; }
    ```

  - **Remove the Underline from Navigation Anchor Tags.** Configure the a element selector to display text without an underline:

    ```
    #nav a { text-decoration: none; }
    ```

  - **Style Unvisited Navigation Hyperlinks.** Configure the `:link` pseudo-class with navy blue text color (#000033):

    ```
    #nav a:link { color: #000033; }
    ```

  - **Style Visited Navigation Hyperlinks.** Configure the `:visited` pseudo-class with dark blue text color (#344873):

    ```
    #nav a:visited { color: #344873; }
    ```

  - **Style Interactive Hyperlinks.** Configure the `:hover` pseudo-class with white text color (#FFFFFF):

    ```
    #nav a:hover {color: #FFFFFF; }
    ```

Save the pacific.css file.

FIGURE 8.35 The new Pacific Trails Home page with a two-column layout.

Step 3: Edit the Web Pages. Launch a text editor and open the index.html file. Configure the navigation hyperlinks using an unordered list. Remove the   special characters. Save the file. Modify the yurts.html and activities.html files in a similar manner.

Test your web pages in a browser. Your home page should be similar to the example in Figure 8.35 with a two-column page layout!

Step 4: OPTIONAL—Configure with HTML5 Structural Elements. Get more practice with the new HTML5 structural elements by creating a new version of the Pacific Trails Resort website. Create a folder called ch8pacificHTML5 to contain your Pacific Trails Resort website files. Copy the files from this case study's ch8pacific folder.

- Modify the pacific.css file in a text editor. Configure new styles, and use HTML element selectors for the header, nav, and footer elements.
  - All style declarations previously associated with the h1 HTML selector will apply to the header HTML selector. Replace the h1 selector with the header selector.
  - Configure a new h1 HTML selector with a zero bottom margin to eliminate extra space in the header area.
  - Replace all instances of the #nav selector with the HTML nav selector.

- Replace the #footer selector with the HTML footer selector.
- Configure the figure HTML selector to float left with 20 pixels of padding on the right and 10 pixels of padding on the bottom.
- Configure the figcaption HTML selector for block display with centered, italic text using size .80em font.
- Remove the #content img style declaration.
- Add the following CSS to be compatible with current browsers (other than IE 8 and earlier): header, nav, figure, footer { display: block; }
  - Modify each web page file in a text editor. Configure HTML5 elements.
    - Configure an HTML5 header element to contain the h1 element.
    - Replace the opening and closing tags for the div assigned to the nav id with the HTML5 nav element.
    - Replace the opening and closing tags for the div assigned to the footer id with the HTML5 footer element.
    - Note the large image on each page. Use the HTML5 figure element to contain the img element with an HTML5 figcaption element below the image. Configure each figcaption element to display a text caption appropriate for its corresponding image, such as "Scenic Pacific Coast", "Yurt with Pacific Ocean View", and "Serene Trail in the Redwoods".

Save your files. Display your web pages in a modern browser. Figure 8.36 shows the home page rendered in the Safari browser. With the exception of the image caption, your case study web pages should look similar to those you created in Step 1 through Step 3.

The optional Step 4 in this case study provided you with additional practice using new HTML5 elements. Be aware that if you display your pages in a nonsupporting browser (such as Internet Explorer 8 or earlier), you may not be pleased with the result.

FIGURE 8.36 HTML5 elements structure the content in this web page.

Explore Further

Internet Explorer 9 and current versions of Safari, Chrome, Firefox, and Opera offer good support for HTML5. However, older browsers do not. Remy Sharp offers a solution to enhance the support of Internet Explorer version 8 and earlier (see http://remysharp.com/2009/01/07/html5-enabling-script). The technique uses conditional comments that are only supported by Internet Explorer and are ignored by other browsers. The conditional comments cause Internet Explorer to interpret JavaScript (see Chapter 11) statements that configure it to recognize and process CSS for the new HTML5 element selectors. Remy Sharp has uploaded the script to Google's code project and has made it available for anyone to use. Add the following code to the head section of a web page to cause Internet Explorer (versions 8 and earlier) to correctly render your HTML5 code:

```
<!--[if lt IE 9]>
<script src="http://html5shim.googlecode.com/svn/trunk/html5.js"></script>
<![endif]-->
```

What's the drawback to this approach? Be aware that your web page visitors using Internet Explorer (version 8 and earlier) may see a warning message and must have JavaScript enabled for this method to work.

Table Basics

While back in the day tables were often used to format the layout of a web page, CSS is the page layout tool of choice for modern web designers. In this chapter, you'll become familiar with coding HTML tables to organize information on a web page.

You'll learn how to . . .

- Create a table on a web page
- Apply attributes to format tables, table rows, and table cells

- Increase the accessibility of a table
- Style an HTML table with CSS

Table Overview

The purpose of a table is to organize information. In the past, before CSS was well-supported by browsers, tables were also used to format web page layouts. An HTML table is composed of rows and columns, like a spreadsheet. Each individual table cell is at the intersection of a specific row and column.

- Each table begins with a `<table>` tag and ends with a `</table>` tag.
- Each table row begins with a `<tr>` tag and ends with a `</tr>` tag.
- Each cell (table data) begins with a `<td>` tag and ends with a `</td>` tag.
- Table cells can contain text, graphics, and other HTML elements.

Name	Birthday	Phone
Jack	5/13	857-555-5555
Sparky	11/28	303-555-5555

FIGURE 9.1 Table with three rows, three columns, and a border.

Figure 9.1 shows a sample table with three rows, three columns, and a border. The sample HTML for the table shown in Figure 9.1 is

```html
<table border="1">
  <tr>
    <td>Name</td>
    <td>Birthday</td>
    <td>Phone</td>
  </tr>
  <tr>
    <td>Jack</td>
    <td>5/13</td>
    <td>857-555-5555</td>
  </tr>
  <tr>
    <td>Sparky</td>
    <td>11/28</td>
    <td>303-555-5555</td>
  </tr>
</table>
```

Notice how the table is coded row by row. Also, each row is coded cell by cell. This attention to detail is crucial to the successful use of tables. An example can be found in the student files (chapter9/table1.html).

The Table Element

Table elements are block-level elements that contain tabular information. The table begins with a `<table>` tag and ends with a `</table>` tag. See Table 9.1 for common attributes of the table element.

Attribute	Value	Purpose
align	left (default), right, center	Horizontal alignment of the table (obsolete in HTML5)
bgcolor	Valid color value	Background color of the table (obsolete in HTML5)
border	0	Default; there is no visible border (obsolete in HTML5)
	1–100	Visible border with pixel width specified
cellpadding	Numeric value	Specifies the number of pixels of padding between the content of a table cell and its border (obsolete in HTML5)
cellspacing	Numeric value	Specifies the number of pixels of space between the borders of each cell in a table (obsolete in HTML5)
summary	Text description	Provides for accessibility; a text description that provides an overview of and context for the information in the table
title	Text description	A brief text description that provides an overview of the table; may be displayed in some browsers as a tooltip
width	Numeric value or percentage	Specifies the width of the table (obsolete in HTML5)

TABLE 9.1 Commonly Used Attributes of the Table Element

Table Captions

The **caption element** is often used with a data table to describe its contents. The table shown in Figure 9.2 uses `<caption>` tags to set the caption to "Bird Sightings". Notice that the caption element is coded on the line immediately after the opening `<table>` tag. An example can be found in the student files (chapter9/table2.html). The HTML for the table is

```
<table border="1">
<caption>Bird Sightings</caption>
  <tr>
   <td>Name</td>
   <td>Date</td>
  </tr>
  <tr>
   <td>Bobolink</td>
   <td>5/25/10</td>
  </tr>
  <tr>
   <td>Upland Sandpiper</td>
   <td>6/03/10</td>
  </tr>
</table>
```

Bird Sightings

Name	Date
Bobolink	5/25/10
Upland Sandpiper	6/03/10

FIGURE 9.2 The caption for this table is Bird Sightings.

Table Rows, Cells, and Headers

The **table row element** configures a row within a table on a web page. The table row begins with a `<tr>` tag and ends with a `</tr>` tag. See Table 9.2 for common attributes of the table row element.

Attribute	Value	Purpose
align	left (default), right, center	Horizontal alignment of the table row (obsolete in HTML5)
bgcolor	Valid color value	Background color of the table row (obsolete in HTML5)

TABLE 9.2   Commonly Used Attributes of the Table Row Elements

The **table data element** configures a cell within a row in a table on a web page. The table cell begins with a `<td>` tag and ends with a `</td>` tag. See Table 9.3 for common attributes of the table data cell element.

Attribute	Value	Purpose
align	left (default), right, center	Horizontal alignment of the table cell (obsolete in HTML5)
bgcolor	Valid color value	Background color of the table cell (obsolete in HTML5)
colspan	Numeric	The number of columns spanned by a cell
headers	The id value(s) of a column or row heading cell	Associates the table data cells with table header cells; may be accessed by screen readers
rowspan	Numeric	The number of rows spanned by a cell
scope	row, col	The scope of the table header cell contents (row or column); may be accessed by screen readers
valign	top, middle (default), bottom	The vertical alignment of the contents of the cell (obsolete in HTML5)
width	Numeric value or percentage	Width of the cell (obsolete in HTML5)

TABLE 9.3   Commonly Used Attributes of the Table Data and Table Header Cell Elements

Name	Birthday	Phone
Jack	5/13	857-555-5555
Sparky	11/28	303-555-5555

FIGURE 9.3   Using `<th>` tags to indicate column headings.

The **table header element** is similar to a table data element and configures a cell within a row in a table on a web page. Its special purpose is to configure column and row headings. Text displayed within a table header element is centered and bold. The table header element begins with a `<th>` tag and ends with a `</th>` tag. See Table 9.3 for common attributes of the table data cell element. Figure 9.3 shows a table with column headings configured by `<th>` tags. The HTML for the table shown in Figure 9.3 is as follows (also see chapter9/table3.html in the student files). Notice that the first row uses <th> instead of <td> tags:

```
<table border="1">
  <tr>
    <th>Name</th>
    <th>Birthday</th>
    <th>Phone</th>
  </tr>
  <tr>
    <td>Jack</td>
    <td>5/13</td>
    <td>857-555-5555</td>
  </tr>
  <tr>
    <td>Sparky</td>
    <td>11/28</td>
    <td>303-555-5555</td>
  </tr>
</table>
```

HANDS-ON PRACTICE 9.1

Create a web page similar to Figure 9.4 that describes two schools you have attended. Use the caption "School History Table." The table has three rows and three columns. The first row will have table header elements with the headings School Attended, Years, and Degree Awarded. You will complete the second and third rows with your own information within table data elements.

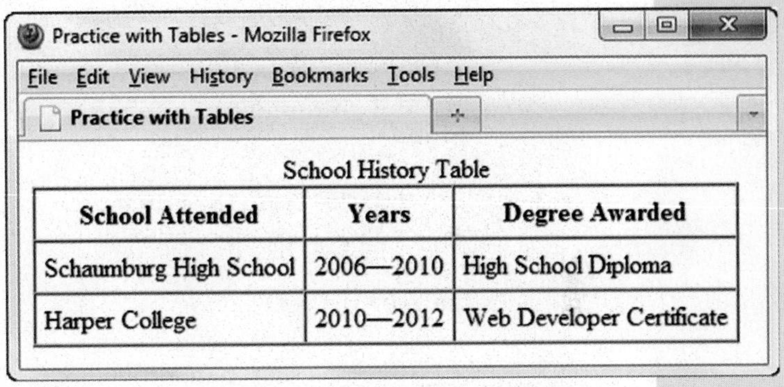

To get started, launch a text editor and open the template file located at chapter1/template.html

FIGURE 9.4 School History Table.

in the student files. Modify the title element. Use table, table row, table header, table data, and caption elements to configure a table similar to Figure 9.4.

Hints: The table has three rows and three columns. To configure a border, use border="1" on the <table> tag. To eliminate space between the cell borders, use cellspacing="0" on the <table> tag. To configure padding within each cell, use cellpadding="5" on the <table> tag. Use the table header element for the cells in the first row.

A sample solution is found in the student files (chapter9/table4.html). Your HTML5 code will not pass W3C validation testing when using obsolete attributes such as border, cellspacing, and cellpadding. This chapter introduces these "obsolete" attributes because they are still valid in XHTML and are still used often on the Web. Don't worry, you'll get practice configuring a table with CSS properties later in the chapter.

Span Rows and Columns

You can alter the gridlike look of a table by applying the `colspan` and `rowspan` attributes to table data or table header elements. As you get into more complex table configurations like these, be sure to sketch the table on paper before you start typing the HTML.

This spans two columns	
Column 1	Column 2

FIGURE 9.5 Table with a row that spans two columns.

The **colspan attribute** specifies the number of columns that a cell will occupy. Figure 9.5 shows a table cell that spans two columns.

The HTML for the table is

```
<table border="1">
  <tr>
    <td colspan="2">This spans two columns</td>
  </tr>
  <tr>
    <td>Column 1</td>
    <td>Column 2</td>
  </tr>
</table>
```

This spans two rows	Row 1 Column 2
	Row 2 Column 2

FIGURE 9.6 Table with a column that spans two rows.

The **rowspan attribute** specifies the number of rows that a cell will occupy. An example of a table cell that spans two rows is shown in Figure 9.6.

The HTML for the table is

```
<table border="1">
  <tr>
    <td rowspan="2">This spans two rows</td>
    <td>Row 1 Column 2</td>
  </tr>
  <tr>
    <td>Row 2 Column 2</td>
  </tr>
</table>
```

An example of the tables in Figures 9.5 and 9.6 can be found in the student files (chapter9/table5.html).

HANDS-ON PRACTICE 9.2

To create the web page shown in Figure 9.7, launch a text editor and open the template file located at chapter1/template.html in the student files. Modify the title element. Use table, table row, table head, and table data elements to configure the table.

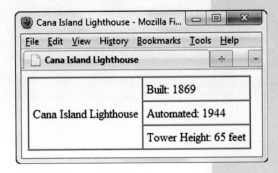

1. Code the opening `<table>` tag. Configure a border with `border="1"`, eliminate space between the cell borders with `cellspacing="0"`, and configure padding within each cell with `cellpadding="5"`.

2. Begin the first row with a `<tr>` tag.

3. The table data cell with "Cana Island Lighthouse" spans three rows. Code a table data element. Use the `rowspan="3"` attribute.

4. Code a table data element that contains the text "Built: 1869".

5. End the first row with a `</tr>` tag.

6. Begin the second row with a `<tr>` tag. This row will only have one table data element because the cell in the first column is already reserved for "Cana Island Lighthouse"

7. Code a table data element that contains the text "Automated: 1944".

8. End the second row with a `</tr>` tag.

9. Begin the third row with a `<tr>` tag. This row will only have one table data element because the cell in the first column is already reserved for "Cana Island Lighthouse".

10. Code a table data element that contains the text "Tower Height: 65 feet".

11. End the third row with a `</tr>` tag.

12. Code the closing `</table>` tag.

FIGURE 9.7 Practice with the rowspan attribute.

Save the file and view it in a browser. A sample solution is found in the student files (chapter9/table6.html). The use of the border, cellpadding, and cellspacing attributes will cause your web page to fail HTML5 validation. However, these attributes are still valid in XHTML syntax.

Notice how the "Cana Island Lighthouse" text is vertically aligned in the middle of the cell—this is the default vertical alignment. You can modify the vertical alignment using the valign attribute on the td element. The modern method is to configure tables using CSS—see the section "Style a Table with CSS" later in this chapter.

Configure an Accessible Table

Tables can be useful to organize information on a web page, but what if you couldn't see the table and were relying on assistive technology like a screen reader to read the table to you? You'd hear the contents of the table just the way it is coded—row by row, cell by cell. This might be difficult to understand. This section discusses coding techniques to improve the accessibility of tables.

Bird Sightings	
Name	**Date**
Bobolink	5/25/10
Upland Sandpiper	6/03/10

FIGURE 9.8 This simple data table uses `<th>` tags and the summary attribute to provide for accessibility.

For a simple informational data table like the one shown in Figure 9.8, the W3C's Web Accessibility Initiative (WAI) Web Content Accessibility Guidelines 2.0 (WCAG 2.0) recommend the following:

- Use table header elements (`<th>` tags) to indicate column or row headings.
- Use the summary attribute on the table element to provide an overview of the purpose and organization of the table.
- Use the caption element to provide a text title or caption for the table.

An example web page is in the student files (chapter9/table7.html). The HTML is

```
<table border="1" summary="A list of bird sightings with one bird
listed in each row. The first column contains the name of the bird.
The second column contains the date the bird was identified.">
<caption>Bird Sightings</caption>
   <tr>
    <th>Name</th>
    <th>Date</th>
   </tr>
   <tr>
    <td>Bobolink</td>
    <td>5/25/10</td>
   </tr>
   <tr>
    <td>Upland Sandpiper</td>
    <td>6/03/10</td>
   </tr>
</table>
```

However, for more complex tables the W3C recommends specifically associating the table data cell values with their corresponding headers. The technique that is recommended uses the `id` attribute (usually in a <th> tag) to identify a specific header cell and the **headers attribute** in a <td> tag. The code to configure the table in Figure 9.8 using headers and ids is as follows (also found in the student files chapter9/table8.html):

```
<table border="1" summary="A list of bird sightings with one bird
listed in each row. The first column contains the name of the bird.
The second column contains the date the bird was identified.">
<caption>Bird Sightings</caption>
   <tr>
     <th id="name">Name</th>
     <th id="date">Date</th>
   </tr>
   <tr>
     <td headers="name">Bobolink</td>
     <td headers="date">5/25/10</td>
   </tr>
   <tr>
     <td headers="name">Upland Sandpiper</td>
     <td headers="date">6/03/10</td>
   </tr>
</table>
```

 FAQ

What about the scope attribute?

The scope attribute specifies the association of table cells and table row or column headers. It is used to indicate whether a table cell is a header for a column (scope="col") or row (scope="row"). An example of the code for the table in Figure 9.8 that uses this attribute is as follows (also see the student files chapter9/table9.html):

```
<table border="1" summary="A list of bird sightings with one bird listed in each row. The
first column contains the name of the bird. The second column contains the date the bird
was identified.">
<caption>Bird Sightings</caption>
   <tr>
     <th scope="col">Name</th>
     <th scope="col">Date</th>
   </tr>
   <tr>
     <td>Bobolink</td>
     <td>5/25/10</td>
   </tr>
   <tr>
     <td>Upland Sandpiper</td>
     <td>6/03/10</td>
   </tr>
</table>
```

As you reviewed the code sample above, you may have noticed that using the scope attribute to provide for accessibility requires less coding than implementing the headers and id attributes. However, due to inconsistent screen reader support of the scope attribute, the WCAG 2.0 recommendations for coding techniques encourage the use of headers and id attributes rather than the scope attribute.

Style a Table with CSS

Back in the day, it was common practice to configure the visual aesthetic of a table with HTML attributes. A more modern approach is to use CSS to style a table. In this section you'll explore using CSS to style the border, padding, alignment, width, height, vertical alignment, and background of table elements. Table 9.4 lists corresponding CSS properties with HTML attributes used to style tables.

XHTML Attribute	CSS Property
align	To align a table, configure the width and margin properties for the table element selector. For example, to center a table, use `table { width: 75%;   margin: auto; }` To align content within table cells, use text-align
width	width
height	height
cellpadding	padding
cellspacing	border-spacing; a numeric value (px or em) or percentage. If you set a value to 0, omit the unit. One numeric value with unit (px or em) configures both horizontal and vertical spacing. Two numeric values with unit (px or em): The first value configures the horizontal spacing, and the second value configures the vertical spacing.
bgcolor	background-color
valign	vertical-align
border	border, border-style, border-spacing
none	background-image

TABLE 9.4   Configuring Tables with XHTML Attributes and CSS Properties

HANDS-ON PRACTICE 9.3

Lighthouse Island Bistro Specialty Coffee Menu		
Specialty Coffee	**Description**	**Price**
Lite Latte	Indulge in a shot of organic, locally roasted espresso with steamed, skim milk.	$3.50
Mocha Latte	Chocolate lovers will enjoy a shot of organic, locally roasted espresso, steamed milk, and your choice of melted dark, milk, or white chocolate.	$4.00
Turtle Treasure	A lucious mocha latte with caramel and pecan syrup — a candy bar in a cup.	$4.50

FIGURE 9.9   The table is configured with XHTML attributes.

In this Hands-On Practice you will code CSS style rules to configure an informational table on a web page. Create a folder named ch9table. Copy the starter.html file from the chapter9 folder to your ch9table folder. We'll use embedded styles for ease of editing and testing your page. Display the starter.html file in a browser; the display should look similar to the one shown in Figure 9.9.

Launch a text editor and open the starter.html file from your ch9table folder.

1. Review the web page code and notice the attributes on the <table> tag that configure the border, width, alignment, cellpadding, and cellspacing of the table. Delete these attributes from the <table> tag. You will code embedded CSS style rules to replace their function.

2. Configure the table element selector. Locate the embedded styles in the head section of the web page. Add a style rule for the table element selector in this area that configures the table to be centered, have a border, and have a width of 600px:

```
table { margin: auto; border: 1px solid #5c743d;  width: 600px;  }
```

Save the file and display your page in a browser. Notice that there is a border surrounding the entire table but not surrounding each table cell.

3. Configure the td and th element selectors. Add a style rule that configures a border and padding. Configure these selectors to use Arial or the default sans-serif font typeface:

```
td, th { border: 1px solid #5c743d;    padding: 5px;
        font-family: Arial, sans-serif;}
```

Save the file as menu.html and display your page in a browser. Each table cell should now be outlined with a border and should display text in a sans serif font.

4. Notice the empty space between the borders of the table cells. The **border-spacing property** can be used to eliminate this space. Add a `border-spacing: 0;` declaration to the table element selector. Save the file and display your page in a browser.

5. Configure the caption to be displayed with Verdana or the default sans-serif font typeface, bold font weight, font size 1.2 em, and 5 pixels of bottom padding. Configure a style rule as follows:

```
caption { font-family: Verdana, sans-serif; font-weight: bold;
        font-size: 1.2em; padding-bottom: 5px; }
```

6. Let's experiment and configure background colors for the rows instead of cell borders. Modify the style rule for the td and th element selectors and remove the border declaration. The new style rule for the cells is

```
td, th {  padding: 5px; font-family: Arial, sans-serif;}
```

7. Create a new class called `altrow` that sets a background color:

```
.altrow { background-color:#eaeaea;  }
```

8. Modify the <tr> tags in the HTML: assign the second and fourth <tr> tags to the `altrow` class. Save the file. Display your page in a browser. The table area should look similar to the one shown in Figure 9.10.

Notice how the background color of the alternate rows adds subtle interest to the web page. Compare your work with the sample located in the student files (chapter9/menu.html). In this Hands-On Practice you configured the display of an HTML table using CSS. You'll see this coding technique used increasingly in the future.

Lighthouse Island Bistro Specialty Coffee Menu

Specialty Coffee	Description	Price
Lite Latte	Indulge in a shot of organic, locally roasted espresso with steamed, skim milk.	$3.50
Mocha Latte	Chocolate lovers will enjoy a shot of organic, locally roasted espresso, steamed milk, and your choice of melted dark, milk, or white chocoloate.	$4.00
Turtle Treasure	A luscious mocha latte with caramel and pecan syrup — a candy bar in a cup.	$4.50

FIGURE 9.10 Rows are configured with alternating background colors.

CSS3 Structural Pseudo-classes

In the previous section you configured CSS and applied a class to every other table row to configure alternating background colors, often referred to as "zebra striping." You may have found this to be a bit inconvenient and wondered if there was a more efficient method. Well, there is! CSS3 **structural pseudo-class selectors** allow you to select and apply classes to elements based on their position in the structure of the document, such as every other row. CSS3 pseudo-classes are supported by current versions of Firefox, Opera, Chrome, Safari, and Internet Explorer 9. Earlier versions of Internet Explorer do not support CSS3 pseudo-classes, so consider using this coding technique only for enhancements to a web page. Table 9.5 lists common CSS3 structural pseudo-class selectors and their purpose.

Pseudo-class	Purpose
:first-of-type	Applies to the first element of the specified type
:first-child	Applies to the first child of an element (*CSS2 selector*)
:last-of-type	Applies to the last element of the specified type
:last-child	Applies to the last child of an element
:nth-of-type(n)	Applies to the "nth" element of the specified type. Values: a number, odd, or even

TABLE 9.5   Common CSS3 Structural Pseudo-classes

To apply a pseudo-class, write it after the selector. The following code sample will configure the first item in an unordered list to display with red text.

```
li:first-of-type { color: #FF0000; }
```

HANDS-ON PRACTICE 9.4 ─────────────────────────

In this Hands-On Practice you will rework the table you configured in Hands-On Practice 9.3 to use CSS3 structural pseudo-class selectors to configure color.

1. Launch a text editor, and open the menu.html file in your ch9table folder (also found in the student files chapter9/menu.html). Save the file as menu2.html.

2. View the source code, and notice that the second and fourth tr elements are assigned to the altrow class. You won't need this class assignment when using CSS3 structural pseudo-class selectors. Delete class="altrow" from the tr elements.

3. Examine the embedded CSS and locate the altrow class. Change the selector to use a structural pseudo-class that will apply the style to the even-numbered table rows. Replace `.altrow` with `tr:nth-of-type (even)` as shown in the following CSS declaration:

```
tr:nth-of-type(even) { background-color:#eaeaea; }
```

4. Save the file. Display your page in a browser. The table area should look similar to the one shown in Figure 9.10 if you are using a modern browser that supports CSS3 structural pseudo-classes.

5. Let's configure the first row to have a dark gray background (#666) and light gray text (#eaeaea) with the `:first-of-type` structural pseudo-class. Add the following to the embedded CSS:

```
tr:first-of-type { background-color: #666;
                   color: #eaeaea; }
```

6. Save the file. Display your page in a browser. The table area should look similar to the one shown in Figure 9.11 if you are using a modern browser that supports CSS3 structural pseudo-classes. A sample solution is available in the student files (chapter9/menucss3.html).

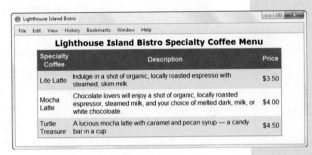

FIGURE 9.11 CSS3 pseudo-class selectors style the table rows.

CSS structural pseudo-classes are convenient to use, but be aware that Internet Explorer 8 (and earlier versions) does not support this technology. Although browser support will increase in the future, today it's best to apply these pseudo-classes with progressive enhancement in mind.

Configuring the First Letter

Ever wonder how to easily style the first letter of a paragraph to be different from the rest? It's easy using the CSS2 **:first-letter pseudo-element.** Use the following code to configure the text as shown in Figure 9.12:

```
p:first-letter { font-size: 3em;
font-weight: bold; color: #F00; }
```

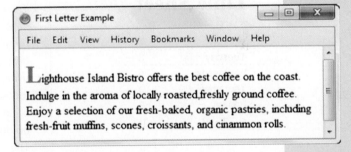

FIGURE 9.12 Configure the first letter with CSS.

Configure Table Sections

There are lots of configuration options when coding tables. Table rows can be put together into three types of table row groups: table head with `<thead>`, table body with `<tbody>`, table footer with `<tfoot>`.

These groups can be useful when you need to configure the areas in the table in different ways, using either attributes or CSS. The `<tbody>` tag is required if you configure a `<thead>` or `<tfoot>` area, although you can omit either the table head or table footer if you like. When you use table row groups, the `<thead>` and `<tfoot>` sections must be coded *before* the `<tbody>` section to pass W3C XHTML validation. The code sample in this section uses HTML5 syntax with the `<tfoot>` coded after the `<tbody>` which is more intuitive.

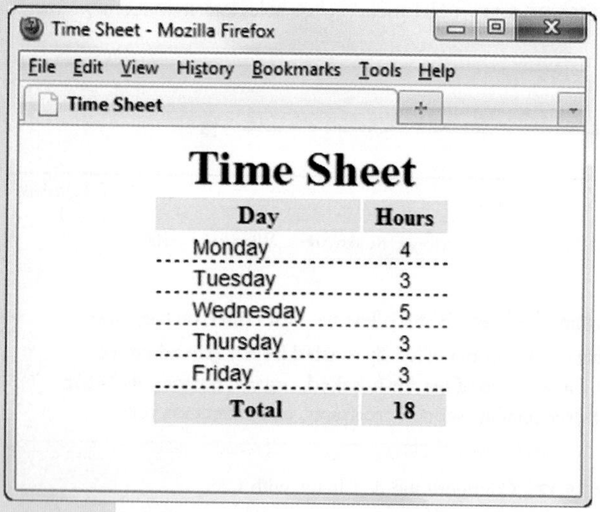

FIGURE 9.13 CSS configures the thead, tbody, and tfoot element selectors.

The following code sample (see chapter9/tfoot.html in the student files) configures the table shown in Figure 9.13 and demonstrates the use of CSS to configure a table head, table body, and table footer with different styles.

The CSS styles a centered 200-pixel-wide table with a caption that is rendered in large, bold font; a table head section with a light-gray (#eaeaea) background color; a table body section styled with slightly smaller text (.90em) using Arial or sans-serif font; table body td element selectors set to display with some left padding and a dashed bottom border; and a table footer section that has centered, bolded text and a light gray background color (#eaeaea). The CSS code is

```
table { width: 200px; margin: auto;}
caption { font-size: 2em; font-weight: bold;}
thead { background-color: #eaeaea;}
tbody { font-family: Arial, sans-serif; font-size:.90em;}
tbody td { border-bottom: 1px #000033 dashed; padding-left: 25px;}
tfoot { background-color: #eaeaea; font-weight: bold; text-align: center;}
```

The HTML for the table is

```
<table summary="This table presents a time sheet. Rows contain days
of the week and the total hours. Columns contain days and hours.">
<caption>Time Sheet</caption>
<thead>
   <tr>
      <th id="day">Day</th>
      <th id="hours">Hours</th>
      </tr>
</thead>
<tbody>
   <tr>
      <td headers="day">Monday</td>
      <td headers="hours">4</td>
   </tr>
   <tr>
      <td headers="day">Tuesday</td>
      <td headers="hours">3</td>
   </tr>
   <tr>
      <td headers="day">Wednesday</td>
      <td headers="hours">5</td>
   </tr>
   <tr>
      <td headers="day">Thursday</td>
      <td headers="hours">3</td>
   </tr>
   <tr>
      <td headers="day">Friday</td>
      <td headers="hours">3</td>
   </tr>
</tbody>
<tfoot>
   <tr>
      <td headers="day">Total</td>
      <td headers="hours">18</td>
   </tr>
</tfoot>
</table>
```

This example demonstrates the power of CSS in styling documents. The <td> tags within each table row group element selector (thead, tbody, and tfoot) inherited the font styles configured for their parent group element selector. Notice how a contextual selector (refer back to Chapter 5) configures padding and border only for <td> tags that are contained within (actually, "children of") the <tbody> element. Sample code is located in the student files (chapter8/tfoot.html). Take a few moments to explore the web page code and display the page in a browser.

CHAPTER 9

Review and Apply

Review Questions

Multiple Choice. Choose the best answer for each item.

1. Which HTML attribute specifies the distance between the edges of each cell?
   - **a.** cellpad
   - **b.** cellpadding
   - **c.** cellspacing
   - **d.** cellborder

2. Which HTML attribute specifies the distance between the cell text and the cell border?
   - **a.** cellpad
   - **b.** cellpadding
   - **c.** cellspacing
   - **d.** cellborder

3. Which HTML tag pair is used to group rows in the footer of a table?
   - **a.** <footer> </footer>
   - **b.** <tr> </tr>
   - **c.** <tfoot> </tfoot>
   - **d.** none of the above

4. Which HTML element uses a border attribute to display a table with a border?
   - **a.** <td>
   - **b.** <tr>
   - **c.** <table>
   - **d.** <tableborder>

5. Which HTML tag pair is used to specify table headings?
   - **a.** <td> </td>
   - **b.** <th> </th>
   - **c.** <head> </head>
   - **d.** <tr> </tr>

6. Which CSS property replaces the use of the cellpadding attribute?
   - **a.** cell-padding
   - **b.** border-spacing
   - **c.** padding
   - **d.** none of the above

7. Which HTML tag pair is used to begin and end a table row?
   - **a.** <td> </td>
   - **b.** <tr> </tr>
   - **c.** <table> </table>
   - **d.** none of the above

8. Which of the following is the intended use of tables on web pages?
   - **a.** configuring the layout of an entire page
   - **b.** organizing information
   - **c.** forming hyperlinks
   - **d.** configuring a resume

9. Which CSS property specifies the background color of a table?
   - **a.** background
   - **b.** bgcolor
   - **c.** background-color
   - **d.** none of the above

10. Which HTML attribute associates a table data cell with a table header cell?
    - **a.** head
    - **b.** headers
    - **c.** align
    - **d.** rowspan

Hands-On Exercises

1. Write the HTML for a two-column table that contains the names of your friends and their birthdays. The first row of the table should span two columns and contain the following heading: Birthday List. Include at least two people in your table.

2. Write the HTML for a three-column table to describe the courses you are taking this semester. The columns should contain the course number, course name, and instructor name. The first row of the table should use th tags and contain descriptive headings for the columns. Use the table row grouping tags <thead> and <tbody> in your table.

3. Use CSS to configure a table that has a border around both the entire table and the table cells. Write the HTML to create a table with three rows and two columns. The cell in the first column of each row will contain one of the following terms: HTML5, XML, and XHTML. The corresponding cell in the second column of each row will contain a definition of the term.

4. Review the web page you created in Hands-On Practice 9.1 and create a new version that uses embedded styles to configure CSS properties instead of the obsolete HTML border, cellpadding, and cellspacing attributes. Save the file as table4css.html.

5. Review the web page you created in Hands-On Practice 9.2 and create a new version that uses embedded styles to configure CSS properties instead of the obsolete HTML border, cellpadding, and cellspacing attributes. Save the file as table6css.html.

6. Create a web page about your favorite sports team with a two-column table that lists the positions and starting players. Use embedded CSS to style the table border, background color, and center the table on the web page. Place an e-mail link to yourself in the footer area. Save the file as sport9.html.

7. Create a web page about your favorite movie that uses a two-column table containing details about the movie. Use embedded CSS to style the table border and background color. Include the following in the table:

   ▪ Title of the movie
   ▪ Director or producer
   ▪ Leading actor
   ▪ Leading actress
   ▪ Rating (R, PG-13, PG, G, NR)
   ▪ A brief description of the movie
   ▪ An absolute link to a review about the movie

   Place an e-mail link to yourself on the web page. Save the page as movie9.html.

Focus on Web Design

Good artists view and analyze many paintings. Good writers read and evaluate many books. Similarly, good web designers view and scrutinize many web pages. Surf the Web and find two web pages—one that is appealing to you and one that is unappealing to you. Print out each page. Create a web page that answers the following questions for each of your examples:

   a. What is the URL of the website?
   b. Does this page use tables? If so, for what purpose—page layout, organization of information, or another reason?
   c. Does this page use CSS? If so, for what purpose—page layout, text and color configuration, or another reason?
   d. Is this page appealing or unappealing? List three reasons for your answer.
   e. If this page is unappealing, what would you do to improve it?

PACIFIC TRAILS RESORT CASE STUDY ————————

In this chapter's case study you will use the Pacific Trails existing website (Chapter 8) as a starting point and add an informational table to the Yurts page on the Pacific Trails website. Your new page will be similar to Figure 9.14 when you have completed this case study.

Step 1: Create a folder called ch9pacific to contain your Pacific Trails Resort website files. Copy the files from the Chapter 8 Case Study ch8pacific folder.

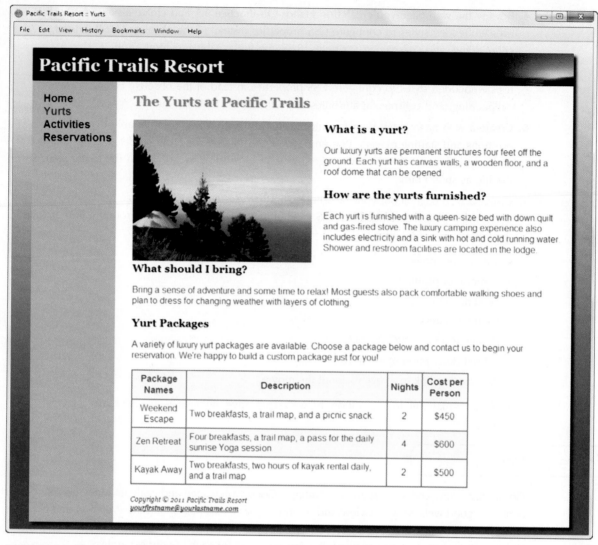

FIGURE 9.14   The new Pacific Trails Yurts page.

Step 2:   Configure the CSS. You will add styles to configure the table on the Yurts page. Launch a text editor and open the pacific.css external style sheet file.

- **Configure the table.** Code a new style rule for the `table` element selector that configures a centered table with a 1-pixel solid blue border (#3399cc), 600 pixel width, and no cellspacing (use `border-spacing: 0;`).

- **Configure the table cells.** Code a new style rule for the `td` and `th` element selectors that configures 5 pixels of padding and a 1-pixel solid blue border (#3399cc).

- **Center the td content.** Code a new style rule for the `td` element selector that centers text (use `text-align: center;`).

- **Configure the .text class.** Notice that the content in the table data cells that contain the text description is not centered. Code a new style rule for a class named `text` that will override the td style rule and left-align the text (use `text-align: left;`).

- **Configure alternate-row background color.** The table looks more appealing if the rows have alternate background colors but is still readable without them. Apply the :nth-of-type CSS3 pseudo-class to configure the odd table rows with a light blue background color (#F5FAFC).

Save the pacific.css file.

Step 3: Update the Yurts Page. Open the yurts.html page for the Pacific Trails Resort website in a text editor.

- Add a blank line above the footer div. Configure a h3 element with the following text: "Yurt Packages".
- Below the new h3 element, configure a paragraph with the following text:
  A variety of luxury yurt packages are available. Choose a package below and contact us to begin your reservation. We're happy to build a custom package just for you!
- You are ready to configure the table. Position your cursor on a blank line under the paragraph and code a table with four rows and four columns. Use the table, th, and td elements. Assign the td elements that contain the detailed descriptions to the class named text. The content for the table is as follows.

Package Name	Description	Nights	Cost per Person
Weekend Escape	Two breakfasts, a trail map, and a picnic snack.	2	$450
Zen Retreat	Four breakfasts, a trail map, a pass for the daily sunrise Yoga session.	4	$600
Kayak Away	Two breakfasts, two hours of kayak rental daily, and a trail map.	2	$500

Save your yurts.html file. Launch a browser and test your new page. It should look similar to Figure 9.14.

CHAPTER 10

Form Basics

Forms are used for many purposes all over the Web. They are used by search engines to accept keywords and by online stores to process e-commerce shopping carts. Websites use forms to help with a variety of functions—accepting visitor feedback, encouraging visitors to send a news story to a friend or colleague, collecting e-mail addresses for a newsletter, and accepting order information. This chapter introduces a very powerful tool for web developers—forms that accept information from web page visitors.

You'll learn how to . . .

- Describe common uses of forms on web pages
- Create forms on web pages using the form, input, textarea, and select elements
- Associate form controls and groups using label, fieldset, and legend elements
- Use CSS to style a form

- Describe the features and common uses of server-side processing
- Invoke server-side processing to handle form data
- Configure new HTML5 form controls including the email, URL, datalist, range, spinner, and calendar controls

Form Overview

Every time you use a search engine, place an order, or join an online mailing list, you use a form. A **form** is an HTML element that contains and organizes objects called **form controls**—such as text boxes, check boxes, and buttons—that can accept information from website visitors.

FIGURE 10.1 The search form on Google's home page.

For example, you may have used Google's search form (Figure 10.1) many times but never thought about how it works. The form is quite simple; it contains just three form controls—the text box that accepts the keywords used in the search, and two buttons. The "Google Search" button submits the form and invokes a process to search the Google databases to display a results page. The whimsical "I'm Feeling Lucky" button submits the form and displays the top page for your keywords.

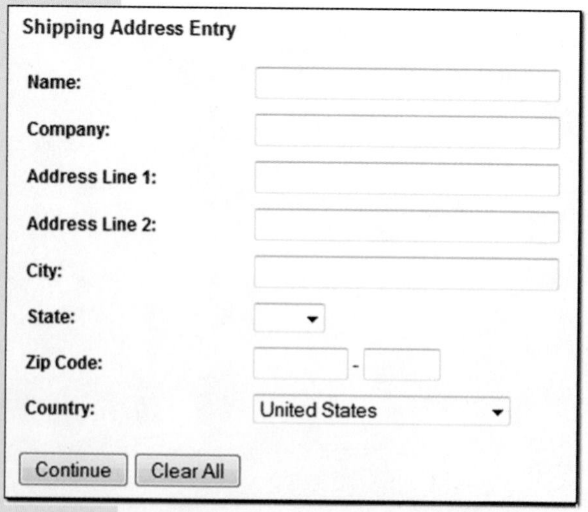

FIGURE 10.2 This form accepts order information.

Figure 10.2 shows a more detailed form, used to enter shipping information at irs.gov. This form contains text boxes to accept information such as name and address. Select lists are used to capture information with a limited number of correct values, such as state and country information. When a visitor clicks the continue button, the form information is submitted and the ordering process continues.

Whether a form is used to search for web pages or to place an order, the form alone cannot do all the processing. The form needs to invoke a program or script on the server in order to search a database or record an order. There are usually two components of a form:

1. The HTML form itself, which is the web page user interface

2. The server-side processing, which works with the form data and sends e-mail, writes to a text file, updates a database, or performs some other type of processing on the server

The Form Element

Now that you have a basic understanding of what forms do, let's focus on the HTML to create a form. The **form element** contains a form on a web page. The `<form>` tag specifies the beginning of a form area. The closing `</form>` tag specifies the end of a form area. There can be multiple forms on a web page, but they cannot be nested inside each other. The form element can be configured with attributes that specify what server-side program or file will process the form, how the form information will be sent to the server, and the name of the form. These attributes are listed in Table 10.1.

Attribute	Value	Purpose
`action`	URL or file name/path of server-side processing script	Required; indicates where to send the form information when the form is submitted; mailto:youre-mailaddress will launch the visitor's default e-mail application to send the form information
`autocomplete`	on	HTML5 attribute; default value; browser will use autocompletion to fill form fields
	off	HTML5 attribute; browser will not use autocompletion to fill form fields
`id`	Alphanumeric, no spaces; the value must be unique and not used for other id values on the same web page document	Optional; provides a unique identifier for the form
`method`	get	Default value; the value of `get` causes the form data to be appended to the URL and sent to the web server
	post	The `post` method is more private and transmits the form data in the body of the HTTP response; this method is preferred by the W3C
`name`	Alphanumeric, no spaces, begins with a letter; choose a form name value that is descriptive but short; for example, OrderForm is better than Form1 or WidgetsRUsOrderForm	Optional; names the form so that it can be easily accessed by client-side scripting languages, such as JavaScript, to edit and verify the form information before the server-side processing is invoked

TABLE 10.1 Attributes of the Form Element

For example, to configure a form with the name of order, using the post method, and invoking a script called demo.php on your web server, the code is

```
<form name="order" method="post" id="order" action="demo.php">
. . . form controls go here . . .
</form>
```

Form Controls

The purpose of a form is to gather information from a web page visitor; form controls are the objects that accept the information. Types of form controls include text boxes, scrolling text boxes, select lists, radio buttons, check boxes, and buttons. HTML5 offers new form controls including those customized for e-mail addresses, URLs, dates, times, numbers, and even date selection. HTML elements that configure form controls will be introduced in the following sections.

Text Box

Sample Text Box

E-mail: [   ]

FIGURE 10.3 The `<input>` tag with type="text" configures this form element.

The **input element** is a stand-alone tag that is used to configure several different types of form controls. The input element is coded as `<input>` when using HTML5 syntax and as `<input />` when using XHTML syntax. Use the `type` attribute to specify the type of form control that the browser should display. The `<input>` tag with `type="text"` configures a text box. The **text box** form control accepts text or numeric information such as names, e-mail addresses, phone numbers, and other text. A sample text box is shown in Figure 10.3. The code for the text box is shown below.

```
E-mail: <input type="text" name="email" id="email">
```

Common input element attributes for text boxes are listed in Table 10.2. Several attributes are new in HTML5. The new **required attribute** is exciting because it will cause supporting browsers to perform form validation. Browsers that support the HTML5 required attribute will automatically verify that information has been entered in the text box and display an error message when the condition is not met. A code sample is

```
E-mail: <input type="text" name="email" id="email" required="required">
```

FIGURE 10.4 The Firefox 4 browser displayed an error message.

Figure 10.4 shows an error message automatically generated by Firefox 4 that displayed after the user clicked the form's submit button without entering information in the required text. Browsers that do not support HTML5 or the required attribute will ignore the attribute.

Quick Tip

Although web designers are enthusiastic about the `required` attribute and other new form processing functions offered by HTML5, it will be some time before all browsers support these new features. In the meantime, be aware that verification and validation of form information also must be done the old-fashioned way—with client-side or server-side scripting.

Attribute	Value	Usage
type	text	Configures the text box
name	Alphanumeric, no spaces, begins with a letter	Names the form element so that it can be easily accessed by client-side scripting languages (such as JavaScript) or by server-side processing; the name should be unique
id	Alphanumeric, no spaces, begins with a letter	Provides a unique identifier for the form element
size	Numeric	Configures the width of the text box as displayed by the browser; if size is omitted, the browser displays the text box with its own default size
maxlength	Numeric	Configures the maximum length of data accepted by the text box
value	Text or numeric characters	Assigns an initial value to the text box that is displayed by the browser; accepts information typed in the text box; this value can be accessed by client-side scripting languages and by server-side processing
disabled	disabled	Form control is disabled
readonly	readonly	Form control is for display; cannot be edited
autocomplete	on	HTML5 attribute; default; browser will use autocompletion to fill the form control
	off	HTML5 attribute; browser will not use autocompletion to fill the form control.
autofocus	autofocus	HTML5 attribute; browser places cursor in the form control and sets focus.
list	Datalist element id value	HTML5 attribute; associates the form control with a datalist element
placeholder	Text or numeric characters	HTML5 attribute; brief information intended to assist the user
required	required	HTML5 attribute; browser verifies entry of information before submitting the form
accesskey	Keyboard character	Configures a hot key for the form control
tabindex	Numeric	Configures the tab order of the form control

TABLE 10.2 Common Input Element Attributes

Why use both the name and id attributes on form controls?

The name attribute names the form element so that it can be easily accessed by client-side scripting languages such as JavaScript or by server-side processing languages such as PHP. The value given to a name attribute for a form element should be unique for that form. The id attribute is included for use with CSS and scripting. The value of the id attribute should be unique to the entire web page document that contains the form.

Typically, the values assigned to the name and id attribute on a particular form element are the same.

Submit Button and Reset Button

The Submit Button

The **submit button** form control is used to submit the form. When clicked, it triggers the action method on the `<form>` tag and causes the browser to send the form data (the name and value pairs for each form control) to the web server. The web server will invoke the server-side processing program or script listed on the form's action property.

The `<input>` tag with `type="submit"` configures a submit button. For example,

```
<input type="submit">
```

The Reset Button

The **reset button** form control is used to reset the form fields to their initial values. A reset button does not submit the form.

The `<input>` tag with `type="reset"` configures a reset button. For example,

```
<input type="reset">
```

Sample Form

A form with a text box, a submit button, and a reset button is shown in Figure 10.5. Common attributes for submit buttons and reset buttons are listed in Table 10.3.

FIGURE 10.5 The form contains a text box, a submit button, and a reset button.

Attribute	Value	Usage
type	submit	Configures a submit button
	reset	Configures a reset button
name	Alphanumeric, no spaces, begins with a letter	Names the form element so that it can be easily accessed by client-side scripting languages (such as JavaScript) or by server-side processing; the name should be unique
id	Alphanumeric, no spaces, begins with a letter	Provides a unique identifier for the form element
value	Text or numeric characters	Configures the text displayed on the button; a submit button displays text "Submit Query" by default; a reset button displays "Reset" by default
accesskey	Keyboard character	Configures a hot key for the form control
tabindex	Numeric	Configures the tab order of the form control

TABLE 10.3 Common Attributes for Submit Buttons and Reset Buttons

HANDS-ON PRACTICE 10.1 ———————————

You will code a form in this Hands-On Practice. To get started, launch a text editor and open the template file located at chapter1/template.html in the student files. Save the file with the name form1.html. You will create a web page with a form similar to the example in Figure 10.6.

FIGURE 10.6 The text on the submit button says, "Sign Me Up!"

1. Modify the title element to display the text "Form Example".
2. Configure an h1 element with the text "Join Our Newsletter".
3. You are ready to configure the form area. A form begins with the form element. Place your cursor on a blank line under the heading you just added and type in a `<form>` tag as follows:

   ```
   <form method="get">
   ```

   As you read through the chapter you will find that a number of attributes can be used with the `<form>` element. In your first form, we are using the minimal HTML needed to create the form.

4. To create the form control for the visitor's e-mail address to be entered, type the following code on a blank line below the form element:

   ```
   E-mail: <input type="text" name="email" id="email"><br><br>
   ```

   This places the text "E-mail:" in front of the text box used to enter the visitor's e-mail address. The input element has a `type` attribute with the value of `text` that causes the browser to display a text box. The `name` attribute assigns the name `email` to the information entered into the text box (the `value`) and could be used by server-side processing. The `id` attribute uniquely identifies the element on the page. The `<br>` elements configure line breaks.

5. Now you are ready to add the submit button to the form on the next line. Add a `value` attribute set to "Sign Me Up!":

   ```
   <input type="submit" value="Sign Me Up!">
   ```

   This causes the browser to display a button with "Sign Me Up!" instead of the default value of "Submit Query".

6. Add a blank space after the submit button and code a reset button:

   ```
   <input type="reset">
   ```

7. Next, code the closing form tag:

   ```
   </form>
   ```

Save your form1.html file. Test your page in a browser. It should look similar to the page shown in Figure 10.6.

You can compare your work with the solution found in the student files (chapter10/form1.html) folder. Try entering some information into your form. Try clicking the submit button. Don't worry if the form redisplays but nothing seems to happen when you click the button—you haven't configured this form to work with any server-side processing. Connecting forms to server-side processing is demonstrated later in this chapter. The next sections will introduce you to more form controls.

———————————————————————————————— ∎

Check Box and Radio Button

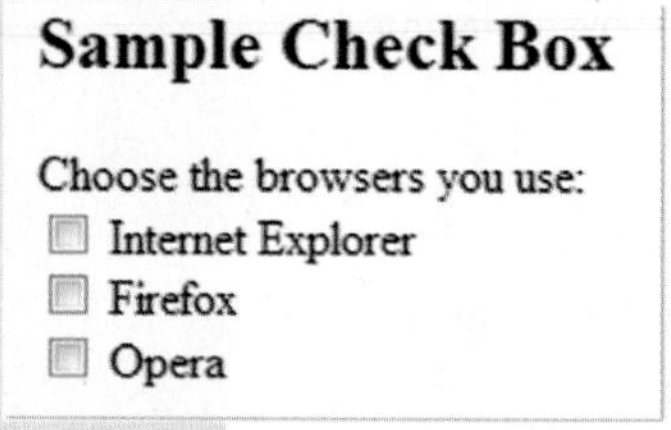

Sample Check Box

Choose the browsers you use:
- ☐ Internet Explorer
- ☐ Firefox
- ☐ Opera

FIGURE 10.7 Check box.

The Check Box

The **check box** form control allows the user to select one or more of a group of pre-determined items. The `<input>` tag with `type="checkbox"` configures a check box. Figure 10.7 shows an example with several check boxes—note that more than one check box can be selected by the user. Common check box attributes are listed in Table 10.4. The HTML is

```
Choose the browsers you use: <br>
<input type="checkbox" name="IE" id="IE" value="yes">Internet Explorer<br>
<input type="checkbox" name="Firefox" id="Firefox" value="yes">Firefox<br>
<input type="checkbox" name="Opera" id="Opera" value="yes"> Opera<br>
```

Attribute	Value	Usage
type	checkbox	Configures the check box
name	Alphanumeric, no spaces, begins with a letter	Names the form element so that it can be easily accessed by client-side scripting languages or by server-side processing; the name of each check box should be unique
id	Alphanumeric, no spaces, begins with a letter	Provides a unique identifier for the form element
checked	checked	Configures the check box to be checked by default when displayed by the browser
value	Text or numeric characters	Assigns a value to the check box that is triggered when the check box is checked; this value can be accessed by client-side and by server-side processing
disabled	disabled	Form control is disabled and will not accept information
autofocus	autofocus	HTML5 attribute; browser places cursor in the form control and sets focus
required	required	HTML5 attribute; browser verifies entry of information before submitting the form
accesskey	Keyboard character	Configures a hot key for the form control
tabindex	Numeric	Configures the tab order of the form control

TABLE 10.4 Common Check Box Attributes

The Radio Button

The **radio button** form control allows the user to select exactly one (and only one) choice from a group of predetermined items. Each radio button in a group is given the same `name` attribute and a unique `value` attribute. Because the `name` attribute is the same, the elements are identified as part of a group by the browsers and only one may be selected.

The `<input>` tag with `type="radio"` configures a radio button. Figure 10.8 shows an example with a radio button group—note that only one radio button can be selected at a time by the user. Common radio button attributes are listed in Table 10.5. The HTML is

Sample Radio Button

Select your favorite browser:
- ○ Internet Explorer
- ○ Firefox
- ○ Opera

FIGURE 10.8 Use radio buttons when only one choice is an appropriate response.

```
Select your favorite browser:<br>
<input type="radio" name="favbrowser" id="favIE" value="IE"> Internet Explorer<br>
<input type="radio" name="favbrowser" id="favFirefox" value="Firefox"> Firefox<br>
<input type="radio" name="favbrowser" id="favOpera" value="Opera"> Opera<br>
```

Notice that all the `name` attributes have the same value: `favbrowser`. Radio buttons with the same `name` attribute are treated as a group by the browser. Each radio button in the same group can be uniquely identified by its `value` attribute.

Attribute	Value	Usage
`type`	`radio`	Configures the radio button
`name`	Alphanumeric, no spaces, begins with a letter	Required; all radio buttons in a group must have the same `name`; names the form element so that it can be easily accessed by client-side scripting languages or by server-side processing
`id`	Alphanumeric, no spaces, begins with a letter	Provides a unique identifier for the form element
`checked`	`checked`	Configures the radio button to be selected by default when displayed by the browser
`value`	Text or numeric characters	Assigns a value to the radio button that is triggered when the radio button is selected; this should be a unique value for each radio button in a group; this value can be accessed by client-side and by server-side processing
`disabled`	`disabled`	Form control is disabled and will not accept information
`autofocus`	`autofocus`	HTML5 attribute; browser places cursor in the form control and sets focus
`required`	`required`	HTML5 attribute; browser verifies entry of information before submitting the form
`accesskey`	Keyboard character	Configures a hot key for the form control
`tabindex`	Numeric	Configures the tab order of the form control

TABLE 10.5 Common Radio Button Attributes

Hidden Field and Password Box

The Hidden Field

The **hidden field** form control stores text or numeric information, but it is not visible in the browser viewport. Hidden fields can be accessed by both client-side and server-side scripting.

The `<input>` tag with `type="hidden"` configures a hidden field. Common hidden field attributes are listed in Table 10.6.

The HTML to create a hidden form control with the `name` attribute set to "sendto" and the `value` attribute set to an e-mail address as follows:

```
<input type="hidden" name="sendto" id="sendto" value="order@site.com">
```

Attribute	Value	Usage
type	hidden	Configures the hidden form element
name	Alphanumeric, no spaces, begins with a letter	Names the form element so that it can be easily accessed by client-side scripting languages (such as JavaScript) or by server-side processing; the name should be unique
id	Alphanumeric, no spaces, begins with a letter	Provides a unique identifier for the form element
value	Text or numeric characters	Assigns a value to the hidden control; this value can be accessed by client-side scripting languages and by server-side processing
disabled	disabled	Form control is disabled

TABLE 10.6 Common Hidden Field Attributes

The Password Box

The **password box** form control is similar to the text box, but it is used to accept information that must be hidden as it is entered, such as a password. The `<input>` tag with `type="password"` configures a password box.

When the user types information in a password box, asterisks (or another symbol, depending on the browser) are displayed instead of the characters that have been typed, as shown in Figure 10.9. This hides the information from someone looking over the shoulder of the person typing. The actual characters typed are sent to the server, and the information is not really secret or hidden. Common password box attributes are listed in Table 10.7.

The HTML is

```
Password: <input type="password" name="pword" id="pword">
```

Sample Password Box

Password: ●●●●●●●

FIGURE 10.9 The characters secret9 were typed, but the browser displays ******* (Note: Your browser may use a different symbol, such as an asterisk, to hide the characters.)

Attribute	Value	Usage
type	password	Configures the password box
name	Alphanumeric, no spaces, begins with a letter	Names the form element so that it can be easily accessed by client-side scripting languages or by server-side processing; the name should be unique.
id	Alphanumeric, no spaces, begins with a letter	Provides a unique identifier for the form element
size	Numeric	Configures the width of the password box as displayed by the browser; if size is omitted, the browser displays the password box with its own default size
maxlength	Numeric	Optional; configures the maximum length of data accepted by the password box
value	Text or numeric characters	Assigns an initial value to the text box that is displayed by the browser; accepts the information typed in the password box; This value can be accessed by client-side and by server-side processing
disabled	disabled	Form control is disabled
readonly	readonly	Form control is for display; cannot be edited
autocomplete	on	HTML5 attribute; default; browser will use autocompletion to fill the form control
	off	HTML5 attribute; browser will not use autocompletion to fill the form control.
autofocus	autofocus	HTML5 attribute; browser places cursor in the form control and sets focus.
placeholder	Text or numeric characters	HTML5 attribute; brief information intended to assist the user
required	required	HTML5 attribute; browser verifies entry of information before submitting the form
accesskey	Keyboard character	Configures a hot key for the form control
tabindex	Numeric	Configures the tab order of the form control

TABLE 10.7 Common Password Box Attributes

Textarea Element

Sample Scrolling Text Box

Comments:

```
Enter your comments here
```

FIGURE 10.10   Scrolling text box.

The **scrolling text box** form control accepts free-form comments, questions, or descriptions. The **textarea element** configures a scrolling text box. The `<textarea>` tag denotes the beginning of the scrolling text box. The closing `</textarea>` tag denotes the end of the scrolling text box. Text contained between the tags will display in the scrolling text box area. A sample scrolling text box is shown in Figure 10.10. Common attributes are listed in Table 10.8. The HTML is

```
Comments:<br>
<textarea name="comments" id="comments" cols="40" rows="2">Enter your comments here</textarea>
```

Attribute	Value	Usage
name	Alphanumeric, no spaces, begins with a letter	Names the form element so that it can be easily accessed by client-side scripting languages (such as JavaScript) or by server-side processing; the name should be unique.
id	Alphanumeric, no spaces, begins with a letter	Provides a unique identifier for the form element
cols	Numeric	Required; configures the width in character columns of the scrolling text box; if cols is omitted, the browser displays the scrolling text box with its own default width
rows	Numeric	Required; configures the height in rows of the scrolling text box; if rows is omitted, the browser displays the scrolling text box with its own default height
maxlength	Numeric	Maximum number of characters accepted
disabled	disabled	Form control is disabled
readonly	readonly	Form control is for display; cannot be edited
autofocus	autofocus	HTML5 attribute; browser places cursor in the form control and sets focus
placeholder	Text or numeric characters	HTML5 attribute; brief information intended to assist the user
required	required	HTML5 attribute; browser verifies entry of information before submitting the form
wrap	hard or soft	HTML5 attribute; configures line breaks within the information entered
accesskey	Keyboard character	Configures a hot key for the form control
tabindex	Numeric	Configures the tab order of the form control

TABLE 10.8   Common Scrolling Text Box Attributes

HANDS-ON PRACTICE 10.2

In this Hands-On Practice you will create a contact form with the following form controls: a First Name text box, a Last Name text box, an E-mail text box, and a Comments scrolling text box. You'll use the form you created in Hands-On Practice 10.1 (see Figure 10.6) as a starting point. Launch a text editor and open the form1.html file located at chapter10/form1.html in the student files. Save the file with the name form2.html. The new contact form is shown in Figure 10.11.

FIGURE 10.11 A typical contact form.

1. Modify the title element to display the text "Contact Form".

2. Configure the h1 element with the text "Contact Us".

3. A form control for the e-mail address is already coded. Refer to Figure 10.11 and note that you'll need to add text box form controls for the first name and last name above the e-mail form control. Position your cursor after the opening form tag and press the enter key twice to create two blank lines. Add the following code to accept the name of your web page visitor:

```
First Name: <input type="text" name="fname" id="fname"><br><br>
Last Name: <input type="text" name="lname" id="lname"><br><br>
```

4. Now you are ready to add the scrolling text box form control to the form using a `<textarea>` tag on a new line below the e-mail form control. The code is

```
Comments:<br>
<textarea name="comments" id="comments"></textarea><br><br>
```

Save your file and display in a browser to view the default display of a scrolling text box. Note that this default display will differ by browser. At the time this was written, Internet Explorer always rendered a vertical scroll bar, but the Firefox browser only rendered scroll bars once enough text was entered to require them. The writers of browser rendering engines keep the lives of web designers interesting!

5. Let's configure the `rows` and `cols` attributes for the scrolling text box form control. Modify the `<textarea>` tag and set `rows="4"` and `cols="40"` as follows:

```
Comments:<br>
<textarea name="comments" id="comments" rows="4" cols="40"></textarea><br><br>
```

6. Next, modify the text displayed on the submit button. Set the value attribute to "Contact". Save your form2.html file. Test your page in a browser. It should look similar to the page shown in Figure 10.11.

You can compare your work with the solution found in the student files (chapter10/form2.html) folder. Try entering some information into your form. Try clicking the submit button. Don't worry if the form redisplays but nothing seems to happen when you click the button—you haven't configured this form to work with any server-side processing. Connecting forms to server-side processing is demonstrated later in this chapter.

Format a Form with a Table

FIGURE 10.12 The form controls are well aligned.

The form in Figure 10.11 (refer to the previous section) looks a little "messy"—and you might be wondering how that can be improved.

Back in the day, web designers always used a table to configure the design of form elements—typically placing the text labels and form field elements in separate table data cells. An example of this technique is shown in Figure 10.12 and found in the student files at chapter10/formtable.html.

The HTML is

```
<form method="get">
<table border="0">
 <tr>
  <td align="right">First Name: </td>
  <td><input type="text" name="fmail" id="fmail"></td>
 </tr>
 <tr>
  <td align="right">Last Name:</td>
  <td><input type="text" name="lmail" id="lmail"></td>
 </tr>
 <tr>
  <td align="right">E-mail:</td>
  <td><input type="text" name="email" id="email"></td>
 </tr>
 <tr>
  <td align="right" valign="top">Comments:</td>
  <td><textarea name="comments" id="comments" rows="4" cols="40"></textarea></td>
 </tr>
 <tr>
  <td> </td>
  <td><input type="submit" value="Contact">   <input type="reset"></td>
 </tr>
</table>
</form>
```

HTML Tables Meet CSS Properties

Another approach is to organize a form with an HTML table but configure it with CSS rather than with HTML attributes. While this is not a completely tableless design, using a table to configure a small portion of a page that otherwise uses CSS is a method to consider. It would be best to reserve the use of a table for pure tabular data—such as price lists and budgets. However, the purpose of this example is to show how CSS can be used to streamline even the HTML needed by a table. Later in the chapter you'll explore how to configure the layout and styling of a form with only CSS—without using an HTML table.

Figure 10.13 shows a web page (see chapter10/formtable2.html in the student files) with the form area coded with a table but styled with CSS.

FIGURE 10.13 This page uses a table styled with CSS.

The CSS to style the table configures table and td element selectors with properties that would otherwise be defined with HTML attributes. A class was created to configure the table cells that contained the text labels for right and top alignment. The CSS is as follows:

```
table { background-color: #eaeaea; width: 20em;  font-family: Arial, sans-serif; }
td { padding: 5px; }
.myLabel { text-align: right; vertical-align: top; }
```

In the following HTML code, the `<table>` tag has no attributes since it is styled with CSS. The only attribute on the `<td>` tags is a class attribute to render the myLabel class styles:

```
<form method="post">
<table>
 <tr>
  <td class="myLabel">Name:</td>
  <td><input type="text" name="Name" id="Name"></td>
 </tr>
 <tr>
  <td class="MyLabel">E-mail:</td>
  <td><input type="text" name="myEmail" id="myEmail"></td>
 </tr>
 <tr>
  <td class="MyLabel">Comments:</td>
  <td><textarea name="myComments" id="myComments" rows="2"
cols="20"></textarea></td>
 </tr>
 <tr>
  <td> </td>
   <td><input type="submit" value="Submit"></td>
 </tr>
</table>
</form>
```

Select Element and Option Element

The **select list** form control shown in Figures 10.14 and 10.15 is also known by several other names, including select box, drop-down list, drop-down box, and option box. A select list is configured with one select element and multiple option elements.

The Select Element

The **select element** contains and configures the select list form control. The `<select>` tag denotes the beginning of the select list. The closing `</select>` tag denotes the end of the select list. Attributes configure the number of options to display and whether more than one option item may be selected. Common attributes are listed in Table 10.9.

Attribute	Value	Usage
name	Alphanumeric, no spaces, begins with a letter	Names the form element so that it can be easily accessed by client-side scripting languages (such as JavaScript) or by server-side processing; the name should be unique
id	Alphanumeric, no spaces, begins with a letter	Provides a unique identifier for the form element
size	Numeric	Configures the number of choices the browser will display; if set to 1, element functions as a drop-down list (see Figure 10.14); scroll bars are automatically added by the browser if the number of options exceeds the space allowed
multiple	multiple	Configures a select list to accept more than one choice; by default, only one choice can be made from a select list
disabled	disabled	Form control is disabled
tabindex	Numeric	Configures the tab order of the form control

TABLE 10.9 Common Select Element Attributes

The Option Element

The **option element** contains and configures an option item displayed in the select list form control. The `<option>` tag denotes the beginning of the option item. The closing `</option>` tag denotes the end of option item. Attributes configure the value of the option and whether they are preselected. Common attributes are listed in Table 10.10.

Attribute	Value	Usage
value	Text or numeric characters	Assigns a value to the option; this value can be accessed by client-side and by server-side processing
selected	selected	Configures an option to be initially selected when displayed by a browser
disabled	disabled	Form control is disabled

TABLE 10.10 Common Option Element Attributes

The HTML for the select list in Figure 10.14 is

```
<select size="1" name="favbrowser" id="favbrowser">
  <option>Select your favorite browser</option>
  <option value="Internet Explorer">Internet Explorer</option>
  <option value="Firefox">Firefox</option>
  <option value="Opera">Opera</option>
</select>
```

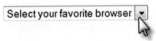

Select List: One Initial Visible Item

FIGURE 10.14 A select list with size set to 1 functions as a drop-down box when the arrow is clicked.

The HTML for the select list in Figure 10.15 is

```
<select size="4" name="jumpmenu" id="jumpmenu">
  <option value="index.html">Home</option>
  <option value="products.html">Products</option>
  <option value="services.html">Services</option>
  <option value="about.html">About</option>
  <option value="contact.html">Contact</option>
</select>
```

Select List: Four Items Visible

FIGURE 10.15 Since there are more than four choices, the browser displays a scroll bar.

Label Element

The **label element** is a container tag that associates a text description with a form control. This is helpful to visually challenged individuals using assistive technology such as a screen reader to match up the text descriptions on forms with their corresponding form controls. The label element also benefits individuals without fine motor control. Clicking anywhere on either a form control or its associated text label will set the cursor focus to the form control.

There are two different methods to associate a label with a form control.

1. The first method places the label element as a container around both the text description and the HTML form element. Notice that both the text label and the form control must be adjacent elements. The code is

   ```
   <label>E-mail: <input type="text" name="email" id="email"></label>
   ```

2. The second method uses the `for` attribute to associate the label with a particular HTML form element. This is more flexible and is does not require the text label and the form control to be adjacent. The code is

   ```
   <label for="email">E-mail: </label>
   <input type="text" name="email" id="email">
   ```

   Notice that the value of the **for attribute** on the label element is the same as the value of the `id` attribute on the input element. This creates the association between the text label and the form control. The input element uses both the `name` and `id` attributes for different purposes. The `name` attribute can be used by client-side and by server-side scripting. The `id` attribute creates an identifier that can be used by the label element, anchor element, and CSS selectors.

The label element does not display on the web page—it works behind the scenes to provide for accessibility.

HANDS-ON PRACTICE 10.3

In this Hands-On Practice you will add the label element to the text box and scrolling text area form controls on the form you created in Hands-On Practice 10.2 (see Figure 10.11) as a starting point. Launch a text editor and open the form2.html file located at chapter10/form2.html in the student files. Save the file with the name form3.html.

1. Locate the text box for the first name. Add a label element to wrap around the input tag as follows:

```
<label>First Name: <input type="text" name="fname" id="fname"></label>
```

2. Using the method shown previously, add a label element for the last name and e-mail form controls.

3. Configure a label element to contain the text "Comments". Associate the label with the scrolling text box form control. Sample code is

```
<label for="comments">Comments:</label><br>
<textarea name="comments" id="comments" rows="4" cols="40"></textarea>
```

Save your form3.html file. Test your page in a browser. It should look similar to the page shown in Figure 10.11—the label elements do not change the way the page displays, but a web visitor with physical challenges should find the form easier to use.

You can compare your work with the solution found in the student files (chapter10/form3.html) folder. Try entering some information into your form. Try clicking the submit button. Don't worry if the form redisplays but nothing seems to happen when you click the button—you haven't configured this form to work with any server-side processing. Connecting forms to server-side processing is demonstrated later in this chapter.

Fieldset Element and Legend Element

Fieldset and legend elements work together to visually group form controls together and increase the usability of the form.

The Fieldset Element

A technique that can be used to create a more visually pleasing form is to group elements of a similar purpose together using the **fieldset element**, which will cause the browser to render a visual cue, such as an outline or a border, around form elements grouped together within the fieldset. The `<fieldset>` tag denotes the beginning of the grouping. The closing `</fieldset>` tag denotes the end of the grouping.

The Legend Element

The **legend element** provides a text description for the fieldset grouping. The `<legend>` tag denotes the beginning of the label. The closing `</legend>` tag denotes the end of the text description.

The HTML to create the grouping shown in Figure 10.16 is

```
<fieldset>
    <legend>Billing Address</legend>
    <label>Street: <input type="text" name="street" id="street"
                size="54"></label><br><br>
    <label>City: <input type="text" name="city" id="city"></label>
    <label>State: <input type="text" name="state" id="state" maxlength="2"
                size="5"></label>
    <label>Zip: <input type="text" name="zip" id="zip" maxlength="5"
                size="5"></label>
</fieldset>
```

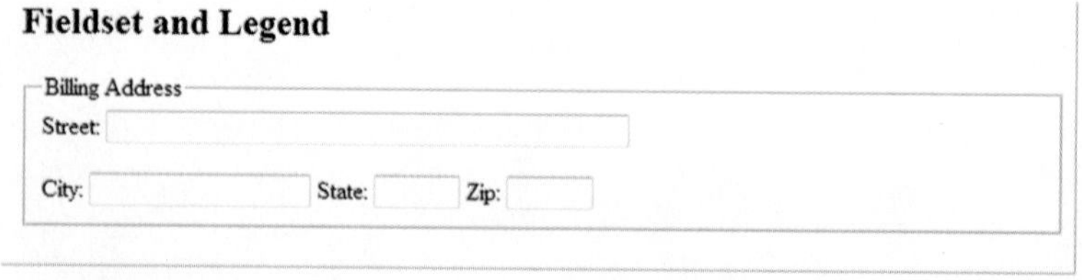

FIGURE 10.16 Form controls that are all related to a mailing address.

The grouping and visual effect of the fieldset element creates an organized and appealing web page containing a form. Using the fieldset and legend elements to group form controls enhances accessibility by organizing the controls both visually and semantically. The fieldset and legend elements can be accessed by screen readers and are useful tools to configure groups of radio buttons and check boxes on web pages.

A Look Ahead—Styling a Fieldset Group with CSS

The next section focuses on styling a form with CSS. But how about a quick preview?

Figures 10.17 and 10.16 show the same form elements, but the form in Figure 10.17 is styled with CSS— the same functionality with increased visual appeal. Access the example page at chapter10/form4.html in the student files. The style rules are

Fieldset and Legend Styled with CSS

Billing Address

Street: [   ]

City: [   ] State: [   ] Zip: [   ]

FIGURE 10.17 The fieldset, legend, and label elements are configured with CSS.

```
fieldset { width: 500px; border: 2px ridge #ff0000;
           font-family: Arial, sans-serif; padding: 10px;}
legend { font-family: Georgia, "Times New Roman", serif; font-weight: bold; }
label { padding-left: 10px; }
```

Accessibility and Forms

Using the HTML elements label, fieldset, and legend will increase the accessibility of your web forms. This makes it easier for individuals with vision and mobility challenges to use your form pages. An added benefit is that the use of label, fieldset, and legend elements may increase the readability and usability of the web form for all visitors. Be sure to include contact information (e-mail address and/or phone number) just in case a visitor is unable to submit your form successfully and requires additional assistance.

Some of your website visitors may have difficulty using the mouse and will access your form with a keyboard. The Tab key can be used to move from one form control to another. The default action for the Tab key within a form is to move to the next form control in the order in which the form controls are coded in the web page document. This is usually appropriate. However, if the tab order needs to be changed for a form, use the **tabindex attribute** on each form control.

Another technique that can make your form keyboard-friendly is the use of the **accesskey attribute** on form controls. Assigning accesskey a value of one of the characters (letter or number) on the keyboard will create a hot key that your website visitor can press to move the cursor immediately to a form control. Windows users will press the Alt key and the character key. Mac users will press the Ctrl key and the character key. When choosing accesskey values, avoid combinations that are already used by the operating system (such as Alt+F to display the File menu). Testing hot keys is crucial.

Style a Form with CSS

Many web developers cruise along using CSS for page layout until they need to code a form. As discussed in a previous section, tables (although usually avoided when coding CSS page layouts) have long been used to configure forms. This section will demonstrate a more modern approach—using CSS to style a form layout without using an HTML table.

Styling Forms with Only CSS

In this method, the CSS box model is used to create a series of boxes, as shown in Figure 10.18. The outermost box defines the form area. Other boxes indicate label elements, various form controls, and div elements. CSS is used to configure these components.

- The myForm id declares properties for the entire form area.
- The label element selector is the key to aligning the text—this selector is configured to float on the left with text aligned to right.
- The input and textarea element selectors are configured with a top margin.
- The mySubmit id configures the display of the submit button with declarations for the left margin and bottom padding.

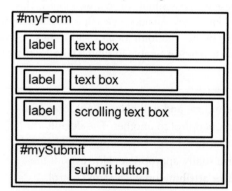

FIGURE 10.18   A sketch of the box model used to configure the form.

Figure 10.19 displays a web page with a form configured in this manner (see chapter10/formcss.html in the student files). As you view the following CSS and HTML, note the alignment of the text labels and form controls.

FIGURE 10.19 The layout and format of this form are configured with CSS.

The CSS is

```
#myForm { background-color: #eaeaea;
          font-family: Arial, sans-serif;
          width: 400px; }
label { float: left;
        width: 120px; clear: left;
        text-align: right;
        padding-right: 10px;
        margin-top: 10px; }
input, textarea { margin-top: 10px; }
#mySubmit { margin-left: 130px;
            padding-bottom: 10px; }
```

The HTML follows. Note the use of div elements to organize the form elements.

```
<form method="post" id="myForm">
 <div>
  <label for="myName">Name:</label>
  <input type="text" name="myName" id="myName">
 </div>
 <div>
  <label for="myEmail">E-mail:</label>
  <input type="text" name="myEmail" id="myEmail">
 </div>
 <div>
  <label for="myComments">Comments:</label>
  <textarea name="myComments" id="myComments"
  rows="2" cols="20"></textarea>
 </div>
 <div id="mySubmit">
  <input type="submit" value="Submit">
 </div>
</form>
```

This section provided you with a method to style a form with CSS. Testing the way that different browsers render the form is crucial.

As you've coded and displayed the forms in this chapter, you may have noticed that when you click the submit button, the form just redisplays—the form doesn't "do" anything. This is because there is no action attribute in the <form> tag. The next section focuses on the second component of using forms on web pages—server-side processing.

Server-Side Processing

Your web browser requests web pages and their related files from a web server. The web server locates the files and sends them to your web browser. Then the web browser renders the returned files and displays the requested web pages. Figure 10.20 illustrates the communication between the Web browser and the Web server.

Browser Request

Server Response

Web Client   **Web Server**

FIGURE 10.20   The web browser (client) communicates with the web server.

Sometimes a website needs more functionality than static web pages—possibly a site search, order form, e-mail list, database display, or other type of interactive, dynamic processing. This is when server-side processing is needed. Early web servers used a protocol called **Common Gateway Interface** (CGI) to provide this functionality. CGI is a protocol, or standard method, for a web server to pass a web page user's request (which is typically initiated through the use of a form) to an application program and to accept information to send to the user. The web server typically passes the form information to a small application program that is run by the operating system and processes the data, and it usually sends back a confirmation web page or message. Perl and C are popular programming languages for CGI applications.

Server-side scripting is a technology in which a server-side script is run on a web server to dynamically generate web pages. Examples of server-side scripting technologies include PHP, Ruby on Rails, Microsoft Active Server Pages, Adobe ColdFusion, Sun JavaServer Pages, and Microsoft.NET. Server-side scripting differs from CGI in that it uses **direct execution**—the script is run either by the web server itself or by an extension module to the web server.

A web page invokes server-side processing by either an attribute on a form or by a hyperlink—the URL of the script is used. Any form data that exists is passed to the script. The script completes its processing and may generate a confirmation or response web page with the requested information. When invoking a server-side script, the web developer and the server-side programmer must communicate about the form `method` **attribute** (`get` or `post`), form `action` **attribute** (URL of the server-side script), and any special form element control(s) expected by the server-side script. The `name` attribute and the `value` attribute associated with each form control are passed to the server-side script. The `name` attribute may be used as a variable name in the server-side processing.

Server-Side Processing Resources

Sources of Free Remote-Hosted Form Processing

If your web host provider does not support server-side processing, free remotely hosted scripts may be an option. Try out the free form processing offered by http://formbuddy.com, http://www.expressdb.com, or http://www.formmail.com.

Sources of Free Server-Side Scripts

To use free scripts, you need to have access to a web server that supports the language used by the script. Contact your web host provider to determine what is supported. Be aware that many free web host providers do not support server-side processing (you get what you pay for!). Visit http://scriptarchive.com and http://php.resourceindex.com for free scripts and related resources.

Privacy and Forms

A **privacy policy** lists the guidelines that you develop to protect the privacy of your visitors' information. Websites either indicate this policy on the form page itself or create a separate page that describes the privacy policy (and other company policies). For example, the order form page at mymoney.gov (http://mymoney.gov/mymoneyorder.shtml) indicates the following:

> "WE WILL NOT SHARE OR SELL ANY PERSONAL INFORMATION OBTAINED FROM YOU WITH ANY OTHER ORGANIZATION, UNLESS REQUIRED BY LAW TO DO SO."

If you browse popular sites such as Amazon.com or eBay.com you'll find links to their privacy policies (sometimes called a privacy notice) in the page footer area. The Better Business Bureau provides a sample privacy notice at http://www.bbbonline.org/privacy/sample_privacy.asp. Include a privacy notice in your site to inform your visitors how you plan to use the information they share with you.

Practice with a Form

HANDS-ON PRACTICE 10.4

In this Hands-On Practice you will modify the form page that you created earlier in this chapter, configuring the form so that it uses the post method to invoke a server-side script. Your computer must be connected to the Internet when you test your work. The post method is more secure than the get method because the post method does not pass the form information in the URL; it passes it in the entity-body of the HTTP Request, which makes it more private.

When using a server-side script you will need to obtain some information, or documentation, from the person or organization providing the script. You will need to know the location of the script, whether it requires the get or post method, whether it requires any specific names for the form controls, and whether it requires any hidden form elements. The action attribute is used on the `<form>` tag to invoke a server-side script. A server-side script has been created at http://webdevbasics.net/scripts/demo.php for students to use for this exercise. The documentation for the server-side script is listed in Table 10.11.

Script URL	http://webdevbasics.net/scripts/demo.php
Form method	`post`
Script purpose	This script will accept form input and display the form control names and values in a web page. This is a sample script for student assignments. It demonstrates that server-side processing has been invoked. A script used by an actual website would perform a function such as sending an e-mail message or updating a database.

TABLE 10.11 Server-Side Script Documentation

Launch a text editor and open the form3.html file you created in Hands-On Practice 10.3, also found in the student files (chapter10/form3.html). Modify the `<form>` tag by adding a method attribute with a value of "post" and an action attribute with a value of "http://webdevbasics.net/scripts/demo.php". The HTML for the revised `<form>` tag is

```
<form method="post" action="http://webdevbasics.net/scripts/demo.php">
```

Save your page as contact.html and test it in a browser. Your screen should look similar to Figure 10.10. Now you are ready to test your form. You must be connected to the Internet to test your form successfully. Enter information in the form controls and click the submit button. You should see a confirmation page similar to the one shown in Figure 10.21.

FIGURE 10.21   The server-side script has created this page in response to the form.

The demo.php script creates a web page that displays a message and the form information you entered. This confirmation page was created by the server-side script on the action attribute in the `<form>` tag. Writing scripts for server-side processing is beyond the scope of this textbook. However, if you are curious, visit http://webdevbasics.net/chapter10.html to see the source code for the demo. php script.

What should I do if nothing happened when I tested my form?

Try these troubleshooting hints:

- Verify that your computer is connected to the Internet.
- Verify the spelling of the script location in the action attribute.
- Recall that attention to detail is crucial!

HTML5 Text Form Controls

FIGURE 10.22 The Opera 11 browser displays an error message.

The E-mail Address Input Form Control

The **e-mail address** form control is similar to the text box. Its purpose is to accept information that must be in e-mail format, such as "DrMorris2010@gmail.com". The `<input>` element with `type="email"` configures an e-mail address form control. Only browsers that support the HTML5 email attribute value will verify the format of the information. Other browsers will treat this form control as a text box. Figure 10.22 (see chapter10/email.html in the student files) shows an error message displayed by Firefox 4 when text other than an e-mail address is entered. Note that the browser does not verify that the e-mail address actually exists—just that the text entered is in the correct format. The HTML is

```
<label for="email">E-mail:</label>
<input type="email" name="myEmail" id="myEmail">
```

FIGURE 10.23 The Firefox 4 browser displays an error message.

The URL Form Input Control

The **URL** form control is similar to the text box. It is intended to accept any type of URL or URI, such as http://webdevbasics.net". The `<input>` element with `type="url"` configures a URL form control. Only browsers that support the HTML5 url attribute value will verify the format of the information. Other browsers render this form control as a text box. Figure 10.23 (see chapter10/url.html in the student files) shows an error message displayed by Firefox 4 when text other than a URL is entered. Note that the browser does not verify that the URL actually exists—just that the text entered is in the correct format. The HTML is

```
<label for="myWebsite">Suggest a Website:</label>
<input type="url" name="myWebsite" id="myWebsite">
```

The Telephone Number Input Form Control

The **telephone number** form control is similar to the text box. Its purpose is to accept a telephone number. The `<input>` element with `type="tel"` configures a telephone number form control. An example is in the student files (chapter10/tel.html). Browsers that do not support `type="tel"` will render this form control as a text box. The HTML is

```
<label for="mobile">Mobile Number:</label>
<input type="tel" name="mobile" id="mobile">
```

The Search Input Form Control

The **search** form control is similar to the text box and is used to accept a search term. The `<input>` element with `type="search"` configures a search input form control. An example is in the student files (chapter10/search.html). Browsers that do not support `type="search"` will render this form control as a text box. The HTML is

```
<label for="keyword">Search:</label>
<input type="search" name="keyword" id="keyword">
```

Valid Attributes for HTML5 Text Form Controls

Attributes supported by the HTML5 text form controls are listed in Table 10.2.

How can I tell which browsers support the new HTML5 form elements?

There's no substitute for testing. With that in mind, several resources are listed below that provide information about browser support for new HTML5 elements:

- http://caniuse.com (*also CSS3 browser support information*)
- http://findmebyip.com/litmus (*also CSS3 browser support information*)
- http://html5readiness.com
- http://html5test.com
- http://www.standardista.com/html5

HTML5 Datalist Element

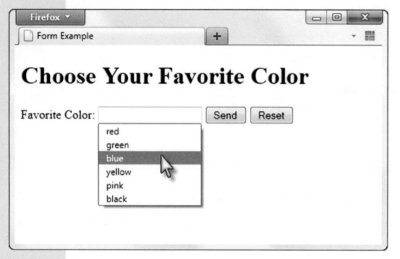

FIGURE 10.24 Firefox 4 displays the datalist form control.

Figure 10.24 shows the **datalist** form control in action. Notice how a selection of choices is offered to the user along with a text box for entry. The datalist is configured using three elements: an input element, the datalist element, and one or more option elements. Only browsers that support the HTML5 datalist element will display and process the datalist items. Other browsers ignore the datalist element and render the form control as a text box.

The source code for the datalist is available in the student files (chapter10/list.html). The HTML is

```
<label for="color">Favorite Color:</label>
<input type="text" name="color" id="color" list="colors">
   <datalist id="colors">
      <option value="red">
      <option value="green">
      <option value="blue">
      <option value="yellow">
      <option value="pink">
      <option value="black">
   </datalist>
```

Notice that the value of the **list** attribute on the input element is the same as the value of the id attribute on the datalist element. This creates the association between the text box and the datalist form control. One or more option elements can be used to offer predefined choices to your web page visitor. The option element's value attribute configures the text displayed in each list entry. The web page visitor can choose an option from the list (see Figure 10.24) or type directly in the text box, as shown in Figure 10.25.

FIGURE 10.25   The list disappeared when the user began typing in the text box.

The datalist form control offers a convenient way to offer choices yet provide for flexibility on a form. At the time this was written, only the Firefox 4 beta browser supported this new HTML5 element. Check out http://webdevbasics.net/chapter10.html for new developments on this intriguing form control.

Why should I learn about the new HTML5 form controls if they are not yet supported by all browsers?

The display and support of the new HTML5 form controls will vary by browser, but you really can use them right now! The new form controls offer increased usability for your web page visitors who have modern browsers. For example, some new form controls offer built-in browser edits and validation. Future web designers will probably take these features for granted some day, but you are right in the middle of this huge advance in web page coding—so now is a great time to become familiar with

FIGURE 10.26   Browsers that do not support the datalist form control display a text box.

these new elements. Finally, browsers that do not support the new input types will display them as text boxes and ignore unsupported attributes or elements. Figure 10.26 depicts the display of a datalist in the Google Chrome browser. Notice that, unlike Firefox 4, this version of the Chrome browser does not render the list—it only renders a text box.

HTML5 Slider and Spinner Controls

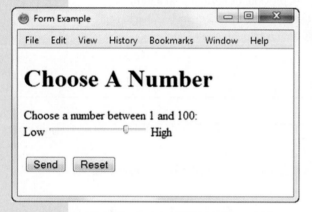

FIGURE 10.27 The Safari browser displays the range form control.

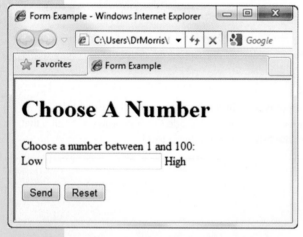

FIGURE 10.28 Internet Explorer 8 renders the range form control as a text box.

The Slider Input Form Control

The **slider** form control provides a visual, interactive user interface that accepts numerical information. The `<input>` element with `type="range"` configures a slider control in which a number within a specified range is chosen. The default range is from 1 to 100. Only browsers that support the HTML5 range attribute value will display the interactive slider control, shown in Figure 10.27 (see chapter10/range.html in the student files). Note the position of the slider in Figure 10.27; this resulted in the value 80 being chosen. The nondisplay of the value to the user may be a disadvantage of the slider control. Nonsupporting browsers render this form control as a text box, as shown in Figure 10.28.

The slider control accepts attributes listed in Tables 10.2 and 10.12. The min, max, and step attributes are new. Use the **min attribute** to configure the minimum range value. Use the **max attribute** to configure the maximum range value. Use the **step attribute** to configure a value for the step between values to be other than 1. The HTML for the slider control rendered in Figures 10.27 and 10.28 is shown below.

```
<label for="myChoice">Choose a number between 1 and 100:</label><br>
Low <input type="range" name="myChoice" id="myChoice"> High
```

The Spinner Input Form Control

The **spinner** form control displays an interface that accepts numerical information and provides feedback to the user. The <input> element with type="number" configures a spinner control in which the user can either type a number into the text box or select a number from a specified range. Only browsers that support the HTML5 number attribute value will display the interactive spinner control, shown in Figure 10.29 (see chapter10/spinner.html in the student files). Other browsers render this form control as a text box. Expect increased support in the future.

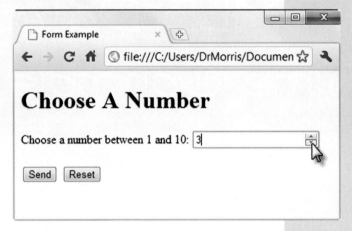

FIGURE 10.29 A spinner control displayed in the Google Chrome browser.

The spinner control accepts attributes listed in Tables 10.2 and 10.12. Use the min attribute to configure the minimum value. Use the max attribute to configure the maximum value. Use the step attribute to configure a value for the step between values to be other than 1. The HTML for the spinner control displayed in Figure 10.29 is

```
<label for="myChoice">Choose a number between 1 and 10:</label>
<input type="number" name="myChoice" id="myChoice" min="1" max="10">
```

Attribute	Value	Usage
max	Maximum value	HTML5 attribute for range, number, and date/time input controls; specifies a maximum value
min	Minimum value	HTML5 attribute for range, number, and date/time input controls; specifies a minimum value
step	Incremental step value	HTML5 attribute for range, number, and date/time input controls; specifies a value for incremental steps

TABLE 10.12 Additional Attributes for Slider, Spinner, and Date/Time Form Controls

HTML5 and Progressive Enhancement

Use HTML5 form elements with the concept of progressive enhancement in mind. Nonsupporting browsers will display text boxes in place of form elements that are not recognized. Supporting browsers will display and process the new form controls. This is progressive enhancement in action—everyone sees a usable form, and those using modern browsers benefit from enhanced features.

HTML5 Date and Time Controls

HTML5 provides a variety of date and time input form controls to accept date- and time-related information. Use the `<input>` element and configure the `type` attribute to specify a date or time control. Table 10.13 lists the HTML5 date and time controls.

Type Attribute Value	Purpose	Format
`date`	A date	YYYY-MM-DD Example: January 2, 2010, is represented by "20100102"
`datetime`	A date and time with time zone information; note that the time zone is indicated by the offset from UTC time	YYYY-MM-DDTHH:MM:SS-##:##Z Example: January 2, 2010, at exactly 9:58 AM Chicago time (CST) is represented by "2010-01-02T09:58:00-06:00Z"
`datetime-local`	A date and time without time zone information	YYYY-MM-DDTHH:MM:SS Example: January 2, 2010, at exactly 9:58 AM is represented by "2010-01-02T09:58:00"
`time`	A time without time zone information	HH:MM:SS Example: 1:34 PM is represented by "13:34"
`month`	A year and month	YYYY-MM Example: January, 2011, is represented by "2011-01"
`week`	A year and week	YYYY-W##, where ## represents the week in the year Example: The third week in 2010 is represented by "2010-W03"

TABLE 10.13 Date and Time Controls

The form in Figure 10.30 (see chapter10/date.html in the student files) uses the `<input>` element with `type="date"` to configure a calendar control with which the user can select a date.

The HTML for the date control displayed in Figure 10.30 is

```
<label for="myDate">Choose a Date</label>
<input type="date" name="myDate" id="myDate">
```

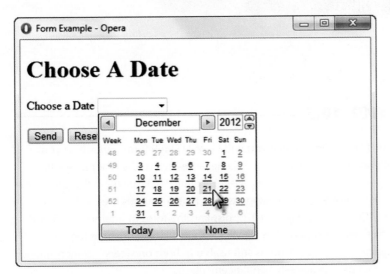

FIGURE 10.30   A date form control displayed in the Opera browser.

The date and time controls accept attributes listed in Tables 10.2 and 10.12. At the time this was written, only the Opera browser displayed a calendar interface for date and time controls. Other browsers currently render the date and time form controls as a text box, but you should expect increased support in the future.

Explore
Further

According to the W3C HTML5 specification, the `<input>` element with `type="color"` should configure a color picker control to provide a visual interface for color selection. At the time this was written, there was still no support for this intriguing new input form control. The Opera browser (version 10.5+) is currently the only browser to support the color picker form control. Perhaps this will have changed by the time you read this. Visit one of more of the following websites to determine the current state of browser support:

- http://www.standardista.com/html5-web-forms
- http://caniuse.com
- http://findmebyip.com/litmus

Practice with an HTML5 Form

HANDS-ON PRACTICE 10.5

FIGURE 10.31 The form displayed in Opera 11.

FIGURE 10.32 The form displayed in Internet Explorer 8.

In this Hands-On Practice you will code HTML5 form controls as you configure a form that accepts a name, an e-mail address, a rating value, and comments from a website visitor. Figure 10.31 displays the form in the Opera 11 browser, which supports the HTML5 features used in the Hands-On Practice. Figure 10.32 displays the form in Internet Explorer 8, which does not support the HTML5 features. Notice that the form is enhanced in Opera 11 but is still usable in both browsers—demonstrating the concept of progressive enhancement.

To get started, launch a text editor, and open the file located at chapter10/formcss.html in the student files, shown in Figure 10.19. Save the file with the name form5.html. You will modify the file to create a web page similar to the examples in Figures 10.31 and 10.32.

1. Modify the title element to display the text "Comment Form". Configure the text contained within the h1 element to be "Send Us Your Comments". Add a paragraph to indicate "Required fields are marked with an asterisk *.".

2. Modify the form element to submit the form information to the text-book's form processor at http://webdevbasics.net/scripts/demo.php.

   ```
   <form method="post" id="myForm"
    action="http://webdevbasics.net/scripts/demo.php">
   ```

3. Modify the form controls. Configure the name, e-mail, and comment information to be required. Use an asterisk to inform your web page visitor about the required fields. Code `type="email"` instead of `type="input"` for the e-mail address. Use the placeholder attribute to provide hints to the user in the name and e-mail form controls. Add a slider control (use `type="range"`) to generate a value from 1 to 10 for the rating. Modify the HTML as follows:

```
<form method="post" id="myForm"
 action="http://webdevbasics.net/scripts/demo.php">
<div>
   <label for="myName">Name*:</label>
   <input type="text" name="myName" id="myName"
    required="required" placeholder="your first and last name">
</div>
<div>
   <label for="myEmail">E-mail*:</label>
   <input type="email" name="myEmail" id="myEmail"
    required="required" placeholder="you@yourdomain.com">*
</div>
<div>
   <label for="myRating">Rating (1 - 10):</label>
   <input type="range" name="myRating" id="myRating"
   min="1" max="10">*
</div>
<div>
   <label for="myComments">Comments*:</label>
   <textarea name="myComments" id="myComments"
    required="required"
    rows="2" cols="20"></textarea>*
</div>
<div id="mySubmit">
   <input type="submit" value="Submit">
</div>
</form>
```

4. Save your form5.html file. Test your page in a browser. If you use a browser that supports the HTML5 features used in the form (such as Opera 11), your page should look similar to Figure 10.31. If you use a browser that does not offer support of the form's HTML5 attributes (such as Internet Explorer 8), your form should look similar to Figure 10.32. The display in other browsers will depend on the level of HTML5 support. See http://www.standardista.com/html5/html5-web-forms for an HTML5 for a browser support list.

5. Try submitting the form without entering any information. Figure 10.33 shows the result when using Opera 11. Note the error message that indicates the name field is required.

Compare your work with the solution in the student files (chapter10/form5.html). As this Hands-On Practice demonstrated, support of the new HTML5 form control attributes and values is not uniform. It will be some time before all browsers support these new features. Design forms with progressive enhancement in mind and be aware of both the benefits and the limitations of using new HTML5 features.

FIGURE 10.33 The Opera browser displays an error message.

Review and Apply

Review Questions

Multiple Choice. Choose the best answer for each item.

1. Which of the following form controls would be appropriate for an area that your visitors can use to type in comments about your website?
   a. text box
   b. select list
   c. radio button
   d. scrolling text box

2. Which attribute of the `<form>` tag is used to specify the name and location of the script that will process the form field values?
   a. `action`
   b. `process`
   c. `method`
   d. `id`

3. Forms contain various types of _____, such as text boxes and buttons, that accept information from a web page visitor.
   a. hidden elements
   b. labels
   c. form controls
   d. legends

4. Choose the tag that would configure a text box with the name "city" and a width of 40 characters.
   a. `<input type="text" id="city" width="40">`
   b. `<input type="text" name="city" size="40">`
   c. `<input type="text" name="city" space="40">`
   d. `<input type="text" width="40">`

5. Which of the following form controls would be appropriate for an area that your visitors can use to type in their e-mail address?
   a. select list
   b. text box
   c. scrolling text box
   d. none of the above

6. You would like to conduct a survey and ask your web page visitors to vote for their favorite search engine. Which of the following form controls is best to use for this purpose?
   a. check box
   b. radio button
   c. text box
   d. scrolling text box

7. You would like to accept a number that's in a range from 1 to 50. The user needs visual verification of the number they selected. Which of the following form controls is best to use for this purpose?
   a. spinner
   b. radio button
   c. check box
   d. slider

8. What will happen when a browser encounters a new HTML5 form control that it does not support?
   a. The computer will shut down.
   b. The browser will crash.
   c. The browser will display an error message.
   d. The browser will display an input text box.

9. Which tag would configure a scrolling text box with the name comments, two rows, and thirty characters?
   a. `<textarea name="comments" width="30" rows="2"></textarea>`
   b. `<input type="textarea" name="comments" size="30" rows="2">`
   c. `<textarea name="comments" rows="2" cols="30"></textarea>`
   d. `<textarea name="comments" width="30" rows="2">`

10. Choose the item that would associate a label displaying the text E-mail: with the text box named email.
    a. `E-mail <input type="textbox" name="email" id="email">`
    b. `<label>E-mail: <input type="text" name="email" id="email"></label>`
    c. `<label for="email">E-mail </label> <input type="text" name="email" id="email">`
    d. both b and c

Hands-On Exercises

1. Write the code to create the following:

   a. A text box named username that will accept the user name of web page visitors. The text box should allow a maximum of thirty characters to be entered.

   b. A group of radio buttons that website visitors can check to vote for their favorite day of the week.

   c. A select list that asks website visitors to select their favorite social networking website.

   d. A fieldset and legend with the text "Shipping Address" around the form controls for the following fields: AddressLine1, AddressLine2, City, State, Zip Code.

   e. A hidden form control with the name of userid.

   f. A password form control with the name of password.

   g. A form tag to invoke server-side processing using http://webdevbasics.net/scripts/demo.php and the post method.

2. Create a web page with a form that accepts requests for a brochure to be sent in the mail. Use the HTML5 required attribute to configure the browser to verify that all fields have been entered by the user. Sketch out the form on paper before you begin.

3. Create a web page with a form that accepts feedback from website visitors. Use the HTML5 input `type="email"` along with the required attribute to configure the browser to verify the data entered. Also configure the browser to require user comments with a maximum length of 1600 characters accepted. Sketch out the form on paper before you begin.

4. Create a web page with a form that accepts a website visitor's name, e-mail, and birthdate. Use the HTML5 `type="date"` attribute to configure a calendar control on browsers that support the attribute value.

Focus on Web Design

1. Search the Web for a web page that uses an HTML form. Print the browser view of the page. Print out the source code of the web page. Using the printout, highlight or circle the tags related to forms. On a separate sheet of paper, create some notes by listing the tags and attributes related to forms found on your sample page along with a brief description of their purpose. Place your name in an e-mail link on the web page.

2. Choose one server-side technology mentioned in this chapter: Ruby on Rails, PHP, JSP, or ASP.NET. Use the resources listed in the chapter as a starting point, but also search the Web for additional resources on the server-side technology you have chosen. Create a web page that lists at least five useful resources along with information about each that provides the name of the site, the URL, a brief description of what is offered, and a recommended page (such as a tutorial, free script, and so on). Place your name in an e-mail link on the web page.

PACIFIC TRAILS RESORT CASE STUDY ———

In this chapter's case study you will use the existing Pacific Trails website (Chapter 9) as a starting point. You will add a new page to the Pacific Trails website—the Reservations page. Refer back to the site map for the Pacific Trails website in Chapter 2, Figure 2.17. Your task is to create a new

FIGURE 10.34   The new Pacific Trails Reservations page.

page—the Reservations page (reservations.html). The Reservations page will use the same page layout as the other Pacific Trails web pages. You'll apply your new skills from this chapter and code a form in the content area of the Reservations page. Your new page will be similar to Figure 10.34 when you have completed this case study.

Step 1:   Create a folder called ch10pacific to contain your Pacific Trails Resort website files. Copy the files from the Chapter 9 Case Study ch9pacific folder.

Step 2:   Configure the CSS. View Figure 10.35 for a sketch of the form layout. You will add styles to configure the form. Launch a text editor and open the pacific.css external style sheet file.

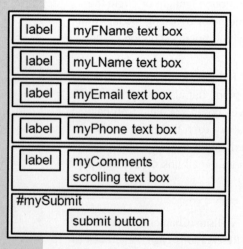

FIGURE 10.35   The sketch of the form.

- **The `label` element selector.** Configure the label elements to float on the left side of the form. Code a new style rule for the `label` selector that configures left float, 100 pixel width, text aligned to the right, 10 pixels of padding on the right side, and 10 pixels of top margin.

- **The `input` and textarea element selector.** Code a new style rule for the `input` and `textarea` element selectors that sets 10 pixels of top margin. The top margin adds visual empty space between the rows of form controls.

- **Clear floating elements.** Configure each div in the form to clear the left float.
  form div { clear: left; }

- **Configure the #mySubmit id.** Notice that the submit button is aligned vertically with the textboxes. Code a new style rule for an id named `mySubmit` with 110 pixels of margin on the left side and 10 pixels of padding on the bottom.

Save the pacific.css file.

Step 3: Create the Reservations Page. A productivity technique is to create new pages based on existing pages so you can benefit from your previous work. Your new Reservations page will use the index.html page as a starting point. Open the index.html page for the Pacific Trails Resort website in a text editor. Select File > Save As and save the file with the new name of reservations.html in the ch10pacific folder.

Now you are ready to edit the reservations.html file.

- Modify the page title. Change the text contained between the `<title>` and `</title>` tags to Pacific Trails Resort :: Reservations.
- Replace the text contained within the `<h2>` tags with: Reservations at Pacific Trails
- Delete the image, the paragraph, and the unordered list. Do not delete the logo, navigation, address, or page footer areas of the page.
- Position your cursor on a blank line below the h2 element. Configure an h3 element with the following text: Contact Us Today!
- Position your cursor on a blank line under the h3 element. You are ready to configure the form.. Begin with a `<form>` tag that uses the `post` method and the `action` attribute to invoke server-side processing. Unless directed otherwise by your instructor, use http://webdevbasics.net/scripts/pacific.php as the value of the `action` attribute.
- Configure the form control for the First Name information. Code a div element to contain the form control and label for the first name of your web page visitor. Create a `<label>` tag that is associated with the id myFName. Next, use an input element to code a textbox with the value of myFName for the `id` and `name` attributes.
- In a similar way, configure the div elements to contain a form control and label element to collect the following information: Last Name, E-mail Address, and Phone Number. Use the diagram in Figure 10.35 as a guide for the `id` and `name` values. Also set the `size` of the e-mail text box to 40 and the `maxlength` of the phone text box to 12.
- Configure a div element to contain the form control and label element for the comments scrolling text box. Use `rows="4"` and `cols="60"`.
- Configure the submit button on the form. Code a div element that is assigned to the `mySubmit` id. Code an input element with `type="submit"` and `value="Submit"`.
- Code an ending `</form>` tag on a blank line after the closing tag for the `mySubmit` div.

Save your reservations.html page and test it in a browser. It should look similar to the page shown in Figure 10.34. If you are connected to the Internet, submit the form. This will send your form information to the server-side script configured in the `<form>` tag. A confirmation page that lists the form information and their corresponding names will be displayed.

Step 4: OPTIONAL—Configure the form with HTML5 attributes and values. Get more practice with the new HTML5 elements by modifying the form on the Reservations page to use HTML5 attributes and values You'll also improve the form by adding form controls to accept the date and number of nights. Modify the reservations.html file in a text editor.

- Add a paragraph above the form to indicate "Required fields are marked with an asterisk *.".
- Use the required attribute to require the first name, last name, e-mail, and comment form controls to be entered.
- Configure the input element for the e-mail address with `type="email"`.

- Configure the input element for the phone number with `type="tel"`.
- Add a calendar form control to process a reservation request date (use `type="date"`).
- Add a spinner form control to process a value between 1 and 14 to indicate the number of nights for the length of stay (use `type="number"`). Use the min and max attributes to configure the range of values.

Save your file. Display your web page in browser. Submit the form with missing information or only a partial e-mail address. Depending on the browser's level of HTML5 support, the browser may perform form validation and display an error message. Figure 10.36 shows the Reservations page rendered in the Opera 11 browser with an incorrectly formatted e-mail address.

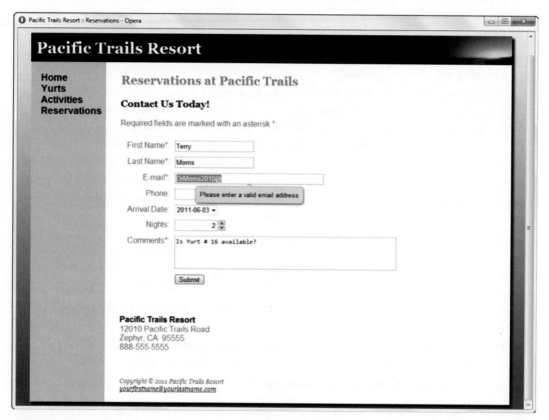

FIGURE 10.36 HTML5 attributes and values are coded in the form.

The optional Step 4 in this case study provided you with additional practice using new HTML5 attributes and values. The display and functioning of browsers will depend on the level of HTML5 support. See http://www.standardista.com/html5/html5-web-forms for an HTML5 browser support list.

Media and Interactivity Basics

Videos and sounds on your web pages can make them more interesting and informative. This chapter introduces you to working with multimedia and interactive elements on web pages. Methods to add audio, video, and Flash to your web pages are introduced. Sources of these media types, the HTML code needed to place the media on a web page, and suggested uses of the media are discussed. You're already familiar with using the CSS hover pseudo-class to add interactivity to hyperlinks. In this chapter you'll create an interactive image gallery with CSS and explore the CSS3 transform and transition properties. Adding the right touch of interactivity to a web page can make it engaging and compelling for your visitors.

You'll learn how to . . .

- Describe types of multimedia files used on the Web
- Configure hyperlinks to multimedia files
- Apply the object element to display audio and video files
- Apply the object element to display Flash multimedia on a web page
- Configure audio and video on a web page with HTML5 elements
- Configure a Flash animation on a web page
- Create an interactive image gallery with CSS
- Use the CSS3 transform and transition properties
- Describe the purpose of the HTML5 canvas element

Plug-ins, Containers, and Codecs

Helper Applications and Plug-Ins

Web browsers are designed to display certain file types such as .html, .htm, .gif, .jpg, and .png, among others. When the media is not one of these file types, the browser searches for a **plug-in** or **helper application** configured to display the file type. If it cannot find a plug-in or helper application (which runs in a separate window from the browser) on the visitor's computer, the web browser offers the visitor the option of saving the file to their computer. Several commonly used plug-ins are as follows:

- **Adobe Flash Player** (http://www.adobe.com/products/flashplayer). The Flash Player displays **.swf** format files. These can contain audio, video, and animation, along with interactivity.
- **Adobe Shockwave Player** (http://www.adobe.com/products/shockwaveplayer). The Shockwave Player displays high-performance multimedia created using the Adobe Director application.
- **Adobe Reader** (http://www.adobe.com/products/acrobat/readstep2.html). Adobe Reader is commonly used to exchange information stored in .pdf format.
- **Java Runtime Environment** (http://www.java.com/en/download/manual.jsp). The Java Runtime Environment (JRE) is used to run applications and applets using Java technology.
- **RealPlayer** (http://real.com). The RealPlayer plug-in plays streaming audio, video, animations, and multimedia presentations.
- **Windows Media Player** (http://www.microsoft.com/windows/windowsmedia/download). The Windows Media plug-in plays streaming audio, video, animations, and multimedia presentations.
- **Apple QuickTime** (http://www.apple.com/quicktime/download). The Apple QuickTime plug-in displays QuickTime animation, music, audio, and video directly within the web page.

The plug-ins and helper applications listed above have been used on the Web for many years. What is new about HTML5 video and audio is that it is native to the browser—with no plug-in needed. When working with native HTML5 video and audio, you need to be aware of the **container** (which is designated by the file extension) and the **codec** (which is the algorithm used to compress the media). There is no single codec that is supported by all popular browsers. For example, the H.264 codec requires licensing fees and is not supported by the Firefox and Opera web browsers, which support royalty-free Vorbis and Theora codecs. Explore Tables 11.1 and 11.2, which list common media file extensions, the container file type, and a description with codec information (if applicable for HTML5).

Extension	Container	Description
.wav	Wave	This format was originally created by Microsoft. It is a standard on the PC platform but is also supported by the Mac platform.
.aiff or .aif	Audio Interchange	A popular audio file format on the Mac platform. It is also supported on the PC platform.
.mid	Musical Instrument Digital Interface	Contain instructions to recreate a musical sound rather than a digital recording of the sound itself. However, a limited number of types of sounds can be reproduced.
.au	Sun UNIX Sound File	This is an older type of sound file that generally has poorer sound quality than the newer audio file formats.
.mp3	MPEG-1 Audio Layer-3	This sound file format is popular for music files due to the MP3 codec which supports two-channels and advanced compression.
.ogg	Ogg	An open-source audio file format (see http://www.vorbis.com) that uses the Vorbis codec.
.m4a	MPEG 4 Audio	This audio-only MPEG-4 format uses the Advanced Audio Coding (AAC) codec; supported by QuickTime, iTunes, and mobile devices such as the iPod and iPad.

TABLE 11.1 Common Audio File Types

Extension	Container	Description
.mov	QuickTime	Created by Apple and initially used on the Macintosh platform; also supported by Windows.
.avi	Audio Video Interleaved	Microsoft's original standard video format for PC platforms.
.flv	Flash Video	A Flash-compatible video file container; supports H.264 codec.
.wmv	Windows Media Video	A streaming video technology developed by Microsoft. The Windows Media Player supports this file format.
.mpg	MPEG	Developed under the sponsorship of the Moving Picture Experts Group (MPEG), http://www.chiariglione.org/mpeg; supported on both Windows and Mac platforms.
.m4v and .mp4	MPEG-4	MPEG4 (MP4) codec; H.264 codec; played by QuickTime, iTunes, and mobile devices such as the iPod and iPad.
.3gp	3GPP Multimedia	H.264 codec; a standard for delivery of multimedia over third-generation, high-speed wireless networks.
.ogv or .ogg	Ogg	This open-source video file format (see http://www.theora.org) uses the Theora codec.
.webm	WebM	This open media file format (see http://www.webmproject.org), sponsored by Google, uses the VP8 video codec and Vorbis audio codec.

TABLE 11.2 Common Video File Types

Configure Audio and Video

Accessing an Audio or Video File

The easiest way to give your website visitors access to an audio or a video file is to create a simple hyperlink to the file. For example, the code to hyperlink to a sound file named WDFpodcast.mp3 is

```
<a href="WDFpodcast.mp3">Podcast Episode 1</a> (MP3)
```

When your website visitor clicks on the link, the plug-in for .mp3 files that is installed on the computer (such as QuickTime) typically will display embedded in a new browser window or tab. Your web page visitor can then use the plug-in to play the sound.

HANDS-ON PRACTICE 11.1

FIGURE 11.1 The default MP3 player will launch in the browser when the visitor clicks on Podcast Episode 1.

In this Hands-On Practice you will create a web page similar to Figure 11.1 that contains an h1 tag and a hyperlink to an MP3 file. The web page will also provide a hyperlink to a text transcript of that file to provide for accessibility. It's useful to your web page visitors to also indicate the type of file (such as an MP3) and, optionally, the size of the file to be accessed.

Copy the podcast.mp3 and podcast.txt files from the chapter11/starters folder in the student files and save them to a folder named podcast. Use the chapter1/template.html file as a starting point and create a web page with the heading Web Design Podcast, a hyperlink to the MP3 file, and a hyperlink to the text transcript. Save your page as podcast2.html and display it in a browser. Try to test your page in different browsers and browser versions. When you click on the MP3 hyperlink, an audio player (whichever player or plug-in is configured for the browser) will launch to play the file. When you click on the hyperlink for the text transcript, the text will display in the browser. Compare your work to the sample in the student files (chapter11/podcast/podcast.html).

Multimedia and accessibility

Provide alternate content for the media files you use on your website in either transcript, caption, or printable PDF format. Provide a text transcript for audio files such as podcasts. Often you can use the podcast script as the basis of the text transcript file that you create as a PDF and upload to your website. Provide captions for video files. Apple QuickTime Pro includes a captioning function—view an example in the student files at chapter11/starters/sparkycaptioned.mov. Captions can be added to your YouTube Videos using http://captiontube.appspot.com. Visit http://www.webaim.org/techniques/captions for more information about video captioning.

Multimedia and Browser Compatibility Issues

Providing your website visitor a hyperlink to download and save a media file is the most basic method to provide access to your media, although your visitor will need an application installed on their computer (such as Adobe Quicktime, Apple iTunes, or Windows Media Player) to play the file after download. In the next section, you'll learn how to use the object element to configure audio and video players on a web page. You may find differences with the way modern browsers support the object element, and older browsers may not support it at all! It is critical that you test your page in the browsers (and browser versions) you expect your web page visitors to use. When you configure the object element to embed audio or video on a page, you are dependent on whether your website visitors have installed the corresponding player. For this reason, many websites, such as http://youtube.com and http://last.fm, use the Adobe Flash file format to share video and audio files. You'll work with Flash later in this chapter.

In a response to these browser plug-in compatibility issues and in an effort to reduce reliance on a proprietary technology like Adobe Flash, HTML5 introduces new audio and video elements that are native to the browser. However, because HTML5 is not yet a standard and not yet well supported by browsers, web designers still need to provide for a fallback option, such as providing a hyperlink to the media file or displaying a Flash version of the multimedia. You'll work with HTML5 video and audio later in this chapter.

FAQ

Why doesn't my audio or video file play?

Playing audio and video files on the Web depends on the plug-ins installed in your visitor's web browsers. A page that works perfectly on your home computer may not work for all visitors—depending on the configuration of their computer. Some visitors will not have the plug-ins properly installed. Some visitors may have file types associated with incorrect plug-ins or incorrectly installed plug-ins. Some visitors may be using low bandwidth and have to wait an overly long time for your media file to download. Are you detecting a pattern here? Sometimes media on the Web can be problematic.

XHTML Audio: Object Element

The Object Element

Another way to include multimedia on your web page is to embed the audio or video file in the page and optionally display a control panel or player for the multimedia. When coding in XHTML syntax (refer to Chapter 1), the object element is used for this purpose. The code in this section uses XHTML syntax but the object and param elements may also be used in HTML5. The **object element** is a multipurpose container tag for adding various types of objects to a web page. The object element begins with the `<object>` tag and ends with the `</object>` tag. Additional configuration values, called parameters, will usually need to be coded using the param element. Table 11.3 lists useful attributes of the object element.

Attribute	Value	Usage
data	Valid file name, name of media file	Required; provides the name of the file to be played.
classid	Uniquely identifies the player software	Optional; used with Windows. The classid identifies an ActiveX control that must be installed on the visitor's PC.
codebase	Specifies a relative path for the location of the plug-in	Optional; facilitates the location and download of plug-in if needed.
height	Numeric, number of pixels	Optional; configures the height of media control console.
title	Brief text description	Optional; may be displayed by browsers or assistive technologies.
type	A valid MIME type	Optional; specifies the MIME type of the media file; such as audio/mpeg or video/quicktime.
width	Numeric, number of pixels	Optional; configures the width of media console.

TABLE 11.3 Common Attributes of Media Object Elements

The Param Element

The **param element** is a self-contained tag with two attributes: `name` and `value`. Use `<param />` for XHTML syntax and `<param>` for HTML5 syntax. All the `<param />` tags for the object appear before the ending `</object>` tag. The player's documentation will indicate if parameters are needed and the format you should use. Table 11.4 lists common param element attribute values.

Name Attribute	Value Attribute	Usage
src	Valid file name, name of media file	Required; provides the name of the file to be played
autoplay	true, false	Optional; determines whether the media will play automatically when the page is loaded—if omitted, media may not automatically play
controller	true, false (not uniformly supported)	Optional; indicates whether the media console will display
hidden	true (not uniformly supported)	Optional; hides the default media console
loop	Numeric value, or true for continuous play (not uniformly supported)	Optional; determines how many times the media file will repeat

TABLE 11.4 Param Element Media Attribute Values

Embedding an Audio File on a Web Page

The basic XHTML code to use the `<object>` tag to embed a sound loop in a web page follows:

```
<object data="soundloop.mp3" height="50" width="100"
type="audio/mpeg" title="Music Sound Loop">
   <param name="src" value="soundloop.mp3" />
   <param name="controller" value="true" />
   <param name="autoplay" value="false" />
</object>
```

A sample page can be found in the student files at chapter11/music.html. See Figure 11.2 for a screenshot of this page displayed in the Chrome browser.

Review Figures 11.2 and 11.3. Notice that the Chrome browser correctly renders the `<object>` tag and displays a media player for the MP3. However, even though the web page code is valid and satisfies W3C recommendations, Internet Explorer 8 displays an ActiveX control warning— click through the warnings and the browser will display the media player.

Older versions of Internet Explorer require additional workarounds; see http://www.alistapart.com/articles/byebyeembed for more information. If you see warning messages when the object element is used to play media, consult your network administrator or lab support staff for recommended security settings and/or plug-in installation.

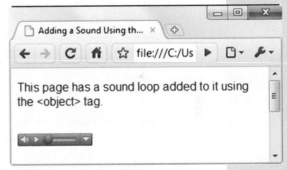

FIGURE 11.2 The Google Chrome browser correctly renders the multimedia object.

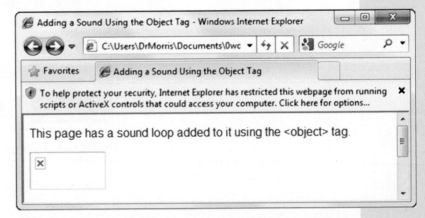

FIGURE 11.3 Internet Explorer 8 displays an ActiveX control warning.

XHTML Video: Object Element

Embedding video using an object element and param element is similar to embedding audio in a web page. Refer to the previous section for an overview of these elements. The code in this section uses XHTML syntax. Keep in mind that the object and param elements may also be used in HTML5, although HTML5 introduces new video and audio elements which you'll work with later in this chapter.

The XHTML code to play a QuickTime .mov video named sparky.mov is

```
<object data="sparky.mov" height="150" width="160" type="video/quicktime"
classid="clsid:02BF25D5-8C17-4B23-BC80-D3488ABDDC6B"
codebase="http://www.apple.com/qtactivex/qtplugin.cab"
title="Video of a cute Pekingese dog barking">
   <param name="src" value="sparky.mov" />
   <param name="controller" value="true" />
   <param name="autoplay" value="false" />
   <p>A video of a cute Pekingese dog barking.</p>
</object>
```

A sample can be found in the student files at chapter11/sparky.html. See Figure 11.4 for a screenshot of this page displayed in the Chrome browser.

FIGURE 11.4 Playing a video file.

Not everyone will have their browser plug-ins configured to display media. Sometimes there are compatibility issues between browser versions and multimedia. What happens if a browser or other user agent cannot display the video? Carefully review the code and notice that there is a descriptive phrase coded before the closing `</object>` tag. This phrase will display on the web page if the object (in this case the video player) cannot be rendered. Also, to help provide for accessibility, the title attribute has been configured with a brief text description of the video. This area will be read by some assistive technologies such as screen readers.

Multimedia and copyright issues

It is very easy to copy and download an image, audio, or video file from a website. It may be very tempting to place someone else's file in one of your projects, but that may not be ethical or lawful. Only publish web pages, images, and other media that you have personally created or have obtained the rights or license to use. If another individual has created an image, sound, video, or document that you think would be useful on your website, ask permission to use the material instead of simply taking it. All work (web pages, images, sounds, videos, and so on) is copyrighted—even if there is no copyright symbol and date on the material.

The Fair Use Clause of the Copyright Act

Be aware that there are times when students and educators can use portions of another's work and not be in violation of copyright law. This is called **fair use**. Fair use is use of a copyrighted work for purposes such as criticism, reporting, teaching, scholarship, or research. Criteria used to determine fair use are as follows:

- The use must be educational rather than commercial.
- The nature of the work copied should be factual rather than creative.
- The amount copied must be as small of a portion of the work as possible.
- The copy does not impede the marketability of the original work.

It is considered good netiquette to contact the owner of the original work to obtain permission even if your use is considered to be fair use. Visit http://copyright.gov and http://www.copyrightwebsite.com for more information on copyright issues.

Creative Commons—A New Approach to Copyright

Some individuals may want to retain ownership of their work but make it easy for others to use or adapt it. Creative Commons, http://creativecommons.org, provides a free service that allows authors and artists to register a type of a public copyright license called a **Creative Commons license**. There are several licenses to choose from, depending on the rights you wish to grant as the author. The Creative Commons license informs others exactly what they can and cannot do with the creative work. See http://meyerweb.com/eric/tools/color-blend for a web page licensed under a Creative Commons Attribution-ShareAlike 1.0 License with "Some Rights Reserved."

Configure Flash Multimedia

Adobe Flash is a popular application that creates multimedia that adds visual interest and interactivity to web pages with slideshows and multimedia effects. Flash multimedia uses a .swf file extension and requires a browser plug-in, which is free and readily available for download from Adobe. According to Adobe, 99 percent of Internet-enabled desktops have a Flash plug-in installed (http://adobe.com/products/player_census/flashplayer). Recently, there has been an increasing use of Adobe Flash technology to play video (http://youtube.com) and audio (http://last.fm) files on web pages. With the nearly ubiquitous Flash Player installed on most web browsers, website developers are confident when using Flash technology.

Adding a Flash Animation to a Web Page

Modern browsers support the display of Flash media with the object and param elements. As previously discussed, the object element is a multipurpose tag for adding various types of objects to a web page. The object element's attributes vary, depending on the type of object being referenced. The minimum attributes required when working with Flash media are described in Table 11.5.

Attribute	Description and Value
data	File name of the Flash media (.swf file)
height	Specifies the height of the object area in pixels
type	The MIME type of the object; use type="application/x-shockwave-flash"
width	Specifies the width of the object area in pixels
title	Optional; specifies a brief text description

TABLE 11.5 Minimal Flash Media Attributes for the Object Element

The Flash object uses special values, called parameters, to configure the name of the .swf file, quality of the media, and background color of the page areas. These are configured with the param element using <param> tags. Parameters used with Flash media are shown in Table 11.6.

Name Attribute	Value Attributes
movie	File name of the Flash media (.swf file)
bgcolor	Optional; background color of the Flash media area
loop	Optional; indicates whether the .swf loops; values are "true" and "false"
quality	Optional; describes the quality of the media; usually the value "high" is used
wmode	Optional; configures transparent background; value is "transparent"

TABLE 11.6 Param Element Flash Media Attribute Values

The following code sample configures the Flash .swf file shown in Figure 11.5:

```
<object type="application/x-shockwave-flash" data="flashlogo.swf"
width="300" height="70">
   <param name="movie" value="flashlogo.swf">
   <param name="bgcolor" value="#ffffff">
   <param name="quality" value="high">
   <p>Add a little Flash to your web page.</p>
</object>
```

Notice the code placed before the closing </object> tag in this example. It is displayed if the browser does not support the multimedia object. Include a link to a web page containing alternate text content if needed. While the developers of assistive technologies such as screen readers are working toward the support of Flash media, it is not yet universal.

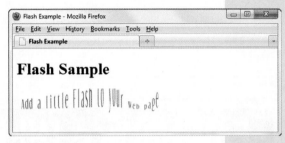

FIGURE 11.5   This web page displays a Flash .swf.

HANDS-ON PRACTICE 11.2

In this Hands-On Practice you will create a web page that displays a Flash slideshow of photographs. Your page will look like the one shown in Figure 11.6. Let's get started. Create a folder called lighthouse. Copy the lighthouse.swf file from the student files chapter11/starters folder and save it in your lighthouse folder.

Use the chapter1/template.html file as a starting point and create a web page with the heading Door County Lighthouse Cruise and the appropriate <object> and <param> tags to display a Flash file named lighthouse.swf which is 320 pixels wide and 240 pixels high. A sample follows:

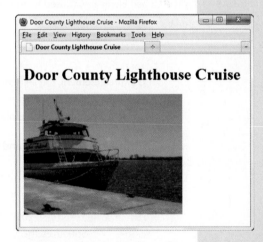

FIGURE 11.6   Flash slideshow of images.

```
<object type="application/x-shockwave-flash" data="lighthouse.swf"
width="320" height="240" title="Door County Lighthouse Cruise">
   <param name="movie" value="lighthouse.swf">
   <param name="bgcolor" value="#ffffff">
   <param name="quality" value="high">
   <p>Door County Lighthouse Cruise</p>
</object>
```

Save your page as lighthouse2.html and test it in a browser. Compare your work to the sample in the student files (chapter11/lighthouse/lighthouse.html).

HTML5 Embed Element

FIGURE 11.7 The embed element was used to configure the Flash media.

Although used for many years to configure media and Flash on web pages, the embed element was never an official W3C element until HTML5. One of the design principles of HTML5 is to "pave the cowpaths"—meaning to smooth the way for valid use of techniques that, although supported by browsers, were not part of the official W3C standard. Figure 11.7 (also in the student files at chapter11/flashembed.html) shows a web page using an embed element to display a Flash .swf file.

The **embed element** is a self-contained, or void, element that provides a way to add content which requires a plug-in or player to a web page. The embed element can be used to display a Flash .swf file on a web page. The attributes of the embed element commonly used with Flash media are listed in Table 11.7.

Attribute	Description and Value
src	File name of the Flash media (.swf file)
height	Specifies the height of the object area in pixels
type	The MIME type of the object; use type="application/x-shockwave-flash"
width	Specifies the width of the object area in pixels
bgcolor	Optional; background color of the Flash media, using a hexadecimal color value
quality	Optional; describes the quality of the media, usually set to "high"
title	Optional; specifies a brief text description that may be displayed by browsers or assistive technologies
wmode	Optional; set to "transparent" to configure transparent background in supporting browsers

TABLE 11.7 Embed Element Attributes

The following code sample configures the Flash .swf file shown in Figure 11.7:

```
<embed type="application/x-shockwave-flash"
       src="fall5.swf"
       width="640"
       height="100"
       quality="high"
       title="Fall Nature Hikes">
```

Notice the value of the title attribute in the code sample. The descriptive text could be accessed by assistive technologies such as a screen reader application.

HANDS-ON PRACTICE 11.3

In this Hands-On Practice you will launch a text editor and create a web page that displays a Flash slideshow of photographs. Your page will look like the one shown in Figure 11.8.

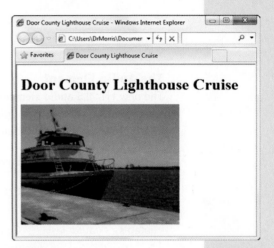

Create a folder called embed. Copy the lighthouse.swf file from the student files chapter11/starters folder and save it in your embed folder.

Use the chapter1/template.html file as a starting point, and create a web page with the heading Door County Lighthouse Cruise and an <embed> tag to display a Flash file named lighthouse.swf that is 320 pixels wide and 240 pixels high. A sample is as follows:

```
<embed type="application/x-shockwave-flash"
       src="lighthouse.swf" quality="high"
       width="320" height="240"
       title="Door County Lighthouse Cruise">
```

FIGURE 11.8 Flash slideshow of images configured with the embed element.

Save your page as index.html in the embed folder. Test it in a browser. Compare your work to the sample in the student files (chapter11/lighthouse/embed.html).

FAQ

What will happen if my web page visitor uses a browser that does not support Flash?

If you used the code in this section to display Flash media on a web page and your visitor's browser does not support Flash, the browser typically will display a message about needing a missing plug-in. The code in this section passes W3C HTML5 conformance checks and is the minimum code needed to display Flash media on a web page. If you'd like more features, such as being able to offer an express install of the latest Flash player to your visitors, explore SWFObject at http://code.google.com/p/swfobject/wiki/documentation, which uses JavaScript to embed Flash content and is W3C XHTML standards compliant.

At the time this was written there was no Flash support in the iPhone, iTouch, or iPad; however, these devices have been configured to support the new HTML5 video and audio elements that are introduced next in this chapter.

HTML5 Audio Element

The Audio Element

The new HTML5 **audio element** supports native play of audio files in the browser—without the need for plug-ins or players. The audio element begins with the `<audio>` tag and ends with the `</audio>` tag. Table 11.8 lists the attributes of the audio element.

Attribute	Value	Description
src	file name	Optional; audio file name
type	MIME Type	Optional; the MIME type of the audio file, such as audio/mpeg or audio/ogg
autoplay	autoplay	Optional; indicates whether audio should start playing automatically; use with caution
controls	controls	Optional; indicates whether controls should be displayed; recommended
loop	loop	Optional; indicates whether audio should be played over and over
preload	none, auto, metadata	Optional; values: none (no preload), metadata (only download media file metadata, and auto (download the media file)
title		Optional; specifies a brief text description that may be displayed by browsers or assistive technologies

TABLE 11.8 Audio Element Attributes

You'll need to supply multiple versions of the audio due to browser support of different codecs. Plan to supply audio files in at least two different containers, including ogg and mp3. It is typical to omit the src and type attributes from the audio tag and, instead, configure multiple versions of the audio file with the source element.

The Source Element

The **source element** is a self-contained, or void, tag that specifies a media file and a MIME type. The `src` attribute identifies the file name of the media file. The `type` attribute indicates the MIME type of the file. Code `type="audio/mpeg"` for an MP3 file. Code `type="audio/ogg"` for audio files using the Vorbis codec. Configure a source element for each version of the audio file. Place the source elements before the closing audio tag.

The following code sample configures the web page shown in Figure 11.9 (also in the student files chapter11/audio.html) to display a controller for an audio file:

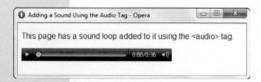

FIGURE 11.9 The Opera browser supports the HTML5 audio element.

```
<audio controls="controls">
   <source src="soundloop.mp3" type="audio/mpeg">
   <source src="soundloop.ogg" type="audio/ogg">
   <a href="soundloop.mp3">Download the Audio File</a> (MP3)
</audio>
```

Current versions of Safari, Chrome, Firefox, and Opera support the HTML5 audio element. The controls displayed by each browser are different. While Internet Explorer 9 supports the audio element, earlier versions of Internet Explorer offer no support. Review the code sample just given and note the hyperlink placed between the second source element and the closing audio tag. Any HTML elements or text placed in this area is rendered by browsers that do not support the HTML5 audio element. This is referred to as "fallback content"—if the audio element is not supported, the MP3 version of the file is made available for download. Figure 11.10 shows a screen shot of Internet Explorer 8 displaying the web page.

FIGURE 11.10 Internet Explorer 8 does not recognize the audio element.

HANDS-ON PRACTICE 11.4

In this Hands-On Practice you will launch a text editor and create a web page (see Figure 11.11) that displays an audio control to play a podcast.

Copy the podcast.mp3, podcast.ogg, and podcast.txt files from the chapter11/starters folder in the student files and save them to a folder named audio. Use the chapter1/template.html file as a starting point and create a web page with the heading Web Design Podcast, an audio control (use the audio element and two source elements), and a hyperlink to the text transcript. Configure a hyperlink to the MP3 file as the fallback content. The code for the audio element is

FIGURE 11.11 Using the audio element to provide access to a podcast.

```
<audio controls="controls">
      <source src="podcast.mp3" type="audio/mpeg">
      <source src="podcast.ogg" type="audio/ogg">
      <a href="podcast.mp3">Download the Podcast</a> (MP3)
</audio>
```

Save your page as index.html in the audio folder. Display the file in a browser. Try to test your page in different browsers and browser versions. Recall that Internet Explorer versions prior to Version 9 do not support the audio element but will display the fallback content. When you click on the hyperlink for the text transcript, the text will display in the browser. Compare your work to the sample in the student files (chapter11/podcast/audio.html).

How can I convert an audio file to the Ogg Vorbis codec?

The open-source Audacity application supports Ogg Vorbis. See http://audacity.sourceforge.net for download information. If you upload and share an audio file at the Internet Archive (http://archive.org), an .ogg format file will automatically be generated.

HTML5 Video Element

The Video Element

The new HTML5 **video element** supports native play of video files in the browser— without the need for plug-ins or players. The video element begins with the `<video>` tag and ends with the `</video>` tag. Table 11.9 lists the attributes of the video element.

Attribute	Value	Description
src	file name	Optional; video file name
type	MIME Type	Optional; the MIME type of the video file, such as video/mp4 or video/ogg
autoplay	autoplay	Optional; indicates whether video should start playing automatically; use with caution
controls	controls	Optional; indicates whether controls should be displayed
height	number	Optional; video height in pixels
loop	loop	Optional; indicates whether video should be played over and over
poster	file name	Optional; specifies an image to display if the browser cannot play the video
preload	none, auto, metadata	Optional; values: none (no preload), metadata (only download media file metadata, and auto (download the media file)
title		Optional; specifies a brief text description that may be displayed by browsers or assistive technologies
width	number	Optional; video width in pixels

TABLE 11.9 Video Element Attributes

You'll need to supply multiple versions of the video due to browser support of different codecs. Plan to supply video files in at least two different containers, including mp4 and ogg (or ogv). It is typical to omit the src and type attributes from the video tag and, instead, configure multiple versions of the audio file with the source element.

The Source Element

The **source element** is a self-contained, or void, tag that specifies a media file and a MIME type. The `src` attribute identifies the file name of the media file. The `type` attribute indicates the MIME type of the file. Code `type="video/mp4"` for video files using the MP4 codec. Code `type="video/ogg"` for video files using the Theora codec. Configure a source element for each version of the video file. Place the source elements before the closing video tag.

The following code sample configures the web page shown in Figure 11.12 (student files chapter11/sparky2.html) with the native HTML5 browser controls to display and play a video.

```html
<video controls="controls" poster="sparky.jpg"
     width="160" height="150">
  <source src="sparky.m4v" type="video/mp4">
  <source src="sparky.ogv" type="video/ogg">
  <a href="sparky.mov">Sparky the Dog</a> (.mov)
</video>
```

FIGURE 11.12 The Opera browser.

Current versions of Safari, Chrome, Firefox, and Opera support the HTML5 video element. The controls displayed by each browser are different. Internet Explorer 9 supports the video element, but earlier versions do not. Review the code sample just given and note the anchor element placed between the second source element and the closing video tag. Any HTML elements or text placed in this area is rendered by browsers that do not support the HTML5 video element. This is referred to as "fallback content". In this case, a hyperlink to a QuickTime (.mov) version of the file is supplied for the user to download. Another fallback option is to configure an embed element to play a Flash .swf version of the video. Figure 11.13 shows Internet Explorer 8 displaying the web page.

FIGURE 11.13 Internet Explorer 8 displays the "fallback".

HANDS-ON PRACTICE 11.5

In this Hands-On Practice you will launch a text editor and create the web page in Figure 11.14, which displays a video control to play a movie. Copy the lighthouse.m4v, lighthouse.ogv, lighthouse.swf, and lighthouse.jpg files from the chapter11/starters folder in the student files and save them to a folder named video. Open the chapter1/template.html file in a text editor and configure a web page with the heading Lighthouse Cruise and a video control (use the video element and two source elements). Configure an embed element to display the Flash content, lighthouse.swf, as fallback content. Configure the lighthouse.jpg file as a poster image, which will display if the browser supports the video element but cannot play any of the video files. The code for the video element is

```html
<video controls="controls" poster="lighthouse.jpg"
     width="320" height="240">
  <source src="lighthouse.m4v" type="video/mp4">
  <source src="lighthouse.ogv" type="video/ogg">
  <embed type="application/x-shockwave-flash"
    src="lighthouse.swf" quality="high" width="320" height="240"
    title="Door County Lighthouse Cruise">
</video>
```

FIGURE 11.14 HTML5 video element.

Save your page as index.html in the video folder. Display the index.html page in a browser. Try to test your page in different browsers and browser versions. Compare your work to Figure 11.13 and the sample in the student files (chapter11/video/video.html).

How can I convert a video file to the Ogg Theora codec?

Firefogg (http://firefogg.org) and TinyOgg (http://tinyogg.org) are two free web-based options to convert your video file to the Ogg Theora codec.

Embed a YouTube Video

YouTube (http://www.youtube.com) is a popular website for sharing videos for both personal and business use. When a video is uploaded to YouTube the creator can choose to allow for video embedding by others. It's easy to embed a video—just look for the embed code provided on the YouTube page and paste it into your web page source code. However, many mobile devices (such as the iPad, iTouch, and iPhone) do not support Flash and will not be able to display the video when you embed it in this manner.

According to the YouTube API Blog (http://apiblog.youtube.com/2010/07/new-way-to-embed-youtube-videos.html), there is another way for you to provide an embedded video, even to those devices that do not support Flash. Use an iframe element to display a web page configured by YouTube to detect the browser and operating system of your web page visitor and serve the content in an appropriate format—with either Flash or HTML5 video.

FIGURE 11.15 Embedding a YouTube video.

The iframe Element

The **iframe element** configures an **inline frame** that displays the contents of another web page within your web page document, referred to as *nested browsing*. The iframe element begins with the `<iframe>` tag and ends with the `</iframe>` tag. Fallback content that should be displayed if the browser does not support inline frames (such as a text description or hyperlink to the actual web page) should be placed between the tags. Figure 11.15 depicts a web page that displays a YouTube video within an iframe element. See Table 11.10 for a list of iframe element attributes.

Attribute	Description
src	URL of the web page to display in the inline frame
height	Inline frame height in pixels
width	Inline frame width in pixels
id	Optional; text name, alphanumeric, beginning with a letter, no spaces—the value must be unique and not used for other id values on the same web page document
name	Optional; text name, alphanumeric, beginning with a letter, no spaces—this attribute names the inline frame
sandbox	Optional; disallow/disable features such as plug-ins, scripts, forms (new in HTML5)
seamless	Optional; set seamless="seamless" to configure the browser to more "seamlessly" display the inline frame content (new in HTML5)
title	Optional; specifies a brief text description that may be displayed by browsers or assistive technologies

TABLE 11.10 iframe Element Attributes

HANDS-ON PRACTICE 11.6

In this Hands-On Practice you will launch a text editor and create the web page in Figure 11.15 that displays a YouTube video within an iframe element. This example embeds the video found at http://www.youtube.com/watch?v=rtCZloFmHB. You can choose to embed this video or select a different video. The process is to display the YouTube page for the video and copy the video identifier which is the text after the "=" in the URL. In this example, the video identifier is "rtCZloFmHB".

Use the chapter1/template.html file as a starting point and configure a web page with the heading YouTube Video and an iframe element that displays the video. Code the src attribute to display http://www.youtube.com/embed/ followed by the video identifier. In this example set the src attribute to the value http://www.youtube.com/embed/rtCZloFmHB. Configure a hyperlink to the YouTube video page as fallback content. The code to display the video shown in Figure 11.15 is

```
<iframe src="http://www.youtube.com/embed/rtCZloFmHB"
   width="640" height="385">
   View the
   <a href="http://www.youtube.com/watch?v=rtCZloFmH">YouTube Video</a>
</iframe>
```

Save your page as youtubevideo.html and display it in a browser. Try to test your page in different browsers and browser versions. Compare your work to Figure 11.15 and the sample in the student files (chapter11/iframe.html).

In addition to playing multimedia that is hosted on another server, such as the YouTube video in this example, inline frames are widely used on the Web for a variety of marketing and promotional purposes, including displaying ad banners and serving content for associate and partner sites. The advantage is separation of control. The dynamic content—such as the ad banner or multimedia clip—can be modified by the partner site at any time, just as YouTube dynamically configures the format of the video display in this section.

CSS Image Gallery

FIGURE 11.16 An interactive image gallery with CSS.

Recall from Chapter 8 that the CSS :hover pseudo-class provides a way to configure styles to display when the web page visitor moves the mouse over an element. You'll use this basic interactivity along with CSS positioning and display properties to configure an interactive image gallery with CSS and HTML. Figure 11.16 shows the gallery in action (available in the student files (chapter11/gallery/gallery.html). When you place the mouse over a thumbnail image, the larger version of the image is displayed along with a caption. If you click on the thumbnail, the image displays in its own browser window.

HANDS-ON PRACTICE 11.7 ————————————

In this Hands-On Practice you will create the image gallery web page in Figure 11.16. Copy the following images from the chapter11/starters folder in the student files: photo1.jpg, photo2.jpg, photo3.jpg, photo4.jpg, photo5.jpg, photo6.jpg, photo1thumb.jpg, photo2thumb.jpg, photo3thumb.jpg, photo4thumb.jpg, photo5thumb.jpg, and photo6thumb.jpg. Save them to a folder named gallery.

Launch a text editor and modify the chapter1/template.html file to configure a web page as indicated:

1. Configure the text, Image Gallery, within an h1 element.
2. Code a div assigned to the id named gallery. This div will contain the thumbnail images, which will be configured within an unordered list.
3. Configure an unordered list within the div. Code six li elements, one for each thumbnail image. The thumbnail images will function as image links with a :hover pseudo-class that causes the larger image to display on the page. We'll make this all happen by configuring a hyperlink element containing both the thumbnail image and a span element that comprises the larger image along with descriptive text. An example of the first li element is

```
<li><a href="photo1.jpg"><img src="photo1thumb.jpg"
    width="100" height="75" alt="Golden Gate Bridge">
    <span><img src="photo1.jpg" width="400" height="300"
    alt="Golden Gate Bridge"><br>Golden Gate Bridge
    </span></a>
</li>
```

4. Configure all six li elements in a similar manner. Substitute the actual name of each image file for the href and src values in the code. Write your own descriptive text for each image. Use photo2.jpg and photo2thumb.jpg in the second li element. Use photo3.jpg and photo3thumb.jpg in the third li element, and so on. Save the file as index.html in the gallery folder. Display your page in a browser. You'll see an unordered list with the thumbnail images, the larger images, and the descriptive text. Figure 11.17 shows a partial screen capture.

5. Now, let's add embedded CSS. Open your file in a text editor and code a style element in the head section.

The gallery id will use relative positioning. This does not change the location of the gallery but sets the stage to use absolute positioning on the span element in relation to its container (#gallery) instead of in relation to the entire web page document. This won't matter too much for our very simple example, but it would be very helpful if the gallery was part of a more complex web page. Code embedded CSS to configure the gallery with relative positioning; the unordered list with a width of 300 pixels and no

FIGURE 11.17 The web page display before CSS.

list marker; the list items with inline display, left float, and 10 pixels of padding; the images with no border; the anchor tags with no underline, dark gray color (#333), and italic font; and the span to not display by default. The CSS is

```
#gallery { position: relative; }

#gallery ul { width: 300px; list-style-type: none; }

#gallery li { display: inline; float: left; padding: 10px; }

#gallery img { border-style: none; }

#gallery a { text-decoration: none; color: #333; font-style: italic; }

#gallery span {display: none; }
```

Next, configure the span to display *only* when the web visitor hovers the mouse over the thumbnail image link. Set the location of the span to use absolute positioning. Locate the span 10 pixels down from the top and 300 pixels in from the left. Center the text within the span:

```
#gallery a:hover span { display: block; position: absolute;
                        top: 10px; left: 300px; text-align: center; }
```

Save your page and display it in a browser. Your gallery should work well in modern browsers. Note that the outdated Internet Explorer 6 does not support the dynamic display of the larger image but displays the unordered list and processes the thumbnail image links. Compare your work to Figure 11.16 and the sample in the student files (chapter11/gallery/gallery.html).

CSS3 Transform Property

CSS3 provides a method to change or transform the display of an element. The **transform** property allows you to rotate, scale, skew, or move an element. Both two-dimensional (2D) and three-dimensional (3D) transforms are possible. Transforms are often used in conjunction with the CSS3 transition property, which is introduced in the next section.

Browser vendor prefixes are needed to configure this property. This section will provide an example of a CSS3 transform along with links to resources for further study.

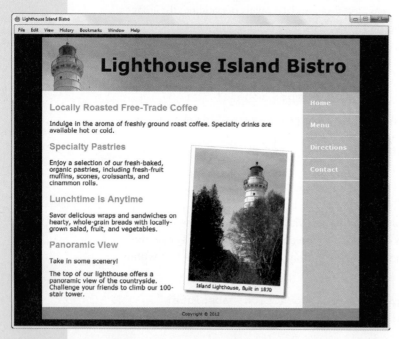

The web page in Figure 11.18 (available in the student files, chapter11/transform/transform.html) demonstrates the use of the CSS3 transform property to slightly rotate the figure. CSS is also used to configure a border, text caption, and box shadow for the div that contains the image.

FIGURE 11.18 The transform property in action.

Configuring a CSS3 Rotation Transform

Code four style declarations to configure a transform:

> `-webkit-transform` (for Webkit browsers)
>
> `-moz-transform` (for Gecko browsers)
>
> `-o-transform` (for the Opera browser)
>
> `-ms-transform` (for Internet Explorer 9)
>
> `transform` (W3C draft syntax)

Configure the transform type and value for each item listed. The `rotate()` transform type takes a value in degrees (like an angle in geometry). Rotate right with a positive value. Rotate left with a negative value. The rotation is around the origin, which by default is the middle of the element. The following CSS code first configures a class named figure to float to the right, with a 260-pixel width, 20-pixel margin, 5 pixels of padding, a white background, a gray, solid 1-pixel border, and centered text .80em in size. CSS3 is configured next to rotate 3 degrees and apply a box shadow. The code is

```
.figure {float: right;
        width: 260px;
        margin: 20px;
        padding: 5px;
        background-color: #FFF;
        border: 1px solid #CCC;
        text-align: center;
        font-size: .80em;
        -webkit-transform: rotate(3deg);
        -moz-transform: rotate(3deg);
        -o-transform: rotate(3deg);
        -ms-transform: rotate(3deg);
        transform: rotate(3deg);
        -webkit-box-shadow: 5px 5px 5px #828282;
        -moz-box-shadow: 5px 5px 5px #828282;
        box-shadow: 5px 5px 5px #828282; }
```

As shown in the code sample, the syntax for configuring transforms varies by browser engine. It is expected that eventually all browsers will support W3C syntax CSS3 and transform, so code this declaration last in the list. Recall that the browser proprietary CSS syntax in this section is nonstandard. Your CSS code will not pass W3C validation when you use these properties.

Explore Further

This section provided an overview of one type of transform—the rotation of an element.
Visit http://www.westciv.com/tools/transforms/index.html to generate the CSS for rotate, scale, translate, and skew transforms.
For more information about the syntax used in transforms, visit the corresponding websites:

- **Webkit**
  http://webkit.org/blog/130/css-transforms

- **Mozilla**
  https://developer.mozilla.org/en/CSS/-moz-transform

- **Opera**
  http://dev.opera.com/articles/view/css3-transitions-and-2d-transforms/#transforms

- **Internet Explorer**
  http://msdn.microsoft.com/en-us/ie/ff468705.aspx#_CSS3_2D_Transforms

- **W3C**
  http://www.w3.org/TR/css3-2d-transforms and http://www.w3.org/TR/css3-3d-transforms

CSS3 Transition Property

CSS3 **transitions** provide for changes in property values to display in a smoother manner over a specified time. Four different properties can be used with transitions: transition-property, transition-duration, transition-timing-function, and transition-delay. The properties can be combined in a single transition shorthand property. Table 11.11 lists the transition properties and their purpose.

Property	Description
transition-property	Indicates the CSS property to which the transition applies; a list of applicable properties is available at http://www.w3.org/TR/css3-transitions
transition-duration	Indicates the length of time to apply the transition; default value 0 configures an immediate transition; otherwise use a numeric value to specify time (usually in seconds)
transition-timing-function	Configures changes in the speed of the transition by describing how intermediate property values are calculated; common values include ease (default), linear, ease-in, ease-out, ease-in-out
transition-delay	Indicates the beginning of the transition; default value 0 configures no delay; otherwise use a numeric value to specify time (usually in seconds)
transition	Shorthand property; list the value for transition-property, transition duration, transition-timing-function, and transition-delay separated by spaces; default values can be omitted, but the first time unit applies to transition-duration

TABLE 11.11 CSS Transition Properties

Browser vendor prefixes are needed to configure transitions. Transitions are supported by current versions of most modern browsers. However, transitions are not currently supported by Internet Explorer. Code four style declarations to configure a transition:

```
-webkit-transition (for Webkit browsers)
-moz-transition (for Gecko browsers)
-o-transition (for the Opera browser)
transform (W3C draft syntax)
```

The web page in Figure 11.19 (see the student files, chapter11/transform/transition.html) demonstrates the use of the CSS3 transition property to "straighten" the lighthouse photo when the web page visitor hovers over it with the mouse. Compare the position of the lighthouse photo in Figures 11.18 and 11.19 to see the result of the transition.

Configuring a CSS3 Transition

The transition was applied to the transform property and uses the shorthand transition property to configure a rotation back to 0 degrees in 1/2 second with a smooth, linear timing. The key is to configure a style rule for the `.figure:hover` pseudo-class with a style declaration with the ending value of the transform property in addition to style declarations for the transition property. The new CSS code has a lot of repetition due to the browser vendor prefixes on the CSS3 properties:

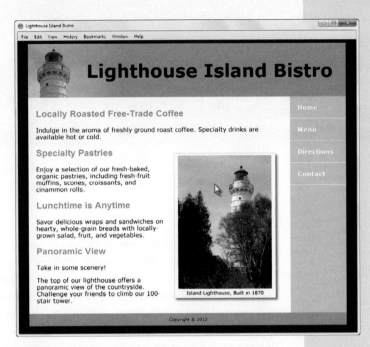

FIGURE 11.19 The interactive CSS3 transition effect.

```
.figure:hover { -webkit-transform: rotate(0deg);
          -moz-transform: rotate(0deg);
          -o-transform: rotate(0deg);
          transform: rotate(0deg);
          -webkit-transition: -webkit-transform .5s linear;
          -moz-transition: -moz-transform .5s linear;
          -o-transition: -o-transform .5s linear;
          transition: transform .5s linear; }
```

As shown in the code sample, the syntax for configuring transforms varies by browser engine. It is expected that eventually all browsers will support W3C syntax CSS3 and `transition`, so code this declaration last in the list. Recall that the browser proprietary CSS syntax in this section is nonstandard. Your CSS code will not pass W3C validation when you use these properties.

Explore
Further

You are not limited to configuring a single transition. Explore the example in the student files (chapter11/transform/transition2.html) which changes both the transform property and the background-color property of the lighthouse figure. See the following resources for more examples of CSS transforms and transitions:

http://www.webdesignerdepot.com/2010/01/css-transitions-101,

http://return-true.com/2010/06/using-css-transforms-and-transitions, and

http://net.tutsplus.com/tutorials/html-css-techniques/css-fundametals-css-3-transitions.

HTML5 Canvas Element

The HTML5 **canvas element** configures dynamic graphics. It provides a way to dynamically draw and transform lines, shapes, images, and text on web pages. If that wasn't enough, the canvas element also provides methods to interact with actions taken by the user, like moving the mouse. The promise of the canvas element is that it can be used to create interactions as sophisticated as those developed with Adobe Flash. At the time this was written, all modern browsers with the exception of Internet Explorer support the canvas element. Use a browser other than Internet Explorer to see virtuoso examples of the canvas element in action at the following websites:

- http://www.chromeexperiments.com (look for experiments with "canvas" in the title)
- http://blog.webreakstuff.com/2010/11/building-a-canvas-snowglobe
- http://www.canvasdemos.com

The canvas element begins with the `<canvas>` tag and ends with the `</canvas>` tag. However, the canvas element is configured through an **application programming interface** (API), which means that a programming or scripting language, such as JavaScript, is needed to implement it. **JavaScript** is an object-based scripting language interpreted by a web browser. It's used to work with the objects associated with a web page document—the browser window, the document itself, and the elements—including form, img, and canvas. These elements are all part of the **document object model** (DOM). JavaScript is associated with a web page using the **script element**.

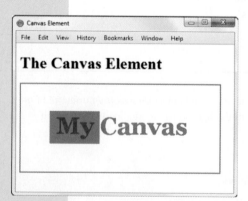

FIGURE 11.20 The canvas element.

The canvas API provides methods for two-dimensional (2D) bitmap drawing, including lines, strokes, arcs, fills, gradients, images, and text. However, instead of drawing visually using a graphics application, you draw programmatically by writing JavaScript statements. A very basic example of using JavaScript to draw within the canvas element is provided in this section. Although you need to understand JavaScript to use the canvas element, learning to code JavaScript is outside of the scope of this book. We'll explore the very basic example of configuring the canvas element shown in Figure 11.20 (see the student files chapter11/canvas.html). The code is

```
<!DOCTYPE html>
<html lang="en">
<head>
<title>Canvas Element</title>
<meta charset="utf-8">
<style>
canvas { border: 2px solid red; }
</style>
<script type="text/javascript">
function drawMe() {
   var canvas = document.getElementById("myCanvas");
   if (canvas.getContext) {
      var ctx = canvas.getContext("2d");
      ctx.fillStyle = "rgb(255, 0, 0)";
      ctx.font = "bold 3em Georgia";
      ctx.fillText("My Canvas", 70, 100);
      ctx.fillStyle = "rgba(0, 0, 200, 0.50)";
      ctx.fillRect(57, 54, 100, 65);
   }
}
</script>
</head>
<body onload="drawMe()">
<h1>The Canvas Element</h1>
<canvas id="myCanvas" width="400" height="175"></canvas>
</body>
</html>
```

If some of the code looks like a foreign language to you, don't worry—JavaScript IS a different language than CSS and HTML, with its own syntax and rules. Here's a quick overview of the code sample:

The red outline was created by applying CSS to the canvas selector.

The JavaScript function drawMe() is invoked when the browser loads the page.

JavaScript looks for a canvas element assigned to the "myCanvas" id.

- Test for browser support of canvas and, if true, perform the actions listed below.
- Set the canvas context to 2d.
- Draw the "My Canvas" text.
  - Use the fillStyle attribute to set the drawing color to red.
  - Use the font attribute to configure font-weight, font-size, and font-family.
  - Use the fillText method to specify the text to display, followed by the x-value (pixels in from the left) and y-value (pixels down from the top).
- Draw the rectangle.
  - Use the fillStyle attribute to set the drawing color to blue with 50% opacity.
  - Use the fillRect method to set the x-value (pixels in from the left), y-value (pixels down from the top), width, and height of the rectangle.

This section provided a very quick overview of the canvas element. Visit http://www.html5canvastutorials.com, http://diveintohtml5.org/canvas.html, and http://blog.nihilogic.dk/2009/02/html5-canvas-cheat-sheet.html if you'd like additional examples and practice with this intriguing new element.

CHAPTER 11

Review and Apply

Review Questions

Multiple Choice. Choose the best answer for each item.

1. Which property provides a way for you to rotate, scale, skew, or move an element?
   a. display
   b. transition
   c. transform
   d. list-style-type

2. Which of the following is the file extension for a Flash animation?
   a. .swf
   b. .ogg
   c. .flash
   d. .mov

3. What happens when a browser does not support the <video> or <audio> element
   a. The computer crashes.
   b. The web page does not display.
   c. The fallback content, if it exists, will display.
   d. none of the above

4. What element provides a way to add content which requires a plug-in or player to a web page?
   a. object
   b. source
   c. iframe
   d. none of the above

5. Which of the following is an open-source video codec?
   a. Theora
   b. MP3
   c. Vorbis
   d. Flash

6. Which of the following is a void element that specifies a media file name and MIME type?
   a. iframe
   b. anchor
   c. param
   d. source

7. Which of the following configures an area on a web page to not display?
   a. hide: yes;
   b. display: no;
   c. display: none;
   d. display: block;

8. What type of files are .webm, .ogv, and .m4v?
   a. audio files
   b. video files
   c. Flash files
   d. none of the above

9. Which of the following should you do to provide for usability and accessibility?
   a. Use video and sound whenever possible.
   b. Supply text descriptions of audio and video files that appear in your web pages.
   c. Never use audio and video files.
   d. none of the above

10. Which of the following elements displays the contents of another web page document?
    a. iframe
    b. div
    c. document
    d. object

Hands-On Exercises

1. Write the HTML for a hyperlink to a video called lighthouse.mov on a web page.

2. Write the HTML to embed an audio file called soundloop.mp3 on a web page that can be controlled by the visitor.

3. Write the HTML to display a video on a web page. The video files are named movie.m4v and movie.ogv. The width is 480 pixels. The height is 360 pixels. The poster image is movie.jpg.

4. Write the HTML to display a Flash file named flashbutton.swf on a web page.

5. Write the HTML to configure an inline frame to display the home page of http://webdevbasics.net in your web page.

6. Create a web page about your favorite movie that contains an audio file with your review of the movie. Use an application of your choice to record your review (visit http://audacity.sourceforge.net/download for a free download of Audacity). Place an e-mail hyperlink to yourself on the web page. Save the page as review.html

7. Create a web page about your favorite music group that contains either a brief audio file with your review or an audio clip of the group. Use an application of your choice to record your review (visit http://audacity.sourceforge.net/download for a free download of Audacity). Place an e-mail hyperlink to yourself on the web page. Save the page as music.html.

8. Visit the textbook website at http://webdevbasics.net/flashcs5 and follow the instructions to create a Flash logo banner.

9. Add a new transition to the Lighthouse Bistro home page (found in the student files at chapter11/transform/transition2.html). Configure the opacity property to display the lighthouse figure at 50% opacity and slowly change the opacity to 100% when the visitor places their mouse over the figure area.

Focus on Web Design

This chapter mentioned, "pave the cowpaths" as one of the design principles of HTML5. You may be wondering about the others. The W3C has a list of the HTML5 Design Principles at http://www.w3.org/TR/html-design-principles. Review the page and write a one-page summary and reaction to these principles and what they mean to you as a web designer.

PACIFIC TRAILS RESORT CASE STUDY ————

In this chapter's case study you will use the existing Pacific Trails (Chapter 10) website as a starting point to create a new version of the website that incorporates multimedia and interactivity.

Step 1: Create a folder called ch11pacific to contain your Pacific Trails Resort website files. Copy the files from the Chapter 10 Case Study ch10pacific folder. Copy the following files from the chapter11/casestudystarters folder in the student files and save them in your ch11pacific folder: pacifictrailsresort.mp4, pacifictrailsresort.ogv, pacifictrailsresort.jpg and pacifictrailsresort.swf. Copy the following files from the Chapter11/starters folder in the student files and save them in your ch11pacific folder: photo2.jpg, photo3.jpg, photo4.jpg, photo6.jpg, photo2thumb.jpp, photo3thumb.jpg, photo4thumb.jpg, and photo6thumb.jpg.

Step 2: The Home Page. Launch a text editor and open the home page, index.html. Replace the image with an HTML5 video control. Configure the video, source, and embed elements to work with the following files: pacifictrailsresort.mp4, pacifictrailsresort.ogv, pacifictrailsresort.swf, and pacifictrailsresort.jpg. The dimensions of the video are 320 pixels wide by 240 pixels high. Save the file. Check your HTML syntax in the W3C validator (http://validator.w3.org). Correct and retest if necessary.

Next, configure the CSS. Launch a text editor and open pacific.css. Locate the #content img selector which is configured with style rules to float to the left and have padding on the right. Add the #content video, and #content embed selectors to the style rule as shown below:

```
#content img, #content video, #content embed { float: left;
        padding-right: 20px; }
```

Save the pacific.css file. Launch a browser and test your new index.html page. It should look similar to Figure 11.21.

FIGURE 11.21   Pacific Trails Resort home page.

Step 3: The Activities Page. Launch a text editor and open the activities.html file. Modify the page by adding an image gallery above the footer area. You'll need to modify both the activities. html file and the pacific.css file.

Use Hands-On Practice 11.7 as a guide and configure a div assigned to the gallery id. This gallery will display four thumbnail images. Code an unordered list within the gallery div that has four li elements, one for each thumbnail image. The thumbnail images will function as image links with a :hover pseudo-class that causes the larger image to display on the page. Within each li element, configure a hyperlink element to contain both the thumbnail image and a span element that comprises the larger image along with descriptive text. Configure the dimensions of the larger images to be 200 pixels wide by 150 pixels high. Save the activities.html file.

Open the pacific.css file in a text editor. Code the CSS for the gallery as shown in Hands-On Practice 11.7 but configure the position of the span to be located farther in from the left (use left: 340px;). By default, the images in the gallery inherit the left float configured for the #content img selector. To remove this inheritance code a float:none; style rule on the #gallery img selector. Also add a style declaration to the #footer selector to clear all floats. Save the pacific.css file.

Launch a browser and test your new activities.html page. It should look similar to Figure 11.22.

FIGURE 11.22 New Pacific Trails Resort activities page.

 Explore Further

You were briefly introduced to using JavaScript to configure the canvas element in this chapter. JavaScript is often used to respond to events such as moving the mouse, clicking a button, and loading a web page. As you continue your web design studies, a good next step would be to explore client-side scripting with JavaScript. Visit the following resources to get started: http://www.echoecho.com/javascript.htm, http://www.w3schools.com/js, and http://www.tizag.com/javascriptT.

Just as JavaScript was needed to configure the HTML5 canvas element in this section, other more advanced features of HTML5 also provide APIs that work with JavaScript. These include web storage, web databases, offline application caching, drag and drop, geolocation, and web messaging.

JavaScript is also the "J" in **AJAX**, which stands for Asynchronous JavaScript and XML, a technology that powers interactive web applications including Gmail (http://gmail.google.com), Flickr (http://flickr.com, and Delicious (http://del.icio.us). Recall the client/server model discussed in Chapters 1 and 10. The browser makes a request to the server (often triggered by clicking a hyperlink or a submit button), and the server returns an entire new web page for the browser to display. AJAX pushes more of the processing on the client (browser) with JavaScript and XML and often uses "behind the scenes" asynchronous requests to the server to refresh a portion of the browser display instead of the entire web page. The key is that when using AJAX technology, JavaScript code (which runs on the client computer within the confines of the browser) can communicate directly with the server—exchanging data and modifying parts of the web page display without reloading of the entire web page.

For example, as soon as a website visitor types a Zip code into a form, the value could be looked up on a Zip code database and the city/state automatically populated using AJAX—and all this takes place while the visitor is entering the form information before he or she clicks the submit button. The result is that the visitor perceives the web page as being more responsive and has a more interactive experience. Visit the following websites to explore this topic further: http://www.w3schools.com/ajax/ajax_intro.asp, http://www.alistapart.com/articles/gettingstartedwithajax, and http://www.tizag.com/ajaxTutorial.

CHAPTER 12

Web Publishing Basics

Well, you've designed and built a website, but there is still much more to do. You need to obtain a domain name, select a web host, publish your files to the Web, and submit your site to search engines. In addition to discussing these tasks, this chapter introduces you to evaluating the accessibility and usability of your website.

You'll learn how to . . .

- Describe criteria to consider when you're selecting a web host
- Obtain a domain name for your website
- Publish a website using FTP
- Design web pages that are friendly to search engines
- Submit a website for inclusion in a search engine
- Determine whether a website meets accessibility requirements
- Evaluate the usability of a website

Register a Domain Name

FIGURE 12.1   Your domain name establishes your presence on the Web.

A crucial part of establishing an effective web presence is choosing a **domain name;** it serves to locate your website on the Internet (Figure 12.1). If your business or organization is brand new, then it's often convenient to select a domain name while you are deciding on a company name. If your organization is well established, you should choose a domain name that relates to your existing business presence. Although many domain names have already been purchased, there are still many options available.

Choosing a Domain Name

Describe Your Business

Although there is a long-standing trend to use "fun" words as domain names (for example, yahoo.com, google.com, bing.com, woofoo.com, and so on), think carefully before doing so. Domain names for traditional businesses and organizations are the foundation of the organization's web presence and should include the business name or purpose.

Be Brief, If Possible

Although most people find new websites with search engines, some of your visitors will type your domain name in a browser. A shorter domain name is preferable to a longer one—it's easier for your web visitors to remember.

Avoid Hyphens ("-")

Using the hyphen character (commonly called a dash) in a domain name makes it difficult to pronounce the name. Also, someone typing your domain name may forget the dash and end up at a competitor's site! If you can, avoid the use of dashes in a domain name.

There's More Than .com

While the .com top-level domain name (TLD) is still the most popular for commercial and personal websites, consider also registering your domain name with other TLDs, such as .biz, .net, .us, .mobi, and so on. Commercial businesses should avoid the .org TLD, which is the first choice for nonprofit organizations. You don't have to create a website for each domain name that you register. You can arrange with your domain name registrar (for example, http://register.com) for the "extra" domain names to point visitors to the domain name where your website is located. This is called **domain name redirection**.

Brainstorm Potential Keywords

Think about words that a potential visitor might type into a search engine when looking for your type of business or organization. This is the starting point for your list of **keywords**. If possible, work one or more keywords into your domain name (but still keep it as short as possible).

Avoid Trademarked Words or Phrases

The U.S. Patent and Trademark Office (USPTO) defines a **trademark** as a word, phrase, symbol, or design, or a combination of words, phrases, symbols, or designs, that identifies and distinguishes the source of the goods of one party from those of others. A starting point in researching trademarks is the USPTO Trademark Electronic Search System (TESS); visit http://www.uspto.gov/web/trademarks/workflow/start.htm and click on the link to TESS. See http://www.uspto.gov for more information about trademarks.

Know the Territory

Explore the way your potential domain name and keywords are already used on the Web. It's a good idea to type your potential domain names (and related words) into a search engine to see what may already exist.

Verify Availability

Check with one of the many **domain name registrars** to determine whether your domain name choices are available. A few of the many sites that offer domain name registration services are as follows:

- http://register.com
- http://networksolutions.com
- http://godaddy.com

Each of these sites offers a WHOIS search feature that provides a way to determine whether a potential domain name is available and, if it is owned, who owns it. Often the domain name is already taken. If that's the case, the sites listed here will provide alternate suggestions that may be appropriate. Don't give up; a domain name is out there waiting for your business.

Registering a Domain Name

Once you've found your perfect domain name, don't waste any time in registering it. The cost to register a domain name varies but is quite reasonable. The top rate for a .com one-year registration is currently $35 (and there are numerous opportunities for discounts with multiyear packages or bundled web hosting services). It's perfectly OK to register a domain name even if you are not ready to publish your website immediately. There are many companies that provide domain registration services, as listed earlier. When you register a domain name, your contact information (such as name, phone number, mailing address, and e-mail address) will be entered into the WHOIS database and available to anyone unless you choose the option for private registration. While there is usually a small annual fee for **private registration**, it shields your personal information from unwanted spam and curiosity seekers.

Obtaining a domain name is just one part of establishing a web presence—you also need to host your website somewhere. The next section introduces you to factors involved in choosing a web host.

Choose a Web Host

A **web host provider** is an organization that offers storage for your website files along with the service of making them available on the Internet. Your domain name, such as webdevbasics.net, is associated with an IP address that points to your website on the web server at the web host provider.

It is common for web host providers to charge a setup fee in addition to the monthly hosting fee. Hosting fees vary widely. The cheapest hosting company is not necessarily the one to use. Never consider using a "free" web host provider for a business website. These free sites are great for kids, college students, and hobbyists, but they are unprofessional. The last thing you or your client wants is to be perceived as unprofessional or not serious about the business at hand. As you consider different web host providers, try contacting their support phone numbers and e-mail addresses to determine just how responsive they really are. Word of mouth, web searches, and online directories such as http://www.hosting-review.com are all resources in your quest for the perfect web host provider.

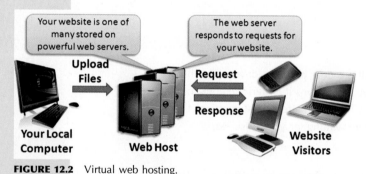

FIGURE 12.2   Virtual web hosting.

Types of Web Hosting

- **Virtual Hosting**, or shared hosting, is a popular choice for small websites (Figure 12.2). The web host provider's physical web server is divided into a number of virtual domains, and multiple websites are set up on the same computer. You have the authority to update files in your own website space, while the web host provider maintains the web server computer and Internet connectivity.

- **Dedicated Hosting** is the rental and exclusive use of a computer and connection to the Internet that is housed on the web hosting company's premises. A dedicated server is usually needed for a website that could have a considerable amount of traffic, such as tens of millions of hits a day. The server can usually be configured and operated remotely from the client company, or you can pay the web host provider to administer it for you.

- **Co-Located Hosting** uses a computer that your organization has purchased and configured. Your web server is housed and connected to the Internet at the web host's physical location, but your organization administers this computer.

Choosing a Virtual Host

There are a number of factors to consider when choosing a web host. Table 12.1 provides a checklist.

TABLE 12.1 Web Host Checklist

Operating system	☐ UNIX ☐ Linux ☐ Windows	Some web hosts offer a choice of these platforms. If you need to integrate your web host with your business systems, choose the same operating system for both.
Web server	☐ Apache ☐ IIS	These two web server applications are the most popular. Apache usually runs on a UNIX or Linux operating system. Internet Information Services (IIS) is bundled with selected versions of Microsoft Windows.
Bandwidth	☐ ___ GB per month ☐ ___ Charge for overage	Some web hosts carefully monitor your data transfer bandwidth and charge you for overages. While unlimited bandwidth is great, it is not always available. A typical low-traffic website varies between 100GB and 200GB per month. A medium-traffic site should be OK with about 500GB of data transfer bandwidth per month.
Technical support	☐ E-mail ☐ Chat ☐ Forum ☐ Phone	Review the description of technical support on the web host's site. Is it available 24 hours a day, 7 days a week? E-mail or phone a question to test it. If the organization is not responsive to you as a prospective customer, be leery about the availability of its technical support later.
Service agreement	☐ Uptime guarantee ☐ Automatic monitoring	A web host that offers a Service Level Agreement (SLA) with an uptime guarantee shows that they value service and reliability. The use of automatic monitoring will inform the web host technical support staff when a server is not functioning.
Disk space	☐ ___ GB	Many virtual hosts routinely offer 100GB+ disk storage space. If you have a small site that is not graphic intensive, you may never even use more than 50MB of disk storage space.
E-mail	☐ ___ Mailboxes	Most virtual hosts offer multiple e-mail mailboxes per site. These can be used to filter messages—customer service, technical support, general inquiries, and so on.
Uploading files	☐ FTP access ☐ Web-based file manager	A web host that offers FTP access will allow the most flexibility. Others only allow updates through a web-based file manager application. Some web hosts offer both options.
Canned scripts	☐ Form processing	Many web hosts supply canned, prewritten scripts to process form information.
Scripting support	☐ PHP ☐ .NET ☐ ASP	If you plan to use server-side scripting (refer back to Chapter 10) on your site, determine which, if any, scripting is supported by your web host.
Database support	☐ MySQL ☐ MS Access ☐ MS SQL	If you plan to access a database with your scripting, determine which, if any, database is supported by your web host.
E-commerce packages	☐ _____	If you plan to enter into e-commerce, it may be easier if your web host offers a shopping cart package. Check to see if one is available.
Scalability	☐ Scripting ☐ Database ☐ E-commerce	You probably will choose a basic (low-end) plan for your first website. Note the scalability of your web host—are there other plans with scripting, database, e-commerce packages, and additional bandwidth or disk space available as your site grows?
Backups	☐ Daily ☐ Periodic ☐ No backups	Most web hosts will back up your files regularly. Check to see how often the backups are made and if they are accessible to you. Be sure to make your own site backups as well.
Site statistics	☐ Raw log file ☐ Log reports ☐ No log	The website log contains useful information about your visitors, how they find your site, and what pages they visit. Check to see if the log is available to you. Some web hosts provide reports about the log.
Domain name	☐ Included ☐ On your own	Some web hosts offer a package that includes registering your domain name. You may prefer to register your domain name yourself (see http://register.com or http://networksolutions.com) and retain control of your domain name account.
Price	☐ $___ setup fee ☐ $___ per month	Price is last in this list for a reason. Do not choose a web host based on price alone—the old adage "you get what you pay for" is definitely true here. It is not unusual to pay a one-time setup fee and then a periodic fee—monthly, quarterly, or annually.

Publish with File Transfer Protocol

Once you obtain your web hosting, you'll need to upload your files. While your web host may offer a web-based file manager application for client use, a common method of transferring files is to use **File Transfer Protocol** (FTP). A **protocol** is a convention or standard that enables computers to speak to one another. **FTP** is used to copy and manage files and folders over the Internet. FTP uses two ports to communicate over a network—one for the data (typically port 20) and one for control commands (typically port 21). See http://www.iana.org/assignments/port-numbers for a list port numbers used on the Internet.

FTP Applications

There are many FTP applications available for download or purchase on the Web; several are listed in Table 12.2.

Application	Platform	URL	Cost
FileZilla	Windows, Mac, Linux	http://filezilla-project.org	Free download
SmartFTP	Windows	http://www.smartftp.com	Free download
CuteFTP	Windows, Mac	http://www.cuteftp.com	Free trial download, academic pricing available
WS_FTP	Windows	http://www.ipswitchft.com	Free trial download

TABLE 12.2 FTP Applications

Connecting with FTP

Your web host will provide you with the following information along with any other specifications, such as whether the FTP server requires the use of active mode or passive mode:

FTP Host: Your FTP Host
Username: Your Account Username
Password: Your Account Password

Overview of Using an FTP Application

This section focuses on FileZilla, a free FTP application with versions for the Windows, Mac, and Linux platforms. A free download of FileZilla is available at http://filezilla-project.org/download.php?type=client. After you download an FTP application of your choice, install the program on your computer using the instructions provided.

Launch and Login

Launch Filezilla or another FTP application. Enter the information required by your web host (such as FTP host, username, and password) and initiate the connection. An example screenshot of FileZilla after a connection is shown in Figure 12.3.

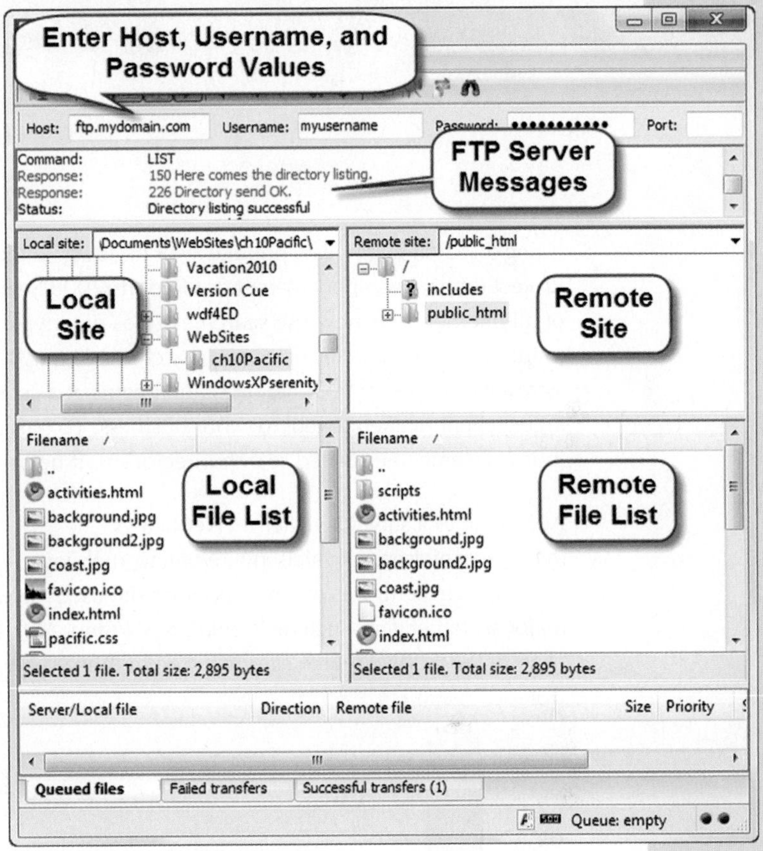

As you examine Figure 12.3, notice the text boxes near the top of the application for the Host, Username, and Password information. Under this area is a display of messages from the FTP server. Review this area to confirm a successful connection and the results of file transfers. Next, notice that the application is divided into a left panel and a right panel. The left panel is the local site—it displays information about your local computer and allows you to navigate to your drives, folders, and files. The right panel is the remote site—it displays information about your website and provides a way to navigate to its folders and files.

FIGURE 12.3 The FileZilla FTP application.

Uploading a File

It's really easy to transfer a file from your local computer to your remote website—just select the file with your mouse in the left panel (local site list) and drag it to the right panel (remote site list).

Downloading a File

If you need to download a file from your website to your local computer, just drag the file from the right panel (remote site list) to the left panel (local site list).

Deleting a File

To delete a file on your website, right-click on the file name (in the right panel) and select Delete from the context-sensitive menu.

And There's More!

Feel free to explore the other functions offered by FileZilla (and most FTP applications)—right-click on a file in the remote site list to display a context-sensitive menu with several options, including renaming a file, creating a new directory (also known as a folder), and viewing a file.

Search Engine Submission

Using a search engine is a popular way to navigate the Web and find websites. The PEW Internet Project (http://www.pewinternet.org/Reports/2008/Search-Engine-Use.aspx) reports "almost half of all Internet users now use search engines on a typical day." A Direct Marketing News report (http://dmnews.com/cms/dm-news/search-marketing/37367.html) on a Harris Interactive study states that 80 percent of Internet traffic begins at a search engine. Search engine listings can be an excellent marketing tool for your business. To harness the power of search engines and search indexes (sometimes called search directories), it helps to know how they work.

According to a survey by Nielsen/NetRatings (http://blog.nielsen.com/nielsenwire/online_mobile/top-u-s-search-sites-for-june-2010), Google (http://google.com) was the most popular site used to search the Web during a recent month. Other major search engines include Yahoo!, MSN/Bing, AOL Search, and Ask.com Search. Figure 12.4 is a chart of the top five search sites reported in this survey.

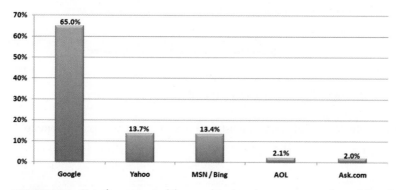

FIGURE 12.4 Sixty-five percent of the searches done in a recent month used Google.

Components of a Search Engine

The components of a search engine (robot, database, and search form) work together to obtain information about web pages, store information about web pages, and provide a graphical user interface to facilitate searching for and displaying a list of web pages relevant to given keywords.

Robot

A **robot** (sometimes called a spider or bot) is a program that automatically traverses the hypertext structure of the Web by retrieving a web page document and following the hyperlinks on the page. It moves like a robot spider on the Web, accessing and storing information about the web pages in a database. Visit The Web Robots Pages at http://www.robotstxt.org if you'd like more details about web robots.

Database

A **database** is a collection of information organized so that its contents can easily be accessed, managed, and updated. Database management systems (DBMSs) such as Oracle, Microsoft SQL Server, or IBM DB2 are used to configure and manage the database. The web page that displays the results of your search, called the Search Engine Results Page (SERP), lists information from the database accessed by the search engine.

Search Form

The search form is the graphical user interface that allows a user to type in the word or phrase he or she is searching for. It is typically a text box and a submit button. The visitor to the search engine types words (called keywords) related to his or her search into the text box. When the form is submitted, the keywords are sent to a server-side script that searches the database for matches. The results are displayed on a SERP and formatted with a hyperlink to each page along with additional information that might include the page title, a brief description, the first few lines of text, or the size of the page. The order in which the results are displayed may depend on paid advertisements, alphabetical order, and link popularity. The link popularity of a website is a rating determined by a search engine based on the quantity and quality of incoming hyperlinks. Each search engine has its own policy for ordering the search results. Be aware that these policies can change over time.

Listing Your Site in a Search Engine

According to a study by The Direct Marketing Association (http://www.the-dma.org), 66 percent of web marketers surveyed rated search engines as the top method used to drive traffic to their sites.

Step 1:   Visit the search engine site (such as http://google.com or http://yahoo.com) and look for the "Add site" or "List URL" link. This is typically on the home page (or About Us page) of the search engine. Be patient—these links are sometimes not obvious. At Google, click the "About Google" link, click on the "Submit your content to Google" link, and then click on the "Submit a URL" link.

Step 2:   Follow the directions listed on the page and submit the form to request that your site be added to the search engine. At other search engines there may be a fee for an automatic listing, called paid inclusion—more on this later. Currently, there is no fee to submit a site to Google.

Step 3:   The spider from the search engine will index your site. This may take several weeks.

Step 4:   Several weeks after you submit your website, check the search engine or search directory to see if your site is listed. If it is not listed, review your pages and check whether they are optimized for search engines (see the next section) and display in common browsers.

Is advertising on a search engine worth the cost?

It depends. How much is it worth to your client to appear on the first page of the search engine results? You select the keywords that will trigger the display of your ad. You also set your monthly budget and the maximum amount to pay for each click. While costs and charges vary by search engine, at this time Google charges are based on cost per click—you'll be charged each time a visitor to Google clicks on your advertisement. Visit http://google.com/adwords for more information about their program.

Search Engine Optimization

If you have followed recommended web design practices, you've already designed your website so that the pages are appealing and compelling to your target audience. How can you also make your site work well with search engines? Here are some suggestions and hints on designing your pages for optimal ranking by search engines—a process called **Search Engine Optimization (SEO)**.

Keywords
Spend some time brainstorming about terms and phrases that people may use when searching for your site. These terms or phrases that describe your website or business are your **keywords**.

Page Titles
A descriptive page title (the text between the `<title>` tags) that includes your company and/or website name will help your site market itself. It's common for search engines to display the text in the page title in the SERP. The page title is also saved by default when a visitor bookmarks your site and is often included when a visitor prints a page of your site. Avoid using the exact same title for every page; include keywords in the page title that are appropriate for the page.

Heading Tags
Use structural tags such as `<h1>`, `<h2>`, and so on to organize your page content. If it is appropriate for the web page content, also include some keywords in the text contained within heading tags. Some search engines will give a higher list position if keywords are included in a page title or headings. Also include keywords as appropriate within the page text content. However, avoid spamming keywords—that is, do not list them over and over again. The programs behind search engines become more sophisticated all the time, and you can actually be prevented from being listed if it is perceived that you are not being honest or are trying to cheat the system.

Description
What is special about your website that would make someone want to visit? With this in mind, write a few sentences about your website or business. This description should be inviting and interesting so that a person searching the Web will choose your site from the list provided by a search engine or search directory. Some search engines will display your description on the SERP. You can configure a description for your web page by coding a meta tag in the page header area.

The Meta Tag
A **meta tag** is a self-contained tag that is placed in the header section of a web page. You've been using a meta tag to indicate character encoding. There are a number of other uses for a meta tag.

We'll focus here on providing a description of a website for use by search engines. The description meta tag content is displayed on the SERP by some search engines, such as Google. The **name** attribute indicates the purpose of the meta tag. The **content** attribute provides the value needed for the specific purpose. For example, the description meta tag for a website about a web development consulting firm called Acme Design could be configured as follows:

```
<meta name="description" content="Acme Design, a web consulting
group that specializes in e-commerce, website design,
development, and redesign.">
```

What if I don't want a search engine to index a page?

Sometimes there will be pages that you don't want indexed, perhaps test pages or pages only meant for a small group of individuals (such as family or coworkers). Meta tags can be used for this purpose also. To indicate to a search engine robot that a page should not be indexed and the links should not be followed, do not place keywords and description meta tags in the page. Instead, add a "robots" meta tag to the page as follows:

```
<meta name="robots" content="noindex,nofollow">
```

Linking

Verify that all hyperlinks are working and not broken. Each page on your website should be reachable by a text hyperlink. The text should be descriptive—avoid phrases like "more info" and "click here"—and should include keywords as appropriate. Inbound links (sometimes called incoming links) are also a factor in SEO. The link popularity of your website can determine its order in the search engine results page.

Images and Multimedia

Be mindful that search engine robots do not "see" the text embedded within your images and multimedia. Configure meaningful alternate text for images. Include relevant keywords in the alternate text. Although some search engine robots, such as Google's Googlebot, have recently added functionality to index text and hyperlinks contained within Flash media, be aware that a website that depends on the use of technologies such as Flash and Silverlight will be less visible to search engines and may rank lower as a result.

Valid Code

Search engines do not require that your HTML and CSS code pass validation tests. However, code that is valid and well structured is likely to be more easily processed by search engine robots. This may help with your placement in the search engine results.

Content of Value

Probably the most basic, but often overlooked, component of SEO is providing content of value that follows web design best practices (see Chapter 4). Your website should contain high-quality, well-organized content that is of value to your visitors.

Accessibility Testing

Universal Design and Accessibility

The Center for Universal Design defines universal design as "the design of products and environments to be usable by all people, to the greatest extent possible, without the need for adaptation or specialized design." Web pages that follow the principle of universal design are **accessible** to all individuals, including those with visual, hearing, mobility, and cognitive challenges. As you've worked this book, accessibility has been an integral part of your web page design and coding rather than an afterthought. You've configured headings and subheadings, navigation within unordered lists, images with alternate text, alternate text for multimedia, and associations between text and form controls. These techniques all increase the accessibility of a web page.

Web Accessibility Standards

Recall from Chapter 4 that the accessibility recommendations presented in this text are intended to satisfy Section 508 of the Rehabilitation Act and the W3C's Web Content Accessibility Guidelines.

Section 508 of the Rehabilitation Act

Section 508 (http://www.access-board.gov) requires electronic and information technology, including web pages, that are used by federal agencies to be accessible to people with disabilities. At the time this was written the Section 508 standards were undergoing revision.

Web Content Accessibility Guidelines (WCAG 2.0)

WCAG 2.0 (http://www.w3.org/TR/WCAG20) considers an accessible web page to be perceivable, operable, and understandable for people with a wide range of abilities. The page should be robust to work with a variety of browsers and other user agents, such as assistive technologies (for example, screen readers) and mobile devices. The guiding principles of WCAG 2.0 are as follows:

1. Content must be **P**erceivable.
2. Interface components in the content must be **O**perable.
3. Content and controls must be **U**nderstandable.
4. Content should be **R**obust enough to work with current and future user agents, including assistive technologies.

What is assistive technology and what is a screen reader?

Assistive technology is a term that describes any tool that a person can use to help him or her to overcome a disability and use a computer. Examples of assistive technologies include screen readers, head- and mouth-wands, and specialized keyboards, such as a single-hand keyboard. A screen reader is a software application that can be controlled by the user to read aloud what is displayed on the computer screen. JAWS is a popular screen reader application. A free time-restricted download of JAWS is available at http://www.freedomscientific.com/downloads/jaws/jaws-downloads.asp. A free download of the open-source NVDA screen reader is available at http://www.nvda-project.org. Visit http://www.doit.wisc.edu/accessibility/video/intro.asp for a video introduction to the screen reader.

Testing for Accessibility Compliance

No single testing tool can automatically test for all web standards. The first step in testing the accessibility of a web page is to verify that it is coded according to W3C standards with the (X)HTML syntax validator (http://validator.w3.org) and the CSS syntax validator (http://jigsaw.w3.org/css-validator).

Automated Accessibility Testing

An automated accessibility evaluation tool is no substitute for your own manual evaluation but can be useful to quickly identify potential issues with a web page. WebAim Wave (http://wave.webaim.org) and ATRC AChecker (http://www.achecker.ca/checker) are two popular free online accessibility evaluation tools. The online applications typically require the URL of a web page and reply with an accessibility report. Several browser toolbars are available that can be used to assess accessibility, including the Web Developer Extension (http://chrispederick.com/work/web-developer), WAT Toolbar (http://www.wat-c.org/tools), and the AIS Web Accessibility Toolbar (http://www.visionaustralia.org.au/ais/toolbar). The browser toolbars are all multifunctional, with options to validate HTML, validate CSS, disable images, view alt text, outline block level elements, resize the browser viewport, disable styles, and more. Figure 12.5 shows the Web Developer Extension toolbar in action.

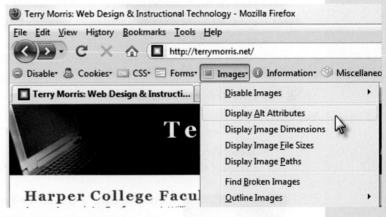

FIGURE 12.5 Selecting the Images > Display Alt Attributes feature.

Manual Accessibility Testing

It's important not to rely completely on automated tests—you'll want to review the pages yourself. For example, while an automated test can check for the presence of an alt attribute, it takes a human to critically think and decide whether the text of the alt attribute is an appropriate description for a person who cannot view the image. WebAIM provides a detailed checklist at http://www.webaim.org/standards/wcag/checklist that prompts you with items to review in order to verify compliance with WCAG 2.0 requirements.

Usability Testing

An addition to accessibility, another aspect of universal design is the usability of the website. **Usability** is the measure of the quality of a user's experience when interacting with a website. It's about making a website that is easy, efficient, and pleasant for your visitors. Usability.gov describes five factors that affect the user's experience: ease of learning, efficiency of use, memorability, error frequency and severity, and subjective satisfaction.

- **Ease of Learning**
  How easy is it to learn to use the website? Is the navigation intuitive? Does a new visitor consider it easy to learn to perform basic tasks on the website or is he or she frustrated?

- **Efficiency of Use**
  How do experienced users perceive the website—once they are comfortable, are they able to complete tasks efficiently and quickly or are they frustrated?

- **Memorability**
  When a visitor returns to a website, does he or she remember enough to use it productively or is the visitor back at the beginning of the learning curve (and frustrated)?

- **Error Frequency and Severity**
  Do website visitors make errors when navigating or filling in forms on the website? Are they serious errors? Is it easy to recover from errors or are visitors frustrated?

- **Subjective Satisfaction**
  Do users "like" using the website? Are they satisfied? Why or why not?

Conducting a Usability Test

Testing how people use a website is called **usability testing**. It can be conducted at any phase of a website's development and is often performed more than once. A usability test is conducted by asking users to complete tasks on a website, such as placing an order, looking up the phone number of a company, or finding a product. The exact tasks will vary depending on the website being evaluated. The users are monitored while they try to perform these tasks. They are asked to think out loud about their doubts and hesitations. The results are recorded (often on video tape) and discussed with the web design team. Often changes are made to the navigation and page layouts based on these tests.

FIGURE 12.6 Observing a user perform a task on a website.

If usability testing is done early in the development phase of a website, it may use the printed page layouts and site map. If the web development team is struggling with a design issue, sometimes a usability test can help to determine which design idea is the better choice. When usability is done during a later phase after the pages have been built, the actual website is tested. This can lead to a confirmation that the site is easy to use and well designed, to last-minute changes in the website, or to a plan for website enhancements in the near future.

HANDS-ON PRACTICE 12.1 ——————————————

Perform a small-scale usability test with a group of other students. Decide who will be the "typical users," the tester, and the observer. You will perform a usability test on your school's website.

- The "typical users" are the test subjects.
- The tester oversees the usability test and emphasizes that the users are not being tested—the website is being tested.
- The observer takes notes on the user's reactions and comments.

Step 1:　The tester welcomes the users and introduces them to the website they will be testing.

Step 2:　For each of the following scenarios, the tester introduces the scenario and questions the users as they work through the task. The tester should ask the users to indicate when they are in doubt, confused, or frustrated. The observer takes notes.

- Scenario 1: Find the phone number of the contact person for the Web Development program at your school.
- Scenario 2: Determine when to register for the next semester.
- Scenario 3: Find the requirements to earn a degree or certificate in Web Development or a related area.

Step 3:　The tester and observer organize the results and write a brief report. If this were a usability test for an actual website, the development team would meet to review the results and discuss necessary improvements to the site.

Step 4:　Hand in a report with your group's usability test results. Complete the report using a word processor. Write no more than one page about each scenario. Write one page of recommendations for improving your school's website.

 Explore Further

Continue to explore the topic of usability testing at the following resources:

- Keith Instone's Classic Presentation on How to Test Usability: http://instone.org/files/KEI-Howtotest-19990721.pdf
- Advanced Common Sense—the website of usability expert Steve Krug http://www.sensible.com
- Interview with Steve Krug: http://www.marketingsherpa.com/sample.cfm?contentID=3165
- Usability Basics: http://usability.gov/basics/index.html
- Usability Resources: http://www.infodesign.com.au/usabilityresources
- Usability Testing Materials: http://www.infodesign.com.au/usabilityresources/usabilitytestingmaterials

Review and Apply

Review Questions

Multiple Choice. Choose the best answer for each item.

1. Which of the following is the design of products and environments to be usable by all people, to the greatest extent possible, without the need for adaptation or specialized design?
   a. accessibility
   b. usability
   c. universal design
   d. assistive technology

2. In which of the following sections of a web page should meta tags be placed?
   a. head
   b. body
   c. comment
   d. none of the above

3. Which of the following statements is true?
   a. No single testing tool can automatically test for all web standards.
   b. Include as many people as possible when you conduct usability tests.
   c. Search engine listings are effective immediately after submission.
   d. None of the above statements is true.

4. Which are the four principles of the Web Content Accessibility Guidelines?
   a. contrast, repetition, alignment, proximity
   b. perceivable, operable, understandable, robust
   c. accessible, readable, maintainable, reliable
   d. hierarchical, linear, random, sequential

5. Which of the following is a protocol commonly used to transfer files over the Internet?
   a. port
   b. HTTP
   c. FTP
   d. SMTP

6. Which of the following is the most popular method used by visitors to find websites?
   a. banner ads
   b. hearing about websites on television
   c. search engines
   d. RSS feeds

7. What is the purpose of private registration for a domain name?
   a. It protects the privacy of your web host.
   b. It is the cheapest form of domain name registration.
   c. It protects the privacy of your contact information.
   d. none of the above

8. Which of the following is true about domain names?
   a. It is recommended to register multiple domain names that are redirected to your website.
   b. It is recommended to use long, descriptive domain names.
   c. It is recommended to use hyphens in domain names.
   d. There is no reason to check for trademarks when you are choosing a domain name.

9. Which web hosting option is appropriate for the initial web presence of an organization?
   a. dedicated hosting
   b. free web hosting
   c. virtual hosting
   d. co-located hosting

10. What is the measure of the quality of a user's experience when interacting with a website?
    a. accessibility
    b. usability
    c. validity
    d. functionality

Hands-On Exercises

1. Run an automated accessibility test on the home page of your school website. Use both the WebAim Wave (http://wave.webaim.org) and ATRC AChecker (http://www.achecker.ca/checker) automated tests. Describe the differences in the way these tools report the results of the test. Did both tests find similar errors? Write a one-page report that describes the results of the tests. Include your recommendations for improving the website.

2. Search for web host providers and report on three that meet the following criteria:

- Support PHP and MySQL
- Offer e-commerce capabilities
- Provide at least 1GB hard disk space

Use your favorite search engine to find web host providers or visit web host directories such as http://www.hosting-review.com and http://www.hostindex.com. The web host survey results provided by http://uptime.netcraft.com/perf/reports/Hosters may also be useful. Create a web page that presents your findings. Include links to the three web host providers you selected. Your web page should include a table of information such as setup fees, monthly fees, domain name registration costs, amount of hard disk space, type of e-commerce package, and cost of e-commerce package. Use color and graphics appropriately on your web page. Place your name and e-mail address at the bottom of your web page.

Focus on Web Design

1. Explore how to design your website so that it is optimized for search engines (Search Engine Optimization, or SEO). Visit the following resources as a starting point as you search for three SEO tips or hints:

- http://www.sitepoint.com/article/skool-search-engine-success
- http://www.digital-web.com/articles/designing_for_search_engines_and_stars
- http://www.seoconsultants.com/seo/tips
- http://www.youtube.com/watch?v=65PQpHcAonw

Write a one-page report that describes three tips that you found interesting or potentially useful. Cite the URLs of the resources you used.

2. Explore how to reach out to your current and potential website visitors with **Social Media Optimization** (SMO), which is described by Rohit Bhargava as optimizing a website so that it is "more easily linked to, more highly visible in social media searches on custom search engines (such as Technorati), and more frequently included in relevant posts on blogs, podcasts and vlogs." Benefits of SMO include increased awareness of your brand and/or site along with an increase in the number of inbound links (which can help with SEO). Visit the following resources as a starting point as you search for three SMO tips or hints:

- http://social-media-optimization.com
- http://rohitbhargava.typepad.com/weblog/2006/08/5_rules_of_soci.html
- http://www.toprankblog.com/2009/03/sxswi-interview-rohit-bhargava

Write a one-page report that describes three tips that you found interesting or potentially useful. Cite the URLs of the resources you used.

Answers to Review Questions

Chapter 1

1. b **2.** b **3.** b
4. True **5.** False **6.** XHTML
7. HTML5 **8.** HTML **9.** .htm, .html
10. index.htm, index.html

Chapter 2

1. b **2.** a **3.** c
4. c **5.** b **6.** b
7. b **8.** c **9.** b
10. b

Chapter 3

1. c **2.** c **3.** b
4. b **5.** b **6.** a
7. a **8.** b **9.** c
10. b

Chapter 4

1. c **2.** b **3.** b
4. b **5.** d **6.** d
7. c **8.** a **9.** c
10. b

Chapter 5

1. d **2.** b **3.** b
4. a **5.** c **6.** b
7. b **8.** d **9.** a
10. a

Chapter 6

1. b **2.** b **3.** b
4. a **5.** c **6.** d
7. d **8.** d **9.** b
10. b

Chapter 7

1. c **2.** c **3.** b
4. b **5.** a **6.** b
7. c **8.** a **9.** b
10. a

Chapter 8

1. c **2.** c **3.** b
4. d **5.** d **6.** a
7. b **8.** d **9.** c
10. b

Chapter 9

1. c **2.** b **3.** c
4. c **5.** b **6.** c
7. b **8.** b **9.** c
10. b

Chapter 10

1. d **2.** a **3.** c
4. b **5.** b **6.** b
7. a **8.** d **9.** c
10. d

Chapter 11

1. c **2.** a **3.** c
4. b **5.** a **6.** d
7. c **8.** b **9.** b
10. a

Chapter 12

1. c **2.** a **3.** a
4. b **5.** c **6.** c
7. c **8.** a **9.** c
10. b

XHTML Cheat Sheet

COMMONLY USED XHTML TAGS

Tag	Purpose	Commonly Used Attributes
`<!-- -->`	Comment	
`<a>`	Anchor tag: configures hyperlinks	accesskey, class, href, id, name, style, tabindex, target, title
`<abbr>`	Configures an abbreviation	class, id, style
`<acronym>`	Configures an acronym	class, id, style
`<address>`	Configures contact information	class, id, style
`<area />`	Configures an area in an image map	accesskey, alt, class, coords, href, id, nohref, shape, style, tabindex, target
`<b>`	Configures bold text	class, id, style
`<big>`	Configures large text size	class, id, style
`<blockquote>`	Configures a long quotation	class, id, style
`<body>`	Configures the body section	alink (deprecated), background (deprecated), bgcolor (deprecated), class, id, link (deprecated), style, text (deprecated), vlink (deprecated)
` `	Configures a line break	class, id, style
`<button>`	Configures a button	accesskey, class, disabled, id, name, type, style, value
`<caption>`	Configures a caption for a table	align (deprecated) class, id, style
`<cite>`	Configures the title of a cited work	class, id, style, title
`<dd>`	Configures a definition area in a definition list	class, id, style
`<del>`	Configures deleted text (with strikethrough)	cite, class, datetime, id, style
`<div>`	Configures a section or division in a document	align (deprecated), class, id, style
`<dl>`	Configures a definition list	class, id, style
`<dt>`	Configures a term in a definition list	class, id, style
`<em>`	Configures emphasized text (usually displays in italics)	class, id, style
`<fieldset>`	Configures a grouping of form elements with a border	class, id, style
`<form>`	Configures a form	accept, action, class, enctype, id, method, name, style, target (deprecated)

Tag	Purpose	Commonly Used Attributes
`<h1>` … `<h6>`	Configures headings	align (deprecated), class, id, style
`<head>`	Configures the head section	
`<hr />`	Configures a horizontal line	align (deprecated), class, id, size (deprecated), style, width (deprecated)
`<html>`	Configures a web page document	lang, xmlns, xml:lang
`<i>`	Configures italic text	class, id, style
`<iframe>`	Configures an inline frame	align (deprecated), class, frameborder, height, id, marginheight, marginwidth, name, scrolling, src, style, width
`<img />`	Configures an image	align (deprecated), alt, border (deprecated), class, height, hspace (deprecated), id, name, src, style, width, vspace (deprecated)
`<input />`	Configures a text box, scrolling text box, submit button, reset button, password box, or hidden field form control	accesskey, class, checked, disabled, id, maxlength, name, readonly, size, style, tabindex, type, value
`<ins>`	Configures text that has been inserted with an underline	class, id, style, cite
`<label>`	Configures a label for a form control	class, for, id, style
`<legend>`	Configures a caption for a fieldset element	align (deprecated), class, id, style
`<li>`	Configures a list item in an unordered or ordered list	class, id, style
`<link />`	Associates a web page document with an external resource	class, href, id, rel, media, style, type
`<map>`	Configures an image map	class, id, name, style
`<meta />`	Configures meta data	content, http-equiv, name
`<noscript>`	Configures content for browsers that do not support client-side scripting	
`<object>`	Configures an embedded object	align, classid, codebase, data, height, name, id, style, title, tabindex, type, width
`<ol>`	Configures an ordered list	class, id, start (deprecated), style, type (deprecated)
`<optgroup>`	Configures a group of related options in a select list	class, disabled, id, label, style
`<option>`	Configures an option in a select list	class, disabled, id, selected, style, value
`<p>`	Configures a paragraph	align (deprecated), class, id, style
`<param />`	Configures a parameter for an object element	name, value
`<pre>`	Configures preformatted text	class, id, style
`<script>`	Configures a client-side script (typically JavaScript)	src, type
`<select>`	Configures a select list form control	class, disabled, id, multiple, name, size, style, tabindex

(Continued)

Tag	Purpose	Commonly Used Attributes
`<small>`	Configures small text size	class, id, style
`<span>`	Configures an inline-level section of a document	class, id, style
`<strong>`	Configures strong text (typically displayed as bold)	class, id, style
`<style>`	Configures embedded styles in a web page document	type, media
`<sub>`	Configures subscript text	class, id, style
`<sup>`	Configures superscript text	class, id, style
`<table>`	Configures a table	align (deprecated), bgcolor (deprecated), border, cellpadding, cellspacing, class, id, style, summary, title, width
`<tbody>`	Configures the body section of a table	align, class, id, style, valign
`<td>`	Configures a table data cell in a table	align, bgcolor (deprecated), class, colspan, id, headers, height (deprecated), rowspan, style, valign, width (deprecated)
`<textarea>`	Configures a scrolling text box form control	accesskey, class, cols, disabled, id, name, readonly, rows, style, tabindex
`<tfoot>`	Configures the footer section of a table	align, class, id, style, valign
`<th>`	Configures a table header cell in a table	align, bgcolor (deprecated), class, colspan, id, height (deprecated), rowspan, scope, style, valign, width (deprecated)
`<thead>`	Configures the head section of a table	align, class, id, style, valign
`<title>`	Configures the title of a web page document	
`<tr>`	Configures a row in a table	align, bgcolor (deprecated), class, id, style, valign
`<ul>`	Configures an unordered list	class, id, style, type (deprecated)

HTML5 Cheat Sheet

COMMONLY USED HTML5 TAGS

Tag	Purpose	Commonly Used Attributes
`<!-- -->`	Comment	
`<a>`	Anchor tag: configures hyperlinks	accesskey, class, href, id, name, rel, style, tabindex, target, title
`<abbr>`	Configures an abbreviation	class, id, style
`<address>`	Configures contact information	class, id, style
`<area>`	Configures an area in an image map	accesskey, alt, class, href, hreflang, id, media, rel, shape, style, tabindex, target, type
`<article>`	Configures an independent section of a document as an article	class, id, style
`<aside>`	Configures tangential content	class, id, style
`<audio>`	Configures an audio control native to the browser	autoplay, class, controls, id, loop, preload, src, style, title
`<b>`	Configures bold text with no implied importance	class, id, style
`<blockquote>`	Configures a long quotation	class, id, style
`<body>`	Configures the body section	alink (deprecated), background (deprecated), bgcolor (deprecated), class, id, link (deprecated), style, text (deprecated), vlink (deprecated)
` `	Configures a line break	class, id, style
`<button>`	Configures a button	accesskey, autofocus, class, disabled, format, formaction, formenctype, mormmethod, formtarget, formnovalidate id, name, type, style, value
`<canvas>`	Configures dynamic graphics	class, height, id, style, title, width
`<caption>`	Configures a caption for a table	align (deprecated) class, id, style
`<cite>`	Configures the title of a cited work	class, height, id, style, title
`<code>`	Configures a fragment of computer code	class, id, style
`<col>`	Configures a table column	class, id, span, style
`<colgroup>`	Configures a group of one or more columns in a table	class, id, span, style
`<command>`	Configures an area to represent commands	class, id, style, type

(Continued)

Tag	Purpose	Commonly Used Attributes
`<datalist>`	Configures a control that contains one or more option elements	class, id, style
`<dd>`	Configures a description area in a description list	class, id, style
`<del>`	Configures deleted text (with strikethrough)	cite, class, datetime, id, style
`<details>`	Configures a control to provide additional information to the user on demand	class, id, open, style
`<dfn>`	Configures the definition of a term	class, id, style
`<div>`	Configures a generic section or division in a document	class, id, style
`<dl>`	Configures a description list (formerly called a definition list)	class, id, style
`<dt>`	Configures a term in a description list	class, id, style
`<em>`	Configures emphasized text (usually displays in italics)	class, id, style
`<fieldset>`	Configures a grouping of form elements with a border	class, id, style
`<figcaption>`	Configures a caption for a figure	class, id, style
`<figure>`	Configures a figure	class, id, style
`<footer>`	Configures a footer area	class, id, style
`<form>`	Configures a form	accept-charset, action, autocomplete class, enctype, id, method, name, novalidate, style, target
`<h1> ... <h6>`	Configures headings	class, id, style
`<head>`	Configures the head section	
`<header>`	Configures a header area	class, id, style
`<hgroup>`	Configures a heading group	class, id, style
`<hr>`	Configures a horizontal line; indicates a thematic break in HTML5	class, id, style
`<html>`	Configures the root element of a web page document	lang, manifest
`<i>`	Configures italic text	class, id, style
`<iframe>`	Configures an inline frame	class, height, id, name, sandbox, seamless, src, style, width
`<img>`	Configures an image	alt, class, height, id, ismap, name, src, style, usemap, width
`<input>`	Configures an input control; text box, email text box, URL text box, search text box, telephone number text box, scrolling text box, submit button, reset button, password box, calendar control, slider control, spinner control, color picker control, or hidden field form control	accesskey, autocomplete, autofocus, class, checked, disabled, form, id, list, max, maxlength, min, name, pattern, placeholder, readonly, required, size, step, style, tabindex, type, value

Tag	Purpose	Commonly Used Attributes
`<ins>`	Configures text that has been inserted with an underline	cite, class, datetime, id, style
`<kbd>`	Configures a representation of user input	class, id, style
`<keygen>`	Configures a control that generates a public-private key pair or submits the public key.	autofocus, challenge, class, disabled, form, id, keytype, style
`<label>`	Configures a label for a form control	class, for, form, id, style
`<legend>`	Configures a caption for a fieldset element	class, id, style
`<li>`	Configures a list item in an unordered or ordered list	class, id, style, value
`<link>`	Associates a web page document with an external resource	class, href, hreflang, id, rel, media, sizes, style, type
`<map>`	Configures an image map	class, id, name, style
`<mark>`	Configures text as marked (or highlighted) for easy reference	class, id, style
`<menu>`	Configures a list of commands	class, id, label, style, type
`<meta>`	Configures meta data	charset, content, http-equiv, name
`<meter>`	Configures visual gauge of a value	class, id, high, low, max, min, optimum, style, value
`<nav>`	Configures an area with navigation hyperlinks	class, id, style
`<noscript>`	Configures content for browsers that do not support client-side scripting	
`<object>`	Configures a generic embedded object	classid, codebase, data, form, height, name, id, style, title, tabindex, type, width
`<ol>`	Configures an ordered list	class, id, reversed, start, style, type
`<optgroup>`	Configures a group of related options in a select list	class, disabled, id, label, style
`<option>`	Configures an option in a select list	class, disabled, id, selected, style, value
`<output>`	Configures result of processing in a form	class, for, form, id, style
`<p>`	Configures a paragraph	class, id, style
`<param>`	Configures a parameter for plug-ins	name, value
`<pre>`	Configures preformatted text	class, id, style
`<progress>`	Configures a visual progress indicator	class, id, max, style, value
`<q>`	Configures quoted text	cite, class, id, style
`<rp>`	Configures a ruby parentheses	class, id, style
`<rt>`	Configures ruby text component of a ruby annotation	class, id, style
`<ruby>`	Configures a ruby annotation	class, id, style
`<samp>`	Configures sample output from a computer program or system	class, id, style
`<script>`	Configures a client-side script (typically JavaScript)	async, charset, defer, src, type

(Continued)

Tag	Purpose	Commonly Used Attributes
`<section>`	Configures a section of a document	class, id, style
`<select>`	Configures a select list form control	class, disabled, form, id, multiple, name, size, style, tabindex
`<small>`	Configures a disclaimer in small text size	class, id, style
`<source>`	Configures a media file and MIME type	class, id, media, src, style, type
`<span>`	Configures a generic section of a document with inline display	class, id, style
`<strong>`	Configures text with strong importance (typically displayed as bold)	class, id, style
`<style>`	Configures embedded styles in a web page document	media, scoped, type
`<sub>`	Configures subscript text	class, id, style
`<summary>`	Configures text as a summary, caption, or legend for a details control	class, id, style
`<sup>`	Configures superscript text	class, id, style
`<table>`	Configures a table	class, id, style, summary
`<tbody>`	Configures the body section of a table	class, id, style
`<td>`	Configures a table data cell in a table	class, colspan, id, headers, rowspan
`<textarea>`	Configures a scrolling text box form control	accesskey, autofocus, class, cols, disabled, id, maxlength, name, placeholder, readonly, required, rows, style, tabindex, wrap
`<tfoot>`	Configures the footer section of a table	class, id, style
`<th>`	Configures a table header cell in a table	class, colspan, id, headers, rowspan, scope, style
`<thead>`	Configures the head section of a table	class, id, style
`<time>`	Configures a date and/or time	class, datetime, id, pubdate, style
`<title>`	Configures the title of a web page document	
`<tr>`	Configures a row in a table	class, id, style
`<ul>`	Configures an unordered list	class, id, style
`<var>`	Configures text as a variable or placeholder text	class, id, style
`<video>`	Configures a video control native to the browser	autoplay, class, controls, height, id, loop, poster, preload, src, style, width
`<wbr>`	Configures a line-break opportunity	class, id, style

CSS Cheat Sheet

COMMONLY USED CSS PROPERTIES

Property	Description
background	Shorthand to configure all the background properties of an element Value: `background-color` `background-image` `background-repeat` `background-position`
background-attachment	Configures a background image as fixed-in-place or scrolling Value: `scroll` (default) or `fixed`
background-clip	CSS3; configures the area to display the background Value: `border-box`, `padding-box`, or `content-box`
background-color	Configures the background color of an element Value: Valid color value
background-image	Configures a background image for an element Value: `url` (*file name or path to the image*), none (default) Optional new CSS3 functions: `linear-gradient()` and `radial-gradient()`
background-origin	CSS3; configures the background positioning area. Value: `padding-box`, `border-box`, or `content-box`
background-position	Configures the position of a background image Value: Two percentages, pixel values, or position values (`left`, `top`, `center`, `bottom`, `right`)
background-repeat	Configures how the background image will be repeated Value: `repeat` (default), `repeat-y`, `repeat-x`, or `no-repeat`
background-size	CSS3; configures the size of the background images. Value: Numeric value (px or em), percentage, contain, cover
border	Shorthand to configure the border of an element Value: `border-width` `border-style` `border-color`
border-bottom	Configures the bottom border of an element Value: `border-width` `border-style` `border-color`
border-collapse	Configures the display of borders in a table Value: `separate` (default) or `collapse`
border-color	Configures the border color of an element Value: Valid color value
border-image	CSS3; configures an image in the border of an element. See http://www.w3.org/TR/css3-background/#the-border-image
border-left	Configures the left border of an element Value: `border-width` `border-style` `border-color`

(Continued)

Property	Description
border-radius	CSS3; configures rounded corners Value: One or two numeric values (px or em) or percentages that configure horizontal and vertical radius of the corner. If one value is provided, it applies to both horizontal and vertical radius. Related properties: `border-top-left-radius`, `border-top-right-radius`, `border-bottom-left-radius`, and `border-bottom-right-radius`
border-right	Configures the right border of an element Value: `border-width` `border-style` `border-color`
border-spacing	Configures the space between table cells in a table. Value: Numeric value (px or em)
border-style	Configures the style of the borders around an element Value: `none` (default), `inset`, `outset`, `double`, `groove`, `ridge`, `solid`, `dashed`, or `dotted`
border-top	Configures the top border of an element Value: `border-width` `border-style` `border-color`
border-width	Configures the width of an element's border Value: Numeric pixel value (such as 1 px), `thin`, `medium`, or `thick`
bottom	Configures the offset position from the bottom of a containing element Value: Numeric value (px or em), percentage, or `auto` (default)
box-shadow	CSS3; configures a drop shadow on an element Values: Three or four numerical values (px or em) to indicate horizontal offset, vertical offset, blur radius, (optional) spread distance, and a valid color value. Use the `inset` keyword to configure an inner shadow.
caption-side	Configures the placement of a table caption Value: `top` (default), or `bottom`
clear	Configures the display of an element in relation to floating elements Value: `none` (default), `left`, `right`, or `both`
color	Configures the color of text within an element Value: Valid color value
display	Configures how and if an element will display Value: `inline`, `none`, `block`, `list-item`, `table`, `table-row`, or `table-cell`
float	Configures the horizontal placement (left or right) of an element Value: `none` (default), `left`, or `right`
font	Shorthand to configure the font properties of an element Value: `font-style` `font-variant` `font-weight` `font-size/line-height` `font-family`
font-family	Configures the font typeface of text Value: List of valid font names or generic font family names
font-size	Configures the font size of text Value: Numeric value (px, pt, em), percentage value, `xx-small`, `x-small`, `small`, `medium` (default), `large`, `x-large`, `xx-large`, `smaller`, or `larger`

Property	Description
font-stretch	CSS3; configures a normal, condensed, or expanded face from a font family Values include: normal, wider, narrower, condensed, semi-condensed, expanded, ultra-expanded
font-style	Configures the font style of text Value: normal (default), italic, or oblique
font-variant	Configures whether text is displayed in small-caps font Value: normal (default) or small-caps
font-weight	Configures the weight (boldness) of text Value: normal (default), bold, bolder, lighter, 100, 200, 300, 400, 500, 600, 700, 800, or 900
height	Configures the height of an element Value: Numeric value (px or em), percentage, or auto (default)
left	Configures the offset position from the left of a containing element Value: Numeric value (px or em), percentage, or auto (default)
letter-spacing	Configures the space between text characters Value: Numeric value (px or em) or normal (default)
line-height	Configures the line height of text Value: Numeric value (px or em), percentage, multiplier numeric value, or normal (default),
list-style	Shorthand to configure the properties of a list list-style-type list-style-position list-style-image
list-style-image	Configures an image as a list marker Value: url (*file name or path to the image*) or none (default)
list-style-position	Configures the position of the list markers Value: inside, or outside (default)
list-style-type	Configures the type of list marker displayed Value: none, circle, disc (default), square, decimal, decimal-leading-zero, Georgian, lower-alpha, lower-roman, upper-alpha, or upper-roman
margin	Shorthand to configure the margin of an element Value: One to four numeric values (px or em), percentages, auto or 0
margin-bottom	Configures the bottom margin of an element Value: Numeric value (px or em), percentage, auto or 0
margin-left	Configures the left margin of an element Value: Numeric value (px or em), percentage, auto or 0
margin-right	Configures the right margin of an element Value: Numeric value (px or em), percentage, auto or 0
margin-top	Configures the top margin of an element Value: Numeric value (px or em), percentage, auto or 0
max-height	Configures the maximum height of an element Value: Numeric value (px or em), percentage, or none (default)
max-width	Configures the maximum width of an element Value: Numeric value (px or em), percentage, or none (default)

(Continued)

Property	Description
min-height	Configures the minimum height of an element Value: Numeric value (px or em), or percentage
min-width	Configures the minimum width of an element Value: Numeric value (px or em), or percentage
opacity	CSS3; configures the transparency of an element. Values: Numeric value between 1 (fully opaque) and 0 (completely transparent).
overflow	Configures how content should display if it is too large for the area allocated. Value: `visible` (default), `hidden`, `auto`, or `scroll`
padding	Shorthand to configure the padding of an element Value: One to four numeric values (px or em), percentages, or 0
padding-bottom	Configures the bottom padding of an element Value: Numeric value (px or em), percentage, or 0
padding-left	Configures the left padding of an element Value: Numeric value (px or em), percentage, or 0
padding-right	Configures the right padding of an element Value: Numeric value (px or em), percentage, or 0
padding-top	Configures the top padding of an element Value: Numeric value (px or em), percentage, or 0
page-break-after	Configures the page break after an element Value: `auto` (default), `always`, `avoid`, `left`, or `right`
page-break-before	Configures the page break before an element Value: `auto` (default), `always`, `avoid`, `left`, or `right`
page-break-inside	Configures the page break inside an element Value: `auto` (default) or `avoid`
position	Configures the type of positioning used to display an element Value: `static` (default), `absolute`, `fixed`, or `relative`
right	Configures the offset position from the right of a containing element Value: Numeric value (px or em), percentage, or `auto` (default)
text-align	Configures the horizontal alignment of text Value: `left`, `right`, `center`, `justify`
text-decoration	Configures the decoration added to text Value: `none` (default), `underline`, `overline`, `line-through`, or `blink`
text-indent	Configures the indentation of the first line of text Value: Numeric value (px or em), or percentage
text-outline	CSS3; configures an outline around text displayed within an element Values: One or two numerical values (px or em) to indicate thickness and (optionally) blur radius, and a valid color value
text-shadow	CSS3; configures a drop shadow on the text displayed within an element Values: Three or four numerical values (px or em) to indicate horizontal offset, vertical offset, blur radius, (optional) spread distance, and a valid color value.

Property	Description
text-transform	Configures the capitalization of text Value: none (default), capitalize, uppercase, or lowercase
top	Configures the offset position from the top of a containing element Value: Numeric value (px or em), percentage, or auto (default)
transform	CSS3; configures change or transformation in the display of an element. Values: A transform function such as scale(), translate(), matrix(), rotate(), skew(), or perspective()
transition	CSS3; Shorthand property to configure the presentational transition of a CSS property value Value: list the value for transition-property, transition duration, transition-timing-function, and transition-delay separated by spaces; default values can be omitted, but the first time unit applies to transition-duration.
transition-delay	CSS3; Indicates the beginning of the transition; default value 0 configures no delay, otherwise use a numeric value to specify time (usually in seconds)
transition-duration	CSS3; Indicates the length of time to apply the transition; default value 0 configures an immediate transition, otherwise use a numeric value to specify time (usually in seconds)
transition-property	CSS3; Indicates the CSS property that the transition applies to; a list of applicable properties is available at http://www.w3.org/TR/css3-transitions
transition-timing-function	CSS3; Configures changes in the speed of the transition by describing how intermediate property values are calculated; common values include ease (default), linear, ease-in, ease-out, ease-in-out
vertical-align	Configures the vertical alignment of an element Value: Numeric value (px or em), percentage, baseline (default), sub, super, top, text-top, middle, bottom, or text-bottom
visibility	Configures the visibility of an element Value: visible (default), hidden, or collapse
white-space	Configures white space inside an element Value: normal (default), nowrap, pre, pre-line, or pre-wrap
width	Configures the width of an element Value: Numeric value (px or em), percentage, or auto (default)
word-spacing	Configures the space between words within text Value: Numeric value (px or em) or auto (default)
z-index	Configures the stacking order of an element Value: A numeric value or auto (default)

Commonly Used CSS Pseudo-Classes and Pseudo-Elements

Name	Purpose
:active	Configures an element that is being clicked
:after	Inserts and configures content after an element
:before	Inserts and configures content before an element
:first-child	Configures an element that is the first child of another element
:first-letter	Configures the first character of text
:first-line	Configures the first line of text
:first-of-type	CSS3; Configures the first element of the specified type
:focus	Configures an element that has keyboard focus
:hover	Configures an element that has a mouse placed over it
:last-child	CSS3; configures the last child of an element
:last-of-type	CSS3; configures the last element of the specified type
:link	Configures a hyperlink that has not been visited
:nth-of-type(n)	CSS3; configures the "nth" element of the specified type. Values: a number, odd, or even
:visited	Configures a hyperlink that has been visited

WCAG 2.0 Quick Reference

Perceivable

- **1.1 Text Alternatives:** Provide text alternatives for any nontext content so that it can be changed into other forms people need, such as large print, Braille, speech, symbols, or simpler language. *You configure images (Chapter 6) and multimedia (Chapter 11) on web pages and provide for alternate text content.*

- **1.2 Time-Based Media:** Provide alternatives for time-based media. *We don't create time-based media in this textbook, but keep this in mind for the future if you create animation or use client-side scripting for features such as interactive slide shows.*

- **1.3 Adaptable:** Create content that can be presented in different ways (for example, simpler layout) without losing information or structure. *In Chapter 2 you use block elements (such as headings, paragraphs, and lists) to create single-column web pages. You create multicolumn web pages in Chapter 8. You use HTML tables in Chapter 9 to configure information.*

- **1.4 Distinguishable:** Make it easier for users to see and hear content, including separating foreground from background. *You are aware of the importance of good contrast between text and background.*

Operable

- **2.1 Keyboard Accessible:** Make all functionality available from a keyboard. *In Chapter 3 you configure hyperlinks to named fragment identifiers on a web page. The label element is introduced In Chapter 10.*

- **2.2 Enough Time:** Provide users enough time to read and use content. *We don't create time-based media in this textbook, but keep this in mind for the future if you create animation or use client-side scripting for features such as interactive slide shows.*

- **2.3 Seizures:** Do not design content in a way that is known to cause seizures. *Be careful when you use animation created by others; web pages should not contain elements that flash more than three times in a one-second period.*

- **2.4 Navigable:** Provide ways to help users navigate, find content, and determine where they are. *In Chapter 2 you use block elements (such as headings and lists) to organize web page content. In Chapter 3 you configure hyperlinks to named fragment identifiers on a web page.*

Understandable

- **3.1 Readable:**   Make text content readable and understandable. *You explore techniques used when writing for the Web in Chapter 4.*

- **3.2 Predictable:**   Make web pages appear and operate in predictable ways. *The web pages you create are predictable, with clearly labeled and functioning hyperlinks.*

- **3.3 Input Assistance:**   Help users avoid and correct mistakes. *We don't validate form input in this textbook, but keep this in mind for the future—client-side scripting can be use to edit web page forms and provide feedback to users.*

Robust

- **4.1 Compatible:**   Maximize compatibility with current and future user agents, including assistive technologies. *You provide for future compatibility by writing code that follows W3C Recommendations (standards).*

The WCAG 2.0 Quick Reference List entries are copyright © 2008 World Wide Web Consortium (Massachusetts Institute of Technology, European Research Consortium for Informatics and Mathematics, Keio University). All Rights Reserved. http://www.w3.org/Consortium/Legal/2002/copyright-documents-20021231.

Explore Further

You'll find the most up-to-date information about WCAG 2.0 at the following resources:

- Overview of WCAG 2.0
  http://www.w3.org/TR/WCAG20/Overview

- Understanding WCAG 2.0
  http://www.w3.org/TR/UNDERSTANDING-WCAG20

- How to Meet WCAG 2.0
  http://www.w3.org/WAI/WCAG20/quickref

- Techniques for WCAG 2.0
  http://www.w3.org/TR/WCAG-TECHS

Index

Web Safe Color Palette

Web safe colors look the most similar on various computer platforms and computer monitors. Back in the day of eight-bit color it was crucial to use web safe colors. Since most modern video drivers support millions of colors the use of web safe colors is now optional. The hexadecimal and decimal RGB values are shown for each color in the palette above.